SOCIAL WORK'S HISTORIES OF COMPLICITY AND RESISTANCE

A Tale of Two Professions

Edited by
Vasilios Ioakimidis and Aaron Wyllie

D1612605

P

First published in Great Britain in 2023 by

Policy Press, an imprint of
Bristol University Press
University of Bristol
1–9 Old Park Hill
Bristol
BS2 8BB
UK
t: +44 (0)117 374 6645
e: bup-info@bristol.ac.uk

Details of international sales and distribution partners are available at
policy.bristoluniversitypress.co.uk

British Library Cataloguing in Publication Data
A catalogue record for this book is available from the British Library

ISBN 978-1-4473-6427-6 hardcover
ISBN 978-1-4473-6428-3 paperback
ISBN 978-1-4473-6429-0 ePub
ISBN 978-1-4473-6430-6 ePdf

Cover design: Robin Hawes
Front cover image: istock/olegganko
Bristol University Press and Policy Press use environmentally responsible print partners.
Printed and bound in Great Britain by CPI Group (UK) Ltd, Croydon, CR0 4YY

Contents

Notes on contributors

Akudo Amadiegwu is Lecturer in Social Work at the University of Essex.

Caroline Bald is Lecturer in Social Work at the University of Essex.

Melisa Campana-Alabarce is a member of CONICET (National Scientific and Technical Research Council) at Universidad Nacional de Rosario.

Victoria Copeland is Senior Policy Analyst at the University of California Los Angeles.

Alan J. Dettlaff is Dean and Maconda Brown O'Connor Endowed Dean's Chair Professor at the University of Huston.

Filipe Duarte is Assistant Professor in Social Work at the University of Windsor.

Pedro Gabriel Silva is Assistant Professor at Universidade de Trás-os-Montes e Alto Douro.

Linda Harms-Smith is Associate Professor of Social Work at the University of Pretoria.

Vasilios Ioakimidis is Professor of Social Work, affiliated with the University of Essex (Founding Professor), the University of West Attica and the University of Johannesburg.

Carola Kuhlmann is Professor in Social Work at Evangelische Hochschule Rheinland-Westfalen-Lippe, Bochum.

Michael Lavalette is Everton Professor of Social and Community Engagement at Liverpool Hope University.

María Inés Martínez Herrero is Lecturer at the International University of La Rioja.

Alcina Martins is Professor of Social Services and Social Work at Instituto Superior Miguel Torga.

Claire McGettrick is Irish Research Council Postgraduate Scholar in the School of Sociology at University College Dublin.

Caroline McGregor is Professor of Social Work at the National University of Ireland Galway.

Rich Moth is Senior Lecturer in Social Work at Royal Holloway University.

Gianinna Muñoz-Arce is Assistant Professor at Universidad de Chile.

Carolyn Noble is Emerita Professor at the Australian College of Applied Psychology, Sydney and Senior Research Associate at University of Johannesburg.

Bob Pease is Honorary Professor at Deakin University, Geelong.

Patrick Selmi is Associate Professor in Social Work at the University of Windsor.

Guy Shennan is a social worker and co-founder of the Solution-Focused Collective.

Nicos Trimikliniotis is Professor of Sociology and Law at the University of Nicosia.

Vassilis Tsianos is Professor of Sociology at Kiel University of Applied Sciences.

Yasmin Turton is Senior Lecturer/Senior Research Associate in Social Work at the University of Johannesburg.

Aaron Wyllie is Lecturer in Social Work and Programme Lead for the BA Social Work at the University of Essex.

Acknowledgements

The main idea behind this book has been shaped by a series of lively events and scholarly debates that long precede its conception and subsequent publication. Most of these discussions have taken place through research, conferences and grassroots activism in the context of the Social Work Action Network (SWAN). SWAN has grown into a truly dynamic radical organisation that brings together researchers, practitioners, students and activists, from all continents, united in their belief that 'another social work is possible'. It is with this inspiration in mind that we attempted to dissect the history of our profession and reimagine its future.

We would like to thank our colleagues at the University of Essex and the University of West Attica who supported this publication in multiple ways.

Colleagues from the International Federation of Social Workers, and Rory Truell in particular, were very generous with their time in sharing ideas and feedback and allowing us access to the organisation's archives.

We would also like to thank our publisher. Policy Press has become an important space for radical social work scholarship and – like in previous projects – they have provided valuable advice and support.

In addition to these organisations we would like thank the following colleagues who, in diverse ways, have supported this publication: Michael Lavalette, Iain Ferguson, Nicos Trimikliniotis, Dora Teloni, Gianinna Munoz, Vassilis Tsianos, Gert Scheepers, Kerry Cuskelly, Lam Chi Leung, Kostis Roussos, Caroline Bald, Rea Maglajlic, Marinilda Rivera Díaz, Jim Campbell, Ruth Seifert, Helen Charnley, John Bates.

Dedicating time to edit and author a book usually means that time needs to be been taken from partners and families, so we would like to record our thanks to Lauren, Scarlett, Zephaniah, Iris, Olga and Eleftheria for their patience and support.

Preface

Social work's history is one of tension, change and re-configuration over time and place. The global definition of social work (International Federation of Social Workers, 2014) articulates a profession committed to the promotion of 'social change and development, social cohesion, and the empowerment and liberation of people', and rooted in principles of 'social justice, human rights, [and] collective responsibility'. As editors, we share this emancipatory and liberatory vision for social work, and this book is motivated, in large part, towards highlighting the need for the continued prioritisation and defence of these foundations in response to current and future crises of occupational identity. For, as the chapters in this volume demonstrate, hesitation or timidity about this vision when faced with the pressures of state coercion and control has too often led to the co-option of social work's identity, and its complicity with unjust and oppressive practices responsible for significant and ongoing harm and despair.

This book documents and attempts to make sense of the economic and sociopolitical context of these histories as a means both of recognising their continued legacy in many fields of contemporary practice and, more critically, for moving towards a meaningful path of healing and reconciliation for those communities affected. While this volume explores many troubling accounts of social work's history around the world, it also details hopeful moments in which social workers have, in solidarity with activists and others, courageously resisted and challenged oppressive systems and structures. As we argue, it is only from an honest and transparent accounting of, and recompense for, social work's contested history that a more hopeful and liberatory vision for its future can be imagined.

Part I provides a framework for approaching this ambitious task by offering a typology for making sense of both the nature and scope of social work's contested histories globally, and of efforts by national social work associations to respond to or acknowledge these histories. While recognising the efforts made by several professional associations, this opening section also presents our central thesis, that there is a need for a more nuanced approach to making amends for social work's past. Such an approach, we argue, must confront the structural and political conditions shaping social work's contested history, its disputed present and its uncertain future. In doing so, we respond directly, and anticipatorily, with the arguments most frequently marshalled against calls for such a meaningful engagement with social work's past.

The individual chapters included in this book represent considerable historical and geographical breadth, and the subsequent three parts of this volume (II–IV) are organised according to the shared sociopolitical conditions from which they arose, and/or the nature of their impact on, and legacy for, affected communities.

Part II explores social work complicity with the systems and practices of colonialism and racism. The chapters in this section document tragically similar histories of social workers as agents of the state within child welfare systems that were systemically weaponised against unwed mothers, and Aboriginal, Black and minority ethnic communities in the United States (US) Canada (Chapter 2), Australia (Chapter 3) and the United States (US) (Chapter 4). South Africa's apartheid regime (Chapter 5) provides perhaps the most blatant case study of social work's dual capacity for complicity and resistance, serving as a cautionary reminder of the need to confront racism and colonialism both within and beyond the bounds of the profession itself. Critically, each of these chapters highlights the long-term intergenerational trauma and inequality resulting from these histories, and their continued legacy in the racialised and colonial logics which remain embedded, to varying degrees, within contemporary social welfare systems.

Part III focuses on episodes of social work's direct engagement in the support of, and/or resistance against, explicitly ideological agendas pursued by dictatorial and authoritarian regimes. These chapters document social work practices that are particularly troubling and challenging to confront, from the horrors of social work involvement in Nazi Germany's eugenics programme (Chapter 6), to complicity in the fervour of Francoist Spain's social control policies (Chapter 7). During the tumultuous years of dictatorship and authoritarianism across Chile, Argentina and Uruguay (Chapter 8) courageous acts of resistance and subterfuge by social workers, often at considerable personal risk, stand in contrast to the actions of those who complied through personal or professional self-interest. Finally, Portugal (Chapter 9) and Palestine (Chapter 10) show the transformative potential of conflict and political upheaval for cleaving social work away from apparatus of the state and reconfiguring new forms of social work 'from below'.

Part IV offers histories of social work's involvement in the targeting of those deemed dangerous, deviant or morally transgressive as objects of state surveillance and control through institutionalisation and detention. Unlike the histories of social work complicity with explicitly racist, authoritarian and exclusionary regimes and practices, the chapters in this section highlight the contested pendulum of 'care' and 'control' which lurks beneath many fields of social work practice. As social work's history within England's mental health system (Chapter 11), Cyprus's asylum system (Chapter 12) and Irish child welfare (Chapter 13) illustrate, social work has rarely found itself in a position of influence in such settings. Instead, social work has often found itself subsumed within, and directed by, the disciplinary inclinations of other professions, religious bodies or the carceral state.

The concluding section (Part V) provides perspectives and reflections both on the personal impact of social work's conflicted histories, and on journeys towards the acknowledgement and redress of the pain, mistrust and ongoing injustice they have fostered. Against the backdrop of the preceding histories of systematic and widespread acts of complicity, these chapters focus on sites and methods where the 'undoing' of these legacies may take shape, such as through the decolonisation and reimagination of social work pedagogy (Chapters 14 and 16), and through partnership and activism with service users (Chapter 15). Drawing the threads of this volume together, the concluding chapter (Chapter 17) underscores the need to understand the 'histories' of social work as living on through both the lives of those harmed and the practices of a profession yet to engage with meaningful processes of reconciliation.

Vasilios Ioakimidis and Aaron Wyllie
Colchester, Essex
February 2023

Reference

International Federation of Social Workers (IFSW) (2014) *Global definition of social work*. Available from: http://ifsw.org/policies/definition-of-social-work/

PART I

Making amends with the past

Learning from the past to shape the future: uncovering social work's histories of complicity and resistance

Vasilios Ioakimidis and Aaron Wyllie

Introduction

This has been a difficult book to prepare. For uncovering the complex political history of social work requires more than archival research, historical analyses and engagement with international scholarship. Making sense of the profession's complex past has been an activity akin to 'soul searching', an emotionally laborious process. At a time when forms of collective soul searching have resulted in the very future of social work being openly debated, we felt a sense of immediacy in approaching this task (Maylea 2021; Garrett 2021). Despite the fact that this book uncovers and interrogates aspects of social work's past that are disturbing, it is important to stress that our starting premise is that social work is a 'profession worth fighting for'. No doubt, like most institutions and professions, social work is a contested activity.

However, unlike many other institutions and professions, social work occupies a critical space between state policies and some of the most vulnerable people in our societies. It is exactly such proximity with people affected by inequality and poverty that has led social workers to witness horrendous state brutality. Many social workers, over the years and across all continents, have challenged violence and oppression and sought to radically transform the profession through their engagement with broader social movements (see Ferguson et al, 2018). Jones et al (2004) in their manifesto that provided the basis for the formation of the Social Work Action Network (SWAN) have suggested that:

> More than any other welfare state profession, social work seeks to understand the links between 'public issues' and 'private troubles' and seeks to address both. It is for this reason that many who hold power and influence in our society would be delighted to see a demoralised and defeated social work, a social work that is incapable of drawing attention to the miseries and difficulties which beset so many in

our society. This alone makes social work worth fighting for. (Jones et al, 2004)

Both editors of this book had qualified as social workers prior to joining academia. Despite our commitment to social work values, the contradictory and contested social work theory and practice led us, early on in our careers, to question the perceived uniformity of the social work profession. Initially, as practitioners, and later, as researchers, we were faced with the reality of a Janus-faced profession. On the one hand, we witnessed truly inspiring, empowering and emancipatory practice that kept fuelling our desire to be part of a 'profession worth fighting for'. On the other hand, we also witnessed the impact of oppressive and often alienating social work practices. The latter informed our decision to research the plight of communities and individuals who had suffered from state violence and injustice directly or indirectly facilitated by social work and social workers.

The initial challenge we faced while working on this book was addressing the following question: 'If social work is a profession of two souls, which one are we to prioritise in this soul-searching exercise?' Histories of emancipatory social work really do offer glimpses into a global profession that places itself unconditionally on the side of the oppressed (Reisch and Andrews, 2002; Ferguson, 2008; Lavalette, 2011). At a time when much of social care is dominated by the tyranny of 'new technocracy' (Gillingham, 2019; Esmark, 2020), recalling and learning from histories of resistance and emancipation can provide our students and colleagues with crucial examples of hope, necessary for reimagining social work alternatives. Conversely, reflecting on histories of complicity, disturbing and distressing as they might be, helps us to understand the complex sociopolitical context within which social work operates. Histories of oppression act as a constant reminder of the social catastrophes that can occur, should social workers stop defending and prioritising fundamental human rights.

In this sense, it became evident that, in order to be fully understood, the 'two souls' of social work needed to be reviewed comparatively rather than in isolation. How are we to cherish the example of Polish social worker Irena Sendler, who confronted the Nazis and saved thousands of Jewish children in the notorious Warsaw Ghetto, if we do not simultaneously concede that the vast majority of German social workers at the time had actively supported Nazism? How can we celebrate the vast contributions of anti-racist social workers throughout the 20th century if we ignore the fact that mainstream social work, in several parts of the world, had operated contentedly and obediently within systems of institutional racism and colonialism?

It is for these reasons that the current book explores the histories both of complicity and of political resistance. Uncovering social work's troubled history not only creates the necessary space for social workers to learn from mistakes of the past but, crucially, also offers an opportunity for the profession to engage with a process of reconciliation and justice, supporting victims of structural violence and accounting for our profession's past in hope of its future. There are three main pillars in this process: (a) mapping and recognising the typologies of institutional oppression, (b) understanding the external and internal factors influencing social work's complicity and (c) working towards justice, reconciliation and change.

Mapping and recognising the typologies of institutional oppression

Categorising the types of institutional violence and oppression that social work has been complicit in is a rather complex exercise, as most (mal)practices naturally overlap with each other. Chapman and Withers (2019, p 7) have described such overlap as interlocking oppressions:

> Real power relations between helping professionals and service users come into being only as they interlock with both the specific stratifications and the violence opened up for that particular service user in receiving that particular service and the service provider's experiences of racism, colonialism, disablism, cisism, capitalism, heteropatriarchy, sexism and ageism.

In fact, as this book presents, multiple dimensions ('stratifications') of the human experience have been targeted by the disciplinary state as unwelcome, problematic and dangerous. However, we should also recognise that the common denominator in most of the histories of oppression categorically refers to the dimension of social class. For working-class communities have been disproportionately targeted by coercive social services – an experience relentlessly exacerbated when additional 'stratifications' such as race, disability and gender identity are also present. Such intersection between multiple human identities, experiences and social roles makes the process of disentangling the different types of oppression rather challenging. For analytical purposes we have proposed a typology of oppressive social work practice, on the basis of its target population, ideological knowledge base and specific practice.

Shaping the ideal-type family

Historically, one of the most fundamental and persistent preoccupations of state social services has been the shaping of the ideal-type family. The use of the term ideal-type does not refer to the Weberian concept of 'comparison via abstract idealisation'. In most contexts within which social work has operated as a state-sponsored profession, the ruling classes maintained a fairly concrete idea of how working-class families should behave and think. Indeed, the history of social work speaks to its evolution as an interclass profession, with its early founders and pioneers emanating from the middle class and focusing primarily on lower-class populations (Kendall, 1998; Strier, 2009). In the industrial metropolises of modernity, the prescribed social roles for the working-class family were informed by the need to ensure the production–consumption binary and, as such, were primarily assigned on the basis of class and gender. The model of patriarchy that emerged from the industrial revolution dictated that men were the uncontested household breadwinners, while women were bound by lifelong caring responsibilities. The children of the working-class family would invariably be seen, at a state level, as either the future workforce or merely a burden – depending on the specific financial and sociopolitical conjecture. The combination and perpetuation of these roles would ensure (a) the consolidation of family as a core production unit for capitalist economies, (b) the dispensing of state caring responsibilities to the family level and (c) the reproduction of moralistic ideas about the function of families.

State social work has been a key activity in the process of ensuring that the family unit abides by the prescribed roles dictated by the capitalist economies, albeit never the most important or prominent. Any family or individual who would deviate from the prescribed moral and social roles would be seen as 'deviant', 'problematic', 'underclass' or, in the most recent addition to the lexicon of repression, 'troubled' (see Crossley, 2018).

Featherstone et al (2018, p 27), in recent work on the development of a social model for child protection, have suggested that 'with the exception of a few decades of the 20th century, history shows a strong tendency towards individual social engineering to produce model citizens, with parenting practices the primary focus of state attention'. It is exactly such relentless emphasis on parenting, or more precisely mothering, that gave substance to a social work toolkit historically characterised by moralism, individualisation and demonisation of the poor. The oppressive repertoire in the formative years of social work included moralistic case-work, strict eligibility criteria and draconian family supervision.

Institutional oppression in social services, as manifested in the historical tension between social care and social control, has been the core characteristic of the welfare state in the era of modernity. This book, however, places particular emphasis on specific episodes in social work history, where the 'care and control' pendulum was firmly fixed towards the latter, episodes that are characterised by unusual brutality and inhumanity. Elsewhere, we have described these episodes as 'social work's horrible' histories (Ioakimidis et al, 2020; Ferguson et al, 2018), for they represent some of the most repugnant examples of social work and social welfare practice.

For example, in the United Kingdom (UK), a context where child protection policies have led to objectionable and contested practices, one would identify the history of forced child migration to Australia and Canada as a concrete case of extraordinary cruelty. The forced migration of children was a policy aimed at reducing the burden of residential care institutions through the relocation of orphaned children to Australia and Canada. Between 1920 and 1970 more than 130,000 children were sent to former British colonies, where they lived

> a life of servitude and hard labour in foster homes. The majority came from deprived backgrounds and were already in some form of social or charitable care. Many ended up on remote farms, or in state-run orphanages and church-run institutions. They were often separated from siblings and some were subjected to physical and sexual abuse. (*The Guardian*, 2019)

Shockingly, according to the Independent Enquiry into the Commonwealth Immigration Scheme, many social workers and local authority children's officers viewed these practices as reasonable and appropriate at the time of migration. During roughly the same period, the Irish state also encouraged and funded the creation of a nexus of abusive institutions aiming at detaining, stigmatising, controlling and punishing working-class women who had become pregnant outside of marriage. These institutions, known as mother-and-baby homes, became spaces of unbearable cruelty and abuse for well over 10,000 young mothers. According to the Commission of Investigation into Mother and Baby Homes (2021), 'around 9,000 children, one in seven of those born in the 18 institutions covered by the Commission's terms of reference, had died in them between 1922 and 1998, double the rate of infant mortality of the general population'. Tragically, many of these children were buried in unmarked graves.

The pattern of the ideal-type family creation and the subsequent demonisation of 'deviant' families had a different focus in countries where the state prioritised a more explicitly ideological agenda. Throughout the 20th century, the battle for winning young people's hearts and minds against the 'communist threat' was particularly pronounced in Latin America and Southern Europe. Spain and Greece are key examples of the latter region. As the painful history of babies stolen from their families during the dictatorship of Francisco Franco continues to unfold in Spain, the role of social services has come under the spotlight. In October 2018, a former doctor was found guilty for his part in the scandal, but escaped punishment, and a recent documentary film, *The Silence of Others*, has shed fresh light on the ongoing struggle for justice by those affected. In the aftermath of the Spanish Civil War (1936–39) and the subsequent defeat of the republican forces, Franco created a sophisticated and extensive system aimed at the ideological and political control of the population. It was based on two main pillars (Ioakimidis, 2020). The first was the ruthless suppression of socialist ideology, mostly through the incarceration and coercion of left-wing citizens. The second was the creation of an ideal type of Spanish family.

In pursuit of both these goals, victims' associations estimate that up to 300,000 new-born babies of left-wing and working-class families were illegally removed from their parents and given for adoption to mostly middle-class nationalist families. This practice continued well into the 1970s. The sheer scale of what happened in Spain belies the direct involvement of several state institutions, and the complicity of thousands of individuals who worked for or alongside the state, including doctors, nurses and social workers. The Spanish Catholic Church held a key role in this vast surreptitious network, and Franco's social services, the Auxilio Social, were directly implicated in the removals. As Martinez (2020, p 7) explains:

> The mission statement of the second school of social work in Spain, founded in Madrid at the beginning of the dictatorship, can serve to illustrate the ideological backlash in the field of social work brought about by the newly established political regime. According to this school's mission statement, social work [asistencia social] was 'a feminine area of study which [sic] aims [were] either a preparation of women for a service to society or an improvement of their education in order to become good and Christian mothers.

In Greece, social work was established as a professional activity at the beginning of the civil war (1944–49), with a key mission to contain families from rebel-controlled regions and establish, particularly within these regions, a child protection system through the physical segregation and eventual separation of families. Research on Greek social work suggests that the profession was so immersed in the politics of 'child-gathering' that nearly all social work practitioners in the 1950s had, in one way or another, been involved in the notorious 'child colonies' (Ioakimidis, 2011). Children from regions controlled by the Greek partisans were forcibly admitted to child protection institutions that resembled 19th-century workhouses. They were separated from their families and were subjected to systematic brainwashing and torture. Mando Dalianis, in her unique longitudinal study that includes interviews with affected children over a period of 30 years, provides evidence of the horrific nature of those institutions (Mazower and Dalianis, 2000). More recently, Gonda Van Steen (2021), in her ground-breaking study of the post-civil war illegal adoptions uncovered the silenced stories of the 3,200 Greek adoptees who were sent to the US between 1949 and 1962. The study suggests that such cruel practice was indeed informed by a number of factors, including the ideological tensions in post-civil war Greece, the destroyed infrastructure and economy and the first large-scale 'business' of adoption to meet increasing demand from the US.

Ideological tensions and the agenda of 'supressing the threat of communism', alongside the 'criminalisation of poverty', also formed a key factor in the development of Latin American histories of violent and arbitrary child removal. In Chile, during Augusto Pinochet's dictatorship, it is estimated that more than 15,000 Chilean babies and young children were arbitrarily offered for international adoption. In most cases, the records of these adoptions were destroyed.

According to the Chilean Adoptees Worldwide (2022):

> In Chile, this phenomenon is referred to as Illegal Adoptions and Child Trafficking and today the results of the official investigation have confirmed that the complete public system of Chile was involved. Doctors, nurses, midwives, hospitals, social workers, lawyers, judges, the child protecting authority and the civil registry, all have been having their involvement as per the findings of investigation team. But also nuns, priests, and even ambassadors and consuls have been identified [as] being involved.

Racist and colonial social services

The second broad category of institutionally and structurally oppressive social services is linked to the implementation of policies enabling colonialism and racial hierarchies. In effect, these policies were aimed toward social engineering, with the main objectives being to (a) absolve early capitalism of criticisms pointing to systemic failures responsible for the perpetuation of inequality, (b) articulate an individualised narrative that pathologised the poorest in society and (c) justify the brutality of colonial expansion and racial hierarchy by presenting people of non-White European race as inferior, ultimately subhuman and, therefore, worthy of exploitation and cruel treatment.

The theorisation of these policies drew its foundational narratives from the grotesque pseudoscience of eugenics, which emerged from the rapid development of natural sciences and engineering, upon which the industrial revolution based its impressive advances. This inspired, in the 19th century, a 'social science' that attempted to mimic and apply the laws of nature to human societies. Charles Darwin's theories of evolution through natural selection and Gregor Mendel's laws of inheritance were seen by the 19th-century ruling classes as safe, appropriate and persuasive ways of explaining poverty, inequality and petty crime. In 1883 Francis Galton coined the term 'eugenics' and defined the discipline as 'the study of agencies under social control that may improve or impair the racial qualities of future generations either physically or mentally' (NIH, 2022, np).

The idea of promoting 'human improvement' via the use of barbaric and invasive interventions gained widespread popularity among elites in Northern Europe and the US. Social work, a professional activity that in the early 20th century was desperately searching for a respectable 'scientific identity', was quick to subscribe to principles of social engineering. Social work practitioners in the UK and the US, up until the 1940s, would routinely use eugenics as the dominant analytical tool for understanding, predicting and 'case-working' working-class families (Welshman, 1999; Starkey, 2000; Kennedy, 2008).

In the US, eugenicists advocated for strict anti-immigration policies and supported racial segregation and discrimination in an effort to prevent the demographic mixing of White and non-White populations. Their alarmist and pseudo-scientific theories, particularly influential within the federal government, led to the adoption of catastrophic interventions such as the forced sterilisation of the 'feeble-minded' and the disproportionate targeting of Black and Latino families by welfare authorities. The legacy of institutional racism is still evident in the child protection system, where research has highlighted the continued over-representation of Black children subject to child welfare processes (Roberts, 2002).

In 2021, the US National Association of Social Workers (NASW) recognised the historical link between social work and theories of eugenics. Such recognition was part of the 'Undoing Racism Through Social Work' report, a brave document that documented histories of racial oppression within and beyond social work, urging the profession to make amends with its troubled past. This report recognised that: 'Many of the leading U.S. social scientists and social reformers of the day supported eugenics theories that were later adopted by the Nazis. In North Carolina, social workers participated in the involuntary sterilization of mostly women of color, women on welfare and in mental institutions' (NASW, 2021, p 3). The report also explains how, up until the 1970s, social problems such as poverty, crime and unemployment were considered as largely 'hereditary' and endemic within the inferior underclasses. Therefore, the 'treatment of choice' would include practices aimed at preventing those communities from 'reproducing'. Forced sterilisation practices lasted until well into the 1970s, permanently affecting more than 7,600 working-class and minority citizens (Boggs, 2013). In the state of North Carolina, sterilisations were recommended by social workers based on their 'diagnoses' of home environments and school performance (Boggs, 2013).

Principles of racial hierarchy were also utilised in the development of colonial social services in Canada, New Zealand, Australia and Latin America, where violent assimilation policies targeted First Nations and Indigenous communities. Implementation of these policies saw the direct involvement of state social services in actively suppressing Indigenous cultures and forcibly extending settler values to native communities (Ioakimidis, 2020). Despite local and contextual variations in each country, the pattern of oppressive social services intervention seemed to broadly adopt the following pattern:

- marginalisation of non-western cultures;
- criminalisation of native/Indigenous communities;
- strict control of parenting, with subsequent suppression of Indigenous models of 'community parenting' as deviant;
- disproportional child removal rates targeting native/Indigenous communities;
- suppression of Indigenous languages and traditions;
- illegal adoptions;
- institutionalisation through abusive residential schools and care institutions.

A characteristic example of violent assimilation is the infamous 'Canada Scoops', referring to the removal of several thousand children from Aboriginal families under the guise of social care. According to The Aboriginal Justice Implementation Commission, within a period of nearly 20 years (from the early 1960s until the late 1980s) the child welfare system:

> removed Aboriginal children from their families, communities and cultures, and placed them in mainstream society. Child welfare workers removed Aboriginal children from their families and communities because they felt the best homes for the children were not Aboriginal homes. The ideal home would instil the values and lifestyles with which the child welfare workers themselves were familiar: white, middle-class homes in white, middle-class neighbourhoods. Aboriginal communities and Aboriginal parents and families were deemed to be 'unfit'. As a result, between 1971 and 1981 alone, over 3,400 Aboriginal children were shipped away to adoptive parents in other societies, and sometimes in other countries. (The Aboriginal Justice Implementation Commission, 1999)

In many respects, the 'Canada Scoops' bring echoes of the Aboriginal Protection Act (1869) that paved the way for the creation of the 'stolen generations' in Australia. For a period spanning almost 100 years, colonial social services implemented a policy and practice of methodically removing Indigenous children from their families in order to 'uproot' whole communities and forcibly assimilate them into western culture. Most of these children were placed in residential schools, whose racist and colonial nature has been responsible for inflicting trauma at both collective and individual levels.

In the African continent, the South African case provides one of the most brutal manifestations of divisive colonial social services. The origins of social services, and consequently social work in South Africa, can be traced back to principles of Social Darwinism so integral to the establishment and domination of apartheid, one of the most extreme expressions of colonial authority. These principles, enshrined in the apartheid system of structural and institutional segregation, dictated that social services were strictly provided along racial lines; they were therefore inherently unequal, hierarchal and ultimately dehumanising. South African social work stands indicted with culpability for its origins in and complicity with colonialism and apartheid in its ideologies, knowledge base, discourse and practice (Harms-Smith, 2014). The historical tension between social work complicity in institutional oppression and social work resistance against apartheid was reflected on the actual split between the white Social Work Association of South Africa (Swasa) and the South African Black Social Workers Association (Sabswa).

Undoubtedly, the most extensive, horrific and murderous case of social engineering in social services is that of Nazi Germany. As Ioakimidis and Trimikliniotis (2020) have highlighted, the German '*Fuersorgerinnen*' ('social carers'), the precursors of the more anglicised post-war 'social workers', were immersed into eugenics discourse and uncritically accepted its principles, believing that this was more about 'public health' improvement rather than an aggressive form of social engineering. In this context, the role of social workers was two-fold. On the one hand, social work contributed to the process of nurturing the ideal-type Aryan family, through ideological indoctrination and 'education'. On the other hand, social work practitioners were directly involved in the process of recording and identifying the racially inferior and 'unworthy citizens' (that is, people with disabilities, mental health challenges, minority communities and so on). Identification of the 'unworthy' would lead to their eventual detention and, in many cases, their extermination. The implicit or explicit involvement of social workers with policies and ideologies that culminated in the Holocaust has been, by some distance, the single most horrendous chapter of social work's global history.

One of the most notable examples of high-profile social work collaboration with the Nazi regime can be traced to the 'Reich Centre for Combating Juvenile Crime', which was created in 1939. The Centre was headed by a social work 'leader', Friederike Wieking, who promoted pseudo-scientific research on the Social Darwinist idea of 'crime heredity' (Wildt, 2002). Part of Wieking's activity saw the development of concentration camps for those whom the Nazis described and classified as deviant youth. These camps provided spaces for unethical experiments, arbitrary detention, torture and execution of young people. Such was the recognition of Friederike Wieking's work within the Nazi leadership that she was eventually promoted to government director in the Reich Criminal Police Headquarters.

Institutionalisation, incarceration and securitisation

The previous two categories of our, admittedly broad and overlapping, typology focused on the ideology, pseudo-science and theoretical conceptualisations underpinning the legacies of oppressive social work. The third major category encapsulates the range of specific practices that were utilised by social work practitioners, among others, in order to materially implement the policies and ideologies of the repressive welfare state. Key dimensions of the practical implementation of those policies were formed through the use of power and coercion. Justification for the use of oppressive techniques aimed at the discipline and control of communities with which social workers were expected to work was based on the existence of 'problematic' or 'troubled' individuals who needed to be 'contained' rather than supported.

Although in recent years there has been a welcome expansion of literature exploring aspects of social work's past and its politically contradictory nature (Reisch, 2002; Chapman and Withers, 2019; Ioakimidis and Trimikliniotis, 2020), there is still a persistent myth surrounding the evolution of the social work profession. This myth relates to the idea that social work is an unconditionally and inherently benevolent activity. The idea that the social worker is an individual who has consciously selected the ethical career of a humanitarian, and therefore automatically qualifies as compassionate and humanitarian practitioner, is as old as the profession itself. Such a conceptualisation of social work has been magnified by the often neutrally presented narrative of its religious and philanthropic origins. One needs to remember that in the formative years of social work in the UK, the public discourse never interrogated the theoretical and philosophical base of the profession, as it was considered unquestionably benevolent. Instead, the emphasis was on the gradual transformation of social workers' 'good intents' into a structured professional activity. Jones (1983, p 81) in his seminal study of the origins of state social work in the UK reminds us that 'One of the principal objectives of the COS [Charity Organisations Society] founding members was to transform philanthropy from an unskilled "duty" of the rich to an expert and professional activity undertaken only by those who were prepared by social theory and appropriate methods'. According to Jones (1983), the emergence of a social work that followed the 'scientific' methodology would be seen by some people, even within the middle classes, as less caring and direct than almsgiving. However, the expectation of the COS, in these formative years, would be that professionalisation of social work would counterbalance the potential risks of creating a more assertive workforce. After all, this narrative held, despite a change in its methods of practice, that the newly formed profession would remain characterised by 'the liberal and compassionate middle-class values' (Jones, 1983). Similarly, Chapman and Withers (2019), in their study about the violent history of benevolence, argue that there is a need for social work to disrupt the profession's 'shared genealogy of morality'.

In many respects, the idea of an unconditionally benevolent and humane profession, immune from the hard-heartedness of other activities, informs more recent ideas of care as 'tough love' directed towards unruly and chaotic service users. The fundamental principle of this rather simplistic and self-serving approach is based on the following logic: social work is an ethical and caring profession; service users are often manipulative; therefore, practice that can be seen as controlling and oppressive is a result of the service users' uncooperativeness rather than the profession's lack of compassion.

The prioritisation of social control over social care, on many occasions, has taken the material form of institutionalisation and containment. The most persistent and characteristic examples of this repressive institutionalisation can be found in the field of mental health (Ferguson, 2017). Oppressive approaches to mental health included the creation of abusive total institutions and the use of coercive and violent medicalised therapies (such us the use of lobotomy and confinement). Carr and Taggart (2017, np), while exploring the case for a truth and reconciliation process in psychiatry, focused on the two pillars upon which power and oppression in mental health services operate:

> *Power* in psychiatry and mental health services is *structural* as well as *interpersonal*. Although operating in the same harmful system, staff nonetheless remained in a position of power within those structures. They had a choice to work where they did, were not subject to containment and compulsion, and could leave the hospital at the end of the working day. They also had a professional (and human) duty to speak out and act if they witnessed abuse within services, as the best staff did and still do. (Original emphasis)

As we highlight in this book, practitioner complicity in oppressive practices usually operates under the guise of technocratic neutrality. It is exactly such pseudo-neutrality that has allowed the development of a sophisticated 'coercive toolkit' entwined with the logic of institutionalisation: the surveillance and securitisation approach. Although, securitisation and surveillance were proclaimed as tools primarily destined for the criminal justice system, it is their historical use – and more recently unprecedented proliferation – in the welfare state that deserves greater attention from the social work literature. Historical examples of strict surveillance of people with whom social services worked have been described in the previous section, where we placed a particular emphasis on colonial residential schools and Nazi social services. However, the securitised social services, borrowing expertise from the military, were not uncommon in post-Second World War Europe. Mazower and Dalianis (2000) describe the development of post-war child protection services ('children villages') in Greece:

> Conditions in these villages in many ways resembled prison life and there was the same rigid sense of a division between 'inside' and 'outside' worlds separated usually by walls or guarded [by] barbed-wire fences. They were run on quasi-military lines, often by former officers, who employed corporal punishment and made the children wear uniforms. Letters were censored, just like in prison, and the atmosphere was generally unfriendly. As in prison, there were no clocks or calendars, and the day was regulated by the ringing of a bell. The children were marched everywhere, even on occasional visits to the world outside, to the cinema or local park. Most teachers were indifferent or cruel to their charges, though there were some exceptions. (Mazower and Dalianis, 2000, p 99)

Italian scholar Giorgio Agamben (2005) provided us with an important conceptualisation of the oppressive nature of practices embedded in the securitisation of services when he referred to the rise of the 'state of exception': a suspension of the juridical order which is exploited by the state in order to curb liberties and justify oppressive measures in the name of a nominal or actual threat to national security and order. It is exactly this state of 'legalised lawlessness' that we have been witnessing in many countries that pledge to fight the so-called enemy within.

More recently, social workers have been appointed in detention centres for asylum seekers – institutions of ambiguous legality have emerged across Europe, often in direct conflict with international conventions for the rights of refugees. In a similar vein, social and community workers in the UK and France have been recruited in order to 'reach out' to Muslim communities and identify potential cases of extremism and radicalisation of young people (Stanley et al, 2018). Within the context of rising Islamophobia and a steady erosion of civil liberties, the proposed collaboration of social workers with intelligence services and law enforcement institutions requires careful interrogation. Indeed, as several of the histories explored within this volume illustrate, uncritical collaboration has the potential to oppress, victimise and stigmatise entire communities (Ioakimidis, 2015; Finch and McKendrick, 2019). There is a risk that social workers involved in such projects could be expected to police and control vulnerable communities instead of working with them in order promote social justice and equality. Certainly, the social work answer to the disproportional levels of inequality, poverty and marginalisation of minority communities cannot be further policing and manipulation.

Conclusion

Exploring the past and, most importantly, making amends with its troubled aspects can be a complex, painful and unsettling journey for social work. It is our contention that, despite the challenges embedded in this process, dealing with contested historical legacies is a journey that social work cannot escape. Proclaimed inevitabilities aside, social work should not try to consciously avoid this journey either. For its contradictory legacies of harm are still present and visible in modern social work theory and practice, albeit largely unspoken. In fact, the most fundamental reason for engaging with the profession's troubled past is not related to the profession itself, whether that be its institutions or practitioners. Rather, it is critical because, outside the microcosm of inter- and intra-professional social work debates, there are whole generations of communities that have been harmed, abused, traumatised and ostracised by social services. Recognising the profession's role in such collective and intergenerational harm is a step towards empathising with, and actively supporting, the healing and liberation of these communities.

The question of 'how to make amends with our past' is a relatively recent one for social work. Social work literature has been slow in responding to broader debates within societies in transition. In most cases, the social work discussion about historical wrongdoings has taken the form of a delayed, reluctant and diluted reaction to broad public debates. Although there are no publicly articulated arguments presenting the case against engagement with its past injustices, let alone to apologise for them, our involvement in international social work fora and professional associations suggests that, anecdotally, there is considerable opposition to making amends with social work's past.

The three main arguments typically posited against a meaningful engagement with the past can be presented as follows:

- Social work is not an activity with significant professional or academic status. Uncovering past legacies will only serve to undermine our professional status even further.
- A possible social work apology for past wrongdoings will open the 'Pandora's box' and will make the professional associations and employers vulnerable to litigation. After all, why should contemporary social work pay for the wrongdoings of past generations?
- Apologies and apologetics are performative and do not lead to meaningful change.

It is crucial that all these arguments are addressed, irrespective of whether they are rooted in genuine and legitimate concerns. The first argument appears to be the most popular within professional associations and societies of social work, and draws its narrative from the more technocratic tradition of social work. The rationale here is that social work has traditionally been a 'lower status – lower power' professional activity, at least in comparison to other professions with which social workers often work on similar territory (psychiatrists, lawyers and so on). Opening up difficult debates, this argument sustains, can create enormous pressures in terms of professional recognition and public trust, and ultimately does more harm than good.

However, this argument adopts several theoretical misconceptions which reflect an uncritical understanding of the context of power imbalance within which social workers operate. Most problematically this argument positions the status and reputation of social work as an institution, rather than the rights and dignity of people it purportedly serves. It also follows the miscalculated fallacy of political neutrality. Social workers, despite the pressures they face as professionals and employees, still retain significantly and disproportionately more power than the individuals and communities they work with. Performing 'damage limitation' activities while there are well-evidenced and widely articulated cases of intergenerational harm infected by social services is also short sighted. Ultimately, such baggage will have the opposite outcome in relation to the status and reputation of social work by undermining relationships and breaching trust with communities. Social work should draw its legitimacy and recognition from the communities it works with, rather than the artificially prescribed hierarchies it operates within. Whenever social work fails to recognise its political dimension and emphasises instead the technical aspects of the profession, it is exposed to the risk of becoming irrelevant or – at worst – oppressive. Therefore, hiding past legacies can be seen as a sign of insecurity and social irrelevance that can only lead to the repetition of the profession's troubled past. Elsewhere, we have described the example of Greek social workers during the dictatorship of the 1970s, who, motivated by an agenda of professional recognition, enthusiastically made themselves available to the authoritarian regime as experts in disciplining the politically unruly youth (Ioakimidis, 2011; Ioakimidis et al, 2020). The military regime, in return, offered this much-desired recognition by promoting social workers to the higher level of senior civil servants. However, this short-sighted quest for recognition meant that social work in the country, despite its temporary promotion within state hierarchies, remained socially irrelevant for decades beyond the dictatorship.

The second argument, that contemporary social work has no moral or ethical responsibility for the profession's past, has been shaped by a mixture of liberal individualism and self-serving managerial 'pragmatism'. The former element is reminiscent of narratives suggesting that contemporary generations should not 'pay for' the wrongdoings of their predecessors. It echoes, for example, the intervention made by Republican Congressman Henry Hyne, who, during a discussion about reparations in response to the legacies of slavery, proclaimed 'I never owned a slave. I never oppressed anybody. I don't know that I should have to pay for someone who did, generations before I was born' (cited in Sandel, 2010).

Ideas of moral individualism, as the basis of denying the continuity of past legacies, can appeal to supporters of the philosophical concept of 'autonomy'. However, when they are applied, in a rather selective manner, to contemporary debates about past wrongdoings, they not hold to scrutiny. In fact, they do a disservice to the liberal thesis on autonomy insofar as they ignore intergenerational and historical aspects that shape and determine individual experiences. Even for the staunchest apologist of this logic, it is difficult to sustain that the White European population, whether in North America, South Africa or Australia have, notwithstanding class inequalities, has not benefited from centuries of racial hierarchy. The impact of 'dividends' created in a system based on racial exploitation and colonialism, although not shared equally across the White population in these countries, is undeniably reflected in the persistence of epidemiological, financial, political and educational advantages related to those of Indigenous and ethnic minority communities.

Social work that operated in racially segregated societies was part of a range of professions that established their professional status, and the benefits that derived from this, through the implementation of repressive and institutionally racist policies. As this book highlights in case study after case study, such levels of complicity were not limited to a small number of 'bad apples'. Rather, engagement with oppressive practice became, given the appropriate conditions and concessions, the accepted norm of social work practice in the given context. Acknowledging the intergenerational continuities not only counters ideas of moral individualism but also addresses the latter part of this argument linked to fears of litigation. Social work as a predominantly state profession cannot be immune from discussions about the judicial aspects of past wrongdoings. Instead of engaging with this discussion from a position of insecurity and reluctance, social work can (and should) proactively create alliances with survivors' movements demanding collective reparation for victims. Not only would supporting survivors' movements provide much-needed space for reconciliation and the rebuilding of trust, it would also demonstrate that social workers, despite the limitations imposed by their proximity to the state, remain committed to human rights and social justice, and prioritise the people they work with.

The third argument adopts a superficially 'radical' approach. Proponents of the 'apology as meaningless performativity' response to calls for a reckoning of the profession's past tend to recognise the significance and lasting impact of past wrongdoings. They also subscribe to a largely helpful analysis that points towards the structural dimensions of oppressive social services. As mentioned earlier in this chapter, histories of oppression within social work are critically linked to the contradictory nature of social services within colonial and capitalist societies. Promoting ruling-class interpretations around deviance, poverty and ill-health had a concrete material basis. These interpretations functioned as conceptualisations supporting the perpetuation of class inequalities and class exploitation. Unless the root causes of historical injustices remain unchallenged, social work will not be able to bring about change within and beyond the profession. Poulantzas, in his classic response to Miliband in their debate about the role of the state in capitalist societies, very eloquently suggested that 'as is always the case when a scientific theory is lacking, bourgeois conceptions of the State and of political power have pre-empted the terrain of political theory almost unchallenged' (Poulantzas, 1969, p 69).

This approach, valuable and valid as it is, remains incomplete when it does not engage with the interpersonal dimensions of structural oppression. It is exactly such dichotomy between the structural and the interpersonal that is bridged through engagement with the survivors' movements and the subsequent recognition and acknowledgement of the profession's past wrongdoings. It is an elitist form of ideological purity to ignore the voices of survivors calling for an apology as a crucial step towards justice and healing. Survivors' movements worldwide have demonstrated the importance of state (and consequently state services') apologies in leading to a 'ripple effect' that can be triggered through official acknowledgement of past wrongdoings.

Dr Fejo King (2011), an aboriginal woman, social worker and active member of the Australian Association of Social Workers, assumed a leading role in The Stolen Generations Alliance in Australia and campaigned tirelessly for a federal apology. Highlighting the symbolic and material importance of an institutional apology, King noted:

> The Stolen Generations Alliance believed an apology would make a difference to all Australians, not just to Indigenous Australia. ... The ripple effect of the Apology as it was reported across Australia and around the world has been phenomenal and is what is lifted up to the light and held as the showpiece of this presentation. The international response was unexpected. The Stolen Generations Alliance received emails from countries torn apart by war in Africa, and Eastern Nations who told that they gathered in their communities and together watched the Apology. (Fejo-King, 2011, p 137)

Beyond the debate surrounding whether a reckoning with social work's past is needed or warranted is the question of what form and process this would take. Historically, processes of acknowledging and making amends for historical injustice and wrongdoing have reflected three distinct political and philosophical approaches: (a) retributive, (b) restorative and (c) emphasis on forgetting.

Retributive approaches to dealing with past injustices emphasise the importance of delivering peace and reconciliation through a process of identifying and persecuting individuals found to have committed serious crimes against humanity. In their most common form, retributive approaches require the setting up of criminal tribunals responsible for delivering justice in relation to the specific political-geographical jurisdiction within which crimes were committed. An early and rather incomplete example of retributive justice in transitional societies was the Nuremberg trials that brought leaders of the Nazi regime to justice. More contemporarily, the International Criminal Tribunal for the former Yugoslavia provides a characteristic case of retributive justice in transitional societies.

In terms of social work responses to past injustices, countries that followed a retributive approach to making amends with the past include Chile, Germany and Argentina. In Argentina, social workers were persecuted for crimes against humanity committed during the dictatorship, while in Germany the only recorded persecution of a Nazi social worker during the denazification process was that of Friederike Wieking, discussed earlier in this chapter.

Restorative approaches to making amends with past wrongdoings follow considerably different philosophical and political principles to those of the retributive strand. Restorative approaches are influenced by First Nation and Indigenous philosophies of collective healing. The emphasis here is not on persecution and punishment of specific individuals but, rather, on recognition of the collective harm inflicted and subsequent encouragement of healing through dialogue. Gilbert and Settles (2007, p 7) describe how

> Restorative justice views crime as a harm to individuals, their neighbourhoods, the surrounding community, and even the offender. Crimes produce injuries that must be repaired by those who caused the injury. In this sense, crimes are more than a violation of law, and justice is more than punishment of the guilty. Restorative justice strives to promote healing through structured communication processes among victims, offenders, community representatives and government officials. It also strives to accomplish these goals in a manner that promotes peace and order for the community, vindication for the victim, and recompense for the offender. Under this restorative perspective, justice is not based on punishment inflicted but the extent to which harms have been repaired and future harms prevented.

The most iconic and representative example of restorative justice in response to state-inflicted violence is the creation of the Truth and Reconciliation

Commission in post-apartheid South Africa. In this country, social workers were involved in discussions about past harms and contributed to the national truth-seeking dialogue, although their contribution was not necessarily social-work specific. National Social Work Associations in Canada and Australia also attempted to follow a restorative and reconciliatory approach, through recognition of social services' complicity in acts of cultural genocide and support for the development of action plans towards making amends. In the case of the US NASW, recognition of past wrongdoing inflicted by institutionally racist social services also followed restorative approaches accompanied by a more assertive political agenda demanding structural change and expecting social workers to fully engage with anti-racist practices.

Other countries have opted to avoid discussions about the past altogether and are characterised by an emphasis on forgetting. In Spain, transition to democracy was characterised by a marked unwillingness of the state to investigate institutional violence during Franco's regime. Such unwillingness was formalised through the Pact of Forgetting (Pacto del Olvido), which ensured the suppression of judicial, academic or even political discussions with regard to holding individuals responsible for past violations of human rights. Consequently, only recently have discussions about illegal adoptions and the role of the church and social work reluctantly resurfaced in the public domain. Greece seems to have followed a relatively similar path. Although the leaders of the 1967–74 military junta were imprisoned, a rather disorganised 'national reconciliation' approach meant that the records referring to violations of human rights were destroyed and questions about suppression of civil liberties during the latter half of the 20th century were not openly addressed by the state.

Table 1.1 provides a summary of the best-known social work responses to making amends with historical injustices that involves social services.

This chapter has presented the typologies of social work's complicity in historical injustices. It has also addressed, in a comparative manner, official social work responses to the profession's troubled past. Our intention has been to reinvigorate the rather anaemic global debate about social work's responses to past legacies, and we have tried to do so by adopting a critical epistemological perspective that sides with communities that have suffered harm at the hands of social work.

Despite the fact that some official social work associations have made efforts towards recognising past injustices, there is still a need for a more structured and nuanced approach to recognising past harms. This should be based on a meaningful and genuine paradigm shift within global social work. Notwithstanding the symbolic reparatory nature of a social work apology, a more material and substantial approach to historical justice should also be forward looking and political, prioritising structural change within social services. The 'liberal peace' approach that emphasises a western conception

Table 1.1: Summary of recognition and responses to historical injustices involving social services

Country	Description of documented social work/social services oppressive practices	State responses	Social work responses
Aotearoa (New Zealand)	Substantial history of removal of Māori children from their whānau (extended families) and placement in pākehā (European) foster homes or institutions. 1986, Pūao-te-Āta-tū report exposed institutional racism within the then Department of Social Welfare. More recent exposure of substantial history of physical, emotional and sexual abuse of children in care, particularly in both state and church institutions. 2019, significant media exposure to increased incidence of Māori children being removed from their mothers at birth by Oranga Tamariki (statutory care and protection agency), as a result of a 'subsequent children' amendment to legislation enacted by previous neoliberal government.	1989, Children, Young Persons and Their Families Act strongly influenced by Pūao-te-Āta-tū report. Implemented innovative process of Family Group Conferences, derived from models of whānau decision making, and provision for 'iwi' (tribal) authorities to undertake statutory care and protection functions. However these were not adequately resourced. 2018, Labour-led government implemented Royal Commission of Inquiry into abuse in care between 1950 and 1999, initial focus on state care subsequently expanded to faith-based care. Hearings ongoing. **February 2021**, Labour-led government commissioned Ministerial Advisory Board to report; Te Kahu Aroha released September 2021, recommending reform to more Māori- and community-led response.	1993, publication of then New Zealand Association of Social Workers Code of Ethics and Code of Bicultural Practice. 1999, name of association changed to Aotearoa New Zealand Association of Social Workers. 2008, Code of Ethics and Code of Bicultural Practice combined into one bilingual (English and Te Reo Māori) Code of Ethics document. 'Responsibility for a Te Tiriti o Waitangi based society' first ethical principle. 2018, ANZASW statement of support for Royal Commission of Inquiry. 2021, ANZASW statement that the association 'fully supports and stands behind the findings and recommendations of Te Kahu Aroha – the Oranga Tamariki Ministerial Advisory Board report. We are saddened and hurt by the continued systemic failings of the Government and previous leadership of Oranga Tamariki that has been harmful to tamariki and whānau. We are pleased to hear the Government has accepted the recommendations and we now call on them to ensure plentiful resourcing and funding to enable the full implementation of the aspirational changes. The voice and value of social work has been systematically stripped out of Oranga Tamariki by both the Government and leadership and we fully embrace the finding that social work must return to the core of Oranga Tamariki'. **Restorative approach**

Table 1.1: Summary of recognition and responses to historical injustices involving social services (continued)

Country	Description of documented social work/social services oppressive practices	State responses	Social work responses
Argentina	State-sponsored illegal adoptions targeting left-wing and working-class families.	Truth and Justice Commission. **1983**, restoration of democracy. Conviction of perpetrators for crimes against humanity committed in the context of the international crime of genocide.	Social Work Association contributes to the 'Never Again' movement for Memory, Truth and Justice. Removal of complicit practitioners from the Association's register. **Retributive approach**
Australia	Colonial social services, forced removal of Aboriginal and Torres Strait Islander children, violent institutionalisation (Stolen Generations).	**2008**, apology from Prime Minister Kevin Rudd.	**2004**, 'Acknowledgment' Statement. **2013**, creation of 'Reconciliation Action Plan' (ongoing). **Restorative approach**
Canada	Colonial social services, forced removal of indigenous children, family separations, violent institutionalisation.	**2008**, Prime Minister Harper offered full apology. **2022**, Pope Francis apologised for the Roman Catholic Church's involvement in abusive Canadian boarding schools.	**2019**, National Association Apology for contributing to the injustices imposed on Indigenous peoples. Commitment to Reconciliation Statement. **Restorative approach**
Chile	State-sponsored illegal adoptions targeting left wing and working-class families	**1990**, transition to democracy. National Committee of Truth and Reconciliation.	Restoration of the democratically elected professional association. **Restorative with a focus on structural change**
Germany	Holocaust, promotion of the Aryan Family, segregation of 'racially inferior families'.	Nuremberg Trials. Denazification. Reparations	Recognition of social work's complicity (through events and publications supported by the professional association). No formal acknowledgement or apology. **Mixed retributive and restorative approach**

(continued)

Table 1.1: Summary of recognition and responses to historical injustices involving social services (continued)

Country	Description of documented social work/social services oppressive practices	State responses	Social work responses
Greece	'Child Gathering', detention of children from rebel-influenced regions, state-sponsored illegal adoptions.	No state recognition of the illegal adoptions. Child protection records are inaccessible or destroyed.	No official response from Hellenic Association of Social Workers. **Emphasis on forgetting**
South Africa	Apartheid, racially segregated social services	1990, release of Nelson Mandela. 1994, first multi-racial elections Establishment of a Truth and Reconciliation.	2007, creation of a unified, non-racial 'National Association of Social Workers, South Africa'. Historical split between the white Social Work Association of South Africa (Swasa) and the South African Black Social Workers Association (Sabswa). **Restorative approach**
Spain	State-sponsored illegal adoptions targeting left-wing and working-class families.	Pact of Forgetting outlaws research on or public scrutiny of abuses committed under Franco.	No official response from Spanish Association of Social Workers. **Emphasis on forgetting**
UK	Commonwealth Child Migration Scheme.	2010, Prime Minister Gordon Brown apologised and announced £6m fund for victims.	The historical involvement of social workers has not been adequately documented. The scheme's abusive nature was revealed by a social worker (Margaret Humphreys), whose contribution has been celebrated by BASW and IFSW. **Moderate restorative approach**
US	Institutional racism, disproportionate rates of child removal from non-White families, institutionalisation, forced sterilisation.	1997, President Bill Clinton apologised for the Tuskegee Syphilis Experiment. 2008, the US House of Representatives apologised for slavery and the impact of the Jim Crow Laws.	2021, NASW apologised for racist practices in US social work. 'Undoing Racism' report (NASW, 2021) proposes Racial Justice Priorities and Action Plan. **Restorative with an emphasis on structural change**

of liberal democracy and marketisation is not fit for purpose in the context of social services. On the one hand, 'liberal peace's' Eurocentric nature suppresses grassroots knowledges and collective participation, perpetuating historical mistakes of state-orchestrated assimilation. On the other hand, the principles of marketisation and profit making are incompatible with social care. It is for these reasons that we invite the global social work community to develop an approach focusing on the following main actions:

- symbolic reparations and recognition of past injustices through an official social work apology. Such apology needs to be expressed by global social work organisations, encouraging and legitimising national associations that are, for various reasons, reluctant or unwilling to deal with past legacies;
- establishing a global Truth, Justice and Reconciliation Commission for social work and social services. The emphasis should be on dialogue, truth seeking, restorative justice and collective reparations;
- supporting arguments for collective material reparations. These reparations may have a different outlook in different countries. For example, Irish movements of survivors prioritise access to historical records as a reparatory gesture, while movements of Greek adoptees who were sent to the US demand Greek citizenship;
- creating meaningful and genuine alliances with survivors' movements and communities that have suffered from past injustices;
- working with broader social movements and trade unions towards countering marketisation and technocratic principles in social services;
- collectively reimagining an inclusive, social justice-based social work.

References

Agamben, G. (2005) *State of exception*. Chicago, IL: University of Chicago Press.

Boggs, B. (2013) *For the public good: The shameful history of forced sterilization in the US*. Available from: https://longreads.com/2014/11/19/for-the-public-good/

Carr, S. and Taggart, D. (2017) Do we need a truth and reconciliation process in psychiatry? Available from: www.nationalelfservice.net/populations-and-settings/service-user-involvement/do-we-need-a-truth-and-reconciliation-process-in-psychiatry/

Chapman, C. and Withers, A.J. (2019) *A violent history of benevolence: Interlocking oppression in the moral economies of social working*. Toronto: University of Toronto Press.

Chilean Adoptees Worldwide (2022) History of the organisation. Available from: https://chileanadoptees.org/history/

Crossley, S. (2018) *Troublemakers: The construction of 'troubled families as a social problem*. Bristol: Policy Press.

Esmark, A. (2020) *The new technocracy*. Bristol: Policy Press.

Featherstone, B. and Gupta, A. (2018) *Protecting children: A social model*. Bristol: Policy Press.

Fejo-King, C. (2011) The national apology to the stolen generations: The ripple effect, *Australian Social Work*, 64: 1, 130–143.

Ferguson, I. (2008) *Reclaiming social work: Challenging neoliberalism and promoting social justice*. London: Sage.

Ferguson, I. (2017) *Politics of the mind: Marxism and mental health*. London: Bookmarks.

Ferguson I., Ioakimidis, V. and Lavalette M. (2018) *Global Social Work in a Political Context: Radical Perspectives*. Bristol: Policy Press.

Finch, J. and McKendrick, D. (2019) Securitising social work: Counter terrorism, extremism and radicalisation. In S. Webb (ed) *Routledge handbook of critical social work* (pp 244–255). London: Routledge.

Garrett, P.M. (2021) 'A world to win': In defence of (dissenting) social work – a response to Chris Maylea. *The British Journal of Social Work*, 51(4): 1131–1149.

Gilbert, M.J. and Settles, T.L. (2007) The next step: Indigenous development of neighborhood restorative community justice. *Criminal Justice Review 32*(5): 5–25.

Gillingham, P. (2019) From bureaucracy to technocracy in a social welfare agency: A cautionary tale. *Asia Pacific Journal of Social Work and Development 29*(2): 108–119.

Ioakimidis, V. (2011) Expanding imperialism, exporting expertise: International social work and the Greek project (1946–1974). *International Social Work 54*(4): 505–519.

Ioakimidis, V. (2015) The two faces of Janus: Rethinking social work in the context of conflict. *Social Dialogue 3*(10): 6–11.

Ioakimidis, V. (2020) From Franco's 'stolen babies' to Nazi Germany, social services have a dark past – it's time for a global reckoning, *The Conversation*. Available from: https://theconversation.com/from-francos-stolen-bab ies-to-nazi-germany-social-services-have-a-dark-past-its-time-for-a-glo bal-reckoning-118008

Ioakimidis, V. and Trimikliniotis, N. (2020) Making sense of social work's troubled past: Professional identity, collective memory and the quest for historical justice. *The British Journal of Social Work 50*(6): 1890–1908.

Ioakimidis, V., Martinez-Herrero I. and Wyllie, A. (2020) Confronting social work's troubled past: Is it time for a Global Truth and Reconciliation Commission? *Social Dialogue*, issue 22 (guest editorial).

Jones, C. (1983) *State social work and the working class*. Basingstoke: Macmillan.

Jones, C., Ferguson, I., Lavalette, M. and Penketh, L. (2004) Social work and social justice: A manifesto for a new engaged practice. Available from: https://socialworkfuture.org/social-work-and-social-justice-a-manifesto-for-a-new-engaged-practice/

Kendall, K.A. (1998) *IASSW: The first fifty years 1928–1978 and: A tribute to the founders.* International Association of Schools of Social Work.

Kennedy, A.C. (2008) Eugenics, 'degenerate girls', and social workers during the progressive era. *Affilia 23*(1): 22–37.

Lavalette, M. (ed) (2011) *Radical social work today: Social work at the crossroads.* Bristol: Policy Press.

Martinez-Herrero, I.M. (2020) Facing a dark and unknown chapter of the history of social work in Spain: social work in times of Franco's eugenics and stolen babies. In V. Ioakimidis, I. Martinez-Herrero and A. Wyllie (eds) 'Confronting social work's troubled past: Is it time for a Global Truth and Reconciliation Commission?' *Social Dialogue*, issue 22.

Maylea, C. (2021) The end of social work. *The British Journal of Social Work 51*(2): 772–789.

Mazower, M. and Dalianis, M. (2000) 'Children in turmoil during the civil war: Today's adults'. In M. Mazower (ed) *After the war was over: Reconstructing the family, nation and state in Greece, 1943–1960.* Princeton, NJ: Princeton University Press.

National Association of Social Workers (2021) Undoing racism through social work: NASW report to the profession. Available from: www.social workers. org/LinkClick.aspx?fileticket ¼29AYH9 qAdXc%3d&portalid1/40

NIH (National Human Genome Research Institute) (2022) Eugenics and scientific racism. Available from: www.genome.gov/about-genomics/fact-sheets/Eugenics-and-Scientific-Racism

Poulantzas, N. (1969) 'The problem of the capitalist state', *New Left Review 58*: 67–78.

Reisch, M. and Andrews, J. (2002) *The road not taken: A history of radical social work in the United States.* London: Brunner-Routledge.

Roberts, D.E. (2002) *Shattered bonds: The color of child welfare.* New York: Basic Books.

Sandel, M. (2010) *Justice: What's the right thing to do?* London: Penguin Books.

Smith, L. (2014) Historiography of South African social work: Challenging dominant discourses. *Social Work 50*(3): 305–331.

Stanley, T., Guru, S. and Gupta, A. (2018) Working with Prevent: Social work options for cases of 'radicalisation risk'. *Practice 30*(2): 131–146.

Starkey, P. (2000) *Families and social workers: The work of Family Service Units, 1940–1985.* Liverpool: Liverpool University Press.

Strier, R. (2009) Class-competent social work: A preliminary definition. *International Journal of Social Welfare 18*(3): 237–242.

The Aboriginal Justice Implementation Commission (1999) The justice system and Aboriginal people. Government of Manitoba. Available from: www.ajic. Mb.ca/reports/final_toc.html

The Commission of Investigation into Mother and Baby Homes (2021) *Final report of the Commission of Investigation into Mother and Baby Homes*, Department of Children, Equality, Disability, Integration and Youth. Available from: www.gov.ie/en/publication/d4b3d-final-report-of-the-commission-of-investigation-into-mother-and-baby-homes/

The Guardian (2019) UK child migrants sent to Australia offered $36k compensation. Available from: www.theguardian.com/uk-news/2019/feb/01/uk-child-migrants-sent-to-australia-offered-just-20k-compensation

Van Steen, G. (2021) *Adoption, memory, and cold war Greece: Kid PRO QUO?* Ann Arbor: University of Michigan Press. Available from: https://www.press.umich.edu/11334015/adoption_memory_and_cold_war_greece

Welshman, J. (1999) The social history of social work: The issue of the 'problem family', 1940–70. *The British Journal Work 50*(6): 1890–1908.

Wildt, M. (2002) Generation des Unbedingten. *Das Führungskorps des Reichssicherheitshauptamtes*, Hamburg: Hamburger Editionen.

PART II

Legacies of colonialism and racism in social work

2

Canadian social work and the Sixties Scoop: reflections on the past, lessons for today

Filipe Duarte and Patrick Selmi

Introduction

Social work's troubled past with Indigenous peoples in Canada represents one of the profession's darkest moments in the 20th century: a chapter that started with the residential schools – created to assimilate Indigenous children into Euro-Canadian society – and continued with the Sixties Scoop, which represented the policies and practices adopted to remove Indigenous children from Indigenous communities and to place them in foster care or to be adopted by White families (Nichols, 2017; Ferguson et al, 2018; Ioakimidis and Trimikliniotis, 2020).

In the early 19th century, when the colonial settlement process in Canada intensified, Indigenous peoples were subjugated to British colonial rule through the imposition of a colonial policy called the Indian Act, which aimed to 'protect' Indigenous people from European settlers (Shewell, 2002). However, such policy and colonial practices were intended primarily to 'civilise the Indians' in the name of Christianisation. This occurred through imposing assimilation strategies and practices, supported by the ideological biases of politicians, administrators and the broader society over the decades (Shewell, 2002).

Such practices of settler colonialism inflicted on Indigenous peoples used child welfare as an approach to solving the 'Indian Problem' (Stevenson, 2020). By the late 1940s the social work profession was already playing a direct role in the child welfare system concerning Indigenous children. Social workers became directly involved in the removal of Indigenous children from Indigenous families and communities (Stevenson, 2020).

This chapter sheds light on social work's troubled past with Indigenous peoples in Canada. It aims to discuss such 'troubled histories' of complicity, oppression and assimilation in an ongoing process of reconciliation with Indigenous peoples and preservation of social work memory (CASW, 2019; Ioakimidis and Trimikliniotis, 2020).

Actions towards reconciliation

The day of 30 September 2021 marked the first National Day for Truth and Reconciliation in Canada, an annual federal statutory holiday passed into federal law in June 2021 by Bill C-5. The creation of such a national day marked another important step in Canada's journey towards reconciliation with Indigenous people. The creation of a National Day for Truth and Reconciliation was one of the 94 Calls to Action made by the Truth and Reconciliation Commission of Canada (TRC) in its final report, released in 2015 (Truth and Reconciliation Commission of Canada, 2015; Canadian Heritage, 2021). The TRC call number 80 stated, 'a National Day for Truth and Reconciliation to honour Survivors, their families, and communities, and ensure that public commemoration of the history and legacy of residential schools remains a vital component of the reconciliation process'.

The TRC Calls to Action addressed the legacy of the social work profession on child welfare by calling upon 'the federal, provincial, territorial, and Aboriginal governments to commit to reducing the number of Aboriginal children in care' and to ensure that 'social workers and others who conduct child-welfare investigations are properly educated and trained about the history and impacts of residential schools' (Truth and Reconciliation Commission of Canada, 2015, p 1).

In response to the TRC Calls to Action, in 2019 the Canadian Association of Social Workers (CASW) released a 'Statement of Apology and Commitment to Reconciliation' on behalf of the social work profession in Canada. In this statement the CASW (2019, p 3) acknowledged 'its role in supporting the implementation of residential schools and affirming the approach to child welfare that led to the Sixties Scoop through the promotion of discriminatory policies with the underlying motivation to dispossess Indigenous peoples from their land'. At the root of CASW's participation is the '1947 Joint Submission of Canadian Association of Social Workers and Canadian Welfare Council to the Senate-Commons Committee on Indian Affairs', where it proposed that 'provincial social services be made available to Indians to improve education, health, and welfare' (CASW, 2019, p 4). CASW's 1947 joint document clearly stated that 'the goal for a national program must be the full assimilation of Indians into Canadian life' (CASW, 2019, p 4). Undoubtedly, CASW's position supported the residential school's system for Indigenous children, while advocating for the extension of provincial child welfare services and foster care to Indigenous children (Blackstock, 2015). The 1947 joint submission recommended that Indigenous children should be submitted to foster care and adoption as white children (CASW, 2019, p 5). The hiring of trained non-Indigenous social workers to work with 'Indian agencies' on 'child welfare, family welfare, recreation and possibly adult education' was also recommended by the CASW (2019, p 6).

The child protection system in Canada falls under provincial jurisdiction, a system that has a dark past when it comes to Indigenous children (Johnston,1983; Walmsley, 2005; Stevenson, 2020). The pattern of the child welfare system in Canada concerning Indigenous children has been very coercive, a tragic legacy of assimilationist and integrationist policies created and imposed by the dominant Euro-Canadian culture that had begun with the Christian residential school system in the late 19th century and continued with the Sixties Scoop (Walmsley, 2005; Stevenson, 2020).

According to the *Report of the Royal Commission on Aboriginal People*, released in 1996, the residential school system had a 'three-part vision of education in the service of assimilation' of Indigenous peoples, first with the removal of children from their communities, then with their 're-socialization' and finally with their integration in mainstream society (report cited in Dussault and Erasmus, 2013a, p 427). Walmsley (2005, p 10) explained that 'throughout its history, the residential school system was chronically underfunded and provided substandard education, housing, education, healthcare and childcare'.

An amendment to the Indian Act in 1951 applied all laws in force in the provinces on-reserves unless conflict with federal laws and treaties existed (Johnston, 1983; Walmsley, 2005). Child welfare services 'were generally not available to Indian people living on-reserve', except on an emergency basis (Dussault and Erasmus, 2013b, p 427). Walmsley (2005, p 13) explains that even such emergency services 'were based on a non-Aboriginal value system and worldview'. However, several changes occurred in the 1960s. The federal government changed its 'Indian' child welfare policy and the residential schools started closing (Walmsley, 2005). Johnston (1983) also explained that the signing of the Canada Assistance Plan with the provinces, a cost-sharing agreement with the provinces to provide social services (Walmsley, 2005), affected immediately 'non-status Indians, Métis people who have mixed European and Indigenous ancestry' (Walmsley, 2005).

The Sixties Scoop and social work: what happened?

Canada's history of colonialism and genocide towards Indigenous people had in the Sixties Scoop another chapter of its darkest times. The Sixties Scoop represented the large-scale apprehension of Aboriginal children that began in the late 1940s, and their placement in 'white' family homes (Johnston, 1983; Sinclair, 2007; Stevenson, 2020). The apprehension of Indigenous children from reserves was almost the norm in the 1960s and 1970s (Johnston, 1983; Stevenson, 2020). Around 70 per cent of those Indigenous children were adopted primarily by non-Indigenous families in Canada, the US and overseas (Sinclair, 2007).

Since the British North American Act of 1867, Canada does not have a unified national child welfare system (Johnston, 1983). The division of powers between provincial and federal governments placed child welfare under the responsibility of provincial and territorial governments, which imposed on Indigenous people different policies and forms of delivering child welfare services (Johnston, 1983).

The harmful legacy of the child protection services in Saskatchewan, Manitoba and British Columbia confirms that the pattern of the child welfare system in Canada concerning Indigenous children was very coercive, a tragic legacy of assimilationist and integrationist policies created and imposed by the dominant Euro-Canadian culture that had begun with the Christian residential school system in the late 19th century and continued with the Sixties Scoop (Walmsley, 2005; Blackstock, 2009, 2015; Choate et al, 2021).

The term 'Sixties Scoop' was coined by Patrick Johnston in his 1983 book, *Native Children and the Child Welfare System* (Johnston, 1983). In his book, a retired social worker from British Columbia admitted that, during the 1960, social workers 'scooped' children from reserves 'almost as a matter of course' (Johnston, 1983, 2016). 'Scooping' around 20,000 Indigenous children from their own communities and placing them in non-Indigenous foster and adoptive care caused severe and irreparable damage on Indigenous children, parents and communities. It aimed to impose the loss of Indigenous identity that, as a result, led to psychiatric disorders, substance abuse, unemployment, violence and numerous suicides (Johnston, 1983; Blackstock, 2009; Choate et al, 2021).

Stevenson (2020, p 3) explains that the province of 'Saskatchewan is the heart of Canada's colonial enterprise'. Other provinces like British Columbia and Manitoba also had rising numbers of Indigenous children being placed in foster care and adopted by non-Indigenous families. However, the case of Saskatchewan represents the best expression of how harmful and how far such policies and practices went with the ultimate goal of seeking transracial adoptions, aiming to place Indigenous children already in foster care with permanent adoptive families (Schulz, 2021).

In 1967, Otto Driedger, a social worker and former director of child welfare for the Saskatchewan Department of Social Services, created with a colleague the Adopt Indian Métis (AIM) Program, a pilot programme introduced in the province of Saskatchewan that aimed to increase adoptions of Indigenous children (Stevenson, 2017). This programme was similar to the approach taken in the 19th century by Dr Thomas Barnardo and other 'childsavers' who took in children living on the streets. Dr Barnardo soon developed a plan to send children to the 'colonies', Canada and Australia (Wencer, 2014). In the west of Canada, the AIM approach was to take in children and then adopt them out to White families (Stevenson, 2017; Nichols, 2017; Finding Cleo, 2019; Schulz, 2021). The AIM Program advertised Indigenous children on television, radio and in newspapers across south-eastern Saskatchewan to induce White families to take on transracial adoption of Indigenous children (Stevenson, 2017). Stevenson (2017) states that the AIM Program 'successfully stimulated interest in transracial adoption as planned (Nichols, 2017)'. Many Euro-Canadian Saskatchewan families were quick to embrace the idea that Indian children were no different than any other child'. Recently, Driedger reflected about his role in the AIM Program as director of child welfare for the Saskatchewan Department of Social Services (Schulz, 2021). He said that his services 'had 3,000 children in care on the basis of neglect or abuse', but he recognised that 'whether [his] judgments were always accurate is another question, but some would have died if they had not been taken from their homes' (Schulz, 2021). He emphasised that 'white families were readily to adopt white children who were in care, but they did not adopt Indigenous children'. Driedger also acknowledged 'that having Indigenous children adopted into white families was not the best solution but he and his colleagues felt it was the best option available to them at the time' (Schulz, 2021).

So, how, and to what extent, were social workers responsible for such a dark history? Baskin (2018, p 38) questioned 'why is [was] social work with Indigenous Peoples so focused on removing children from their families and communities?' For Baskin (2018), social work's complicity with the Sixties Scoop represented just another layer of a 'genocide' that started in the residential schools with social workers 'first assisting in the removal of children from their communities and then by ignoring the conditions and treatment of children within the schools (Baskin, 2018, p 36). Blackstock (2009) describes such policies and practices that social workers were part of as part of Canada's introduction of compulsory attendance at residential schools. Blackstock (2009, p 30) affirms that social workers 'were active participants in the placement of Aboriginal children in the residential schools as late the 1960s'. Such participation and practices in the residential school system and later in the Sixties Scoop are labelled by Blackstock (2009) and Baskin (2018) as 'cultural genocide'. The harm caused by social workers in the residential schools and the Sixties Scoop is often 'justified' by reference to the colonial mindset of such times, the lack of perception about the harm being caused, the lack of power and influence for changing those policies and practices and as being an immoral behaviour practised by few social workers (Blackstock, 2009). Stevenson (2020), a survivor of the Sixties Scoop, offers a first-hand account of the harm inflicted towards Indigenous communities and their children. Stevenson (2020, p 155) claims that 'evidence emerged that Indian mothers and children had become profoundly vulnerable to the heavy-handed tactics of social workers'. She sheds light on the impact of forced apprehensions and transracial adoptions of Indigenous children. Indeed, for Stevenson (2020), social work was an important architect in the Sixties Scoop. Social work as an entity was rooted in a hierarchical professional structure complete with western-style therapeutic approaches that emphasised the need to 'improve' First Nations individuals and families through the removal of their children to proper White Christian families.

While research by Blackstock (2009), Baskin (2018) and Stevenson (2020) provides a compelling and unsettling explanation of how social work could take part in and be a leading force in the Sixties Scoop, a number of additional factors may help to bolster the power of their accounts. At the forefront are the needs of modern, industrial capitalism. Prior research has demonstrated that professional social work needed to conform too, and meet, market forces in order to achieve legitimacy and stability (Lubove, 1965; Wenocur and Reisch, 1989). Scholars highlight the struggles that social work has endured in activating its social justice impulses in significant ways (Wenocur and Reisch, 1989). Yet, social work practice has also had to demonstrate its ability to advance the needs and interest of modern industrial and post-industrial capitalism. As scholars such as Marx and Engels (1947), Harvey (2018) and others have shown, the logic of capital dictates that social relations must be structured to reflect and advance capitalist economies in an intricate and interwoven manner. As Couthard (2014) and others have shown, settler colonialism in Canada was also settler, colonial capitalism and, as such, the need to acquire land through force, illegal treaties, co-optation, displacement, Western law and genocide was essential to the colonial capitalist objectives (Manuel and Derrickson, 2017; Nichols, 2020). Additionally, First Nations collectivist and non-Western capitalist culture that didn't view land as an individual commodity designed for exploitation needed to delegitimised and abandoned (Estes, 2019; Nichols, 2020). Residential schools and transracial adoption and foster care placements served to both displace First Nations from their land and delegitimise their culture. Thus, social work as an architect of the Sixties Scoop was demonstrating its commitment to advancing the needs of Western industrial capitalism even if it wasn't directly stating that that was its purpose.

Within this context, we also must remind ourselves of social work's original purpose and its historical educational structure. Canadian social work, similar to other Western nations, was established in the late 19th century to address the associated social problems and issues of industrial capitalism within its rapidly developing urban centres. It was not then, nor ever, organised for the express purpose of resolving colonial oppression of First Nations and Indigenous populations. First Nations culture simply wasn't a central feature of early social work education and, given the prevailing views at the time of First Nations as 'backwards savages' that needed to be eradicated or assimilated, social workers must be recognised as likely holding and expressing such viewpoints, which would contribute to its support for the Sixties Scoop (Jennissen and Lundy, 2011; Coulthard, 2014; Nichols, 2020).

It should be noted that not all social workers supported the Sixties Scoop. However, those who did oppose it were small in number and struggled to have their voices and discontent heard. As Jennissen and Lundy (2011) have well shown, a host of social work practitioners have rallied to the cause of social justice over time, but many, particularly those in the early post-Second World War period, faced a hostile conservative environment and suffered firings and backlisting for their efforts. As a female-dominated field, social workers also suffered from severe gender discrimination that added to practitioners' struggles to oppose the coercive practices of the Sixties Scoop. It is an irony of Canadian social work that it has both advanced and challenged female oppression over time.

Conclusion

It is our view that the history of Canadian social work highlights the need for the field to become significantly involved in social action and social justice initiatives over and above therapeutic-style activities. Social work needs to challenge the basic social relations of a colonial-capitalist society and seek fundamental change. As Manuel and Derrikson (2017) assert, nothing less than fundamental change will serve to reinforce existing colonial–capital relations. Aiding this process, we believe it would be of critical importance for social work to incorporate history into its education and practice to an extent not yet realised. That is, the understanding and application of social work history as well as general history within Canada and on an international level. This critical history would delve into issues of power, economics, culture, institutions and so on. Thus, in many ways social work might see itself as a form of applied history. Issues associated with colonialism and capitalism are rooted in structures of the past and simply can not be understood outside that knowledge and experience. Indeed, we need to recognise historical scholarship and methodology as a valid means of knowledge building on a par with quantitative empirical scholarship. It is through such fundamental change that truly new and just child welfare practices and structures can be created and established. However, above all else, whatever happens with the future direction of social work, it must involve leadership by First Nations and other oppressed groups. We need to accept that Canadian social work was built through White, Christian, upper-class individuals and institutions largely supporting and advancing a colonial-capitalist society. This approach and structure has not served First Nations and other oppressed groups well over time, and fundamental change is one way to help to avoid repeating past actions –as the thousands of unmarked First Nations residential school burial grounds recently uncovered in Canada cry out to us to do.

References

Baskin, C. (2018) 'Sovereignty, colonization, and resistance: 150 years of social work with Indigenous peoples', *Canadian Social Work Journal*, 20(1): 34–49.

Blackstock, C. (2009) 'The occasional evil of angels: Learning from the experiences of Aboriginal peoples and social work', *First Peoples Child & Family Review*, 4(1): 28–37.

Blackstock, C. (2015) 'Should governments be above the law? The Canadian Human Rights Tribunal on First Nations Child Welfare', *Children Australia*, 40(2): 95–103.

Canadian Heritage (2021) 'National Day for Truth and Reconciliation', *Government of Canada, Canadian Heritage*. Available at: www.canada.ca/en/canadian-heritage/campaigns/national-day-truth-reconciliation.html

CASW (Canadian Association of Social Workers) (2019) 'Statement of apology and commitment to reconciliation'. Available at: www.casw-acts.ca/files/Statement_of_Apology_and_Reconciliation.pdf

Choate, P., Bear Chief, R., Lindstrom, D. and CrazyBull, B. (2021) 'Sustaining cultural genocide – a look at indigenous children in non-indigenous placement and the place of judicial decision making – a Canadian example', *Laws*, 10(3): 59.

Coulthard, G.S. (2014) *Red skin, white masks: rejecting the colonial politics of recognition*. Minneapolis: University of Minnesota Press.

Dussault, R. and Erasmus, G. (2013a) *Report of the Royal Commission on Aboriginal Peoples: Volume 1 – Looking Forward, Looking Back*. Ottawa: Indian and Northern Affairs Canada.

Dussault, R. and Erasmus, G. (2013b) *Report of the Royal Commission on Aboriginal Peoples: Volume 3 – Gathering Strength*. Ottawa: Indian and Northern Affairs Canada.

Estes, N. (2019) *Our history is the future: Standing Rock versus the Dakota Access Pipeline, and the long tradition of Indigenous resistance*. London: Verso.

Ferguson, I., Ioakimidis, V. and Lavalette, M. (2018) *Global social work in a political context*. Bristol: Policy Press.

Finding Cleo (2019) 'Saskatchewan's Adopt Indian Métis program'. *CBC Radio*, 18 March. Available at: www.cbc.ca/radio/findingcleo/saskatchewan-s-adopt-indian-m%C3%A9tis-program-1.4555441

Harvey, D. (2018) *The limits to capital*. London: Verso Press.

Hyslop, K. (2018). How Canada created a crisis in Indigenous child welfare. *The Tyee*, 9 May. Available at: https://thetyee.ca/News/2018/05/09/Canada-Crisis-Indigenous-Welfare/

Ioakimidis, V. and Trimikliniotis, N. (2020) 'Making sense of social work's troubled past: professional identity, collective memory and the quest for historical justice', *The British Journal of Social Work*, 50(6): 1890–1908.

Jennissen, T. and Lundy, C. (2011) *One hundred years of social work: A history of the profession in English Canada*. Kitchener: Wilfred Laurier University.

Johnston, P. (1983) *Native children and the child welfare system*. Toronto: Canadian Council on Social Development in association with James Lorimer & Co.

Johnston, P. (2016) 'Revisiting the "Sixties Scoop" of Indigenous children', *IRPP Policy Options*, 26 July. Available at: https://policyoptions.irpp. org/magazines/july-2016/revisiting-the-sixties-scoop-of-indigenous-children/

Lubove, R. (1965) *The professional altruist: The emergence of social work as a career, 1880–1930*. Cambridge: Harvard University Press.

Manuel, A. and Derrickson, R.M. (2017) *The reconciliation manifesto: Recovering the land, rebuilding the economy*. Toronto: James Lorimer & Company Ltd., Publishers.

Marx, K. and Engels, F. (1947) *Capital: A critical analysis of capitalist production*. New York: International Publishers.

Nichols, R.L. (2017) 'From the Sixties Scoop to Baby Veronica: Transracial adoption of Indigenous children in the USA and Canada', in M. Shackleton (ed) *International Adoption in North American Literature and Culture*. Helsinki: Palgrave Macmillan, pp 1–26.

Nichols, R. (2020) *Theft is property! Dispossession and critical theory*. Durham: Duke University Press.

Rosenblatt, H. (2018) *The lost history of liberalism: From ancient Rome to the twenty-first century*. Princeton: Princeton University Press.

Schulz, D. (2021, October 20) 'Former director of child welfare reflects on actions that contributed to the Sixties Scoop'. *Canadian Mennonite*. Available at: https://canadianmennonite.org/stories/making-best-bad-situation

Shewell, H. (2002) '"Bitterness behind every smiling face": Community development and Canada's First Nations, 1954–1968', *The Canadian Historical Review*, 83(1): 58–84.

Sinclair, R. (2007) 'Identity lost and found: Lessons from the sixties scoop', *First Peoples Child & Family Review*, 3(1): 65–82.

Sinclair, R. (2016) 'The Indigenous child removal system in Canada: An examination of legal decision-making and racial bias', *First Peoples Child & Family Review*, 11(2): 8–18.

Stevenson, A. (2017) 'Selling the Sixties Scoop: Saskatchewan's Adopt Indian and Métis Project. *Active History*', 19 October. Available at: http://active history.ca/2017/10/selling-the-sixties-scoop-saskatchewans-adopt-ind ian-and-metis-project/

Stevenson, A. (2020) *Intimate integration: A history of the Sixties Scoop and the colonization of indigenous kinship*. Toronto: University of Toronto Press.

Truth and Reconciliation Commission of Canada (2015) *Truth and Reconciliation Commission of Canada: Calls to action*. Available at: https:// ehprnh2mwo3.exactdn.com/wp-content/uploads/2021/01/Calls_to_Acti on_English2.pdf

Walmsley, C. (2005) *Protecting Aboriginal children*. Vancouver: University of British Columbia Press.

Wencer, D. (20) 'Historicist: Dr. Barnardo's Children', *Torontoist*, 2 August. Available at: https://torontoist.com/2014/08/historicist-dr-barnardos-children/

Wenocur, S. and Reisch, M. (1989) *From charity to enterprise: The Development of American social work in a market economy*. Urbana: University of Illinois Press.

3

Reconciling systemic abuse of children and young women with social work's commitment to a human rights, transformative practice

Carolyn Noble

Introduction

Historical forced child removals, child migration and child adoptions have a long history in Australia. The systematic removal of Aboriginal and Torres Strait Islander (First Nation) children into state and religious institutional care, the forced migration of British children to Australia and the involuntary adoption of young unwed women's children are features of the welfare landscape for more than 250 years of colonial rule. Known as the 'forgotten ones', 'lost innocents' or 'stolen children', these children consequently experienced lifelong trauma and serious mental ill-health, leaving a trail of hurt rippling through the generations (Human Rights Commission, 2014). To this list we can add the current forced, indefinite detention of children and their families in refugee camps, as a punitive aspect of Australia's current Immigration Detention policy. There is no reason to doubt that children being held in these detention centres will experience the same long-term health and welfare impacts as those before them. What is destressing about this legacy is that these atrocities are still occurring with the over-representation of First Nation children in the criminal justice system and the continued confinement of children in detention camps with little or no attention from social work's professional body.

These past and current atrocities present social work with the challenge of how to deal with the consequences of these policies and institutional failings. An important step to tackle this issue is for the Australian Association for Social Workers (AASW) as well as the international professional bodies such as International Association of Schools of Social Work (IASSW) and International Federation of Social Workers (IFSW) on behalf of the practitioners to offer some form of acknowledgement, recompense and reflection on past hurts so as to protect clients from further harm and build trust in its work. Some responses have seen public apologies emerging from the adverse findings of many Royal Commissions and Senate inquiries, but in the main very little public outcry has emerged from the professional social work and welfare bodies. Healy (2012), referring to the Australian context, says it is no easy task for the profession to adequately address these atrocities, as social work is largely a project of the welfare state and does not exist independently of its action and policies. However, this response is no longer adequate, especially when we now know that the 'state' is guilty of past and current human rights transgressions against its people and marginalised populations (Mendes, 2017a). Given this analysis, social work has an opportunity to reflect on past actions and to acknowledge its complicities in the enactment of racist, sexist and unjust welfare policies and practices, and to advocate for social, political, cultural and policy change. This would require recommitting to a transformative social work practice that prevents these atrocities from occurring again.

Removal of Indigenous children from their homes and culture: a national shame

From the early years of invasion, massacres and warfare and well into the 1970s, post-settlement Indigenous children were forcibly removed from their families and raised in White welfare and religious institutions or fostered into non-Indigenous families. Between 1910 and late 1970s, it is estimated that up to 100,000 Indigenous children were removed from their families as part of Australia's Assimilation Policy (Zubrzycki and Bennett, 2006). In the name of the Eastern colonies and the then states, authority was given to church and welfare officers, including social workers, to remove these children from their 'neglectful' families. Raised in White institutions or in White families, these children were actively taught to reject their Indigenous heritage, language and customs and forced to accept White culture as a process of assimilation into White society (Cemlyn and Briskman, 2003). While some prospered, all were robbed of continuous cultural connectedness and many were traumatised by their removal and experienced individual and systemic abuse and neglect while in care, which resulted in 'unshakable' loss, grief and bereavement through their lifetime (Yu, 2019, p 737).

From the early 1990s, these now-adult children and their families agitated for an investigation (and reckoning) into their experiences of removal. So, when in 1995 the National Inquiry into the Separation of Aboriginal and Torres Strait Children from their Families commenced, it marked a pivotal moment in the healing journey for the many Stolen Generation members (Fego-King, 2017). It was the first time in Australian history that the stolen children and their families were given an opportunity to tell their stories of abuse, grief and trauma publicly and to have their experiences acknowledged in a meaningful way. In a submission to the National Inquiry into the

Separation of Aboriginal and Torres Strait Islander Children from their Home (Bringing them Home Report, 1997), the AASW did acknowledge their role in what is now widely recognised as highly unjust practices in the forced removal of Indigenous children from their families (Cemlyn and Briskman, 2003; Healy, 2012; AASW, 2013). Despite the Bringing Them Home Report (1997) listing over 50 recommendations and several warnings of what 'at-risk' behaviour by government officials (welfare and police) is in dealing with Indigenous children, none of its recommendations was acted upon. This demonstrates a national reluctance on the part of these institutions to address the abuse they were charged with.

In 2008 the then Prime Minister, the Hon. Kevin Rudd, made a historic, national apology to the Stolen Generation and their families. However, no apology or recognition of complicity can ever make amends for the intergenerational trauma and the disruption of Indigenous culture and inferiorisation of Australia's First Nations peoples that these practices have left in their wake. Known as the 'Stolen Generation', many of these children never reconnected with their families, while many of the parents separated from their children never recovered from this practice. The trauma resulting from colonial dispossession, oppression and the removal of children is intergenerational. The impact on First Nations of the colonial violence can be seen in low educational achievement, homelessness, mental health issues such as post-traumatic stress, depression and anxiety, over-policing and incarceration, low self-esteem, substance abuse, poverty and suicide that are endemic in the present time (Bennett et al, 2013, p 13).The over-representation of First Nation children in the current child protection system is further evidence that past policies of forced removals and previous separations from family, culture and language are still reverberating throughout the communities (Bennett et al, 2013, p 11).

Child migration: policy of social engineering

Forced removals of Indigenous children were not the only problematic practices undertaken by health and welfare services and their staff in Australia during the last century. For example, inquiries into child migration practices which occurred from the 1920s to 1970s revealed that between 7,000–10,000 British children were forcibly migrated to Australia and highlighted the terrible abuse perpetuated against many of these child refugees. Coldrey (1999) notes that child migration was a policy of social engineering. It was a social policy which involved the transfer of abandoned youth from orphanages, homes, workhouses and reformatories in the UK to overseas British colonies. Once overseas, the children were placed with colonial employers – usually in rural areas – for preparation and training prior to employment. The care and removal of the children was undertaken by religious and philanthropic organisations, but with government approval and under the law as it was then (Coldey, 1999). These children were part of the Australian Empire Settlement Plan, which was an attempt to populate the vast country with British-born citizens. Children placed in these large, often isolated welfare institutions, rural properties and children's homes (rather than being adopted) were often subjected to harsh and cruel treatment. Many were intentionally bullied, sexually assaulted and treated like slaves on properties requiring casual labour, where most experienced no nurturance, support or kindness (Coldey, 1999).

Known as 'lost innocents', these now-adults have experienced lifelong trauma and mental ill-health. The Commonwealth Report on Lost Innocents (2001) found that while some former child migrants have prospered in Australia, having successful relationships with partners and children, and never losing contact with their family, many others are not in this position. For those who suffered, the report illustrated the consequences of emotional deprivation and abuse in childhood, and 'the struggle such children face as adults to cope and contribute and to live fruitful and constructive lives. The cost both human and economic, of treating our children as described in the report is great. Equally grave, the damage done is passed on to subsequent generations' (Commonwealth of Australia Report on Lost Innocents, 2001, preface).

Child abuse in institutional care: multi-generational trauma

Similarly, Australian children raised in institutional care received the same bullying, abuse and regimented work and discipline routines as the 'stolen' and 'lost' children. Between 1910 and 1960, over 400,000 children born in Australia were removed from their homes and placed in government-run care homes and charitable welfare institutions. These children came into care because of poverty, abuse or absent or ill parents. Most were placed in the care of Barnardos, the Fairbridge Society, the Church of England and the Christian Brothers, to name a few.

As a result of continuing public pressure, the Australian Government set up a Royal Commission into Institutional Responses to Child Abuse in Contemporary Out-of-home Care Institutions (2013–2017). Following on from an earlier inquiry (Forgotten Australians: A report of out-of-care as children, 2004–2007), this inquiry found that these institutions were inadequately supervised, monitored and inspected. Further, the findings of this Commission further exposed the level of abuse and neglect that was suffered by children in foster homes, by family members, visitors, case-workers and other children in care, and identified the almost insurmountable barriers that prevented these children from seeking and receiving help. In the second Commission, schools and children's sporting associations and religious institutions (including the Catholic Church) were also implicated. The Commission showed the broad range of institutions in Australia in which child sexual abuse was carried out over many decades. The now-adults' testimony showed how harrowing this experience was and continues to be for them. This six-year investigation into sexual abuse went to some dark places, such as exposing paedophile rings operating in and out of these institutions with impunity for many decades. These children became known as the 'forgotten Australians' and, along with the 'lost innocents' children, received an apology from the Australian Government in 2013.

Forced adoptions: uncomfortable reality

Remembering our history as social workers presents many challenges and requires that we review it with as much truthful reflection as we can. In 1971, I was in my final year as a social work student, and for my last placement I was selected to go to Crown St. Women's Hospital, attached to the maternity ward for unwed pregnant women. Housed in the basement of the hospital, these young pregnant women waited for several months for their child to be given up for adoption. Social and family contact was discouraged. The role of the social worker was to support these women and facilitate adoption for those who agreed to this option. Our job, as I remember it, was to match the child's appearance, intelligence and social class with the new parents, who were mainly infertile couples. On reflection, I do not remember being too concerned by these young women and their circumstances, as I was assured that they were receiving all appropriate support and advice to help them make a wise and thoughtful decision regarding their welfare and that of their child. I was under the impression that these young mothers were there under their own volition. It was the social worker's role to stipulate their right to free and unpressured consent and that any bullying or coercion was illegal. These young mothers were also told that they could rescind their consent within up to 30 days of signing and that their children would be held in the hospital till such time passed. It was only later that I learned that the legislation protecting these women had a clause that included the phrase 'or until adoption order was made'. Little did I know then that in many cases adoption orders were expedited overriding the birth mothers' right to rescind their consent before the 30 days had passed. These young mothers were tricked into giving up their children by the very professionals charged with their welfare (Senate Inquiry Report, 2012).

I am aware that my memory of that time (now over 50 years ago) could be coloured by history, emotions, new information, critique and exposure to other facts, and that remembering is complicated by the emotionally charged nature of events and instances being recalled. However, it is true that between the 1950s and 1980s 210,000 to 250,000 unwed mothers 'consented' to their babies being adopted. (Gair, 2009). I have put consent in inverted commas because we now know that, for many, this consent was coerced. We now know that these forced adoptions were carried out by doctors, social workers, nurses and religious figures. Family members, primarily the parents, were also active in pushing their pregnant daughters into adopting. Forced adoptions took place though hospitals, maternity homes and adoption agencies, both secular and religious, government funded and private, leaving a trail of hurt and trauma that continues to this today. The Releasing the Past Report (2000) criticised social workers in particular for their role in these forced adoptions, claiming that they were acting in the interests of the adoptive parents rather than of the children and their biological mothers.

Forced adoptions left health and welfare authorities and institutions shamefully exposed, accused of and found wanting by failing to gain free and informed consent from these young women before their newborns were removed. Many of the young mothers did not get to see, touch or say farewell to their children, as the practice of 'clean break' or 'blank slate' was enacted. This was to establish early attachment between the adoptive mother and the child and to provide the birth mother an opportunity for both mother and baby to get on with their lives and forget each other more easily. Ironically, it was also claimed to save the birth mothers from the social stigma attached to the 'illegitimate mother' tag with which they were labelled (Gair, 2009). Adoption work by its very nature is seductive because of the amount of power it transfers to its practitioners (Gair, 2009, p 85).

The AASW, in a response to these events, suggested that as social work is not a registered name, many of those people involved in these practices who called themselves social workers may not have been professionally trained, thereby distancing themselves from the actual impropriety (Healy, 2012). This was not the situation at Crown St. Women's Hospital. The senior workers were all trained social workers!

In 2013 Prime Minister Julia Gillard apologised on behalf of the Australian Government to people affected by forced adoption or removal policies and practices . Acknowledging past harms, a statement coordinated by the Australian Council of Social Service, with AASW as co-signatory, also issued a national apology and sincere regret to the survivors and to relinquishing mothers for their loss (Healy 2012; Tyack, 2017). However, the profession has been and continues to be tainted by this past injustice (Quartly, 2012).

Children in detention centres: ongoing abuse and neglect

The AHRC National Inquiry into Children in Immigration Detention (2014) highlighted the emotional and psychological impact of prolonged detention has on children's well-being and development. In March 2014 there were over 100 children in detention on mainland Australia, Christmas Island or Nauru. No other country mandates the closed and indefinite detention of asylum-seeking children when they arrive, or when they are born in detention after their parents arrive, as a deliberate deterrent to would-be others seeking asylum by 'unauthorised' boat arrival. This mandatory detention policy is hard to justify, given that detention is problematic for everyone, and especially so for children. For example, between 2013 and 2014 there were 233 cases of assaults involving children, 33 incidents of sexual assault, plus many cases of self-harm and voluntary starvation (Refugee Council of Australia, 2021). The Australian Human Rights Commission report documented that the most obvious signs of the impact of children's emotional health were the many incidents of crying, sadness, restlessness, anxiety, difficulties in eating and sleeping, not to mention isolation, lack of education and poor language skills and sexual and emotional abuse (Refugee Council of Australia, 2021). Additionally, there has been continuing abuse suffered by adult asylum seekers and refugees permanently located in detention centres in Australia, a cruel and inhuman regime which social workers and healthcare professionals played a significant role in supporting (Briskman, 2017).

We know that many social workers were privately employed to work with the detainees and their families, and all were required to sign a confidentiality agreement banning them from speaking out about the abuse of human rights that they witnessed. Speaking out was punishable by two years' imprisonment for any worker found to have disclosed any information while doing this work (Briskman and Doe, 2016, p 75). When one such social worker did speak out about the abuse of human rights and the unnecessary and arbitrary brutality she witnessed while working offshore in one of the centres, she chose to use a pseudonym (Jane Doe), fearing professional reprisals. She also documented in her diary the ethical dilemmas she confronted as result of the dual-role conflicts/loyalties she faced while undertaking her employment (Briskman and Doe, 2016) and trying to do 'good work' on behalf of the asylum seekers and her employers.

Challenges for social work

As a result of the findings from these inquiries and commissions, social work struggles to cope with the enormity of the problem because the institutions where all this abuse occurred were in workplaces traditionally staffed by social workers. Indeed, as most social workers are employed in government, non-governmental organisations and charitable institutions, agencies and organisations, it is safe to say these workers were key players (or witnesses) in the unfolding drama concerning these children and young women. While the cloak of shame has been lifted from the survivors of these atrocities of abuse and neglect, and only recently has a fund been set up for compensation for the hurt they have endured, it is to the profession's shame that they had to experience this abuse at all.

Karen Healy, past president of AASW, remarked in 2012 in her Norma Parker Address that the act of remembering is challenging for the profession of social work, given that social work from its beginnings is largely a product of the 20th-century welfare state that we now know was associated with human rights transgressions and 'wicked policies' (Healy, 2012, p 288; Mendes, 2017). Early Australian social work (as in most British colonies) was founded on the concepts of charity, personal culpability and, more specifically, White nationalism and supremacy and social engineering, as the experiences of the 'forgotten ones', 'lost innocents' and 'stolen children' so aptly demonstrate.

It is not that social work was not privy to progressive and challenging ideas to stop and reflect on its role as state sanctioned arbitrator of the status quo. The Universal Declaration of Human Rights was securely in place after 1949, and Vaughan in 1997 acknowledged its relevance for the mother–child bond in their discussion of abortion; feminist Mary Bennett in the 1930s fought against the 'official smashing up of native family life'; and activist social worker John Tomlinson led a strike of social workers in the Northern Territory against the forcible removal of an Indigenous girl from her waiting family in 1973 (in Yu, 2018).

Margolin (1997), in criticising the function and practices of 19th- and 20th-century social work, argues that the role of 'benevolent helper' or 'doing good' was a misnomer. In fact, he argues, these early workers were more interested in maintaining their own hegemonic control in the service of the state and their manipulation of social welfare regulations and work environments as to enforce what have been ubiquitously and disdainfully described as 'middle class values'. As well as having to struggle with poverty, starvation, homelessness, unemployment and ill-health, clients became vulnerable to judgement and victim blaming as social workers took seriously their state-sanctioned role to uplift and rehabilitate the needy (Margolin, 1997, p 97). Margolin's argument that social workers used sympathy and friendliness to enter people's private places, and with what was called the 'social work gaze' used their power and authority to monitor and regulate the poor and marginalised, was a damning criticism of the profession.

This was not the only criticism of social work that was being expressed, as the period of the 1960s to 1980s was a time when the debate about whether social workers were the 'soft cops of capitalism', 'angels of mercy', 'catalysts for change' or all three, was prominent (Baines, 2016). Critical, radical and feminist conceptions of social work practice, exemplified in the works of Corrigan and Leonard (1978) and Dominelli and McLeod (1989), were beginning to exert their influence. The loudest voices then and subsequently were from feminists who raised their voices against patriarchy and male dominance in the private and public lives of women (Orme, 2002) and the terrible effects of unchecked capitalism and imperialism on people's lives and well-being. Social work was regarded as a tool to 'manage' and contain social problems, social relations and class and gender conflict.

The problem of intrusion into and surveillance of the poor and Indigenous communities still reverberates today (Fego-King, 2017). We do not need to look any further than the findings of the Royal Commissions into the lost, forgotten, innocent and stolen children in the name of child protection to see the full impact of this intrusion. The discourse on child protection is obviously intertwined with motives of appropriation, integration, assimilation, social control and state surveillance of White settler and patriarchal norms.

Social work's response

As we can see, social work has a complicated public and private image. While social action and policy advocacy to promote social change and ensure human rights are not violated, especially for vulnerable people and communities, is expressed within the IASSW and IFSW's definition and mission statements, there is mounting scepticism that these statements are evident in practice. In practice, argues Mendes (2017a), social work activism was relegated to the margins or left to the Australian Service Union (earlier Australian Social Welfare Union) to protect its workers and the service users in the human services sector many decades ago. The AASW has sought to meet its responsibility to help to expose past and present 'horrible' practices by writing submissions, letters to relevant ministers, networking and developing partnerships with other welfare bodies and developing position papers on specific issues. However, this is where much of this activity stops (Mendes, 2017a). In relation to past practices with reference to the stolen, lost and innocent children, an apology was delivered by the AASW, but following this, the AASW has failed to publicly call out systemic oppression and its role in supporting these past practices of child abuse and neglect, indicating once again that there is little sign that social activism is a priority, even as these abuses continued to be aired.

In looking back to look forward, I would argue that the profession has almost closed the door on any activist stance. By acquiescing to the current neoliberal hegemonic landscape and new public managerialism, which demands that agencies, institutions and practitioners demonstrate measurable competencies and capabilities, social workers have lost any opportunity to lobby or engage in activism within the confines of their workplace. Instead, the AASW's current focus is on knowledge, skills and training regarding mental health, child protection, cross-cultural practice and Aboriginal and Torres Strait Islander peoples as a means of securing the rights and protection of vulnerable peoples, while placing less emphasis on public debate and a public show of activism. This response highlights the inherent tension between activism and professionalism. By exposing current and past abuses, the profession faces a real contradiction between its commitment to relying on standards, regulation and micromanagement with its move to professionalise, and the proposed human rights agenda of its public face. We can wonder if it is the authoritarian logic that has been baked into the quest to professionalise and gain legitimacy that allows for these atrocities to be ignored or even condoned.

Way forward: hope for the future

There is no doubt that Australian social workers were complicit in the forced adoption of unwed mothers' babies, placing poor and neglected children into out-of-care institutions and the colonial dispossession and oppression of Indigenous children and the abuse, neglect and torment they all suffered. Social work's weakness, as suggested by Healy (2012, p 292), was its inability to contest systemic injustices, despite some evidence that there were a few objections to some of these practices at the time. While it might be true that many practitioners were in powerless positions to influence the hegemonic practices in social welfare institutions, as they had to struggle with the dual-conflict roles they were in, it was not so for the AASW as the peak body, who are in a good position to call out the outright brutality and sexual assaults these children endured at the hands of their carers and guardians. There is little historical evidence that the AASW took it upon itself to advocate for these children oppressed by the systemic violence, oppression and dispossession outlined in this chapter. The practice of forced adoption, for example, was curtailed by activist mothers rather than by the social work practitioners working in adoption (Quartly, 2012).

So, how should we remember the past? And how do we move forward? Healy (2012, p 289) argues that public apologies to the victims of government policies and social welfare institutions and practices 'hold extraordinary symbolic significance and can provide the necessary foundations for nations and institutions to move forward'. But this is only the first step.

There is no shortage of critical theories and pedagogies and postcolonial scholarship (Mullaly, 2007; Bennet, et al, 2013; Pease and Nipperess, Morley et al, 2020) to guide the profession to reignite an activist agenda, especially to ensure that the power structures that allowed abuse and wrongdoing are not replicated in contemporary health and welfare institutions. To embrace a public progressive human rights agenda means that social work must move away from its current imperative to professionalise its workforce, and re-embrace a politics of care, a politics of struggle, a politics of decolonisation of its epistemology, a pedagogy of hope (once more) and a politics of transformative change. Implications centre on the need to incorporate transformative practice and critical reflexivity into reframing its mission, its ethics, its practice standards and epistemology. Further action needs to be linked with resources and policy changes to redress opportunities for social, economic and cultural inclusion. Social work must act as a moral witness to society's failings. It is imperative that social work does not misuse this opportunity.

Conclusion

In this chapter I have highlighted past atrocities and social work's culpability of remaining silent. This can no longer be its legacy. The big question here is 'have we learned anything from these inquiries past and present?' The answer can no longer be 'no'. The truth of these 'harmful' policies and practices is exposed, to our shame. This demands that social workers through the AASW, as well as the international bodies, should speak out forcibly and with the courage of their convictions against injustices witnessed, the violation of human rights and the atrocities of social welfare policies past and present. A new beginning based on the truth of the past and a reconciliation with the harm that has happened is far from the 'finished project', but the most realistic start of what needs to be done and the urgency with which to do it. If the list of these atrocities continues to be exposed and social work's complicities do not change, then social work must lose its persona as a human rights profession.

References

Australian Association for Social Workers (2013) Acknowledging the Prime Minister's apology for forced adoption practice. www.aasw.asn.au/news OLD/latest-news/acknowledging-the-prime-ministers-apology-for-for ced-adoption-practice

Australian Human Rights Commission (2014) The forgotten children: The national inquiry into children in immigration detention. https://humanrig hts.gov.au/our-work/asylum-seekers-and-refugees/national-inquiry-child ren-immigration-detention-2014

Baines, D. (2016) 'Forward'. In B. Pease and S. Nipperess (eds) *Doing critical social work: Transformative practices for justice*. Melbourne: Allen & Unwin, pp i–iv.

Bennett, B., Green, S., Gilbert, S. and Bessarab, D. (2013) *Our voices: Aboriginal and Torres Strait Islander social work*. South Yarra, Melbourne: Palgrave Macmillan.

Bringing Them Home Report (1997) https://humanrights.gov.au/our-work/bringing-them-home-report-1997

Briskman, L. (2017) 'The wisdom of hindsight: Cumulative lessons in activism'. In C. Noble, B. Pease and J. Ife (eds) *Radicals in Australian Social Work: Stories of Lifelong Activism*. Redlands Bay: Connor Court, pp 274–289.

Briskman, L. and Doe, J. (2016) 'Social work in dark places'. *Social Alternatives*, 35(4): 73–79

Cemlyn, S. and Briskman, L. (2003) 'Asylum, children's rights and social work'. *Child and Family Social Work*, 8(3): 163–178.

Coldrey, B.M. (1999) *Good British stock: Child and youth migration to Australia*. Canberra: National Archives of Australia.

Commonwealth of Australia (2001) Lost innocents: Righting the record – Report on child migrants. www.aph.gov.au/Parliamentary_Business/Committees/Senate/Community_Affairs/Completed_inquiries/1999-02/child_migrat/report/index

Commonwealth of Australia (2013) Apology to People Affected by Forced Adoption or Removal Policies and Practices. www.ag.gov.au/families-and-marriage/national-apology-forced-adoptions

Community Affairs References Committee (2004) Forgotten Australians: A report on Australians who experienced institutional or out-of-home care as children. www.parliament.nsw.gov.au/lcdocs/inquiries/2026/Report.PDF

Corrigan, P. and Leonard, P. (1978) *Social work under capitalism: A Marxist approach*. London: Macmillan.

Dominelli, L. and McLeod, E. (1989) *Feminist social work*. Basingstoke: Macmillan Higher Education.

Fego-King, C. (2017) 'Social work with The First Australian and Déjàvu: Or in other words – been there, done that, so why are we here again?' In C. Noble, B. Pease and J. Ife (eds) *Radicals in Australian Social Work: Stories of Lifelong Activism*. Redlands Bay: Connor Court.

Gair, S. (2009) 'Hearing the voices of social workers in past adoption practice with mothers and their babies for adoption: what can we learn?' In C. Spark and D. Cuthbert (eds) *Other people's children: Adoption in Australia*. Melbourne: Australian Scholarly Publishing, pp 73–94.

Healy, K. (2012) 'Remembering, apologies, and truth: Challenges for social work today'. *Australian Social Work*, 65(3): 288–294.

Margolin, L. (1997) *Under the cover of kindness: The invention of social work*. Charlottesville, VA: University Press of Virginia.

Mendes, P. (2017) 'The social policy context of the Norma Parker addresses'. *Australian Social Work*, 70, sup1, 2: 4–45.

Mendes, P. (2017a) *Australian welfare wars revisited: The players, the politics and the ideologies*. Sydney: University of New South Wales Press.

Morley, C., Ablett, P., Noble, C. and Cowden, S. (2020) *The Routledge handbook of critical pedagogies for social work*. London: Routledge.

Mullaly, B. (2007) *The new structural social work*. (3e). Don Mills, ON: Oxford University Press.

National Inquiry into the Separation of Aboriginal and Torres Strait from Their Home (Bringing them Home Report) (1997) https://humanrights.gov.au/our-work/bringing-them-home-report-1997

Orme, J. (2002) 'It's feminism because I say so! Feminism, social work and critical practice in the UK'. *Qualitative Social Work*, 2(2): 131–153.

Pease, B. and Nipperess, S. (eds) (2016) *Doing critical social work: Transformative practices for justice.* Melbourne: Allen & Unwin.

Quartly, M. (2012) 'We find families for children, not children for families: An incident in the long and unhappy history of relations between social workers and adoptive parents'. *Social Policy & Society*, 11(3): 415–427.

Refuge Council of Australia (2021) Statistics on People in Detention in Australia (Children in Detention). www.refugeecouncil.org.au/detention-australia-statistics/4/

Royal Commission into Institutional Responses to Child Abuse in Contemporary Out-of-home Care Institutions (2017) www.childabuseroyalcommission.gov.au/final-report.

Senate Inquiry Report (2012) *Commonwealth Contribution to Former Forced Adoption Policies and Practices.* http://forcedadoptions.naa.gov.au/content/overview-forced-adoption-practices-australia

Standing Committee on Social Issues (2000) Releasing the past: adoption practices 1950–1998: final report. www.parliament.nsw.gov.au/lcdocs/inquiries/2026/Report.PDF

The Stolen Generation (nd) https://australianstogether.org.au/discover/australian-history/stolen-generations

Tyack, L. (2017) Stolen at birth: The painful legacy of Australian forced adoption policy. www.vice.com/en_us/article/evgxx7/stolen-at-birth-the-painful-legacy-of-australias-forced-adoption-policy.

Yu, N. (2019) 'Interrogating social work: Australian social work and the stolen generations'. *Journal of Social Work*, 19(6): 736–750.

Zubrzycki, J. and Bennett, B. (2006) 'Aboriginal Australians'. In W.H. Chui and J. Wilson (eds) *Social work and human services best practice.* Sydney: The Federations Press, pp 192–210.

4

The oppressive history of 'child welfare' systems and the need for abolition

Alan J. Dettlaff and Victoria Copeland

Introduction

The history of the 'child welfare' system in the United States, as is true of the history of most government systems following the abolition of human chattel slavery, centred on maintaining and preserving the system of White supremacy upon which the US was founded. Since its earliest origins, the 'child welfare' system has been designed to maintain the superiority of White Americans while maintaining the oppression of Black Americans, first through intentional exclusion of Black families when services focused largely on poverty relief, and later through intentional over-involvement when those services shifted to surveillance and punishment due to poverty. While the practice of forcibly separating Black children from their parents as an act of racial oppression originated with human chattel slavery, today the 'child welfare' system, which we more accurately refer to as the family policing system,[1] maintains this oppression through the forced removal of Black children from their families at a rate nearly double that of White children (Puzzanchera and Taylor, 2021). This act of racial oppression perpetuates harmful outcomes among Black Americans in the form of poverty, homeless, joblessness and others, which each serve as drivers for their continued involvement in and oppression by this system.

Despite these racist intents and the harm that results, the family policing system has largely avoided critique, due to a highly coordinated and successful campaign to frame family policing intervention as not only a needed intervention but a fundamentally indispensable intervention for children who are being harmed. While this myth of a needed intervention is widely held among the public, it obscures the fact that less than one-fifth (17 per cent) of all children who are forcibly removed from their parents have experienced any form of physical or sexual harm[2] (U.S. Department of Health and Human Services, 2020). In reality, more than 60 per cent of all children in the US who are forcibly separated from their parents are separated due to reasons classified by the state as 'neglect', which is largely associated with family poverty (Pressley, 2020; Slack et al, 2004).

This myth of a needed intervention further obscures the harm that is caused directly by family policing intervention. Multiple studies across decades have documented that anywhere between 25 per cent and 40 per cent of children in foster care are abused in their foster homes or in institutional settings (for example, Pecora et al, 2005; Biehal, 2014). Some of these studies have documented that rates of physical and sexual abuse within foster care are two to four times greater than rates of such abuse in the general population (Spencer and Knudsen, 1992; Benedict et al, 1994). In addition to direct maltreatment while in foster care, research has consistently shown that the act of forcible family separation results in significant harm to children, resulting in cognitive delays, depression, increased aggression and behavioural problems (for example, Adam and Chase-Lansdale, 2002; Howard et al, 2011). Beyond the trauma of family separation, research shows that children who experience time in foster care are at risk for a host of negative outcomes as adults, including low educational achievement, homelessness, unemployment, economic hardship, mental health disorders and incarceration (Ryan and Testa, 2005; Doyle, 2007, 2008; Courtney et al, 2011; Lowenstein, 2018; Bauer and Thomas, 2019). Thus, rather than protecting children from harm, it is the family policing system itself that is responsible for harm. The harm inflicted by this system fundamentally distinguishes foster care and the 'child welfare' system from other interventions or systems intended to provide needed support or help to families.

While not all case-workers within family policing systems are social workers, social work is the profession most closely identified with this field. National estimates suggest approximately 40 per cent of family policing agents are social workers with either a BSW or MSW degree (Barth et al, 2008; Staudt et al, 2015). However, to much of the public, working within this system is viewed as the primary role of social workers (LeCroy and Stinson, 2004). Yet, while the actual presence of social workers within this system is lower than the public perception, there are multiple national efforts to increase the presence of social workers in an attempt to 'professionalise' the child welfare workforce. This occurs through both federally funded educational programmes in schools of social work that cover students' tuition and fees in return for an employment commitment, as well as through advocacy from the National Association of Social Workers (NASW), which recommends that an undergraduate degree in social work be a minimum requirement for all child welfare workers (NASW, 2015).

Yet, given the racist origins of this system and the racist harm that continues to be perpetuated, how long can this support be maintained by a profession that purports to hold social justice among its core set of values? How long can social work continue to be complicit in the racism and harm this system produces? This chapter will explore the racist origins of the family policing system, the harm this system continues to produce today and the need for the social work profession to acknowledge that we can no longer be complicit in this harm.

The racist origins of the child welfare system

The history of the US 'child welfare' system is a complex entanglement of colonialism and labour extraction, exemplified through the differential treatment of families who were not Protestant and White. The initial conceptions of foster care and the 'child welfare' system were designed to control poor immigrant, Indigenous, and Black youth families who were deemed as 'other', a pattern that has been threaded into the structure of our current system. Foundational to the creation of the 'child welfare' system in the US was the adamant adherence to English Poor Laws, which impacted on the treatment of individuals who were categorised as 'dependents' or otherwise 'vagrant, involuntary unemployed, and helpless' (Hansan, 2011). Under the influence of English Poor Laws, the US started pushing poor children into indentured service and apprenticeships (Billingsley and Giovannoni, 1972). Indentured servitude was a system of forced labour extraction for poor and immigrant children as well as some poor and immigrant adults. Individuals would perform labour under a contract until they reached a certain age or, in the case of adults, for a certain number of years. English Poor Laws additionally gave power to local governments, allowing them to increase taxation to pay for the upkeep of almshouses as well as provide relief for the 'worthy poor' (Hansan, 2011). Almshouses were homes where individuals who were poor, abandoned, immigrant, mentally ill or labelled delinquent or insane were placed. Around 1830, and in some states as late as 1850, orphanages were created as an alternative to almshouses (Billingsley and Giovannoni, 1972). The proliferation of orphanages was also due to the need for labour, and acted to control poor individuals, and the influx of immigrants who were coming to the US, for labour production. Moreover, orphanages were a way for the US to coerce newly arriving individuals into the country to adhere to cultural 'norms' through assimilation (Kelly, 2020). Indentured servitude was used in conjunction with orphanages. In many cases, children would age out of or graduate from orphanages and enter a phase of indentured service (Billingsley and Giovannoni, 1972).

The advent of orphanages led to other forms of family separation and regulation, most notably through the Orphan Train movement, created during the mid-19th century by Charles Loring Brace and the New York Children's Aid Society. The purpose of these trains was to 'clean up' cities and 'produce upstanding citizens' (Bates, 2016). Concerned that poor youth were engaging in criminal behaviour, and fearing communist revolts, Brace began to compare children to the proletariat revolutions of Europe. Brace's fears led to a rationalisation that poor children must be removed from cities in the East in order to prevent rebellions and criminal behaviour. He also believed that children of Western European culture were to be treated differently than children of colour, maintaining that Western European children (that is, White children) would fare better in mid-western and south-western foster families (Bates, 2016). He stated:

> Something must be done to meet the increasing crime and poverty among the destitute children of New York ... [who] hardly seem able to distinguish good and evil. ... Immigration is pouring in its multitude of poor foreigners, who leave these young outcasts everywhere abandoned in our midst. For the most part ... no one cares for them, and they care for no one. ... These boys and girls, it should be remembered, will soon form the great lower class of our city. They will influence elections; they may shape the policy of the city; they will assuredly, if unreclaimed, poison society all around them. They will help to form the great multitude of robbers, thieves, vagrants, and prostitutes who are now such a burden upon the law-respecting community. (Brace, 1872)

Due to the lack of protections for unaccompanied migrant youth, many private charitable organisations assumed their care and protection. Thus, charitable organisations were a driving force of the movement to 'save' and assimilate children. Brace's Children's Aid Society took children under its guardianship and placed them on Orphan Trains to be placed with foster families across the country. For children who were not unaccompanied, charities were often given guardianship through parents 'temporarily surrendering' their childcare responsibilities, as well as temporary guardianship for a specified number of years (Trammell, 2009). Children were both displayed in public spaces to prospective foster families for placement and marketed in newspapers with information on Orphan Train arrivals. Prospective foster parents could send requests to the charities, detailing their preferences for a child's age and physical characteristics. Once a child was matched with the requests, a receipt was sent to the family stating when the child would arrive (Trammell, 2009). Various actors were implicated in the Orphan Train Movement. The expansion of railway systems and cooperation from railroad companies helped to make the movement a success. Railroad companies made efforts to draw more immigrants into the country, creating an influx of individuals who could provide labour (Trammel, 2009). Subsequently during the 'new immigration', between the 1880s and the First World War, poverty and unemployment increased substantially. The worsening of conditions for families led to an increase in family separation, with families having to place children in orphanages or foster care out of economic necessity. Frequently, these children were forced into doing labour in dangerous mines, mills and factories (Jani and Reisch, 2018).

Given the increased desire to transport 'deserted' and 'vagrant' children and labour, railroad companies offered reduced and free fares to charities who sought to transport children to the western US. These trips were also sponsored by wealthy investors and charities. The Orphan Train Movement resettled over 200,000 White children until the early 1900s and became the model for foster homes and the foundation of the current system of foster care used today. In the late 19th century people began to criticise the Orphan Train Movement, stating that it both increased correctional expenses in the western US and forcibly removed children from their biological families as a deliberate pattern to break up immigrant families (Trammel, 2009). Further, abolitionists believed that placements of children into families in the western US and into indentureship was a form of slavery. According to historical research, the increase in child labour regulations in the US impacted on the Orphan Train Movement as well, as the movement failed to meet new regulatory standards, thus diminishing the major driving force of the movement (Trammel, 2009).

The complex histories for Black, Indigenous and other children of colour remain different than those of European immigrants. While charitable organisations attempted to assimilate White European immigrants, they simultaneously dismissed immigrants from Mexico and China, and emancipated African American individuals from the southern US, whom they determined to be unable to assimilate (Jani and Reisch, 2018). These 'other' individuals had to depend on their own forms of social service provision and mutual aid. The treatment of unaccompanied immigrant youth, Black youth and Indigenous youth during the creation of the 'child welfare' system is important in understanding the current system, as these groups of families were deemed a threat to the 'social order and national security' within the US (Bates, 2016).

Through the antebellum years (1783–1861), Black individuals were still largely enslaved; the main 'child welfare' system did not exist outside of the confines of slavery. After the Civil War, most orphanages, asylums and private institutions were still not accepting Black children (Billingsley and Giovannoni, 1972). Almshouses were also segregated, with terrible living conditions. Due to this, Black communities turned to one another for care. This care came in the form of Black churches, lodges, women's clubs and individuals. For Indigenous children, child savers argued for large-scale institutionalisation and assimilation through off-reservation boarding schools (Bates, 2016). Child welfare advocates rationalised boarding schools and the ability to diminish tribal solidarity and assimilate Native children into Anglo-Saxon culture. They believed that Native children's claim to 'tribal autonomy' was a threat to the national sovereignty of the US (Bates, 2016). By 1880, compulsory attendance laws were passed that enabled officials to remove Native students from their homes, leaving parents with no choice over their children's attendance in boarding schools. Those who refused to send their children were withheld rations, clothing and annuities (Booth, 2009). These boarding schools for Native children lasted until the mid-1900s.

As Black children and families began to receive more formal service through social welfare programmes, the implementation of racist and classist policies created the racial disproportionality and disparities that we see in the family policing system today. The passage of the Social Security Act in 1935, for example, created the Aid to Families with Dependent Children (AFDC) Program, a federal programme that provided financial assistance to children in low-income families. Implementation of this programme gave states wide discretion in policies related to eligibility requirements for AFDC. These policies often included 'suitable home' or 'man in the house' clauses that were used to disproportionately deny benefits to, or subsequently expel, Black families whose homes were viewed as immoral. As examples of this, in 1959 the state of Florida removed over 14,000 children from its welfare programme, over 90 per cent of whom were Black. The following year, the state of Louisiana expelled 23,000 children from AFDC, the majority of whom were also Black, on the grounds of unsuitability (Lawrence-Webb, 1997). When this occurred, no follow-up services to help families meet their basic needs were provided. Moreover, unsuitability laws ignored how slavery, failed reconstruction and Jim Crow shaped the economic hardships that Black families experienced.

The incident in Louisiana triggered enough public attention to form the basis of the Flemming Rule, named after Arthur Flemming, who spearheaded the law as head of the Department of Health and Human Services. On its surface, the Flemming Rule provided that states could no longer deny eligibility to income assistance programmes due to unsuitability clauses. However, the law also required that states investigate homes that had been deemed unsuitable and, if these were determined to be unsafe, either provide some form of income assistance or place children in foster care to ensure their safety. This was followed in 1962 by the Public Welfare Amendments to the Social Security Act, which further emphasised removal as an intervention when families were deemed neglectful. The combination of these policy changes, along with the disproportionate number of Black families who were expelled from welfare rolls and subsequently deemed unsafe by White case-workers, led to what we now refer to as racial disproportionality, as the majority of children removed and placed in foster care following implementation of the Flemming Rule were Black (Lawrence-Webb, 1997).

Since the 20th century the 'child welfare' system has adopted a protective services and foster home model. Under this model there has been an overhaul of state control over 'child welfare' services, with state-created agencies handling all child maltreatment reports and investigations. Under this new model, the pathologising and individualising framing of child maltreatment has allowed for the proliferation of surveillance, policing and the commodification of family separation, which largely impacts on Black and Indigenous families. Highly influenced by Henry Kempe's 'Battered Child Syndrome' (Kempe et al, 1985), which built upon the ideological claims raised by the Moynihan Report (Office of Planning and Research, 1965), the Child Abuse Prevention and Treatment Act (CAPTA) was passed. CAPTA requires mandatory reporting laws for all states and has been amended several times since its inception in 1974. Under mandatory reporting laws, many individuals are required to report if they suspect or have 'any reason to believe that a child has been abused or neglected' (Child Welfare Information Gateway, 2019a, p 3). CAPTA also established mandatory minimum federal definitions of child abuse and neglect. However, CAPTA allowed states broad discretion to expand on these definitions, resulting in laws that vary widely by state and that often reflect current social problems within the context of these states. Similarly, other policies like the Multiethnic Placement Act of 1994, Interethnic Placement Act of 1996 and the Adoption and Safe Families Act (ASFA) of 1997 have since been passed. These policies have shifted the system from one that was extracting labour to one that profits by the removal of families from homes.

Finally, federal reimbursement for foster care services continues to perpetuate inequity as long as it remains tied to eligibility for AFDC. Even after AFDC was replaced by Temporary Assistance for Needy Families in 1996, eligibility for federal funds to reimburse states for the cost of foster care remained tied to the removal of children who would have been eligible for AFDC in July 1996. Thus, child welfare systems are rewarded for removing the poorest children in the country, a policy that systematically promotes the removal of Black and Native children, who are over-represented in this population because of historic and current racism and disadvantage – lingering artefacts of the legacies of slavery, colonisation and genocide. While the Indian Child Welfare Act passed in 1978 in recognition of the government's targeted, harmful removal of Native children from their families, Native children still make up a disproportionate number of children removed and in foster care, due to lingering racist ideologies about Native families.

How the child welfare system produces and maintains harm

Today, the 'child welfare' system functions as an expansive network of institutions that markets itself as 'strengthening families and protecting children'. The system's adherence to a model of 'child protection' perpetuates a belief that Black children and families are objects for control and regulation. It reifies the notion that Black children need to be saved, and often diminishes the autonomy of Black communities. By taking up a lens of 'protection', the system has been able to prioritise and market tactics of risk prevention and mitigation which have drastically increased the monitoring and surveillance of families. These families who are deemed as high risk continue to face forcible family separation, which is the system's main 'service'. Family separation serves as a consequence or punishment to families who are unable to prove to the agency that they are worthy of parenting their child.

Tactics of risk mitigation, surveillance and punishment have impacted largely on Black and Indigenous families, who continue to be disproportionately targeted by the family policing system. The ongoing treatment of Black and Indigenous families in the system is a consequence of pervasive systemic racism that has been foundational to the policies and practices that still exist today. Rather than diverting attention to the material conditions and needs of families, the system utilises separation and surveillance to regulate those who they believe are a threat. The consequences of risk prevention fall particularly heavily on Black and Indigenous families who are impacted upon by structural racism and are consequently vulnerable to biased standards of risk. Conditions of poverty have become synonymous with an inability to parent, and equated to 'high risk of maltreatment'. Additionally, the system's focus on risk prevention harms Black families, due to an accumulation of generational data that has been collected on them.

A family or individual's level of risk is determined by predictive models and case-worker judgements, which are both inherently biased (Capatosto, 2017; Roberts, 2019). Predictive models rely on historical data collection and have recently been used to calculate the risk of maltreatment for unborn children, to estimate the likelihood of an individual becoming a perpetrator and even to estimate the risk of entire geographical communities (Teixeira and Boyas, 2017). Case-workers calculate and determine risk based on their professional judgement, observations of the family and the environment and input from their supervisors. The broader issue, then, is not that these human and computer-assisted decisions will remain biased; rather, it is that the fate of families lies within the discretion and power of certain people.

Additionally, the influence of capitalism and the context of racist ideologies stimulate and incentivise the punishment system, creating a cycle that is often inescapable for Black and Indigenous families. The passing of policies like ASFA and CAPTA shows how the ideological attachments of the past have had far-reaching implications for Black and Indigenous families. The implementation of CAPTA unleashed a system of surveillance that has been overlooked for decades. Due to the severe consequences that mandated reporters face through CAPTA, many individuals report all their suspicions, regardless of the level of risk or evidence. The punishment for not reporting 'reasonable suspicion' includes incarceration and fines (Child Welfare Information Gateway, 2019b). Further, many mandated reporters fear that, if a child is harmed, they will face responsibility for the child's life (Copeland,

2021). This focus on individualised blame creates a cycle in which mass numbers of children, largely Black and Indigenous, face investigation by the family policing system. This system of reporting does not stop at the hotline. Once reports of maltreatment are confirmed for abuse or neglect, they are sent to various law enforcement agencies like the Department of Justice to stay on Child Abuse registries. Although children who were harmed are likely to be removed from the registry at the age of 18, many parents who have been accused of abuse or neglect remain on the registries indefinitely. These records follow families, showing up on background checks in the future. Additionally, documentation of child abuse or neglect is included on various databases which follow families for generations. These past instances of child abuse or neglect are commonly used as predictor variables for decision-making tools that attempt to predict future risk for children. The presence of any prior allegations of child abuse or neglect adds to family's 'risk' if they are investigated by the system again. These generational tracking mechanisms follow Black families through various systems of 'care', and compound the harm that has already been caused. The proliferation of predictive technologies arises from the growing concern that children will continue to be harmed if the state does not intervene.

The passing of ASFA has similarly perpetuated harm in the current iteration of the 'child welfare' system. ASFA created a 'bounty system' in which state and county agencies were incentivised to remove children from the home and place them for adoption. Under ASFA many agencies felt pressure to meet adoption quotas so that they could receive extra federal funding. This bounty system impacted on systems of kinship care, with many Black children receiving services outside of the home. Because Black families have been deemed as unfit or unworthy to take care of their own children, a cycle of separations began to proliferate through the country. In cases where Black children are not removed from their homes, they are heavily monitored and surveilled, many having to agree to coerced 'voluntary services', drug testing and random visits from family policing agents (Copeland, 2021). CAPTA and ASFA serve as examples of how the foundational ideologies of and attachments to structural racism have continued to exacerbate the disparate treatment of Black and Indigenous families. The power of the system culminates in the ability to determine which families deserve to stay together, which families deserve to be separated and who must endure years of monitoring and regulation.

The racism is in the discretion

The notion of saviourism, particularly White saviourism, remains a major rationalisation for the surveillance, monitoring and forcible separation that Black and Indigenous families endure within the 'child welfare' system. The system's mission of 'protecting children' and its effort to 'determine the best interest of the child' through the courts remain a source of interrogation into the system's role today. Though the phrases 'protection' and 'best interest' seem benevolent, they insidiously provide justification for the policing and regulation of families, both of which rely on discretionary power. Generally, discretionary judgements in the system begin several steps before a case-worker investigates a family's home for proof of maltreatment. Discretion begins with the system's nebulous definitions and criteria for child abuse and neglect. Over the decades following CAPTA, the interpretation of these definitions has been largely influenced by racial narratives including the War on Drugs, 'welfare queens', 'crack babies' and beliefs about appropriate parenting that reflect a White normative parenting standard. These biased standards of child maltreatment act as the backbone to the system, with no decision bypassing their use. Minimum definitions of child maltreatment are set by CAPTA but allow for states to have discretionary power over defining the categories more specifically. Due to this, both algorithmic and human decision making can look vastly different per agency and even per case-worker. Neglect, the primary reason why children are involved in the system, remains a catch-all category of child maltreatment and is a primary example of discretionary power.

Neglect has been defined as 'the failure of a parent or other person with responsibility for the child to provide needed food, clothing, shelter, medical care, or supervision such that the child's health, safety, and well-being are threatened with harm' (Child Welfare Information Gateway, 2019a). Substantiated cases of neglect have included a range of scenarios, including families who are unable to afford food or clothing, and instances where victims of interpersonal violence are harmed in front of their children. Additionally, in human-assisted decision-making tools such as the Structured Decision-Making Tool, neglect includes a range of variables including leaking gas from stoves, exposed electrical wires, excessive garbage and lack of water or utilities. It also includes more vague safety risks such as: 'child is suicidal and caregiver cannot take protective action', 'caregiver is present but does not attend to the child to the extent that need for care goes unmet' and 'caregiver makes inadequate or inappropriate babysitting or childcare arrangements'. Based on these definitions there are a range of cases that are flagged as high risk within the child protection hotline and that are further confirmed for child maltreatment by front-line case-workers. Investigative front-line workers can determine to what extent they personally believe that a child is experiencing safety risk and can even override predictive risk models when they do not agree with the tool's decisions. Furthermore, if a case-worker believes there is not enough proof of maltreatment that they observed, they can increase surveillance of families until they feel confident in their judgement of whether or not the child is truly at risk (Copeland, 2021).

Standards of child maltreatment also play a significant role in the courts. Alongside case-workers, the courts determine the fate of a child who has been abused or neglected. While in the court, judges have a say over what decision will be made in the 'best interests' of the child. The Administration for Children and Families admits that there are no standardised definitions of best interest, though it usually refers to the 'type of services, actions, and orders that will best serve a child as well as who is best suited to take care of a child' (Child Welfare Information Gateway, 2020). Per the Administration, these determinations are generally based on a worker judging the child or parents' 'circumstances and capacity to parent' (Child Welfare Information Gateway, 2020).

This fundamental principle that governs child welfare decision making – the 'best interests of the child' standard – has repeatedly been challenged, due to its potential for bias given its ambiguous definition, which leaves room for substantial subjectivity in application. In an analysis of laws governing child welfare systems, legal scholar Tanya Asim Cooper said of the best interest standard, 'Its lack of definitive guidance allows foster care professionals and even judges to substitute their own judgment about what is in a child's best interest and allows unintended biases to permeate decision-making' (Cooper, 2014, p 107). Even the Supreme Court has acknowledged the potential for bias, stating that the best interest standard 'is imprecise and open to the subjective values of the judge' (Lassiter vs. Department of Social Services, 1981).

Discretion over the fate of Black and Indigenous families continues throughout all decision-making points within the family policing system. Beyond the biased definitions of child maltreatment, research has shown that there is an immense amount of human bias in all decision-making processes within the system (Teixeira and Boyas, 2017; Harp and Bunting, 2019). After case-workers and algorithms decide what hotline calls should be filtered in for investigation, they decide which cases are substantiated for maltreatment. Subsequently workers decide which families get separated, which families get surveilled and which families deserve to be reunited. Due to the documented human bias in these decision-making processes, many researchers have advocated the use of predictive analytic tools. Advocates for predictive analytics state that there is potential to identify and correct for human biases by 'lessening reliance on individual judgments' (Capatosto, 2017). However, these predictive models still rely on biased historical data and discretionary judgements with biased standards, and do little to improve the deteriorating material conditions that many families involved in the system live in.

Social work and the child welfare system

Despite the racism that is deeply embedded within the 'child welfare' system's policies and structures, and the racist harm and oppression that result from family policing intervention, the profession of social work continues to support and uphold this system. In fact, through social work education programmes across the country, the profession has made it a professional obligation to increase the number of social workers in the family policing system. Through federally funded Title IV-E programmes, over 200 schools of social work in 47 states have committed to preparing social workers to enter the 'child welfare' workforce (Cheung, 2021). While Title IV-E programmes vary by state, the purpose of these programmes is to offset the costs of obtaining a social work education in exchange for a commitment to work for a 'child welfare' agency for a specified period upon graduation, which is often one to two times the number of years spent in the educational programme.

Through these programmes, the profession purports that the solution to many of the problems that exist in the family policing system is more and better-trained social workers. A large body of research has been used to document the benefits of a social work workforce within the family policing system; however, the vast majority of this work focuses on outcomes such as case-worker turnover, retention, job preparedness and other employment outcomes, rather than outcomes associated with harm to children or the vast racist inequities that exist in this system (for example, Auerbach et al, 2007; Barbee et al, 2018; Trujillo et al, 2020). Despite this, the National Child Welfare Workforce Institute (2021) claims that 'Child welfare leaders and educators must promote the importance of social work degrees in preparing the child welfare workforce and creating an equitable child welfare system focused on keeping families together', despite the lack of any direct evidence to support this latter claim.

In addition to social work education's support of expanding the presence of social workers within family policing systems, the NASW, the largest membership organisation of social workers in the world, recommends that an undergraduate degree in social work be a minimum requirement for all 'child welfare' workers. Thus, the position of social work's largest professional organisation is that the family policing workforce be solely and entirely comprised of social workers. Specifically, 'Effective services to children and families in child welfare demand the values, knowledge, and skills that are intrinsic to social work education; therefore, a BSW degree is recommended as the minimum requirement for child welfare workers. An MSW degree is recommended at child welfare supervisory and administrative levels' (NASW, 2015).

This stance of the social work profession is wholly inconsistent with social work's mission and professional values. Among the key ethical principles of the profession of social work, as defined by NASW, social workers are called upon to challenge injustice and oppression. This professional obligation is enshrined in the NASW Code of Ethics, which states unequivocally, 'Social workers must take action against oppression, racism, discrimination, and inequities' (NASW, 2021). Yet this mandate must also include taking action against the *systems and structures* that perpetuate and maintain oppression, racism, discrimination and inequities. Social work's long-standing support of the family policing system, as well as the blatant inconsistency between this support and its purported professional values, not only legitimises the harmful and racist outcomes that the family policing system produces, but also harms and delegitimises the social work profession.

How long can social work be complicit?

When viewed in its entirety, the 'child welfare' system in the US can be seen as one that has evolved from intentionally excluding Black and Indigenous children to one that intentionally perpetuates oppression against them. Today, what we refer to as the family policing system operates largely as a means of controlling and regulating Black and Indigenous families through surveillance, separation and the harm that results. Although workforce statistics demonstrate that less than half of the 'child welfare' workforce is comprised of social workers, social work remains largely synonymous with this system to much of the general public, who view this as the primary role social workers hold. Further, throughout its history, the social work profession has unequivocally supported and upheld the child welfare system and the practice of forcibly separating children from their parents, despite long-standing awareness of the deep problem of racism in this system and the harm that results.

For how long can social work continue to be complicit in the forcible separation of Black and Indigenous children from their parents within a racist society, given the racist origins of this practice and the harm and oppression that result?

In the summer of 2020, following the murder of George Floyd and many others, each at the hands of law enforcement, many conversations occurred about the role of social work in policing and the potential for social work to reduce some of the racist outcomes that result from policing through increased collaborations with police. This presented a moment for the profession of social work, and the profession's leaders, to acknowledge its historic complicity with policing and to stand up against the racist violence that results from policing. This further presented a moment for social work to disavow itself from the police and to state that social work would no longer be complicit in the harmful and racist outcomes this system produces. Yet this did not occur. In response to these conversations, Angelo McClain, chief executive of NASW, affirmed the importance of social work collaborations with police, writing in the *Wall Street Journal* in an op-ed titled 'Social Workers Cooperate with Police Forces':

> Social workers already work alongside and in partnership with police departments across the nation. Strengthening social worker and police

partnerships can be an effective strategy in addressing behavioural health, mental health, substance use, homelessness, family disputes and other similar calls to 911 emergency response lines. In fact, social workers are playing an increasingly integral role in police forces, helping officers do their jobs more effectively and humanely and become better attuned to cultural and racial biases. And studies show social workers help police excel in fulfilling their mission to protect and serve. (McClain, 2020)

The murder of George Floyd and the subsequent protests throughout 2020 that gave birth to the #DefundThePolice movement have since been referred to by many as a 'racial awakening' for the US. If this moment in history could not prompt the social work profession to re-evaluate its role in supporting the police, despite all the violence and all the evidence of harm, it is clear that social work lacks the awareness to recognise the inconsistency between its actions and its values. Today, social work as a profession continues to debate whether we should collaborate with the police, as well as whether we should work in jails and prisons. As a profession, social work has cooperated with and supported a system of policing that is responsible for the murders of countless Black Americans, but the profession has yet to meaningfully consider whether this is consistent with our professed values.

This professional stance, as well as social work's long-standing and unequivocal support of the 'child welfare' system, suggests that social workers who recognise the harm, racism and oppression this system produces must act outside of social work's professional organisations to bring about needed change. Yet, given how deeply embedded racism is within the policies and structures of the family policing system, reforms of this system are not sufficient. The family policing system has been engaging in reform efforts for decades, yet the inequities and harm that are inflicted on Black and Indigenous children and families persist.

The racism that is foundational to the origins of the family policing system and is now permeated throughout this system cannot simply be reformed. Further, prior attempts at reform have failed because the system has been unwilling to consider abandoning its foundational intervention of family separation. Yet this practice of forcibly and involuntarily separating children from their families, which originated through human chattel slavery, must be understood through the history from which it came, and recognised for the egregious trauma it continues to produce. The harm that results from the family policing system, and the resulting destruction of families, will end only through abolition of the existing system, and a fundamental reimagining of how society cares for children, families and communities that prioritises support over surveillance and separation.

Thus, abolitionists propose a complete elimination of the existing family policing system. Yet, in its place, this does not mean the creation of a new government system. Rather, abolitionists propose that, rather than a state-sanctioned system with the coercive power to separate children and families, funds be divested from the family policing system and reinvested in families and communities as part of newly created efforts to ensure that all children can remain safely in their homes (for example, Dettlaff et al, 2020; Roberts, 2020). Abolition involves building community-led and community-driven systems of support that ensure families have access to the resources they need to thrive. This includes a universal basic income, a child allowance, safe and affordable housing, jobs that pay sustainable wages, mental health services, quality food, interpersonal violence supports and substance-use services for those who choose them. Ultimately, abolitionist movements believe in building communities where residents of communities intervene when needed, community members provide support to those who need it, a sufficient community array of supports and interventions exists and there is a community system of care that can minimise and address harm when it occurs. In this way, abolition is not about simply ending the family policing system, it is about creating the conditions in society where the need for a family policing system is obsolete.

Conclusion

The profession of social work cannot be true to its professional values while continuing to support and uphold a system responsible for racism, harm and oppression. Yet, in the absence of professional leadership in disavowing this system, social workers who recognise the harm this system produces must work outside of our professional organisations and work towards abolition as a means of ending this harm. Finally, in acknowledging the need for abolition, it is important to acknowledge that the family policing system is just one part of the broader carceral state that exists to harm and punish Black, Indigenous and Latinx Americans. From incarceration by the criminal punishment system to immigration detention by Immigration and Customs Enforcement to surveillance and separation by the family policing system, the harm and punishment these systems produce will end only when these systems no longer exist.

Notes
[1] We use the term family policing system, as we believe this term more accurately captures the roles this system plays in the lives of families, which include surveillance, regulation and punishment, all roles associated with policing rather than children's welfare.
[2] It is important to note that rates of physical and sexual abuse identified by the family policing system are likely inflated, as they are subject to well-documented

biases that may influence the determination of abuse. Thus, actual rates of children who have experienced physical or sexual abuse and subsequently been removed from their homes and placed into foster care are unknown.

References

Adam, E.K. and Chase-Lansdale, P.L. (2002) Home sweet home(s): Parental separations, residential moves, and adjustment problems in low-income adolescent girls. *Developmental Psychology, 38*, 792–805.

Auerbach, C., McGowan, B.G. and LaPorte, H.H. (2007) How does professional education impact the job outlook of public child welfare workers? *Journal of Public Child Welfare, 1*(3), 55–76.

Barbee, A., Rice, C., Antle, B.F., Henry, K. and Cunningham, M.R. (2018) Factors affecting turnover rates of public child welfare front line workers: Comparing cohorts of Title IV-E program graduates with regularly hired and trained staff. *Journal of Public Child Welfare, 12*(3), 354–379.

Barth, R.P., Lloyd, E.C., Christ, S.L., Chapman, M.V. and Dickinson, N.S. (2008) Child welfare worker characteristics and job satisfaction: A national study. *Social Work, 53*(3), 199–209.

Bates, J. (2016) The role of race in legitimizing institutionalization: A comparative analysis of early child welfare initiatives in the United States. *The Journal of History of Childhood and Youth, 9*(1), 15–28

Bauer, L. and Thomas, J.L. (2019, December 15) *Throwaway kids: We are sending more foster kids to prison than college.* The Wichita Eagle. www.kansas.com/news/politics-government/article238206754.html1

Benedict, M.I., Zuravin, S., Brandt, D. and Abbey, H. (1994) Types and frequency of child maltreatment by family foster care providers in an urban population. *Child Abuse & Neglect, 18*(7), 577–585.

Biehal, N. (2014) Maltreatment in foster care: A review of the evidence. *Child Abuse Review, 23*, 48–60.

Billingsley, A. and Giovannoni, J. (1972) *Children of the storm: Black children and American child welfare.* Michigan: Houghton Mifflin Harcourt Publishing.

Booth, T.T. (2009) *Cheaper than bullets: American Indian boarding schools and assimilation policy, 1890–1930.* Native American Symposium, 4 November. Images, Imaginations, and Beyond: Proceedings of the Eighth Native American Symposium, Southeastern Oklahoma State University.

Brace, C.L. (1872) *The dangerous classes of New York, and twenty years' work among them.* New York: Wynkoop & Hallenbeck. https://archive.org/details/dangerousclasses00bracuoft

Capatosto, K. (2017) Foretelling the future: A critical perspective on the use of predictive analytics in child welfare. *Kirwan Institute Research Report.* http://kirwaninstitute.osu.edu/wp-content/uploads/2017/05/ki-predictive-analytics.pdf

Cheung, M. (ed) (2021) *National survey of IV-E stipends and paybacks.* Houston: University of Houston.

Child Welfare Information Gateway (2019a) *Mandatory Reporters of Child Abuse and Neglect.* www.childwelfare.gov/pubPDFs/manda.pdf

Child Welfare Information Gateway (2019b) *Penalties for Failure to Report and False Reporting of Child Abuse and Neglect.* www.childwelfare.gov/pubpdfs/report.pdf

Child Welfare Information Gateway (2020) *Determining the Best Interests of the Child.* www.childwelfare.gov/pubPDFs/best_interest.pdf

Cooper, T.A. (2014) Commentary on chapter 2. In A. Sarat (ed) *Civil rights in American law, history, and politics* (pp 64–112). Cambridge: Cambridge University Press.

Copeland, V. (2021) 'It's the only system we've got': Exploring emergency response decision-making in child welfare. *Columbia Journal for Race and Law Forum, 11*(3), 43–74.

Courtney, M., Dworsky, A., Brown, A., Cary, C., Love, K. and Vorhies, V. (2011) *Midwest evaluation of the adult functioning of former foster youth: Outcomes at ages 26.* Chicago: Chapin Hall at the University of Chicago.

Dettlaff, A.J., Weber, K., Pendleton, M., Boyd, R., Bettencourt, B. and Burton, L. (2020) It is not a broken system, it is a system that needs to be broken: The upend movement to abolish the child welfare system. *Journal of Public Child Welfare, 14*(5), 500–517.

Doyle, J.J. (2007) Child protection and child outcomes: Measuring the effects of foster care. *American Economic Review, 97,* 1583–1610.

Doyle, J.J. (2008) Child protection and adult crime: Using investigator assignment to estimate causal effects of foster care. *Journal of Political Economy, 116,* 746–770.

Hansan, J.E. (2011) *English poor laws: Historical precedents of tax-supported relief for the poor. Social Welfare History Project.* http://socialwelfare.library.vcu.edu/programs/poor-laws/

Harp, K.L. and Bunting, A.M. (2019) The Racialized Nature of Child Welfare Policies and the Social Control of Black Bodies. *Social Politics: International Studies in Gender, State & Society, 27*(2), 258–281. https://doi.org/10.1093/sp/jxz039

Howard, K., Martin, A., Berlin, L.J. and Brooks-Gunn, J. (2011) Early mother–child separation, parenting, and child well-being in early head start families. *Attachment and Human Development, 13,* 5–26.

Jani, J.S. and Reisch, M. (2018) Assisting the least among us: Social work's historical response to unaccompanied immigrant and refugee youth. *Children and Youth Services Review, 92,* 4–14. https://doi.org/10.1016/j.childyouth.2018.02.025

Kelly, V. (2020) *Separation, loss, and trauma: Past, present, and future trends in child welfare.* Child Welfare League of America, Reflections on Child Welfare Areas of Practice, Issues, and Service Populations – Volume 1. www.cwla.org/separation-loss-and-trauma-past-present-and-future-trends-in-child-welfare/

Kempe, C.H., Silverman, F.N., Steele, B.F., Droegemueller, W. and Silver, H.K. (1985) The battered-child syndrome. *Child Abuse & Neglect, 9*, 134–1154.

Lassiter v. Department of Social Services. 1981. 452 U.S. 18.

Lawrence-Webb, C. (1997) African American children in the modern child welfare system: A legacy of the Flemming rule. *Child Welfare, 76*(1), 9–30.

LeCroy, C.W. and Stinson, E.L. (2004) The public's perception of social work: Is it what we think it is? *Social Work, 49*(2), 164–174.

Lowenstein, K. (2018) *Shutting down the trauma to prison pipeline: Early, appropriate care for child-welfare involved youth.* Boston: Citizens for Juvenile Justice.

McClain, A. (2020) Social workers cooperate with police forces. *Wall Street Journal*, 15 June. www.wsj.com/articles/social-workers-cooperate-with-police-forces-11592255480

National Association of Social Workers (2015) *Social work speaks* (10th edn). Chicago: NASW Press.

National Association of Social Workers (2021) *Code of Ethics of the National Association of Social Workers.* www.socialworkers.org/About/Ethics/Code-of-Ethics/Code-of-Ethics-English

National Child Welfare Workforce Institute (2021) Social work degrees are leading the child welfare workforce. www.ncwwi.org/index.php/resourcemenu/resource-library/education-professional-development/1650-social-work-degrees-are-leading-the-child-welfare-workforce-ncwwi-1-page-summary/file

Office of Planning and Research (1965) The Negro family: The case for national action. Washington, DC: Department of Labor.

Pecora, P.J., Kessler, R.C., Williams, J., O'Brien, K., Downs, A.C., English, D., Holmes, K. et al (2005) *Improving family foster care: Findings from the Northwest Foster Care Alumni Study.* Casey Family Programs.

Pressley, N. (2020) *Punished for being poor: The relationship between poverty and neglect in Texas.* Texas Public Policy Foundation. www.texaspolicy.com/punished-for-being-poor-the-relationship-between-poverty-and-neglect-in-texas/

Puzzanchera, C. and Taylor, M. (2021) *Disproportionality rates for children of color in foster care dashboard.* National Council of Juvenile and Family Court Judges.

Roberts, D. (2019) Digitizing the carceral state. *Harvard Law Review, 132,* 1695–1728. https://harvardlawreview.org/wp-content/uploads/2019/04/1695–1728_Online.pdf

Roberts, D. (2020) Abolishing policing also means abolishing family regulation. *The Imprint*, 16 June. https://imprintnews.org/child-welfare-2/abolishing-policing-also-means-abolishing-family-regulation/44480

Ryan, J.P. and Testa, M.F. (2005) Child maltreatment and juvenile delinquency: Investigating the role of placement and placement instability. *Children and Youth Services Review, 27,* 227–249.

Slack, K., Holl, J., McDaniel, M., Yoo, J. and Bolger, K. (2004) Understanding the risks of child neglect: An exploration of poverty and parenting characteristics. *Child Maltreatment, 9*(4), 395–408.

Spencer, J.W. and Knudsen, D.D. (1992) Out-of-home maltreatment: An analysis of risk in various settings for children. *Children and Youth Services Review, 14,* 485–492.

Staudt, M., Jolles, M., Chuang, E. and Wells, R. (2015) Child welfare caseworker education and caregiver behavioral service use and satisfaction with the caseworker. *Journal of Public Child Welfare, 9*(4), 382–398.

Teixeira, C. and Boyas, M. (2017) Predictive analytics in child welfare: An assessment of current efforts, challenges and opportunities. U.S. Department of Health and Human Services. https://aspe.hhs.gov/sites/default/files/private/pdf/257841/PACWAnAssessmentCurrentEffortsChallengesOpportunities.pdf

Trammell, R.S. (2009) Orphan train myths and legal reality. *The Modern American, 5*(2). https://digitalcommons.wcl.american.edu/cgi/viewcontent.cgi?article=1023&context=tma

Trujillo, K.C., Bruce, L., de Guzman, A., Wilcox, C., Melnyk, A. and Clark, K. (2020) Preparing the child welfare workforce: Organizational commitment, identity, and desire to stay. *Child Abuse & Neglect, 110*(3), 104539.

US Department of Health and Human Services, Administration for Children and Families, Administration on Children, Youth and Families, Children's Bureau (2020) *Preliminary estimates for FY2019 as of June 23, 2020.* www.acf.hhs.gov/sites/default/files/documents/cb/afcarsreport27.pdf

5

Colonial and apartheid South Africa: social work complicity and resistance

Linda Harms-Smith and Yasmin Turton[1]

Introduction

South African social work has its historical roots not only in violent and racist coloniality but also in its brutal continuity – that of repressive apartheid. Despite social work being defined as a social justice profession, its historiography points to a range of ideological positions in discourse, knowledge and practice. These positions mean variations in levels of complicity, sense of responsibility and resistance to matters of injustice, oppression and crimes against humanity.

Colonisation of South Africa by the British and Dutch achieved gains for race-based mercantile capitalism through the violent enslavement of local people and 'importation' of thousands. This creation of a Black, servile working class served the interests of White capital during the 19th century, forming the basis for apartheid's legislated racism and inequality which would come to structure South Africa society (Seekings, 2008; Sewpaul, 2013). South African social work, developing from this context of growing inequality and social problems, developed in the early 20th century. Given the class- and race-based structuring of society through colonisation, its early roots and formalisation focused only on the White group (Harms-Smith, 2014).

Various moments and conjunctures before and during the period of apartheid as a crime against humanity emerge. These, among many, seem important for investigating the meanings and actions of complicity, responsibility and resistance, and so this chapter details some of these important antecedents and conjunctures. This task is difficult because textual (and other) discourses occupy the broadest range of ideological positions. The same events, personalities and moments in history are described in contradictory and multiplicities of ways; as writers we must constantly revisit discourses and explore dissenting voices. The other difficulty arises from the personalisation of algorithms in our web-based searches for scholarship (Bozdag, 2013). What we find is often what we wish to see, and so we must be conscious of and find ways to resist this tendency.

73

Complicity and resistance

Arguments about consciousness, responsibility and resistance may be useful with respect to individuals in their personal lives, upholding an ethical code and commitment to professional values and principles such as dignity, social justice and equality, is foundational to social work (Banks, 2012; Sewpaul and Henrickson, 2019). It is expected that social workers should challenge and resist unjust and criminal policies and laws (Reisch, 2002; Ferguson and Lavalette, 2006; Kamali and Jönsson, 2019).

Questions must be posed about why most White social workers either did not feel horror at what the racist and socioeconomic oppression of the apartheid/colonial regimes perpetrated, or did, but failed to have the courage or will to act by resisting or challenging. It would also be true to argue that some Black social workers failed to act in ways that resisted or challenged these systems. Social work education during this era, focusing predominantly on status quo maintenance, remedial and pathologising theoretical positions, and a persistently Western and racist and social control focus, carries some of this responsibility (Lombard, 1998; Harms-Smith, 2014; Turton and Schmid, 2020). It seems that among White social work education institutions, besides a small number that were regarded as liberal, there was no attempt at critical conscientisation (Freire, 1972). Social workers did not generally perceive their role to be one of activism.

Choosing to be aware of the truth and reality of atrocities is a conscious choice. Hill (2009, p 6), drawing on Gramsci's notion of praxis and consciousness, argues that questioning everyday assumptions is a 'deliberate and willed intervention of the mind to move from a passive type of knowing to an active type of understanding which would enrich or even displace 'given thought'. Such turning away from conscious awareness is linked to privilege and affluence. Williams and Briskman (2015, p 5) point to the 'numbing effects of complacency, individualism and indifference as characteristic of 21st-century affluent Western society', which applies equally with respect to the predominant White South African context during the 20th century.

Apartheid

Apartheid cannot be regarded in an ahistorical manner. As will be shown, apartheid was a culmination of significant antecedents of imperialism, coloniality, racist capitalism and Afrikaner nationality (Dubow, 1989; Bundy, 2020). Apartheid arose from explosive capitalist growth and urbanisation and set in place legislation and policy that would determine the quality (and inequality) of lives in a racist hierarchy through structures and institutions. These included the 'native' reserves, land dispossession, migrant labour, pass laws and influx control, job reservation, segregation and unequal resource distribution from 1948 onwards (Bundy 2020).

This South African system of legislated racist violence, repression and segregation that oppressed Black South Africans between 1948 and 1994 was declared a 'crime against humanity' in 1966 by the United Nations General Assembly (resolution 2202 A (XXI)). Additionally, apartheid itself and all its acts were declared criminal by the Apartheid Convention of 1973 (Dugard, 2022). It is interesting to note that, at the time, only four of 95 nations voted against the adoption of the Apartheid Convention. These nations were South Africa, Portugal, the United Kingdom and the United States.

Article 2 of the Apartheid Convention described the 'inhuman acts arising from Apartheid' as international crimes and described these as domination and systematic oppression by one racial group over another. Specific crimes mentioned included, among others,

> murder, torture, inhuman treatment and arbitrary arrest ... living conditions calculated to cause its physical destruction; legislative measures that discriminate in the political, social, economic and cultural fields; ... creation of separate residential areas for racial groups; the prohibition of interracial marriages; and the persecution of persons opposed to apartheid. (Dugard, 2022)

Significantly, the Apartheid Convention also applied to other states practising racial discrimination.

The legislated segregation enforced by apartheid had a systematic and serious impact on social welfare. Ntusi (1997) notes that the institutionalisation of apartheid in 1948 legislated the already entrenched racially based services. It was within this state policy of apartheid that social workers provided fragmented and racially based services and formed professional associations which were also constituted on a racial basis. The South African Black Social Workers Association (SABSWA) was formed in 1945 and acted as the mouthpiece of Black social workers. This organisation would also have provided Black social workers a space to engage in response to the exclusions and racism found in the general order of the day. The Social Workers Association, which started in 1951, was exclusionary and only for White social workers, mainly Afrikaans speaking (Mazibuko, 1998; Mazibuko and Gray, 2004).

Apartheid established a highly brutalised society, dominated by a White minority government that had great power and control through both violence and symbolic violence (Bourdieu, 1988). As Turton and Van Breda (2019, p 2) describe, 'Any form of resistance was met with systematic violence, police harassment, detention without trial and the killing in detention of activist leaders such as Steve Biko'.

The transition to a non-racial democracy in 1994 after a lengthy peaceful and violent struggle for liberation by political formations, social movements, civic society and the international anti-apartheid movement, promised ideals of non-racial equality, redistribution and an agenda based on the Freedom Charter (1955), which included promises that 'the people shall govern', 'the land shall be shared among those that work it' and 'all shall share in the country's wealth' (Freedom Charter, 1955). However, what was to ensue was the acceptance of a neoliberal macro-economic policy which hampered the attainment of those ideas (Magubane, 2000; Bond, 2006).

Historical antecedents: imperialism, coloniality, racist capitalism and Afrikaner nationalism

While social work as a profession itself was not 'present' during early antecedents, it is important to explore how its formation rests on these. However, a chronological view of history as a series of events negates the complex economic and sociopolitical context of this history (Harman, 2008). Furthermore, seeing apartheid as a policy conception of only the Afrikaner Nationalist Government of 1948 is a reification which elides the antecedents of imperialism, colonisation, racist capitalist economic forces, White supremacist nationalism and liberal complicity. Questions of complicity may be raised from the earliest arrival of colonial settlers, including those who sent them and those embarking on the invasion.

Césaire (2000, p 33) describes colonisation as a collective hypocrisy that had nothing to do with philanthropy, evangelisation, extending the rule of law or 'for the greater glory of God', and argues that it was a fulfilling of the needs of mercantile capitalism. That is, it was the 'appetite and force' of a civilisation driven by the 'competition of its antagonistic economies'. He indicts Europe and its brutal, genocidal and violent colonisation and states:

> Europe is morally, spiritually indefensible. And today the indictment is brought against it not by the European masses alone, but on a world scale, by tens and tens of millions of men who, from the depths of slavery, set themselves up as judges. The colonialists may kill in Indochina, torture in Madagascar, imprison in Black Africa, crack down in the West Indies. Henceforth the colonized know that they have an advantage over them. They know that their temporary 'masters' are lying. Therefore, that their masters are weak. (Césaire 2000, p 33)

Conquest by the mercantile Dutch East India Company from 1652, and later by British settler-colonial conquest driven by racist capitalism, was foundational to the formation of the apartheid state. Resistance to White domination in South Africa began from the start of colonialism when the Khoi people used passive resistance in the Cape to refuse trade when it emerged that Dutch traders intended to settle and take their land. However, loss of traditional grazing land meant loss of means of subsistence, and, as a consequence, once conquered, the Khoi people were incorporated into the agricultural economy of the Cape.

Besides being a White settler state, South Africa was also a British colonial and imperialist–capitalist social formation (Wolpe, 1974; Magubane, 2000). The (so-called) discovery of diamonds and, later, gold in the late 19th century served British imperial interests and led to the era of wars of British imperial conquest against local peoples as well as against the Boer republics. Once gold production was established, the Rand mines produced a quarter of the capitalist world's gold. As Magubane argues, 'South Africa was developed by usurious British capital to fulfil the colonial role of mining auxiliary and as a source for raw materials' (Magubane, 2000, p 37).

Unlike other White settler colonies of the British empire such as Canada, Australia and New Zealand, where Indigenous populations were decimated or displaced by larger settler colonies, the South African Black population survived as a majority. It is argued that 'the genocidal wars of the 19th century stopped at the point where their logic might be detrimental to the labour needs of settlers' (Magubane, 2000, p 38).

The work of the London Missionary Society in sending missionaries to Southern Africa is filled with contradictions. Missionaries seemed clear about their role of extending the British Empire, or at least, the expansion of capitalism (Majeke, 1986). The Revd John Philip shows his passion for supporting and extending the British Empire in his report:

> While our missionaries, beyond the borders of the colony of the Cape of Good Hope are everywhere scattering the seeds of civilization, social order, and happiness, they are, by the most unexceptionable means extending British interests, British influence, and the British empire. Wherever the missionary places his standard among a savage tribe, their prejudices against the colonial government give way; their dependence upon the colony is increased by the creation of artificial wants; confidence is restored; intercourse with the colony is established; industry, trade, and agriculture spring up; and every genuine convert from among them made to the Christian religion becomes the ally and friend of the colonial government. (Philip, 1828, p x)

He then signals a contradictory consciousness in relation to his views about the role of missionaries and describes the detrimental effects of European impact on 'the natives' by stating: 'They were deprived of their country; from a state of independence, they were reduced to the miseries of slavery;

their herds of cattle followed their lands and passed over into the hands of the intrusive neighbours' (Philip, 1828, p xi).

The establishment, for example, of Lovedale College in 1824 by the Glasgow Missionary Society is an example of a missionary educational project that played a role in the lives of numerous leading figures of the liberation struggle of African resistance (Cele, 2020). Such missionary educational projects, later taken over by apartheid's Bantu Education, were said to have been 'the breeding ground for the black intelligentsia and many of our struggle leaders' (Archbishop Njongonkulu Ndugane, quoted in Mail and Guardian, 2006). However, the overall aims of missionary educational projects are fraught with contradictions, given the explicit commitment of the missionaries to the extension of the British Empire.

Ironically, Northern/Western social work is indicted with continuing the role of the missionaries in Africa, who sought to remake Africans in their own image (Bar-On, 1999). The imperial and colonial legacy exerted an impact on the development of social welfare policies in South Africa (Patel, 2011). The racist hegemony of White superiority justified policies that protected Whites, while Black South Africans living in poverty received inferior, if any, services (McKendrick, 1990; Patel, 2011). Furthermore, as race-based capitalist industrialisation developed, the system of exploitation of migrant labour, whereby only single men were permitted in the cities, left women and families in the reserves to work to support themselves through subsistence farming. This also impacted on the economies of the reserves and structured cultural roles and gendered care (Patel, 2011).

African workers were forced to supplement their means of subsistence by 'the expropriation of land, imposition of taxation, and similar nonmarket inducements' (Burawoy, 1976, p 1054). This system also benefitted the state substantially, as responsibility for the usual services provided by the state such as welfare, social security and education was passed on to families in rural areas (Burawoy, 1976). This also furthered a post-war welfare system promoting White welfare.

While colonisation and ensuing apartheid used violence to maintain power, these reprehensible systems were finally overcome. However, the emergence of the new democratic South Africa seemed to be a continuity of the same driving forces as the old, in this case neoliberal capitalism (Sewpaul and Holscher, 2004; Bond, 2006; Ashman et al, 2011). The same question must therefore also be posed about the current-day extent of ongoing complicity, responsibility and resistance.

(White) social work foundations: Carnegie and 'the poor White problem'

Social work was no innocent bystander, establishing itself as a profession in the early 1900s and growing as an ideological tool of the state's White supremacy.

Its formalisation after the 'poor White enquiry' in the 1930s meant that South African social work would come to be characterised by contradictions not only in its character but also in the response from social workers.

The ideological position of the Pact Government of the Afrikaner National Party and the pro-British Labour Party had led in 1926 to a structural approach to poverty with welfarist state policies such as old age pensions (only for White and, in lesser amounts, for 'Coloured' people) and national insurance. In this sense the Carnegie Commission of Inquiry into the 'Poor White' question (1929–32) and its report were a backlash against this policy position. The report also played a role 'in solidifying white Afrikaner political and economic dominance' (Harms-Smith, 2014). A Social Darwinist approach was embraced towards White poverty, which was to be regarded as due to 'retarded adjustment', weak personal responsibility and psychological deficiencies (Seekings, 2008). This approach was in keeping with views at the time of the early establishment of social work in Britain.

Dependency was said to have been created among White rural Afrikaners who were seen as being uneducated, lacking competence and not having developed the skills to be able to 'compete with cheap native labour' (Soudien, 2019). The creation of a state department of welfare positioned the function of formal social work education to be the scientific investigation of ways to treat social questions. The Sociological report displaying stereotyping and blame for poverty, authored by, among others, the organising secretary of the welfare organisation Afrikaans Christian Women's Organisation, stated that:

> The detrimental effects of the idea that State aid can take the place of personal effort and initiative are considerable. The sense of responsibility … is immediately weakened, and very soon the poor man [sic] is tempted to shirk all responsibility. In this way all desire for honest labour is eventually lost, and he is tempted to resort to all kinds of deception and trickery. … In the worst cases he becomes a shameless parasite on society without any desire or power to support himself, and as such becomes the despair of the social reformer. (Albertyn et al, 1932, p 76)

This became the basis of social work education and practice: an individualist pathologising approach using remedial services to focus on rehabilitation of the 'poor White'. It could be argued that social workers educated within the ideology of this hegemonic system would struggle to adopt any form of critical perspective.

Social work education: embracing the state

Social work education was racially segregated, focused on the welfare system of the day and performed a role mainly of maintaining the status quo

(Harms-Smith, 2014). Although social work training for White students had been introduced for the first time in 1924 at the University of Cape Town, and in 1931 at the University of the Witwatersrand, it was formalised following the Carnegie Commission of Enquiry report (Seekings, 2008). It was only after 1940 that social work training was available for Black students. The Carnegie report and its hegemonic discourse on personal responsibility and psychological deficiency had an important impact on the foundations of social work (Harms-Smith, 2013). Most social work focused on managing dependency brought about by poverty, and on the rights of individuals and groups (Gray and Mazibuko, 2002). Beyond a few liberal institutions, social work education was limited to the furtherance of the ideologies of the apartheid state (the Stellenbosch University Social Work Department was headed by Prof. Hendrick Verwoerd, the so-called architect of apartheid). Mainly remedial, therapeutic and restorative approaches were used, supporting an individualist liberal ideology, and based on American and British models (Harms-Smith, 2013).

African social workers were trained at separate colleges and training institutions and, in keeping with the hegemony of segregationist ideologies, McKendrick (1990, p 182) seems to have empathy for the aims of a White supremacist social work education: 'early moves were largely stimulated by a genuine desire to train Black social workers to work with the problems experienced by Black people'. Such statements may be interpreted as evidence of (liberal) Gramscian 'common understandings' which are examples of contradictory consciousness which are left uninspected (Hill, 2009).

An example of a prominent institution among these was the Jan Hofmeyr School of Social Work in Johannesburg (affiliated to the University of the Witwatersrand), opened in 1941, with Ray Phillips as director and A.B. Xuma (president-general of the African National Congress (ANC) at the time) on the executive committee. This was one of the few South African social work education institutions that created an environment for critical and political engagement with well-known luminaries including Winne Madikizela Mandela, Ellen Kuzwayo, Joshua Nkomo and Gibson Kente. However, even here, an analysis of the curriculum shows a discourse with an individualist, liberal focus. Although the College offered a diploma rather than a degree education, it was taken over by the state and subsequently closed down for, among other reasons, the admission of 'alien black' students and on the grounds that the educational level was unnecessarily high (Harms-Smith, 2014).

However, the *Bantu World* newspaper ran a report on the need for this institution, demonstrating the capacity of the state machinery and of hegemonic liberal ideologies to shape racist discourse. The newspaper was White owned, controlled mostly by the mining industry and tending to present depoliticised text that catered for a Black elite (Switzer, 1997, p 18). Seeming to offer a measure of critique of colonialism, it went on to use offensive, racist misrecognition:

> The impact of Western civilisation upon us has uprooted us from the anchor of the ancient life of our race, and thus has created social problems that can only be dealt with by trained men and women. ... It is becoming clearer and clearer to many Europeans that the welfare of their race in this country is bound up with that of the African race. They realise that as corn and tare [an undesirable weed] cannot grow side by side without the one overwhelming the other, so civilisation and barbarism cannot be allowed to grow side by side. (*Bantu World*, 1940)

Social work foundations: liberalism, social hygiene and eugenics

Liberalism, with its commitment to secular individualism, individual autonomy and freedoms, was the political ideology of mostly English White South Africans (De Gruchy and De Gruchy, 2005). The involvement of liberals in segregationist policies is clear from the following statement in 1937 by J.H. Hofmeyr (cited by Dubow, 1989, p 46), who rejected

> policies which are based either on the repression of the native or on his identification with the white man. ... The important thing is not the native's inferiority, or his equality, or his superiority; what is important is just the fact that he is different from the white man. The recognition of this difference from the white man. The recognition of this difference should be the starting point in South Africa's native policy.

The development of social work and social welfare in South Africa, while being determined by the outcomes of the 1932 Carnegie Commission (Seekings, 2008) was also influenced by liberal ideals. Liberalism also entailed racism in keeping with overall state policies of segregation. For example, the Race Welfare Society, led by H.B. Fantham (Dean of Science at the University of the Witwatersrand and president of the Eugenics Society), was founded in 1930 on liberal, eugenicist ideologies not only with regard to the Black population but also with respect to 'Poor Whites', who were seen as a threat to White supremacy due to 'breeding uncontrollably, among themselves and with Blacks' (Klausen, 2007, p 182).

This focus, however, changed after 1932 to include maternal health and general health and welfare, largely driven by Winifred Hoernle, who, together with Alfred Hoernle, both leading academics in science and anthropology, founded the South African Institute of Race Relations, which was complicit in the elaboration of a pragmatic, 'liberal' vision of segregation

(Klausen, 2017). Winifred Hoernle's involvement in South African welfare was extensive, as chairman of Non-European Child Welfare, president of Johannesburg Child Welfare, chairman of the South African Council for Child Welfare, member of the National Welfare Organizations Board and chairman of the Johannesburg Indian Welfare Society.

However, at that time, another segregationist Act was passed, The Urban Areas Act 21 of 1923, which decreed that Africans were allowed to reside in urban areas only to minister to White needs. Its contradictory and dishonest discourse is evident in the aims which claimed to 'provide for improved living conditions of residence for natives in or near urban areas and the better administration of native affairs in such areas'. Section 5.1 states that all 'natives' in a specific urban area other than those exempt, must 'reside in a location, native village or native hostel'. Exemptions included those owning immovable property valued at £75 or more and those employed in bona fide domestic service and for whom sleeping and sanitary accommodation was provided (South African Government, 1923, p 142).

Although there was some evidence of the Race Welfare Society having philanthropic concern for the extent of Black urban poverty (Klausen, 2017), no record can be found, of any challenge, resistance or social action by that society or by the South African Institute of Race Relations as leading welfare institutions or by Winifred Hoernle in her capacity as leader of many welfare organisations, around the restrictions imposed by this legislation.

Tracing social work resistance

Resistance to White domination in South Africa began from the start of colonisation when the Khoi people used a form of passive resistance in the Cape and refused to engage in trade when it became evident that the Dutch traders intended to settle and take their land. However, after their conquest due to loss of traditional grazing, and so of their means of subsistence, they were incorporated into the colonial agricultural economy, forming the basis for later segregation and apartheid (Lester, 1996, p 25).

While the history of South African resistance is rich with narratives of all forms of courageous struggles (also of some in social work), these do not appear clearly in formal historical textual discourses, in keeping with the epistemicide and subjugation of histories wrought by colonisation and the repression of apartheid (Harms-Smith, 2014; Ndlovu-Gatsheni, 2018). These require reclaiming through in-depth archival research (Stephens et al, 2013).

An important period of the resistance was the 'final stage', which brought sufficient pressure to bear on government that dialogue was started, eventually leading towards the transition to democracy. The Mass Democratic Movement had formed in 1988 in response to the government's repression of the United Democratic Front (UDF). It was a loose alliance of anti-apartheid groups, made up of UDF and ANC supporters, with strong links to the Congress of South African Trade Unions and comprising up to 600 affiliated organisations (O'Malley, 2022). It was especially during this stage that social workers engaged more openly in political activities, although SABSWA, specifically, had been involved in political processes a good 20 years earlier. For example, the Azanian People's Organisation reported that SABSWA had been one of the parties of the Black People's Convention (BPC) consultative meeting at Hammanskraal around the 'independence' of Bophuthatswana (Mpotseng, 1978).

Inspiration for politicised and radical social work practice was found by many social workers in the work of Paulo Freire's critical conscientisation and Steve Biko's Black Consciousness theories of liberation. Furthermore, a number of leading figures of social work such as Adam Small, Head of Philosophy and later of Social Work at the University of the Western Cape (and supporter of the Black Consciousness Movement) and Winnie Madikizela Mandela as a social worker and political leader (Harms-Smith, 2014).

When considering descriptions of radical social work, which uses political power to work for social change and is based on democracy, empathy, militancy, anti-oppressiveness and structural practice (Ioakimidis, 2016), it is clear that some social workers were practising in this way. This was the case especially in radical community work in oppressed communities and using theorists as described earlier (Bak, 2004).

During the heightened period of resistance in the 1980s, opposition welfare groups that had aligned to the UDF began to 'formulate explicitly what may be referred to as welfare demands based on the Freedom Charter' (Patel, 2011, p 78). These included a non-racial and unitary welfare system using a democratic model. Welfare was seen as being a redistributive strategy, and the need was also emphasised for state involvement in the economy, free education, national healthcare and general welfare provisioning. Some social workers participated in resistance formations from within their employment role as some progressive non-governmental organisations were supportive of this. Others participated as social workers in organisations and alliances created by themselves or by civil society. Resistance was also expressed in a more personal capacity, for example, with some leaving the profession for reasons of conscience or protest (see Turton and Van Breda, 2019). Descriptions of some of the organisations and individuals engaged most actively and visibly in these resistance efforts are provided in the following sections.

Resistance efforts which included social workers

The progressive movement Daughters of Africa (DOA), a women's movement, was formed in 1926 by Lillian Tshabalala, a trained social worker.

She, together with Sibusisiwe Makhanya and Nokutula Dube, was also instrumental in forming the Native Women's Welfare organisation (Healy-Clancy, 2014). Importantly, as DOA had also formed in Alexandra township in Johannesburg, Tshabalala was able to mobilise her organisation to protest a 1943 increase in bus fares in a dramatic public campaign that featured a march of 10,000 women, children and men, including the young Nelson Mandela (Bonner and Nieftagodien, 2008, p 71). They and a number of other welfare leaders from these organisations also spoke out against the 1930 Urban Areas Act, which decreed that African women without a husband or father in an urban area needed permission from municipal officials to reside there. They also called for a more racially inclusive state education and social welfare policies (Healy-Clancy, 2014).

The Hospital Defiance Campaign of 1986, organised by the MDM, protested around segregated hospitals and included social work formations. This arose because of rapid urbanisation due to the lifting of pass laws, and inadequate health services unable to meet the health needs of the people. Some areas had only 'White' hospitals, inaccessible to Black patients, while there were empty White hospitals. They argued that if the desegregation campaign was successful, it would logically lead to changes in the more fundamental issues already mentioned.

It is significant that this campaign was supported by numerous health and welfare bodies, indicating additional gains relating to solidarity, a united expression of grievances and, for social work, an important demonstration of commitment to social justice. The campaign was coordinated by health worker organisations such as the National Medical and Dental Association, the South African Health Workers Congress, the Organisation for Appropriate Social Services in South Africa (OASSSA), the National Education Health and Allied Workers Union, the Concerned Social Workers (CSW) and SABSWA, together with the broad MDM.

The South African Black Social Workers Association played the most important social work role in resistance and social activism. It was formed as early as 1945, acting as a mouthpiece for its members and playing a direct role in advocating for the social welfare of Black communities. For SABSWA, 'Black' meant all the 'race' categorisations other than White in South Africa ('Coloured' (mixed race), African and Indian descent). Already in 1977, there is evidence that SABSWA was politically engaged. TheBPC convened a consultative meeting with various organisations at Hammanskraal, to work out strategies on frustrating the pending 'independence' of Bophuthatswana from the Republic of South Africa. SABSWA were present, among others, (Mpotseng, 1978). SABSWA's political role was one of consistent presence in the anti-apartheid struggle, featuring in numerous reports and records of protest actions and formal engagements with other professionals or government.

Concerned Social Workers (and other social work professional groupings) was a progressive South African anti-apartheid social work organisation active in the 1980s and early 1990s. CSW started as a small discussion group at the University of the Witwatersrand and, as it grew, distinguished itself from the other three professional organisations (the Whites-only Social Workers Association of South Africa; SABSWA; and the Society for Social Workers (with a predominantly White membership but open to all)), arguing that it advocated alongside the poor, that it was anti-apartheid and that it was expressly non-racial (Schmid and Sacco, 2012). CSW, as a small grouping of approximately 50 participants, engaged in many anti-apartheid activities. 'Extra-legal activities were also undertaken, for example, in various conferences hosted by CSW, topics challenging state hegemony were openly addressed. At all times, CSW endeavoured to work in ways that were supported by evidence rather than popular rhetoric' (Schmid and Sacco, 2012, p 298). It is important to note that social workers of CSW valued examples of social workers' contributions to the struggle and were inspired 'by the ways in which Helen Joseph, Ellen Kuzwayo and Winnie Madikizela-Mandela, all members of the profession, had stood against oppression and repression' (Schmid and Sacco, 2012, p 295).

Direct involvement in service provision

Both SABSWA and the CSW offered direct services to specific groups and communities. In the case of CSW, post-detention counselling of political prisoners and newly released detainees, in partnership with the Detainees Counselling Service and OASSSA, were offered. They also provided support for parents of young people in detention; support of family members at funerals; group work with traumatised youth; community-based training and capacity building; and organisation of conferences (with support from the University of the Witwatersrand) (Schmid and Sacco, 2012). Important advocacy work and resistance included delegations to government around welfare planning and appointments, involvement in alliances such as the UDF, Free the Children and End Conscription campaigns. SABSWA, through its many branches across South Africa, rendered welfare services in 'townships', often providing interventions where state and non-governmental organisations were not active. These included work with children and young people and a strong community development and community service focus (Mazibuko and Gray, 2004).

Conferences as a strategy of conscientisation and challenge

Various actions of challenge and resistance were organised and mobilised around proposed New Welfare Policy. The welfare sector rallied. A committee was formed by SABSWA together with the non-racial Society for Social Workers and CSW. They declared that

> the new policy was an attempt to control welfare services along ideological lines, while reducing state responsibility for such services; privatization would mean a massive transfer of wealth from the white government to the White business sector; differential and privatised social welfare services in South Africa would mean no social welfare services for Africans. (Mayadas and Watts, 1997, p 357)

In May 1989 a conference was organised by the Welfare Policy Coordinating Committee on the proposed New Welfare Policy, consisting then of SABSWA, CSW, the Society for Social Workers of South Africa, the Johannesburg Indian Welfare Association, the Cape Town Social Workers Forum and the Durban Committee Against the Welfare Policy.

The Maputo Conference on Health and Welfare was organised by the US-based Committee for Health in Southern Africa with the ANC (still banned at that time) and various other groupings including the Welfare Coordinating committee consisting of SABSWA, CSW, the Social Workers Forum and the Durban Welfare Policy Group. Well-known social workers and academics presented papers (including Leila Patel, Cedric De Beer, Francie Lund, Jackie Loffell and Fikile Mazibuko) around the transformation of social welfare (Critical Health, 1990). Various other conference included a conference on Children's Rights (1988), Towards a Democratic Welfare System (1989) and Development of the Welfare Charter (1991) (Schmid and Sacco, 2012).

Social workers in resistance formations: resisting outside of the profession

Black women's resistance in the Free State was formed in 1983. In 1913, the Orange Free State was the only province in South Africa to require urban residential passes for female Africans and 'coloureds'. Meeting in Bloemfontein, African political leaders of SANNC (South African Native National Congress, later the ANC) from all over the country became aware of the local problem. The women were inspired at the meeting by Charlotte Manye Maxeke, the first Black South African female university graduate and a member of the SANNC executive. In two months, 5,000 signatures were collected for their petition to protest women's passes. Nothing happened for a year after the petition was handed in to the Minister of Native Affairs, and so the women decided to embark on passive resistance. They formed the Orange Free State Native and Coloured Women's Association to raise aid for resisters and their families, and to advocate for the cause. They also appealed to sympathetic Whites for support, which led to a solidarity march by White women in Winberg. They were also inspired by the coverage of the British suffragettes who suffered brutal imprisonment and forced feeding. This had a dramatic effect on the Bloemfontein women, who expressed their willingness to go to jail and even die for their cause. They finally had victory in 1913 (Wells, 1983).

The United Democratic Front (1983) was one of the most prominent movements in South Africa, with over 600 affiliated organisations. It included social workers in both their personal and professional capacities. As a broad-based political movement, the UDF united trade unions together with political and social organisations, and some child welfare organisations joined the UDF at its founding in 1983 (for example, Pietermaritzburg Child Welfare). The UDF identified as being non-racial, and so all could join the movement. This was in contrast with the Black Consciousness Movement, which argued that only Black People could liberate themselves.

Grassroots Newspaper, the country's first community newspaper, was launched as 'the people's paper' in 1980. Mention is made of social workers contributing to advice articles in this politically important newspaper. It worked to promote class consciousness, to develop of a culture of resistance and to empower people to work towards national liberation. Organisers included up to 60 democratic organisations, including trade unions, civic associations, women's and youth organisations and, later, the UDF, and were seen as the 'ideologically trained vanguard' (Van Kessel, 2000, p 239). The Advice Committee performed the role of contributing articles for the 'Advice' page and consisted of professionals with a background in law, medicine, childcare and social work. 'Grassroots fulfilled its potential by providing a voice for these communities, uniting them against oppression and injustice, and building opposition against apartheid' (South African History Online, 1992).

Notable social workers in the long struggle before and during apartheid

Several notable social workers, among many others, engaged in the liberation struggle with such courage and consistent leadership, and at such a personal cost, that they are current-day icons of social work.

Charlotte Maxeke (1871–1939) (Bachelor in Social Science Wilberforce College University of Ohio), the first known South African social worker, worked at the Johannesburg Magistrates Courts. A leader in pass-laws protests and women's issues, she co-founded the Bantu Women's League of the SANNC and the National Council for African Women in 1918 (Harms-Smith, 2014; South African History Online, 2022a).

Mfanasekaya Pearce Linda Gqobose (1917–) (Diploma in Social Work, Jan Hofmeyr College, Johannesburg) is a social worker at the National Council for the Blind; founding member of the Pan African Congress (PAC) in 1960; with Nyathi Pokela, she was tasked to establish the forerunner to the Azanian People's Liberation Army; she was PAC treasurer-general and became member of the High Command of PAC settlements in Tanzania (The Presidency, 2007).

Nothembu Grace Millicent Qunta (1917–89) (Bachelor of Social Science) was involved in the Non-European Unity Movement, active in the National Council for Women and the Christian Institute, committee member for NICRO and founded the Black Women's Federation in 1975 (Department of Arts, Culture, Science and Technology, 2000).

Ellen Kuzwayo (1914–2006) (Diploma in Social Work, Jan Hofmeyr College) was active in the anti-apartheid protest movement, general secretary of the Young Women's Christian Association, member of Soweto Committee of Ten, president of the Black Consumers Forum and a Member of Parliament (Department of Arts, Culture, Science and Technology, 2000, p 56);

Helen Joseph (née Fennell) (1905–92), a social worker from England, was a founding member Council of Democrats, reader of part of Freedom Charter at Congress of the People in Kliptown in 1955, one of four leading women of the 1956 Women's March to Union Buildings, an accused in the treason trial and was under house arrest in 1962 until she was 85 years old (Africa Media Online, 2022).

Sherry McLean, a social worker from Ireland, worked from 1985 to 1987 as a social worker at the ANC Solomon Mahlangu Freedom College in Tanzania, where she counselled and developed social support for children and adults, and was an anti-apartheid activist.

Anne Motlatjie Letsebe (PhD in social work, University of the Witwatersrand), a social worker and activist, participated in Maputo Conference on Welfare transformation. She was lecturer for 17 years, chief director for social sectors in Policy Unit in 1998, Deputy Director-General in the Presidency and Head of the Cabinet Office.

Anne Winifred Nomzamo Zanyiwe Madikizela-Mandela (1934–2018) (Diploma in Social Work Jan Hofmeyr College, Johannesburg) was a medical social worker at Baragwanath Hospital, served in the ANC and was banned in 1962 under the Suppression of Communism Act and detained in 1969 under the Terrorism Act. She was kept in solitary confinement for 17 months, after involvement in 1976/77 protests and the formation of the Black Women's Federation, and later banished to Brandfort in the Orange Free State until 1986. She was elected to the ANC's executive in 1991, President of the Women's League and a Member of Parliament. She is known as the 'Mother of the Nation' (South African History Online, 2022b).

Conclusion

There are complexities and risks involved in developing a discourse of complicity and resistance among individuals and groups which relates to the individualising of responsibility in the face of structural violence that is left unaccounted for. Mamdani (2002) argues in his critique of the Truth and Reconciliation Commission that by individualising those that are complicit or perpetrators, there are also a limited number of victims. Sanders (2002) regards all social relations as comprising of complicity, as it is impossible to resist without being engaged within the very relational dynamic that is the focus of what must be resisted. In that sense, all are complicit to the extent that choices are made willingly. Goldblatt (2017) speaks of structural complicity, due purely to a location in a particular violent political and economic structure. However, the focus of this chapter has beenthe facing and acting upon, or the turning away from, moral and ethical outrage and horror, by social work as a collective or by social workers as professionals. Social work itself, in a powerful way, produces structures and ideologies, as was evident in the Carnegie Commission of Inquiry and is evident in social work education.

It is important that an accountable understanding is developed of the violence perpetrated on Black South Africans by apartheid and its antecedents, and we should avoid constructing a narrative that ignores those choices and actions that consented to and turned away from, or resisted and confronted, the structural violence that was done. The question remains, however, of what future generations of social workers will have to say about complicity and resistance in our current era of neoliberal capitalism with inequalities that mean the majority of the world's population live in unacceptable levels of deprivation; about a world in environmental and climate crisis; and about a global pandemic that saw these ruptures exposed, with little action to change them. It is our hope that a better world is possible.

Note
[1] This chapter is written by two South Africans, one of the racialised category White and the other of the racialised category Black ('mixed race' but defined as 'Coloured' in South Africa), who both trained and practised during the apartheid era. At the time one of us remained in practice, thus at times being complicit and compromising ethical principles by having to work within unequal apartheid welfare policies, while also trying to resist through subversive strategies and participating in resistance movements; the other of us left the profession to pursue resistance from within the social justice liberation movement and returned to social work some years after the transition to democracy.

References
Africa Media Online (2022) *Ten things you need to know about Helen Joseph.* https://artsandculture.google.com/story/GgVRtyjLRjqZLw?hl=en

Albertyn, J.R, with A.D. Luckhoff, T.F. Cronje and M.E. Rothmann (1932) *Sociological Report: (a) The Poor White and Society, Part V (a) of The Poor White Problem in South Africa: Report of the Carnegie Commission.* Stellenbosch: Ecclesia.

Ashman, S., Fine, B. and Newman, S. (2011) The crisis in South Africa: Neoliberalism, financialization and uneven and combined development, *Socialist Register, 47.* https://socialistregister.com/index.php/srv/article/view/14326

Bak, M. (2004) Can developmental social welfare change an unfair world? The South African experience, *International Social Work,* 47(1): 81–94. doi: 10.1177/0020872804039385

Bantu World (1940) School of social work. Johannesburg, 13 July. Cullen Library Historical Papers, University of the Witwatersrand.

Banks, S. (2012) *Ethics and Values in Social Work.* Basingstoke: Macmillan International Higher Education.

Bar-On, A. (1999) Social work and the 'missionary zeal to whip the heathen along the path of righteousness', *The British Journal of Social Work,* 29(1): 5–26, https://doi.org/10.1093/oxfordjournals.bjsw.a011440

Bond, P. (2006) *Looting Africa: The Economics of Exploitation.* Pietermaritzburg: University of Natal Press.

Bonner, P. and Nieftagodien, N. (2008) *Alexandra: A History.* Johannesburg: Witwatersrand University Press.

Bourdieu, P. (1988) Social space and symbolic power, *American Sociological Association,* 7(1): 18–26. https://www2.southeastern.edu/Academics/Faculty/jbell/symbolicpower.pdf

Bozdag, E. (2013) Bias in algorithmic filtering and personalization, *Ethics and Information Technology,* 15(3): 209–227. https://doi.org/10.1007/S10676-013-9321-6

Bundy, C. (2020) Poverty and inequality in South Africa: A history. *Oxford Research Encyclopaedia of African History.* https://doi.org/10.1093/acrefore/9780190277734.013.659.

Burawoy, M. (1976) The functions and reproduction of migrant labour: Comparative material from Southern Africa and the United States, *American Journal of Sociology,* 81(5): 1050–1087.

Cele, M. (2020) Preserving Lovedale Press, a historical compass, *New Frame,* 15 July. www.newframe.com/preserving-lovedale-press-a-historical-compass/

Césaire, A. (2000) *Discourse on Colonialism.* New York: Monthly Review Press.

De Gruchy, J. and De Gruchy, S. (2005) *The Church Struggle in South Africa, Twenty Fifth Anniversary Edition.* Minneapolis: Fortress Press.

Dubow, S. (1989) *Racial Segregation and the Origins of Apartheid in South Africa 1919–1936.* New York: Palgrave MacMillan.

Dugard, J. (2022) Convention on the suppression and punishment of the crime of apartheid, *Audiovisual Library of International Law*. https://legal.un.org/avl/ha/cspca/cspca.html

Ferguson, I. and Lavalette, M. (2006) Globalisation and social justice; towards a social work of resistance, *British Journal of Social Work*, 34(3): 309–318.

Freedom Charter (1955) South African History Online. www.sahistory.org.za/archive/freedom-charter-original-document-scan

Freire, P. (1972) *Pedagogy of the Oppressed*. Harmondsworth: Penguin.

Goldblatt, C. (2017) Beyond the 'memory' of apartheid: Richard Rive and the Jewish mock-monarchs of Cape Town, Journal of Postcolonial Writing. doi: 10.1080/17449855.2017.1307259

Harman, C. (2008) *A People's History of the World*. London: Verso Books.

Harms-Smith, L. (2013) Social Work Education: Critical Imperatives for Social Change. Unpublished PhD thesis, University of the Witwatersrand. https://wiredspace.wits.ac.za/handle/10539/12875

Harms-Smith, L. (2014) Historiography of South African social work: Challenging dominant discourses, *Social Work/Maatskaplike Werk*, 50(3): 305–331. http://hdl.handle.net/10059/2338

Healy-Clancy, M. (2014) The daughters of Africa and transatlantic racial kinship: Cecilia Lilian Tshabalala and the Women's Club movement, 1912–1943, *American Studies*, 59(14): 481–500.

Hill, D.J. (2009) A brief commentary on the Hegelian–Marxist origins of Gramsci's 'Philosophy of Praxis', *Educational Philosophy and Theory*, 41(6): 605–621. doi: 10.1111/j.1469-5812.2008.00495.x.

Human Science Research Council (HSRC) (2000) *Women Marching into the 21st Century: Wathint' abfazi wathint' imbokodo*. Cape Town: Department of Arts and Culture, Science and Technology.

Ioakimidis, V. (2016) A guide to radical social work: Inequality and poverty have a devastating effect on service users. www.theguardian.com/social-care-network/2016/may/24/radical-social-work-quick-guide-change-poverty-inequality

Kamali, M. and Jönsson, J.H. (2019) 'Revolutionary social work: promoting sustainable justice', *Critical and Radical Social Work*, 7(3): 293–314. https://DOI:10.1332/204986019X15688881109268

Klausen, S. (2017) The race welfare society: eugenics and birth control in Johannesburg, 1930–40. In S. Dubow (ed) *Science and Society in Southern Africa*. Manchester: Manchester University Press, pp 164–187.

Lester, A. (1996) *From Colonization to Democracy: A New Historical Geography of South Africa*. London: I.B. Tauris.

Magubane, B. (2000) Race and democratization in South Africa, *Macalester International*, 9(8): 33–82. http://digitalcommons.macalester.edu/macintl/vol9/iss1/8

McKendrick, B.W. (1990) *Introduction to Social Work*, Pretoria: Haum Tertiary.

Majeke, N. (1986) *The Role of Missionaries in Conquest*. University of Cape Town, J.W. Jagger Library.

Mamdani, M. (2002) Amnesty of impunity? A preliminary critique of the report of the Truth and Reconciliation Commission of South Africa (TRC). *Ethics: Special Issue – Diacritics*, 32(3/4): 32–59.

Maputo Conference Coordinating Committee (1990) Maputo conference: Health and welfare in transition, *Critical Health*, 31/32, August. www.sahist ory.org.za/sites/default/files/archive-files4/ChAug90.pdf

Mazibuko, F.N.M. (1998) Transformation or organised fragmentation? Exploring the way forward with social worker formations, *Social Work – Stellenbosch*, 34: 28–34.

Mazibuko, F. and Gray, M. (2004) Social work professional associations in South Africa, *International Social Work*, 47(1): 129–142.

Motlanthe, K. (2017) Reflections on the South African political economy, *New Agenda: South African Journal of Social and Economic Policy*, 67. www. ajol.info/index.php/na/article/view/162971

Mpotseng Jairus Kgokong (1978) *Towards Black Wednesday, 19/10/77, and beyond*. Azanian People's Organisation (AZAPO), O'Malley Archives, Nelson Mandela Foundation. https://omalley.nelsonmandela.org/omal ley/index.php/site/q/03lv02424/04lv02730/05lv02889/06lv02890.htm

Ndlovu-Gatsheni, S. (2018) Dynamics of epistemological decolonisation in the 21st century: Towards epistemic freedom, *Strategic Review for Southern Africa*, 40(1): 16–45. www.up.ac.za/media/shared/85/Strategic%20Rev iew/vol%2040(1)/NdlovuGatsheni.pdf

O'Malley Archives (2022) *Mass Democratic* Front, Nelson Mandela Foundation. https://omalley.nelsonmandela.org/omalley/index.php/site/ q/03lv03445/04lv03446/05lv03480.htm

Philip, J. (1828) *Researches in South Africa illustrating the civil, moral and religious condition of the native tribes together with detailed accounts of the progress of the civilising missions exhibiting the influence of Christianity in promoting civilisation*. London: James Duncan, Paternoster-Row. University of Pretoria repository. https://repository.up.ac.za/bitstream/handle/2263/16709/001_ FrontInfo.pdf?sequence=10&isAllowed=y

Reisch, M. and Andrews, J. (2002) *The Road not Taken: A History of Radical Social Work in the United States*. New York: Brunner-Routledge.

Sanders, M. (2002) *Complicities: The Intellectual and Apartheid*. Durham: Duke University Press.

Schmid, J. and Sacco, T. (2012) A story of resistance: Concerned social workers, *Social Work Practitioner-Researcher*, 24(3): 291–308.

Seekings, J. (2008) The Carnegie Commission and the backlash against welfare state-building in South Africa, 1931–1937, *Journal of Southern African Studies*, 34(3): 515–537.

Sewpaul, V. and Henrickson, M. (2019) The (r)evolution and decolonization of social work. *International Social Work*, 62(6): 1469–1481. doi: 10.1177/0020872819846238.

Sewpaul, V. (2013) Neoliberalism and social work in South Africa, *Critical and Radical Social Work,* 1(1): 15–30.

Sewpaul, V. and Henrickson, M. (2019) The (r)evolution and decolonization of social work ethics: The Global Social Work Statement of Ethical Principles, *International Social Work*, 62(6): 1469–1481. doi: 10.1177/0020872819846238.

Sewpaul, V. and Holscher, D. (2004) *Social Work in Times of Neoliberalism: A Postmodern Discourse.* Pretoria: Van Schaik.

Soudien, C. (2019) *Ninety Years of Social Science Research into Poverty: Revisiting the HSRC and the Carnegie Commission.* Human Sciences Research Council. www.hsrc.ac.za/en/review/hsrc-review-march-2019/ninety-years-social-science-research#:~:text=Carnegie%20findings%3A%20A%20strong%20emphasis,executive%20summary%20of%20124%20points

South African Government (1923) *Native (Urban Areas) Act 21 of 1923.* Aluka Digital Library. http://psimg.jstor.org/fsi/img/pdf/t0/10.5555/al.sff.document.leg19230614.028.020.021_cover.pdf

South African History Online (2022a) Charlotte Maxeke (nee Manye). www.sahistory.org.za/people/charlotte-maxeke-nee-manye

South African History Online (2022b) Winnie Madikizela Mandela. www.sahistory.org.za/people/winnie-madikizela-mandela

South African History Online (1992) Grassroots. www.sahistory.org.za/archive/grassroots

Staff Reporter, Mail and Guardian (2006) Archbishop takes interest in historic SA schools, *Mail and Guardian,* 20 March. https://mg.co.za/article/2007-03-20-archbishop-takes-interest-in-historic-sa-schools/

Stevens, G., Duncan, N. and Hook, D. (eds) (2013) *Race, Memory and the Apartheid Archive: Towards a Transformative Psychosocial Praxis.* London; Johannesburg: Palgrave Macmillan.

Switzer, L. (ed) (1997) *South Africa's Alternative Press: Voices of Protest and Resistance, 1880s–1960s.* New York: Cambridge University Press.

The Presidency (2007) *Mfanasekaya Pearce Linda Gqobose.* www.thepresidency.gov.za/national-orders/recipient/mfanasekaya-pearce-linda-gqobose-1917

Turton, Y. and Schmid, J. (2020) Transforming social work: Contextualised social work education in South Africa, *Social Work/Maatskaplike Werk,* 56(4): 367–382. doi: http://dx.doi.org/10.15270/56-4-880.

Turton Y. and van Breda, A. (2019) The role of social workers in and after political conflict in South Africa: Reflections across the fence. In J. Duffy, J. Campbell and C. Tosone (eds) *International Perspectives on Social Work and Political Conflict.* Abingdon: Routledge, pp 128–141.

Van Kessel, I. (2000) *Beyond Our Wildest Dreams: The United Democratic Front and the Transformation of South Africa.* Charlottesville; London: University Press of Virginia.

Wells, J.K.C. (1983) Why women rebel: A comparative study of South African women's resistance in Bloemfontein (1913) and Johannesburg (1938), *Journal of Southern African Studies,* 10 (1): 55–70.

Williams, C. and Briskman, L. (2015) Reviving social work through moral outrage, *Critical and Radical Social Work,* 3(1): 3–17. doi: https://doi.org/10.1332/204986015X14225321433375.

Wolpe, H. (1974) Capitalism and cheap labour-power in South Africa: From segregation to apartheid, *Economy and Society,* 1(4): 425–456.

PART III

Social work's contested ideologies

6

Social services in Nazi Germany and the role of social workers between complicity and rare resistance

Carola Kuhlmann

This chapter contains references to the abuse and murder of people with disabilities, under the Nazi regime, that readers may find upsetting or disturbing.

What led to national socialist '*Volkspflege*' (People's Care)?

Dividing the 'worthy' and 'unworthy' clients: a modern idea

Social work in Germany has emerged from Christian charity in the monasteries and hospitals of the Middle Ages with their doctrine of the duty to give alms to all who begged for it. Since about 1500 the new idea became established that poor people should be examined to see whether they were 'worthy' of support. Honorary municipal officials proved the willingness to work and the moral way of life of the poor. The 'unworthy poor' were locked up in poorhouses and penitentiaries in order to educate them to work (Kuhlmann, 2013, pp 21). The division into 'worthy' and 'unworthy' finally received a new, eugenic interpretation in the 19th century, and especially during the National Socialist era.

Eugenic thinking and its long tradition

The idea of improving humanity through 'breeding' emerged not only in Germany, but first in England (Francis Galton, 1822–1911), and likewise throughout Europe, in the US, Canada and other immigration countries. Not only conservative or reactionary but also socialist and some feminist thinkers were impressed by the idea of combatting social problems by regulating reproduction. In Germany, the conviction arose, especially in psychiatric research, that criminality and other deviant behaviour could mainly be explained by hereditary diseases. Researchers referred to the examinations of the physique of people who had become criminals, as carried out by the Italian Cesare Lombroso (1876). As a result of the successful fight against cholera and tuberculosis through social hygiene measures, the view spread that hygienic concepts could also be successful in other areas. Thus, healthcare was already been oriented towards 'racial hygiene' from the turn of the 20th century (in marriage counselling centres or in sexual healthcare).

Around 1920, many psychiatrists in Germany were examining the residents of care institutions and categorising them, for example, as 'libidinous, indifferent, brutal or morally inferior'. Most of them concluded that these people were more than 90 per cent hereditarily burdened because their parents and grandparents had already been labelled in a similar way (Kuhlmann, 1989, pp 79). (Of course, the effects of hunger, poverty and trauma were overlooked.) Their investigations were considered as proof justifying the coercive measures taken by the National Socialists after 1933, who did not invent eugenic thinking. They only radicalised and implemented it.

The Weimar Republic in economic and political crisis

The First World War had led to a significant deterioration in the social situation of the population. In 1915 one third of German families were dependent on state assistance, mostly in the form food and clothing (see Sachße/Tennstedt, 1988, p 52). In 1918 almost every second soldier was dead or had been wounded. Many families lacked any income even after the war. Since Germany had started and lost the war, it had to pay reparations, which led to severe inflation around 1923 and further impoverishment of the middle class. Nevertheless, the first democratic state in Germany managed to advance some reform projects in the field of welfare. For example, city administrations were obliged to provide adequate support for single persons, youth and families (1922–24). Unemployment insurance was introduced in 1927. But all these new benefit systems collapsed and were overridden by emergency decrees after the start of the Great Depression.

Unemployment in the German Reich more than tripled during 1929–32, from 1.89 million to 6.13 million. In 1933 many people – one fifth of the German population – were again living on public welfare benefits. Between 1928 and 1933 the benefit per unemployed person fell from RM849 to RM569 per year (Kuczynski, 1982, p 136).

However, Weimar democracy failed not only because of the economic burden, but also because many Germans – brought up in Prussian dutifulness and traumatised by the First World War – rejected democracy and longed for the grandeur of an imperial empire and a strong man at the head of the state. The country was destabilised by numerous emergency governments. Finally, in January 1933, the conservative parties handed over power to the new Reich Chancellor, Adolf Hitler. In the last election in March 1933, 44 per cent of Germans voted for the NSDAP (National Socialist German Workers' Party).

The National Socialists seize power through terror and laws

In many reviews of social work, the leading experts welcomed the new state of Adolf Hitler. One example is an article from the important Deutscher Verein für öffentliche und private Fürsorge (German Association for Public and Private Welfare), who promptly expressed they would like to 'put themselves at the service of the national uprising' (Wilhelm Pollligkeit, cited in Kappeler, 2021, p 25). Many institutions and trade journals in social work were still in the hand of Catholic and Protestant associations, and even though they had a different image of man they expressed enthusiasm that now the socialist criticism of their institutions would end, and authoritarian educational methods and traditional family models would finally strengthened again (Kuhlmann, 1989, p 59).

Nevertheless, the relationship to the churches was complex. From the very start, all institutions that could or would have offered resistance were banned, forcibly dissolved or expropriated and taken over by Nazi organisations – for example, the welfare organisations of the social democrats and the communists, and also liberal welfare institutions. The German Labour Front – Nazi labour organisation – took over the trade unions and the professional associations of social workers. From 1933 onwards the framework of the Association of Women Employees included a group for welfare workers, which was merged in 1935 to form the specialist group 'Soziale Berufsarbeit' (social professional work). The former executive director of the Protestant association and that of the German association continued to be active in the management (Paulini, 2001, p 416).

The Nazis also forced youth associations into the Hitler Youth movement and dissolved the vocational academies of the women's movement. Only the Christian organisations and the Red Cross remained after the takeover struggles of 1933.

The concept of 'Volkspflege' (People's Care)

Herrmann Althaus moved from the Innere Mission (the Protestant Welfare organisation) to the main office of the National Socialist organisation and state headquarter of welfare. He distanced himself from the Christian tradition and complained that too many welfare workers were still Christians: 'We are confronted with the task of turning around two millennia of thinking and giving the work a different, a new spirit. In doing so, we face the very difficult problem of having to come to terms with the welfare idea of the Christian religious creeds' (Althaus, 1937, pp 23–24). Christian-oriented welfare workers should be retrained because they believed in the 'unique personal value of each individual before God'. In contrast, National Socialists believed that it was not religious attitudes or environmental conditions, but 'hereditary disposition that makes people unequal in their value for the good of the whole' (Althaus 1937, p 14). The greater the level of public support, the greater would be the growth in numbers of those who otherwise would not be able to acquire resources in the economic struggle for existence and, as a result, would 'naturally' die out.

To bring the 'new spirit' forward, the National Socialists founded their own welfare association, the Nationalsozialistische Volkswohlfahrt (NSV) (National Socialist People's Welfare), which was to concentrate on the so-called hereditary healthy and became particularly active in maternal counselling, family and infant care. Mothers were to be educated to adopt a 'fighting position' towards their children (Johanna Haarer 1934, cited in Kuhlmann, 2013, p 94).

Exclusion of Jews and others

An above-average number of welfare workers were of Jewish origin, and many of them lost their positions after 1933. Alice Salomon, even though she had converted to Protestantism in 1914, lost her chairmanship of the Nationale Konferenz der sozialen Frauenschulen (National Conference of Women's Social Schools), and thus also the chairmanship of the International Association of Schools of Social Work. In 1933 she noticed how quickly people turned their backs on the fate of the 'non-Aryans'. She suddenly felt as if her former colleagues were speaking in a foreign language and as if she herself came from another planet. The former women's solidarity no longer included solidarity with the 'racially' persecuted. Later, she wrote in her autobiography that this and many similar small experiences meant a 'painful awakening from the dream of "German idealism". ... Could this really happen in the 20th century in the heart of Europe?' (Alice Salomon 1944, quoted in Kuhlmann, 2000, p 207). In all fields of social work socialist, Jewish or feminist colleagues were dismissed overnight and lost their position in public authorities without any serious objections on the part of their colleagues.

From exclusion to persecution and extinction in collaboration with social work

Exclusion of the 'non-Aryan' from welfare care

First and especially, the Jews suffered from exclusion from welfare care. In addition to those who were already impoverished before 1933, there were now also people who had fallen on hard times due to dismissal from public office or the boycott of businesses (Gruner, 2002). Although the Nuremberg Race Laws initially left the welfare obligations toward Jewish citizens untouched, the municipalities used their legal possibilities, arbitrarily cancelled allowances and, for example, imposed forced labour as early as 1933, even in the concentration camps as a 'support measure'. In 1938, a ministerial decree followed that excluded Jews from receipt public welfare benefits. Even the private Jewish charitable associations were no longer able to provide any relief, as many donations failed to materialise due to the wave of emigration.

Impoverished for a longer period, but at the same time living apart from society, were the Sinti and Roma, who had already been systematically recorded since the founding of the Reich and were considered by racial scientists to be the 'second most important alien-racial group'. However, because of their smaller number (20,000), their 'mental inferiority' and their 'antisocial way of life', they were not considered to pose such a strong racial danger and were therefore included in the racist legislation later than the Jews, but then with the same deadly consequences. From the very beginning they were excluded from welfare, many were forcibly sterilised and their 'ruthless extermination' was publicly demanded because of their 'anti-community' hereditary traits (*Wohlfahrtswoche*, 14 May 1939, quoted in König, 1989, p 76).

Municipal public welfare officials offered no resistance or even opposition to the process of deliberate exclusion of the 'non-Aryan'. On the contrary, welfare officials helped to register destitute Jews, who were later the first to be deported (Gruner, 2002, p 95; see also Lehnert, 2003).

Political and moral persecution

Not only racial but also political persecution happened, among others, through the welfare authorities. Jehovah's Witnesses were the few who consistently resisted, for example by refusing the Hitler salute or the National Socialist education of their children, and later by refusing military service. In 1936, the authorities increased the pressure on them and withdrew custody of their children in at least 860 cases (Roth, 2015, p 103). The children were sent to residential care and foster families, often deliberately to Catholic or Nazi families (see also Kuhlmann, 1989, p 186).

But when we speak of persecution in the Third Reich we are talking not only about ethnic minorities, political parties or religious minorities, but also about the group of people classified as 'inferior' for social reasons. The National Socialist kind of racism was also socially based.

The persecution of 'antisocials' was carried out under the auspices of the health offices, which had been nationalised in 1934 and to which the municipal welfare and youth offices had been subordinated. Here, extensive so-called '*Sippentafeln*' (kinship-tables) were compiled by social workers, which tracked conspicuous behaviour up to the grandparents' generation and interpreted it as incriminating testimony for the families concerned.

The cleansing of the street scene of 'antisocials' was accomplished at first by increased levels of incarceration in workhouses, later in 'camps for closed welfare', where living conditions became more severe. Finally, from 1938 onwards, 'antisocial' aid recipients, especially prostitutes and so-called drunkards, were no longer placed under the control of the municipal welfare offices, but directly under the control of the criminal police and Gestapo (*Geheime Staatspolizei* [secret state police]; see Ayaß, 1995, p 224).

As part of the '*Arbeitsscheu Reich*' campaign (anti-workshy campaign), many of these people were transferred to concentration camps and marked with a black triangle (for antisocial behaviour) sewn onto their clothing, some only for a short time as a deterrent, some for longer.

The concentration camp system was the 'central instrument of persecution of the Nazi regime' (Roth, 2015, p 109). Heinrich Himmler expanded it further and further into a 'camp universe'. Their existence was known through propaganda, while their actual conditions were kept secret. At first, the camps primarily targeted the political opposition. The mass incarceration of the 'antisocials' shifted the prisoner structure. In June 1938, for example, the 2,500 prisoners in Sachsenhausen were joined by 6,000 'antisocials'. Welfare administrations and labour offices transferred a total of about 10,000 people and used the opportunity to deport their clients primarily for financial reasons. The Frankfurt welfare office wrote to the city's mayor: 'We have, in the closest liaison with the secret state police and the criminal investigation department, over 150 antisocials ... in preventive detention. ... Financially, this decree has also resulted in a substantial relief of the welfare budget' (cited in Roth, 2015, p 126).

Youth welfare: hereditarily ill or educable?

In contrast to nationalised youth work (Hitler Youth), the majority of youth welfare work continued to take place within the framework of Catholic and Protestant institutions and associations. However, the doctrine of hereditary illness penetrated here – even without political pressure. The representatives and institutions admitted that youth welfare had to be 'cleansed' of the inferior types (about 12 per cent of the children were forcibly sterilised) in order to be able to carry out successful 'nation-building educational work' (see Kuhlmann, 1989, p 85).

Despite these kinds of efforts, public education could not successfully free itself from its historically developed hybrid position as a custodial, punitive and educational measure. However, new, specifically National Socialist institutions emerged at the margins, which were primarily intended to bring about greater differentiation (according to 'racial' criteria) in youth welfare:

• Under the direct auspices of the '*Landesjugendämter*' (youth welfare authorities), 'observation centres' were created in every province under psychiatric management in order to separate the probably successful cases from the 'hereditarily damaged non-successful cases' and to distribute them to decentralised special institutions. The earlier differentiation according to age, gender and education level was to be replaced by a differentiation according to the severity of the 'hereditary burden'.

• In addition, the NSV set up so-called youth homes for the 'hereditarily healthy' cases. In these residential care homes, there were regular meetings of the staff and an individually designed educational plan. The groups comprised no more than 15 children, had a family-like structure and the children attended the local school. In summary, these were better conditions than in the reformatories of the churches. But the educational goals followed the National Socialist ideology of obedience and harshness. Most of the educators came from the Hitler Youth.

• Finally, after 1940, so-called youth concentration camps were set up for the 'uneducable'. The function of these camps, which also existed in a more moderate form in various provinces as work camps for juvenile 'work shirkers' (see Kuhlmann, 1989 p 221), consisted primarily in the threat of being transferred there, as well as in being the 'final stop' for those who no longer seemed tolerable in the reformatories.

'Ballast existences': mentally ill and disabled people

Mentally ill and disabled people were one of the most vulnerable groups during the National Socialist era. They were the main target of propaganda against the so-called 'ballast existences', the 'vermin' in the garden of the eugenic utopia – and many doctors also treated them in this way (see Dörner, 1988). For propaganda reasons, mentally handicapped people were depicted in many magazines against the backdrop of mansion-like care facilities. Next to this, pictures of a 'healthy' family in a poor living environment were shown.

Well over half of the sterilisations ordered by the *'Gesetz zur Verhütung erbkranken Nachwuchses'* (Law for the Prevention of Hereditary Diseased Offspring) were carried out on so-called feeble-minded people, and many blind and deaf people were also included. The unchallenged equation of disability and inferiority had serious consequences for those affected (and their relatives). If they survived at all, they rarely fought for reparations, even after 1945, out of shame and despair (see the following for deaf-mute people as examples: Biesold, 1988; Rudnik, 1990; from the perspective of the victims: Nowak, 1989).

As part of the 'T 4' actions carried out by the Reich Ministry of the Interior under the guise of a 'transport company', the so-called euthanasia actions, more than 250,000 residents (adults and children) of the so-called insane or idiot institutions were gassed or poisoned. These murders took place from 1939 onwards, both on transports and in specially converted killing centres (for general information on euthanasia, see Klee, 2010; Ley and Hinz-Wessels, 2012; Aly, 2013).

Doctors and midwives were obliged to report children with 'congenital severe suffering'. They received a payment of RM2 as a reward for each report. Psychiatrists from the 'T 4' headquarters had previously calculated that for every 1,000 people, five needed psychiatric care in asylums, one of whom was to fall under 'the action' – about 70,000 people all told. In order to register them, the directors of the institutions were supposed to report those residents for transfer who were not even usable for the simplest work and who required particularly intensive care. They were also asked about their religious affiliation and who still received frequent visits from relatives. Only a few managers refused to fill out the forms. In these cases, mobile teams were sent from the headquarters in Berlin for assessment.

The intention to kill did not go unnoticed by the patients themselves. Some resisted loudly and did not want to get on the buses. From an asylum in southern Germany, a patient wrote home to their family in November 1940:

Dear Sister! Since our fear and need are increasing, I want to tell you about my concern. Yesterday the cars came again, and eight days ago they came again, and they took many people where one would not have thought. It became so difficult for us that we all cried, and it was completely difficult for me when I no longer saw M.S. ... Now I would like to ask you to stand up for me, to let me come to you, because we don't know if they won't come back next week. If we ever don't see each other again, I want to express my heartfelt thanks for all you have done for me. (Quoted in Kuhlmann, 2018, p 92)

The experiences gained from the gassing of the sick served the National Socialists as preparatory work for the construction of the killing facilities in the extermination camp at Auschwitz. To prevent resistance from caregivers or relatives, and in order to cover traces, the disabled people were often transferred several times beforehand. There were also no 'published' instructions (only requests for transfer). Anyone who spoke publicly about 'killing' the transferred person could be sentenced to death. Families learned by post of the deaths of their relatives, who had allegedly died of pneumonia or similar diseases. Despite threatened sanctions and attempted secrecy, there were soon protests from families as well as public protests from the churches, which were affected as institutions. In this context, two people must be mentioned who paid for their resistance with their lives or imprisonment: from the Catholic side, Cathedral Provost Bernhard Lichtenberg, and from the Protestant side, Pastor Paul Gerhard

Braune. Both sent letters of protest to responsible authorities as early as 1940, Lichtenberg writing to the government about the 'crimes' reported by parents. Braune, vice-president of the Protestant welfare organisation, member of the *'Bekennende Kirche'* (Confessing Church, an opposition movement within the church) and director of a housing complex for the socially disadvantaged, disabled people and the elderly, refused to transfer the sick and, after extensive research, wrote a memorandum entitled 'Planned transfer of inmates of sanatoriums and nursing homes', which he sent to Adolf Hitler and Hermann Göring on 16 July 1940.

Some directors of institutions also manipulated medical records, others placed disabled people in workshops to prove their 'usefulness' – activities that we can interpret as passive resistance, and which were partly effective. Lichtenberg and Braune show that it was possible to oppose the social racist measures of the National Socialists. It was possible, but dangerous. Lichtenberg paid for his commitment with his life; he died after mistreatment on the way to the concentration camp. Braune had already been interrogated by the Gestapo before, because of his commitment to 'non-Aryan' Christians. Two months after the memorandum he was taken into Gestapo custody. But he was released after three months because the 'Confessing Church' spoke up for him (see Strohm/Thierfelder, 1990; Jenner and Klieme, 1997). As a result of the protests, the official murder campaigns were stopped; however, a phase of 'wild' euthanasia followed, some of which used lethal injections. Many sick people also died of malnutrition during the Second World War.

Conclusion

There are differing opinions on whether and which actions can be described as 'resistance'.

In itself, the term resistance is controversial and is used and graded differently in research. Alternative terms range from 'political opposition' and 'ideological dissidence' to 'dissent'. Some distinguish the concept of resistance from political protest, selective dissatisfaction, nonconformity, flight into the public sphere or breach of loyalty. Others differentiate between active and passive resistance or self-preservation. Detlev Peukert is of the opinion that partial criticism does not yet constitute resistance. And according to Wolfgang Benz, resistance can only be understood as activity that led to persecution by the Nazi regime. Following this, in my opinion the reactions to euthanasia can be understood as only resistance in the case of individuals (Kuhlmann, 2018, p 91).

From the forced sterilisations, because they were largely accepted and carried out, a line can be drawn to the 'euthanasia' actions. On this 'slippery slope' there was no stopping. Resistance would have been necessary from the very beginning. Professional social workers did not offer any resistance to euthanasia. This touches on a systematic problem of research on resistance in social work. Welfare workers were mostly women. As a rule, they were not themselves heads of authorities and institutions, but in youth, health and economic welfare they were subordinate to theologians, lawyers or doctors. Structurally, they were therefore less able than other professional groups to refuse or resist measures, even if they would have wanted to. In addition to this structural situation of the professional group, at that time women in general often did not yet have equal rights and, above all, had been brought up 'apolitically'. Since politics was 'men's business', resistance also appeared to be 'men's business'. Against this background, it must be stated that resistance behaviour by women, especially in social work, looked and had to look fundamentally different than, for example, the resistance behaviour of officers or priests. We find here what historians call 'rescue resistance', that is, persons who offered individuals or groups of people protection from discrimination and persecution. Rescue resistance means organising help for refugees or the children of persecuted people. In recent research we found about 100 people who resisted in such a way (or even politically). Partly because they were affected themselves, they organised emigration for Jews or Socialists. Half of them were professional social workers; others were pastors, lawyers or Kindergarten teachers (Amthor, 2017). At the same time about 10,000 professional '*Volkspflegerinnen*' (people's welfare workers) were registered in the '*Deutsche Arbeitsfront*' (German Labour Front, Paulini, 2001, p 405).

It is quite possible that there was more of this 'rescue resistance' in the field of social work than we are able to discover. Rescue from forced sterilisation, incarceration, transfer and killing had to take place covertly and was not reflected in files. Even after 1945, possibly not everything was reported, out of shame for not having done more or because, in the post-war period, one still had to fear being considered a traitor.

Nevertheless, more than 70 years after the end of the Nazi dictatorship and after decades of research on resistance, no one would disagree with the statement that the Germans – according to Johannes Tuchel, the director of the German Resistance Memorial Center in Berlin – were a 'nation of perpetrators' with 'unfortunately very few resistance fighters'. There was – Tuchel continues – 'no large social group' that stood against the Nazis as a whole. This was always only an attitude of a small minority, of 'individual and often very lonely people' (Tuchel, 2005, p 15).

This also applies to social work. And it also applies to the social work of the churches, which, incidentally, in their self-image at that time still tended to pursue a mission motivated by Christian charity and seldom saw themselves as social work professionals of Social Work. Those who wanted to fight the inhuman measures of the Nazi government remained lone fighters in their institutions (Kuhlmann, 2018).

References

Althaus, H. (1937) *Nationalsozialistische Volkswohlfahrt. Wesen, Aufgaben und Aufbau*, Berlin: Junker & Dünnhaupt.

Aly, G. (2013) *Die Belasteten – Euthanasie 1939–1945. Eine Gesellschaftsgeschichte*, Hamburg: Fischer.

Amthor, R.C. (ed) (2017) *Soziale Arbeit im Widerstand! Fragen, Erkenntnisse und Reflexionen zum Nationalsozialismus*, Weinheim: Beltz Juventa.

Ayaß, W. (1995) *Asoziale im Nationalsozialismus*, Stuttgart: Klett-Cotta.

Biesold, H. (1988) *Klagende Hände. Betroffenheit und Spätfolgen in Bezug auf das Gesetz zur Verhütung erbkranken Nachwuchses, dargestellt am Beispiel der 'Taubstummen'*, Solms-Oberbiel: Jarick.

Dörner, K. (1988) *Tödliches Mitleid. Zur Frage der Unerträglichkeit des Lebens oder: Die Soziale Frage. Entstehung, Medizinisierung, NS-Endlösung, heute, morgen*, Gütersloh: Jakob van Hoddis.

Gruner, W. (2002) *Öffentliche Wohlfahrt und Judenverfolgung. Wechselwirkungen lokaler und zentraler Politik im NS-Staat (1933–1942)*, München: Oldenbourg.

Haarer, J. (1934) *Die deutsche Mutter und ihr erstes Kind*, München: Lehmanns.

Jenner, H. and Klieme, J. (eds) (1997) *Nationalsozialistische Euthanasieverbrechen in Einrichtungen der Inneren Mission. Eine Übersicht*, Reutlingen: Diakonie-Verl.

Kappeler, M. (2021) *Kontinuitäten der Fürsorge. Der 'Nachrichtendienst des Deutschen Vereins' 1932–1946*, Freiburg i. B.: Lambertus.

Klee, E. (2010) *'Euthanasie' im NS-Staat. Die Vernichtung 'lebensunwerten' Lebens* (vollst. überarbeitete Neuaufl.), Frankfurt: Fischer.

König, U. (1989) *Sinti und Roma unter dem Nationalsozialismus. Verfolgung und Widerstand*, Bochum: Brockmeyer.

Kuczynski, J. (1982) *Geschichte des Alltags des deutschen Volkes 1918–1945, Band 5*, Köln: Pahl-Rugenstein.

Kuhlmann, C. (1989) *Erbkrank oder erziehbar? Jugendhilfe zwischen Zuwendung und Vernichtung in der Fürsorgeerziehung in Westfalen 1933–1945*, Weinheim: Juventa.

Kuhlmann, C. (2000) *Alice Salomon. Ihr Lebenswerk als Beitrag zur Entwicklung der Theorie und Praxis Sozialer Arbeit*. Weinheim: Deutscher Studienverlag.

Kuhlmann, C. (2013) *Erziehung und Bildung. Einführung in die Geschichte und Aktualität pädagogischer Theorien*, Wiesbaden: SpringerVS.

Kuhlmann, C. (2018) Konfessionelle Wohlfahrtsorganisationen in der NS-Zeit zwischen konkurrierender Kooperation, christlicher Identitätswahrung und Verweigerung, in A. Lob-Hüdepohl and J. Eurich (eds) *Aufblitzen des Widerständigen. Soziale Arbeit der Kirchen und die Frage des Widerstands während der NS-Zeit* (pp 76–97), Stuttgart: Kohlhammer.

Lehnert, E. (2003) *Die Beteiligung von Fürsorgerinnen an der Bildung und Umsetzung der Kategorie 'minderwertig' im Nationalsozialismus. Öffentliche Fürsorgerinnen in Berlin und Hamburg im Spannungsfeld von Auslese und 'Ausmerze'*, Frankfurt: Mabuse-Verl.

Ley, A. and Hinz–Wessels, A. (eds) (2012) *Die Euthanasie-Anstalt Brandenburg an der Havel. Morde an Kranken und Behinderten im Nationalsozialismus, Schriftenreihe der Stiftung Brandenburgische Gedenkstätten, Band 34*, Berlin: Metropol.

Nowak, K. (ed) (1989) *Ich klage an. Tatsachen- und Erlebnisberichte der 'Euthanasie'-Geschädigten und Zwangssterilisierten*, Detmold: Bund der Euthanasie-Geschädigten und Zwangssterilisierten.

Paulini, C. (2001) *'Der Dienst am Volksganzen ist kein Klassenkampf'. Die Berufsverbände der Sozialarbeiterinnen im Wandel der Sozialen Arbeit*, Wiesbaden: SpringerVS.

Roth, M. (2015) *'Ihr wißt, wollt es aber nicht wissen': Verfolgung, Terror und Widerstand im Dritten Reich*, München: Beck.

Rudnik, M. (ed) (1990*) Aussondern – Sterilisieren – Liquidieren: Die Verfolgung Behinderter im Nationalsozialismus,* Berlin: Edition Marhold.

Sachße, C. and Tennstedt, F. (1988) *Geschichte der Armenfürsorge in Deutschland, Bd.2, Fürsorge und Wohlfahrtspflege 1871 bis 1929*, Stuttgart: Kohlhammer.

Strohm, T. and Thierfelder, J. (eds) (1990) *Diakonie im 'Dritten Reich': Neuere Ergebnisse zeitgeschichtlicher Forschung*, Heidelberg: Heidelberger Verl.-Anst.

Tuchel, J. (ed) (2005) *Der vergessene Widerstand. Zu Realgeschichte und Wahrnehmung des Kampfes gegen die NS-Diktatur*, Göttingen: Wallstein.

7

Social assistance in Franco's fascist Spain (1939–75): a history of social control, family segregation and stolen babies

María Inés Martínez Herrero

Introduction

The first Spanish school of social work was founded in 1932 in the city of Barcelona during the Spanish II Republic (1931–39), which historians consider the first attempt at democratic government in Spanish history. This school was financially supported by Raül Roviralta, who was a doctor and aristocrat, and was linked to a Belgian Catholic school of social work. According to the testimony of one of its students, the teachers at the school were prestigious and held varied ideologies (Estrada, cited in Barbero and Feu, 2016). The founding of this first school of social work in Spain is a well-known and celebrated milestone in the development of the profession in the country, and social work students in Spain are taught about it. It is also widely known that the activity of this first school of social work was short lived, as it came to a halt with the outbreak of the Spanish Civil War (1936–39), just four years after the school's foundation. However, very little is known or discussed about some rather dark ramifications, discussed later in this chapter, of the school's work and the pro-fascist political trajectory that its patron, Roviralta, followed during and after the war. This is just one small reflection of a significant political blindspot affecting most historical accounts of the evolution of social work in Spain: a lack of explicit acknowledgement of social work's history of complicity and collaboration with the social control, oppression and indoctrination methods of the far-right dictatorship which was established at the end of the civil war in 1939 and lasted until 1975. Extreme implications of this complicity include instances of involvement in human rights abuses such as the forced removal and stealing of babies from political prisoners and other families deemed unworthy or incapable to raise their children according to the Spanish religious and cultural values that the dictatorship vowed to protect and enforce. Little is known, either, about the histories of social workers' individual and collective resistance to such abuses.

Historical background: the Spanish Civil War and establishment of the francoist dictatorship

The Spanish Civil War started in 1936 as the result of a coup against the Republican government by a group of generals of the Spanish armed forces supported a number of nationalist conservative groups and political parties. After almost three years of conflict (1936–39) the war ended with the victory of the Nationalist front and the subsequent establishment of the francoist dictatorship (1939–75), ruled by the general and dictator Francisco Franco until his death in 1975. The Spanish Civil War and dictatorship became internationally notorious historical events on account of the political passion and civil division that they raised (both within and outside Spain), and for the many atrocities that were committed (on both sides during the war, and against 'the defeated' afterwards). Political repression aimed at consolidating the francoist political regime, especially in the post-war period, was ferocious and systematic. It involved not only violent crimes such as mass killings of opponents of the regime but also sophisticated family policies and strategies of social control and repression in order to preserve the 'national catholic' fascist ideology of the regime, eliminate the 'degeneration' caused by leftist ideas and educate (or re-educate) women and children to embrace francoist religious, moral and cultural norms and values. The repression was disguised by a powerful regime propaganda machinery which praised Franco's generosity toward 'the defeated' and excellent treatment of their children, as well as the regime's top priority to protect and educate all children because they represented 'the hope of the New Spain' (Armengou and Belis, 2002). Propaganda around the regime's investment in the well-being and education of children continued throughout the dictatorship.

Social assistance and social control in francoist Spain

It is in relation to the promotion of social work (*asistencia social*) as a mechanism for social control and indoctrination in service to the francoist dictatorship that Roviralta played a role. Soon after the closure of the Barcelona social work school during the civil war, Roviralta wrote the first Spanish book on 'Social Assistance', dedicating it to the nationalist leader and future dictator of the country, Francisco Franco. The dedication read: 'To his excellency Francisco Franco Bahamonde, Head of State, genuine representative of the new Spain' (Barbero and Feu, 2016, p 29). The book also extolled the Italian and Portuguese fascist dictators, Mussolini and Oliveira Salazar, and it outlined the curriculum of the Fascist School of Social Assistance founded in Rome in 1928, noting that this was 'a model institution' which the author [Roviralta] had 'had the pleasure' of seeing at work and studying its methods. In 1933, Roviralta explained in his book, 'facing the tone of disorder the republican regime had imposed in the social life of Spain and with the purpose of reducing … its harm, I had the satisfaction … of founding in Barcelona a school of this type, the first of its kind in Spain' (Roviralta, 1938, cited in Barbero and Feu, 2016, p 30).

The establishment of the francoist dictatorship in Spain was followed by a decade marked by the poverty and devastation caused by the war, political repression, political autarchy and ideological indoctrination. In this context, Spain's second school of social work was founded in Madrid, in 1939. If the feminine and confessional character of the studies at the Barcelona school was clear, this was further emphasised in the mission statement of the Madrid school. This established that social assistance was 'a feminine degree aimed at either preparing women for serving society, or extending their knowledge in order to become a good – and Christian – family mother' (Sanz Cintora, 2001, p 11). During this period, both the Catholic Church and the regime party were authorised to develop charitable organisations and initiatives aimed at meeting the basic needs of the poor. According to Pérez Rivero (2010), these developments were characterised by the lack of involvement of adequately trained professionals (and adequately trained volunteers) and the paramount influence of Catholic doctrine. A realisation of the need to involve professionals in the development and delivery of charitable initiatives emerged during the decade within the church and single-party organisation (Pérez Rivero, 2010), and a small number of new 'social assistance' schools were eventually established in the early/mid-1950s as a consequence (Molina Sánchez, 1994). However, from the 1940s until the mid-1950s there was widespread unawareness of the social work profession, and even within the social work schools it was unclear how the role of social workers differed from that of 'apostolic volunteers' (Pérez Rivero, 2010, p 91).

An analysis by Pérez Rivero (2010, pp 91–92) of the few dissertations written as part of the social assistance training programmes available at that time highlights that these:

> placed on the woman–mother the responsibility of the education of children and, therefore … the education of society; took for granted a gender division of labour that assigns women to the world of the home and the care of all those who live in it, and to men the world of work outside the home, as generators of material and economic goods, while women's competence was the diffusion of spiritual goods, love and [harmonious] coexistence.

The importance of women's role at home and their subjection to their husbands' authority was 'poetically praised', Pérez Rivero (2010, p 92) claims, to the extent that one dissertation focused on outlining 'the harmfulness of women's work outside the home, since this results in abortions, disease, loss of Christian morals and disorders of all kinds, leading to social disturbances in consequence of the loss of values by women, who are the guarantors of the spiritual values of society'. As solutions to these types of problems, the dissertations of the period argued for well-organised social assistance and social security, adequate pay and benefits and allowances for workers to be able to meet their obligation as breadwinners for the whole family.

Whereas the repressive ideological context remained unchanged until the latest stages of the dictatorship (late 1960s until the death of Franco in 1975), from the mid-1950s onwards Spain entered a political period of gradual international openness which paved the way for some social policy developments more aligned with the foreign welfare states, which would materialise during the 1960s.

Amid increased awareness and concern on the part of some influential religious institutions and political actors about social needs, the period comprised from the late 1950s to the early 1970s saw an enormous 'investment of effort, zeal, and resources' in the creation of social work schools (Méndez-Bonito, 2005, p 230). At the beginning of 1957 there were only five schools of social work in Spain; between 1957 and 1964, 27 new schools were created (Sanz Cintora, 2001); in 1970 there were 42 schools of social work in Spain, most of them belonging to the Catholic Church.

During this period of unprecedented growth of social work education, international openness allowed for two main critical influences to enter the profession, alongside more conservative/individualistic theoretical developments linked to the case-work tradition. Regarding the critical influences, Sanz Cintora (2001, p 15) refers firstly to the 'breezes' coming from Rome's Catholic Church and introducing social assistance modernising ideas, such as the value of planning and technification, alongside a moderated 'social critique'. Secondly, he points to 'the "winds" coming from Latin America' through the radical social work *Reconceptualization* movement, which understood social work as a science and radical social agent for the achievement of fairer and more inclusive societies (Sanz Cintora, 2001, p 16). This movement, which emerged in the 1960s in Latin America, was deeply intertwined with the movements of liberation theology and popular education (or critical pedagogy). It is claimed that the disciplines of theology, education and social work formed a 'radical triangle', leading to a radical shift in the way practitioners, religious organisations and educators worked and engaged with impoverished communities (Ferguson et al, 2018). These movements developed in an international context of broader social rebellion against Western (US in particular) influenced developmentalist policies.

Interestingly, in her analysis of historical social work dissertations in Spain focused on family, Pérez Rivero (2010) found that, from 1957 onwards, there were increased pushes to incorporate scientific approaches into the religious guiding frameworks for social assistance analysis, design and intervention. Such scientific foundations, Pérez Rivero (2010) states, became more predominant and structural as studies yielded evidence of the need to address the social and political environment in which individual social problems emerge, in order for individual and collective interventions to succeed in solving those social problems. Thus, there was a move away from most dissertations linking family problems 'to a lack of religious, moral and intellectual education of the mother' (Pérez Rivero, 2010, p 96) and towards an understanding of individuals as immersed in a conditioning, multilayered social environment. However, Pérez Rivero claims, such progression was notably non-linear, with dissertations showing enormous differences in their degree of alignment with the prevailing oppressive religious ideology of the regime at any given point in time. Moreover, there were back-and-forth movements in relation to these patterns, including among dissertations from the same school of social work (Pérez Rivero, 2010).

Arguably, these patterns reflect the complexity of the political history of the role that the Catholic Church played in the shaping of social work as a profession during the 20th century, which has been oversimplified. The Catholic Church, together with the military and the regime party, had a fundamental role in sustaining the ideology of the francoist dictatorship. Power was distributed among these three institutions, all of which played key roles in the terror, political repression and imposition of a rigid and authoritative morality that took place during the dictatorship, especially during the first two decades (Casanova and Gil, 2012). It is a main argument of this chapter that the 'dark histories' of the social work profession's complicity with these institutions' oppressive practices in Spain remain unknown and must be explored, owned and acted upon.

Nonetheless, it is also important to acknowledge that from the inception of the profession, and especially as time passed during the dictatorship, the relationship between the Catholic Church and the state became increasingly complex and often antagonistic, with critical sections and movements within the church leading or becoming fundamental parts of social justice and political resistance movements (Sanz Cintora, 2001; Casanova and Gil, 2012; Martinez-Roman, 2012). However, accounts of the history of social work in Spain tend to fail to pay attention to the influence of 'the other church' (Martinez-Roman, 2012, p 2), and the Catholic background of Spanish social work is often referred to as a monolithic obstacle that needed to be overcome for the establishment of the profession (Matos-Silveira, 2013). It is largely within this unexplored part of the history of social work in Spain (that is, the relationships with progressive movements born within the Catholic Church) that I believe many of the histories of individual and collective resistance to the oppression during and surrounding the dictatorship about which we need to learn will possibly be found.

Stolen babies: from Franco's eugenics to economically motivated baby trafficking

It has already been outlined how Roviralta, the founder of the first school of social work in Spain, sought to place his theories around social assistance and social control at the service of the francoist dictatorship. However, more sinister and profound was the influence on the regime of the work of another doctor: the psychiatrist Antonio Vallejo-Nágera, who in 1938 was authorised by Franco to establish a national cabinet of psychological research aimed at discovering 'the psychophysic roots of Marxism'. The Spanish Cabinet of Psychological Research mirrored a recently created research institute of the Nazi German secret services, and its work was underpinned by eugenic theories that Vallejo-Nágera had imported from his experience as an inspector of concentration camps in Germany during the First World War, where he had been in contact with notorious German pioneer eugenic psychiatrists (Gordillo, 2014). As is stated in the Cabinet's records:

> We have exposed before, in other pieces of work the profound relationship between Marxism and mental inferiority. ... The confirmation of our hypothesis has an enormous sociopolitical relevance. If Marxism is preferentially militated by antisocial psychopaths, as it is our belief, then the total segregation of these subjects from their infancy could free society of such terrible plague. (Cabinet of Psychological Research, nd, cited in Gordillo, 2014, p 49)

According to the Cabinet's work, children born in leftist or democratic families should be confined to institutions that would promote 'the exaltation of racial bio-psychical qualities and the elimination of environmental factors that through the generations lead to a degradation of the biotype' (Gordillo, 2014, p 49).

On this basis, the francoist legal system allowed children's segregation and removal from their leftist families (political prisoners and other opponents) (Amnistía Internacional, 2021). It is estimated that between 1940 and 1954 about 30,000 children were forcibly removed from their families (including Spanish refugee children abroad, who were systematically brought back to Spain with the help of fascist European regimes) to be raised in Catholic Church institutions on behalf of the state, or given for adoption by 'suitable' families linked to the regime (Gordillo, 2014).

Carme Figuerola, who was a political prisoner at the time, explains how her three-year-old son was taken from her: '[In this prison], when a child turned three years old, they came to pick him up and take him to an asylum Franco had built in Madrid. They told me ... I would not see him again.' Olivia Rapp speaks about losing her refugee brother during that period: 'My brother was repatriated from Russia without us knowing anything. When my mother tried to bring him home, the Child Protection Board told her there was an order not to let him come, without any explanation. Many years later we saw a report that says my family was not fit for my brother's education.'

Contrary to Franco's propaganda, life in the institutions that aimed to offer these children the 'proper' care and education they would not receive from their families was in fact marked by brainwashing and frequent abuse.

'The Auxilio Social ladies gathered us and told us that we were scum, we were daughters of horrible reds, murderers, atheists and criminals, we deserved nothing, and we were there for pure public charity.' (Francisca Aguirre, interview extract from Armengou and Belis, 2002)

'I was brainwashed to go against my father and the democratic and republican Spain. I had to be like them, like the victors. All my education has been "el Cara al Sol" [Fascist anthem] and "Our Father". They stole my childhood, they killed me in 1936. I am dead as to whom I was going to be.' (Uxenu Álvarez, interview extract from Armengou and Belis, 2002)

Whereas adoptions in application of francoist family law and policy did not, in theory, involve economic transactions, informal payment systems and influence networks developed both within the country and abroad. As business at the expense of the exploitation and plunder of 'the defeated' (including removing their children for adoption) ran out, the systems and networks that developed around 'legal' adoptions (on political grounds) began to reach out for new sources of children to keep up with the demand for adoptions and to feed the economic and influence networks which are being proven to have operated until the late 1980s (Vinyes et al, 2003; González de la Terna, 2014; Gordillo, 2014).

Most of the new victims were from among the poorest, most vulnerable and stigmatised Spanish women (such as single mothers, less educated or socially excluded women or young pregnant women in the care of the state). The maintenance of the trafficking networks required the continuing complicity of health professionals and institutions that assisted births (increasingly in hospitals); of those in charge of the civil registration of the newborns; and of institutions of social assistance that would identify and lure suitable vulnerable, pregnant women from whom to obtain babies either by means of coercive persuasion to give up their babies for adoption or by deceiving them into believing that their children had died (González de la Terna, 2014). However, the consolidated plot could affect any women who gave birth in the many health institutions involved.

An anonymous victim, A., related to the press (Esteso Poves, 2011) what happened when she gave birth in one of the main public hospitals in Madrid, in 1976. Hers is a typical story, rather similar to those reported by many other victims, especially in the later years that the plot operated.

> '[When the girl was born] two nurses came and took her away without showing her to me. I heard her cry in the corridor. Then they quickly came back. ... One told me "the girl is healthy" but the other one gave her a very serious look. ... Then the doctor came ... and told me the baby would stay sometime in the incubator as she had a minor respiratory insufficiency ... but later in the day they told my husband the girl had died. He asked to see the body and was told it had already been cremated.' (A.)

Years later, A. had two other children, and when she told the gynaecologist about the death of her first child he told her, "I see ... I know about those stories". This doctor then asked the hospital where she gave birth the first time for a report on the birth, but what was received back was a report stating that on the date of the birth she had had a miscarriage three months into her pregnancy. "I was in shock", A. explains. "I could not believe that. Back then a doctor was like God. Now I am certain they stole that girl from me."

The full history and extent of baby trafficking in Spain only started to be discovered from 2010 onwards, and the struggle for justice and to find the relatives of those affected has faced almost insurmountable legal challenges, shock and a degree of denial on the part of Spanish society and lack of cooperation from the Spanish authorities. Notably, the Spanish Amnesty Law 46/1977 of 15 October, which granted amnesty to 'all acts of political intent, whatever their result, classified as crimes and misdemeanors carried out prior to December 15, 1976' (Ley 46/1977, Art.1) poses a major obstacle to the prosecution of most of the crimes involved. But legal prescription time frames for those crimes that took place after this date have truncated legal action on these too. However, a recent report by Amnesty International has helped to strengthen the record of some of the facts about this chapter in Spanish history, framing the Spanish 'Stolen Babies'[1] phenomenon as involving crimes which breach numerous human rights, including children's rights (Amnistía Internacional, 2021). Very importantly, this report establishes these crimes as forced disappearances; as such, they are considered continuing crimes which the Spanish government has an international legal obligation to help resolve.

Nonetheless, the total number of 'stolen babies' who are living or have lived with a false identity (mostly in Spain, but some abroad) is unknown and estimates are highly contested (Amnistía Internacional, 2021). However, there have been complaints related to the stealing of babies in more than 175 institutions across Spain between 1950 and 1990, including in hospitals, health centres, institutions for expectant and new mothers and children´s homes (Gordillo, 2014).

Both the apparent great reach of the scandal and the nature of the institutions involved should pose questions for the social work profession, even at this early stage of ongoing discovery of the truth. In fact, fingers have already been pointed at individual social workers in the few court proceedings related to stolen babies that have taken place in recent years.

Sor María (María Gómez Valbuena), a nun and the social worker in a main maternity hospital in Madrid between the early 1970s and 1984, is the best-known character involved in the illegal adoptions scheme. She was taken to court in 2012 but died aged 87 before the end of her trial. During this trial, another social worker was requested to testify, due to her administrative involvement (her signature appearing in falsified documents) in one of the cases Sor Maria was accused of (ABC, 2012).

Another infamous name in the scandal is that of Eduardo Vela, the first doctor to appear in court in 2018 in relation to a stolen baby case (Vela was found guilty but acquitted, as the offence was considered prescribed; he died aged 86 in October 2019). He insisted during his trial that he dealt only with the 'medical' aspects of births, whereas it was the midwives and social workers who dealt with registers and administrative procedures (RTVE, 2018).

These might be seen as pointed accusations towards social workers. However, considering that from the early years of the Spanish dictatorship social workers were trained to fulfil a social assistance and control mission at the service of the regime, and that they received practical training and worked in institutions that played a role in baby-trafficking plots, such as hospitals and new mothers' homes, it can be concluded that some will have witnessed (through a more or less naive lens) and played a part in what was going on. Nevertheless, this is a chapter in the history of social work in Spain that the profession has not yet started to acknowledge or to own.

Conclusion

Accounts of the history of social work in Spain tend to present social work as a technical profession whose development was reversed and halted during the long period comprising the Spanish Civil War (1936–39) and most of the far-right francoist dictatorship (1939–75), when public social assistance and the training of social workers were delegated to the Catholic Church and to a feminine section of the regime's single party in order to fulfil paternalistic roles in relation to the relief of the poor. Accounts tend to report that the development of the profession was re-established and that it expanded rapidly during the last years of the dictatorship (when a decrease in political repression allowed foreign critical influences to enter the profession) and the first decades of Spanish democracy and the welfare state (late 1970s–90s).

As a general characteristic, these accounts, while acknowledging the political context that would either prevent or permit the development of social work as a technical profession, do not explore the role of the profession during the most repressive periods in any depth, nor do they acknowledge the histories of complicity with and resistance to political oppression throughout the history of social work in Spain. There is little recognition, either, that the ideology and practices of many services have remained largely untouched since the time of the dictatorship. And in the same way that the history of the darkest implications of the profession's complicity with the dictatorial regime has not been explored in depth, little is known about the profession's involvement in radical and democratic struggles (including from within critical sectors of the Catholic Church and its social action groups/organisations) during the period of the civil war, the dictatorship and the establishment of Spanish democracy. These are some areas of historical amnesia that require social workers' urgent attention.

Social work as a profession should understand, own and make amendments for its history, including the history of complicity with human rights abuses under repressive political regimes. This is a matter of justice and of the profession's commitments to human rights, democracy and (critical) peace. It is also necessary in order to overcome regressive practices and stigmas affecting the profession and its service users, and to avoid repeating mistakes and falling again into the traps of the past.

Spain has a recent sociopolitical history marked by fear, a pact of silence and repressed collective trauma (Ioakimidis and Trimikliniotis, 2020) that has naturally affected social work and shaped the context of training and practice encountered by the well-intentioned social workers who enrolled in the profession to help those in need during very complicated times. But the time is now ripe for new generations of social workers to engage with historical memory and search for the truth with fresh and willing eyes; the profession's commitment to human rights entails this mandate and offers a helpful lens to embark on it. More urgently, and importantly, this is also the right time for those social workers who were involved, who suffered, who witnessed or who resisted these systems of repression to speak out and contribute their insights and invaluable testimonies to help fill the gaps in the profession's historical memory, before their stories are lost.

Note
[1] Amnesty International includes under this term: 'those children, now adults, who could have been victims of appropriation, forced disappearance and/or replacement of their identity in Spain from the end of the civil war until the mid-1990s of the 20th century' (Amnistía Internacional, 2021, p 3).

References

ABC (2012) 'Una asistente social reconoce su firma en la adopción de una supuesta niña robada', *ABC* [online] 20 September, Available from: www.abc.es/sociedad/abci-bebes-robados-juzgado-201209200 000_noticia.html

Amnistía Internacional (2021) *Tiempo de verdad y de justicia: Vulneraciones de derechos humanos en los casos de 'Bebés Robados'*, Madrid: Amnistía Internacional, Available from: https://doc.es.amnesty.org/ms-opac/recordmedia/1@000032 903/object/44036/raw

Armengou, M. and Belis, R. (2002) Los niños perdidos del franquismo – Documentary. *TV3* [online], Available from: www.youtube.com/watch?v= 0WSM5Q9MezY

Barbero, J.M. and Feu, M. (2016) 'El origen del trabajo social en Cataluña: la escuela de asistencia social para la mujer (1932–1939)', *Pedagogia i Treball Social. Revista de Ciences Socials Aplicades*, 4 (2): 3–33.

Casanova, J. and Gil, C. (2012) *Breve historia de España en el siglo XX*, Barcelona: Ariel.

Esteso Poves, M.J. (2011) 'Entonces un médico era como Dios, no imaginaba que me robaran a mi niña', *Diagonal* [online] 4 Februrary, Available from: www.diagonalperiodico.net/saberes/entonces-medico-era-como-dios-no-imaginaba-robaron-nina.html

Ferguson I., Ioakimidis, V. and Lavalette M. (2018) *Global Social Work in a Political Context: Radical Perspectives*, Bristol: Policy Press.

González de la Terna, F. (2014) *Nos encargamos de todo*, Madrid: Clave Intelectual.

Gordillo, J.L. (2014) *Informe especial: ¿Por qué nadie busca a los bebés robados en España?* Available from: www.todoslosnombres.org/sites/default/files/ por-que-nadie-busca.pdf

Ioakimidis, V. and Trimikliniotis, N. (2020) 'Making sense of social work's troubled past: Professional identity, collective memory and the quest for historical justice', *The British Journal of Social Work*, 50 (6): 1890–1908. https://doi.org/10.1093/bjsw/bcaa040

Ley 46/1977, de 15 de octubre, de Amnistía. Boletín Oficial del Estado, 17 de octubre de 1977, núm. 248, Available from: www.boe.es/buscar/doc. php?id=BOE-A-1977-24937

Martinez-Roman, M.A. (2012) *The Social Work Profession and Its Education Structure*, Universidad de Alicante.

Matos-Silveira, R. (2013) 'Social work in Spain: Historic contexts, singularities and current challenges', *Revista Katálysis*, 16: 110–118.

Méndez-Bonito, P. (2005) 'The history of social work education in Spain: Does harmonisation make sense?', *Portularia*, 5: 205–222.

Molina Sánchez, M.V. (1994) *Las enseñanzas del trabajo social en España 1932–1983*, Madrid: UPCO.

Pérez Rivero, L. (2010) 'Familia: campo de intervención social – Origen y evolución', in C. Acero Sáez, A. Castillo Charfolet, T. García Giráldez, G. Hernández Martín, M. Martín Estalayo, C. Miguel Vicente et al (eds) *El imaginario del trabajo social en las tesinas de fin de estudios 1938–1983,* Departamento de Trabajo Social y Servicios Sociales Escuela Universitaria de Trabajo Social Universidad Complutense de Madrid, pp 84–97.

RTVE (2018) 'El doctor Vela en el primer juicio por bebés robados: "No le he dado una niña a nadie"', *RTVE news*, [online] 26 June, Available from: www.rtve.es/noticias/20180626/doctor-vela-no-reconoce-su-firma-parte-nacimiento-del-bebe-robado/1756321.shtml

Sanz Cintora, Á. (2001) 'Acción social y Trabajo Social en España: Una revisión histórica', *Acciones e Investigaciones Sociales*, 13: 5–42.

Vinyes, R., Armengou, M. and Belis, R. (2003) Los niños perdidos del franquismo, Barcelona: Debolsillo.

8

Social work in times of political violence: dictatorships and acts of resistance from the Southern Cone

Gianinna Muñoz-Arce and Melisa Campana-Alabarce

Introduction

The profession of social work developed in Latin America through crises and upheaval from the beginning of the 20th century. A wave of dictatorships affecting Latin American countries in the 1970s and 1980s severely impacted on social work education and practice, having consequences in professional and political terms that can still be observed (Sepúlveda, 2016). In this chapter we aim to contextualise and revisit the period of dictatorships in the Southern Cone, the geographic and cultural region composed of Chile, Argentina and Uruguay – the southernmost area of South America.[1] These three countries experienced dictatorships in overlapping years (Chile 1973–90, Uruguay 1973–85 and Argentina 1976–83), and their dictators had close reciprocal links, as Operation Condor and the exile of so many people have demonstrated over the decades. Despite the fact that these countries have diverse experiences regarding the politics of memory and reparation, a public agenda for recognition of the recent past and its atrocities has already been established. It is precisely that agenda which has also permitted the observation of practices of resistance, abandoning the idea of victims of dictatorship and recognising the capacity of many people, some of them social workers, to contest, subvert and resist the hegemonic order imposed under conditions of political violence. For our colleagues who were detained and disappeared while fighting for a free and equal society, remembrance it is an act of justice. In particular, it is crucial to remember what happened in the heart of social work during those dark years and ask ourselves why attempts were made to erase our history and our voices were silenced by the military forces.

The chapter is based on an extensive dialogue between the two authors and engagement with primary and secondary sources, as well as interviews with Uruguayan colleagues. The scarcity of written material about the impacts of the dictatorship on the development of social work in Uruguay caught our attention, so their testimonies were invaluable. We are confident that this chapter will contribute to a better understanding of the political and cultural effects of political violence on social work and the critical perspectives that some colleagues were able to uncover in the complex context of dictatorship in this region.

The context of dictatorships in Latin America and the neoliberal turn

According to Naomi Klein (2011), South America was the cradle of a particular form of capitalism, which she describes as 'disaster capitalism'. She argues that the civil–military dictatorships that were imposed on our countries during the 1970s played a central role in removing all obstacles – political, cultural and economic – to the imposition of the neoliberal order. Chile was the first country to experience the 'neoliberal experiment' in the region, combining the fierce military dictatorship led by Pinochet in 1973 with the orthodox recipes of the Chicago School led by Milton Friedman.

Dictatorships have a long history in Latin America. In 1971, in Bolivia, the government of Juan José Torres was overthrown by Banzer, resulting in the establishment of a military junta. Almost 20 years earlier, in Paraguay, Adolfo Stroessner had started a dictatorship that would leave the country in political and social isolation until the end of the 20th century. In Brazil, the government of João Goulart was overthrown in 1964, not only to revoke social programmes for the poor, but mainly to make Brazil completely open to foreign investment. Also in Argentina, the basis for the refoundation of the capitalist accumulation model was laid by a civic–military dictatorship between 1976 and 1983; the complexity of labour protection laws was dismantled, the trade union federations and strikes were banned, the drop in wages was brutal, to which must be added the systematic plan for the disappearance of people and appropriation of children. In Chile, during Pinochet's rule, the state's functions were reduced, social expenditure was considerably diminished, universal social programmes became targeted and education, housing, pensions and healthcare services were privatised. Through the decades, dictatorships in Latin America have caused the precarisation of labour, weakening of labour rights and prohibition and repression of collective action, which facilitated the process of the accumulation of capital and redistribution to the rich (Harvey, 2005).

In particular, the civil–military dictatorship led by Pinochet in Chile between 1973 and 1990 not only produced economic and political damage to vast sectors of the population by the violent imposition of the 'neoliberal experiment' but also provoked a significant fracture in collective trust and social bonds. The fragmentation of Chilean society into factions 'in favour of' and 'against' the dictatorship and neoliberal policies, along with fear, repression and censorship, created an extremely complex political environment.

In a similar vein, three years after the *coup d'état* and the establishment of the right-wing military dictatorship in Chile, Argentina and Uruguay were also impacted upon by the dictatorships of Jorge Rafael Videla and Juan María Bordaberry, respectively. In the case of Uruguay, the civil–military dictatorship lasted from 27 June 1973 to 1 March 1985, launching a period marked by the banning of political parties, trade unions and the press, as well as the persecution and imprisonment of opponents of the regime and intervention in the universities. In June 1973, the then President Juan María Bordaberry, with the support of the armed forces, dissolved the Senate and the House of Representatives and created a Council of State with legislative and administrative functions. Around 1977 the independence of the justice system was attacked, while more brutal repression developed. In 1978, according to Caetano and Rilla (1987), it was decided that the government's actions should be legitimised by calling elections, which culminated in the 1980 constitutional plebiscite. This plebiscite was crucial to the collapse of the dictatorship, as the dictatorial government was roundly rejected at the polls. This milestone started the democratic transition, which ended with the assumption of power by the legitimate authorities in 1985.

In the case of Argentina, on 24 March 1976, in the midst of an agitated social and political climate, the armed forces seized power, overthrowing the constitutional mandate of Estela Martínez de Perón, and imposed a de facto government led by a military junta. Commanded at first by Jorge Rafael Videla, they established as a main goal the reorganisation of the nation using the methodology known as state terrorism. In other words, they used the state's monopoly of violence to discipline and terrorise groups and social sectors considered subversive, that is to say, a threat to the social cohesion of the country. Censorship, violence and political persecution, along with kidnappings and forced disappearance of persons, were the main tools used by the military to install a terror regime.

These plans followed in the footsteps of the Chilean dictatorship of Pinochet, whose main objective, directly influenced by the shock doctrine promoted by the neoliberal think-tanks, was to create the social and political conditions for the application of neoliberal rule. To fulfil this purpose, the military junta needed to undermine the main social and political movements and actors that represented a potential danger. Consequently, they focused on the systematic repression of social organisations, factories, trade unions and the student movement.

When the region emerged 'free' from the dictatorial regimes in the 1980s, it still presented a highly problematic panorama of political, economic and social inclusion. The governments that emerged from the fall of the dictatorships faced serious economic crises that limited the effective scope of democratisation, and instruments of neoliberal economic policy that exacerbated the negative social effects of the crises themselves. This mixture of limited democracy and new-type social exclusion, conditioned by serious fiscal constraints and the explosion of social demands, was a painful beginning for the new democracies (Andrenacci, 2012).

Social workers at the crossroads: victims, collaborators ... survivors

Higher education was one of the most-impacted sectors, in the context of reactionary political reforms that were part of the neoliberal turn in Argentina, Uruguay and Chile. According to Florencia Bossié (2008), institutions linked to education suffered censorship and repression through multiple mechanisms. In the case of universities, military regimes aimed to dismantle the student movement and to reshape academic units that, in the state's view, did not fit the curricular or institutional agenda of the junta. In Argentina, the Ministry of Education and Culture created a plan called 'Operación Claridad' that coordinated the physical disappearance (arbitrary detentions and extra-judicial executions) of persons considered suspicious, as well as the systematic destruction of cultural assets and the attack on publishing houses, universities and libraries (Bossié, 2008). In Argentina, out of a total of 45 academic units, 14 were closed or suspended. One of the most paradoxical cases was that of the Rosario School of Social Work, which was closed in 1976 through a resolution of the provincial government of Santa Fe, which justified their action by 'means of public knowledge'. Also, as part of the attack, historical documents were illegally appropriated (files, books, papers produced by students) and were transferred to the Social Work School of Santa Fe city; these documents were partially recovered in 2004.

According to Claramunt and Acosta (2020), in Uruguay the years prior to the dictatorship were marked by the active political militancy of students in left-wing parties or organisations. The authors highlight the direct involvement of several social work educators and students in leadership roles in political and activist organisations. A characteristic event from the pre-dictatorship period is related to the Second International Seminar, the follow-up event of an initial meeting in Porto Alegre, a milestone in the Reconceptualisation Movement. This important and politically impactful event took place 1966 and was hosted at the university auditorium. The Social Service Union, particularly active in this period (and led by Herman Krusse, Raquel Cortinas and Renée Dupont), also participated in the National Workers' Central. Another milestone in this process was the round table on social work in the midst of the reconceptualisation period, the full text of which was published in the Communist Party newspaper, *El Popular*. Claramunt and Acosta (2020) also point out that from the Pacheco presidency onwards, that is, from 1968, the escalation of repression and authoritarianism increased and this factor also strengthened and motivated the commitment of the militants.

In Chile, in the context of the radical privatisation of higher education, social work was stripped of its university status in 1981; as a consequence, curricula were redesigned in order to remove the theoretical and political content of training courses. New laws were created in the 1980s aimed at restricting the 'manoeuvrability' of social work professional associations (for example establishing the voluntary nature of professional affiliation, limiting the legal authority of associations to establish rules of ethical conduct for their members, among others). Social workers were also stripped of their positions as directors of state social services, which, before the coup, were occupations exclusive to them (Sepúlveda, 2016). It is important to mention that all these restrictions are still in force and pose important obstacles for professional development, recognition and dignity of labour conditions.

This attack on social work education and training can only be explained by the political transformation that the profession had experienced in the years before the military coups: the Reconceptualisation Movement. According to Servio (2009), this process was influenced by radical international developments (the Cuban Revolution, the protests of May 1968 in France, the accession of Salvador Allende to the presidency of Chile), regional political events such as the so-called 'Cordobazo' and 'Rosariazo', as well as the publication of 'new readings' linked to the Marxist tradition. The influence of new Latin American thinkers like Enrique Pichón Riviere and Paulo Freire must also be mentioned.

All these factors contributed to a critical revision of the 'classic' view that had traditionally dominated the social work profession. Until the emergence of Reconceptualisation, social work had taken the shape of a traditional and conservative profession that worked towards preserving the status quo and reproducing the established social order. Although heterogeneous, the Reconceptualisation Movement suggested that social work should be part of the broader processes of social liberation contributing to the organisation, mobilisation and awareness of the Latin American people, who were oppressed by the imperialist countries and the capitalist system. In those years, a significant number of social work students began to take part in a sociopolitical project committed to social transformation and started to participate in student, political and social organisations in order to fight against inequality, injustice and oppression. Within this framework, the arrival of the wave of dictatorships in the Southern Cone led to an abrupt and brutal interruption of the Reconceptualisation Movement.

According to Siede (2015), the more conservative sections of the profession had been critical of the Reconceptualisation Movement, branding it as 'a communist movement', and therefore welcomed its repression. Such stigmatisation of the movement, even within social work, offered an unacceptable and grotesque justification for its violent oppression (Siede, 2015). Many social workers were intimidated, persecuted, arrested, imprisoned and tortured (López, 2012; Castañeda and Salamé, 2013; Aguayo et al, 2018). According to the registers of the Chilean Association of Social Workers, at least 19 colleagues were arrested and 'disappeared' during the dictatorship's first years, including at least four social workers who were pregnant at the time of detention (Vera, 2016). To this day, we do not know what happened to them.

When recounting the political history of the profession, it is important to remember that social workers were not only victims of institutional violence and repression during the dictatorships. As Ioakimidis and Trimikliniotis (2020) assert, there is a dark side of professional development that must also be recognised. The flip side of this history – often the one that is silenced – refers to those social workers who collaborated with the authoritarian rule in either passive or active ways, 'deciding to maintain or even upgrade their positions at the expense of declaring their adherence to the de facto regime or even justifying the repression of their colleagues' (Hernández and Ruz, 2005). In Chile, for example, some social work academics chose to remain in their positions at universities under the rule of chancellors and deans imposed by the military junta, while some of their colleagues were expelled from universities for ideological reasons. Likewise, many front-line social workers continued to work in municipalities under the direction of mayors illegally imposed by Pinochet. Even the actual Board of the National Association of Social Workers was appointed by the military junta, bypassing the democratic procedures of election. This board, formed by unelected social work practitioners who supported Pinochet's rule, led the professional association until 1985 (López, 2012). Some social workers have also been accused of participating in irregular adoptions that occurred during the dictatorship, most of which adoptions were politically motivated. Despite evidence gathered as part of a judicial inquiry which suggests that irregular adoptions continued beyond the period of dictatorship, it has been estimated that there were more than 20,000 victims between just 1981 and 1983 (Inquiry Commission's Report, 2018). In a similar vein, the historian Alfaro-Monsalve (2018) has suggested that 'data provided by international adoption centres indicate that between 1975 and 1982 the percentage of Chilean children who were subject to adoption increased considerably' (Inquiry Commission's Report, 2018, p 63). The judicial procedure, currently in development, indicates that at least nine social workers collaborated in these irregular adoptions, receiving considerable payments for their professional services. According to the Inquiry Commission's Report (2018), social workers would write legal reports indicating that children were neglected by their biological parents and proposing their transfer to families supposedly able to provide them with care and protection, demanding legal entitlement for adoption. Then, social workers would take the children out of Chile – mainly to the United States and European countries – to proceed with the shadowy international adoption process. In most of the cases reviewed, there was a financial contribution for mothers. According to many of the testimonies gathered in the Inquiry Commission's Report (2018, p 54), 'after giving birth, most of the time mothers were told by social workers that their children had died', and 'social workers wrote false reports' to support the cases for adoption. These testimonies claim that children were taken without their parents' consent and that most of these children were not registered in the National Civil Registry as required by Chilean regulations. The Inquiry Commission has not arrived at any conclusion regarding the motivations underlying these irregular adoption procedures, although a working hypothesis is that irregular adoptions were politically motivated and underpinned by an ideological approach inspired by the 'civilising project' and 'class hate' driven by Pinochet's dictatorship (Alfaro-Monsalve, 2018).

The question that arises here is why Chilean social work has been confident in recognising the legacy of heroes and martyrs within its ranks but has failed to explore the darkest side of its history: the stories of those social workers who acted against or declined to act in support of human rights during the dictatorship. Different from professional associations in Argentina and other countries that have experienced institutional violence, Chilean social workers' organisations have been unable to investigate or even speak about that darkest side of their professional history. We can look at structural conditions to find some clues that may help us to understand why we have negated or at least silenced this dimension of our professional inheritance. The Pact of Silence that has protected data related to the crimes committed during the dictatorship may have inhibited disclosure of the truth about those social workers who collaborated with the dictatorship. In addition, if we look at the trials for justice and reparation conducted since the return of the democratic regime, we can see that the results have been generally unsatisfactory for victims, with denial of political crimes and even their vindication as necessary actions for the good of the country (Lira, 2010). This creates an environment of defencelessness, desolation and isolation, which may have also affected social workers in terms of professional trauma. This evidence may contribute to understanding the context, but certainly we need more evidence to deepen this analysis from the voices of those social workers who experienced this brutal episode of social work history.

A window for hope: stories of resistance

Many social workers survived and resisted during a period of political repression, struggling for the recovery of democracy. As Aguayo et al (2018) have expressed, the history of social work is 'a history of lights and shadows', full of conservative, reactionary, colonial and oppressive practices coexisting with critical initiatives committed to the struggle for social justice. Latin American dictatorships not only represented violence and repression but also remind us of the courage of those social workers who followed the path of defending human rights and contributed to the recovery of democratic regimes, as several studies have illustrated (Morales, 2010; Castañeda y Salamé, 2013; Del Villar, 2018; Rubilar, 2018). These social workers worked under dangerous conditions, protecting those people persecuted by the regime, organising community food banks during the economic crisis, creating popular and feminist collectives, producing knowledge from participatory active research and popular education and forming alternative professional associations (López, 2012).

For example, resistance exerted by the social work student movement in Uruguay was significant in that context. As Acosta (2005) has claimed, the implementation of a new curriculum in Uruguay in 1977 meant a regression, as it implied a return to traditional methods and embracing the 'doctrine of national security' promoted by the dictatorship. The 1977 curriculum had a clear medicalised and legalistic orientation. In this sense, it represented a step backwards from the proposals that had influenced training during the Reconceptualisation Movement. Despite the climate of repression in which activities took place at the university and, in particular, at the University School of Social Work, the social work student movement in Uruguay began its rearticulation with the creation of the University Social Work Students Union in 1979. The movement's activities were developed under very special conditions, due to the repression that was exerted on student organisations. Many members of this 'first generation of students', once trained, took on the task of rebuilding the organisation of social workers – the National Association of Social Workers of Uruguay – which had been closed down by the dictatorship in 1973. This initiative was taken up by the first cohort of Uruguayan social workers trained under the dictatorship, starting in 1981. The association, which was officially recognised in 1982, played a key role in the restoration of the legitimate authorities of the University School of Social Work – a process that began in 1984. The association participated actively in the democratisation process, and in particular in the mobilisation of the amnesty of political prisoners, with an emphasis on social workers who were still imprisoned by the dictatorship. For example, when, in 1983, the trade union movement celebrated 1 May with a mass demonstration – thus defying the authorities – the recently founded Association of Social Workers participated formally, and was recognised for its commitment to the fight for freedom, democracy, social justice and human rights. According to Claramunt and Acosta (2020), the Social Work School suffered a major political attack in 1973 when it was suspended for two years by the authorities in order to be 'cleaned up' from communist influence. During this process the teaching staff were 'reselected' and the curriculum was censored. Many social work books from the library were literally burned in campus bonfires. Despite the political clean-up, when the government attempted to reopen the School, there were still considerable pockets of resistance within the teaching staff who demonstrated their commitment to the restoration of democracy, thus resulting in further suspension.

The Argentinian Esquema Conceptual Referencial Operativo (ECRO Group) is a characteristic example of the social work resistance that took place during the dictatorial period in the Southern Cone. The Institute of Social Service of Buenos Aires, and the ECRO Group that arose from it, were formed in the heat of the developmentalist/modernising ideas established from the 1950s under the influence of international organisations such as the Organisation of American States and the United Nations. The ECRO Group played a pivotal role and represents a milestone in the academic inflection experienced by social work, expressing 'the seed of what would become the Reconceptualisation Movement in Latin American Social Work' (Servio, 2014, p 196).

This was due, among other things, to the process of 'radicalisation of positions' (Moljo, 2005), a scholarly and activist wave informed by the theory of dependency and the Marxist tradition, as well as ideas that had emerged from Latin American scholars elsewhere, 'which made it possible to criticise technical intervention on populations [...] and was key to the questioning of "aseptic" methodology' (Alayón in Servio, 2014, p 197). In fact, the ECRO Group started its publication programme with positions that responded to developmental guidelines and the idea of making social work a technical profession involved in the process of development. It supported the opportunity to take part in the liberation of the oppressed populations and the Latin American revolution (Servio, 2014).

In Chile, despite the brutal repression of any act of community organising or political activism, the clandestine work of non-governmental organisations (NGOs) – funded at that time by international organisations related to the defence of human rights – played a crucial role in promoting community engagement and political action against the dictatorship. In such settings, many social workers clandestinely exerted resistance against Pinochet's rule and struggled for the return of democracy through the strengthening of community organisations and the promotion of popular education. Social workers, risking their lives, also played a key role in denouncing human rights violations during the military regime and worked with victims and their families (Del Villar, 2018). The action of the strong citizen movements, supported by NGOs, facilitated the end of the dictatorship through a plebiscite in 1988, which assisted the return of democratic regimes in 1990. The end of Pinochet's 17 years of dictatorship was also understood as the beginning of a promising future for social work and gave rise to great expectation and hope regarding the possibilities that democracy could offer in terms of reparation of the trauma experienced by many in the profession (López, 2012). In that context, the work of the Colectivo de Trabajo Social, a group created by female social workers from different NGOs, is particularly interesting. The so-called 'collective of social work' had the aim of building knowledge about their professional field at a time of fierce repression and intellectual censorship. Their work was based upon the knowledge of poor women, women's movements and community work from a feminist perspective. Drawing upon their work with women, the Colectivo de Trabajo Social created a journal, *Apuntes para el Trabajo Social*. Through this publication these female social workers contested and challenged political and cultural models imposed by the dictatorship, crafting a kind of popular praxis that also interpellated social work education and training underpinned by a technocratic and supposedly neutral political approach (Moyano and Pacheco, 2018).

Conclusion

More than 40 years have passed since the end of the dictatorships in the Southern Cone. However, the marks of this period are still present. In the case of Chile, the legacy of the oppressive and traumatic reforms that the profession experienced in that dark period is still felt. While we appreciate the differences that may exist between Argentina, Chile and Uruguay, this chapter has shown that the wounds of past political violence remain open: we are still searching for the grandchildren appropriated by the dictatorship, the bodies and the graves of the disappeared. We continue to prosecute the genocidal and fight in various ways against the onslaught of neoliberalism. The return of the political Right with Piñera in Chile, with Macri in Argentina and recently with Lacalle Pou in Uruguay places the Southern Cone region in a context of intensification of neoliberal precepts and re-emergence of xenophobia, homophobia and aporophobia. The fight against these new expressions of neoliberalism and the extreme Right – this time democratically elected and not under the cloak of the dictatorship – places us in a scenario of strong challenges in political terms. The defence of the historical memory of the profession of social work and the fight for the realisation of human rights are flags of the struggle that we need to make flesh – to incarnate – in the day-to-day of our professional life.

That's why the memory of struggle and resistance in the profession is so relevant. It seems important to cherish the stories of resistance – those that occurred in the past and those occurring today – because during all these years the profession of social work has made human rights a cornerstone of its identity. This is why 10 December was established as a new 'Social Work Day' in Argentina 'placing the issue of Human Rights as the central axis of our ethical-political project as a professional collective' and stating that 'the issue of Human Rights is, without doubt, the great horizon that gives meaning to our professional practices … many colleagues and Social Work students have lost their lives, who believed and fought for a more just and humane country' (Resolution JG 1/2012 of the Argentine Federation of Professional Associations of Social Service, Paraná, 14 April 2012). Something similar occurs every 11 November, when Chilean social workers commemorate another anniversary of the profession and honour social workers who disappeared and/or were assassinated during the dictatorship. In Uruguay, the Café de la Memoria has been held at the Faculty of Social Sciences of the University De La República since 2009, and is organised jointly by the Social Work School and the student organisations. It is an annual event that brings together prominent personalities, activists and human rights associations to discuss recent history, and particularly the events of the last dictatorship. Many of the classrooms in the faculty bear the names of disappeared teachers and students.

What can we do with our history? Reiterations of and regressions to its past show that social work is a politically unfinished project. The historical and political fractures that have shaped Latin American social work during the last four decades emerge today as a legacy that involves both neoliberal oppressions inherited from the dictatorship and resistance to them. Such a professional legacy places limits on social work but, at the same time, provokes the creation of emancipatory strategies to contest the hegemonic order. Our past is not a sentence. As Cortés (2018) has claimed, the recognition of complex professional legacies compels us to choose, prefer, exclude, let collapse the legacy in order to answer the call of the present. Despite the traumatic professional past and although the consequences of dictatorships are far from ending, social workers are called, from a critical perspective, to examine the 'lights and shadows' of our professional history so as to recompose memory and look forward.

Memoria, verdad, justicia. Nunca más.

Note
[1] Parts of this chapter were previously published in Campana-Alabarce et al (2020) The long night of the last dictatorship in Argentina and in Muñoz-Arce (2020) Chilean social work and the legacies of the dictatorship, both in Ioakimidis et al (eds) *Social Work: Key lessons from its troubled past. Social Dialogue,* Issue 22. https://socialdialogue.online/

References
Acosta, L.E. (2005) O processo de renovacao do Servico Social no Uruguai. Unpublished PhD thesis, Universidade Federal do Rio de Janeiro (Brazil).

Aguayo, C., López, T. and Cornejo, R. (2018) *Luces y sombras del trabajo social chileno: memoria desde finales de la década del 1950 al 2000: identidad, ética, políticas sociales, formación universitaria y derechos humanos.* Buenos Aires: Espacio.

Alfaro-Monsalve, K. (2018) Una aproximación a las apropiaciones de menores y adopciones irregulares bajo la dictadura militar en el sur de Chile (1978–2016). Memorias de Alejandro. *Revista Austral de Ciencias Sociales*, 34, 37–51.

Andrenacci, L. (2012) Del desarrollismo al inclusionismo. Avatares de los regímenes de bienestar en América Latina durante la primera década del siglo XXI. *Journal of Development Studies*, 28 (1), 221–234.

Bossié, F. (2008) Biblioclastía y bibliotecología: Recuerdos que resisten en la ciudad de La Plata. Congreso 'Textos, autores y bibliotecas', 24 al 26 de septiembre de 2008. www.memoria.fahce.unlp.edu.ar/trab_eventos/ev.703/ev.703.pdf

Caetano, G. and Rilla, J. (1987) Breve historia de la dictadura uruguaya (1973–1985). Montevideo: Ediciones de la Banda Oriental.

Campana-Alabarce, M., Muñoa, M. and Tiberi, R. (2020) The long night of the last dictatorship in Argentina. *Social work: Key lessons from its troubled past. Social Dialogue*, 22. https://socialdialogue.online/

Castañeda, P. and Salamé, A. (2013) Trabajo Social en Chile y gobierno militar. 40 años de memoria y olvido. *Revista Trabajo Social*, 84, 55–66.

Claramunt, A. and Acosta, L.E. (2020) Personal communication – interview conducted by Melisa Campana-Alabarce on 17 December.

Cortés, R. (2018) Herencia, acontecimiento y cuerpos políticos en la intervención social: Una deconstrucción desde el trabajo social. *Intervención*, 7, 17–26.

Del Villar, M. (2018) *Las Asistentes Sociales de la Vicaría de la Solidaridad: Una historia profesional (1973–1983)*. Santiago de Chile: Ediciones Universidad Alberto Hurtado.

Harvey, D. (2005) *Breve historia del neoliberalismo*. Madrid: Akal.

Hernández, J. and Ruz, O. (2005) La Reconceptualización en Chile. In N. Alayon (ed) *Trabajo Social Latinoamericano. A 40 años de la Reconceptualización*. Buenos Aires: Espacio.

Inquiry Commission's Report (2018) Informe de la Comisión especial investigadora de los actos de organismos del Estado, en relación con eventuales irregularidades en procesos de adopción e inscripción de menores, y control de su salida del país. www.camara.cl/trabajamos/comis ion_portada.aspx?prmID=2141

Ioakimidis, V., and Trimikliniotis, N. (2020) Making Sense of Social Work's Troubled Past: Professional Identity, Collective Memory and the Quest for Historical Justice. *The British Journal of Social Work*, bcaa040. https://doi.org/10.1093/bjsw/bcaa040

Klein, N. (2011) *La doctrina del shock: el auge del capitalismo del desastre*. Buenos Aires: Paidós.

Lira, E. (2010) Trauma, duelo, reparación y memoria. *Revista de Estudios Sociales*, 36, 14–28.

López, T. (2012) *El camino recorrido. Intervención comunitaria. Cómo es y cómo ha sido la experiencia de los trabajadores sociales chilenos.* Santiago de Chile: Libros de Mentira.

Moljo, C. (2005) *Trabajadores sociales en la historia: Una perspectiva transformadora.* Buenos Aires: Espacio Editorial.

Morales, P. (2010) 'Se hace camino al andar …' Trabajo Social y derechos humanos en Chile: de la atención de casos a la denuncia documentada. In M. González Moya (ed) *Historias del Trabajo Social en Chile 1925–2008: Contribución para nuevos relatos* (pp 179–193). Santiago de Chile: Ediciones Técnicas de Educación Superior – Universidad Santo Tomás.

Moyano, C. and Pacheco, V. (2018) Una mirada a las mujeres intelectuales de las ONG y la generación de conocimiento sobre lo femenino-popular en Chile, 1980–1989. *Revista Apuntes para el Trabajo Social*, 37, e2018007. Epub 25 June. https://doi.org/10.1590/1980-4369e2018007

Muñoz-Arce, G. (2020) Chilean social work and the legacies of the dictatorship. In V. Ioakimidis, M.I. Martínez and A. Wyllie (eds) *Social work: Key lessons from its troubled past. Social Dialogue*, 22. https://socialdialogue.online/

Rubilar, G. (2018) Trabajo Social y Derechos Humanos: Perspectivas, posibilidades y desafíos a partir de la experiencia chilena. *Trabajo Social Global – Global Social Work*, 8, 120–144.

Sepúlveda, L. (2016) Algunas reflexiones acerca del ejercicio profesional del trabajo social durante la dictadura militar. In P. Vidal (ed) Trabajo social en Chile: un siglo de trayectoria (pp 141–154). Santiago de Chile: RIL.

Servio, M. (2009) Trabajo Social y tradición marxista. Apuntes para recuperar la experiencia argentina en los años´60 y´70. En: Revista Cátedra Paralela, N° 6, Rosario, UNR Editora.

Servio, M. (2014) The Latin American reconceptualisation movement. *Critical and Radical Social Work: An International Journal*, 2(2), 193–201.

Siede, M. (2015) *Trabajo Social, marxismo, cristianismo y peronismo.* La Plata: Dynamis.

Vera, A. (2016) Reconstrucción de relatos de vida de asistentes sociales detenidos desaparecidos. Unpublished thesis. Universidad Academia Humanismo Cristiano.

9

Trade union mobilisation, resistance and political action of social workers in Portugal

Pedro Gabriel Silva and Alcina Martins

Introduction

In Portugal, the institutionalisation of social work took place in the 1930s under the veil of the Estado Novo (New State), a right-wing conservative dictatorship. In that context, social workers were expected to act within the ideological and political boundaries of the authoritarian regime. Portuguese social workers were, then, instrumental to the dictatorship's authority and, as such, served the regime's moral order while acting as agents of social conformity and control (Martins, 2010). However, from the 1960s onwards, signs of rupture began to be noticed, corresponding to an increasing involvement of social work professionals, students and educators in political movements, often engaging in oppositional, resistance and subversive activities against the regime (Martins, 2017).

The profession, framed in the context of a fascist-prone corporativist state, was deemed to serve its purposes and was collectively represented, from the 1950s, by a single professional trade union. The leadership of the union, as in many other corporativist organisations, was occupied by high-profile senior social workers trusted by the regime (Ferreira et al 1992; Pimentel, 2001). It remained like that until 1970, when younger social workers pulled the union away from the Estado Novo's political power (Martins, 2017; Silva, 2019b; Matos-Silveira et al, 2020).

This chapter revolves around this process of renovation, steered from the inside of the profession in direct connection with the social and political mobilisations against the dictatorship that were happening outside of the ranks of social work. The changes observed in the Portuguese social workers' trade union at this time show a process of renovation taking place within the profession at a time when collective action and civil liberties were severely limited and violently repressed.

In this chapter, the takeover of the social workers' union will be recalled and contextualised within the frame of the social, political and ideological transformations occurring in Portugal in the final years of the Estado Novo dictatorship. The processes that underpinned the union's new political engagement, both endogenous and exogenous to the profession, will be examined, focusing, especially, on how this movement of young progressive and politicised social workers turned the only organisation representative of the profession into an instrument of class political action.

To write this chapter, earlier research has been drawn upon, bringing together outputs that have been lying scattered. Empirical material collected by the authors in three research projects developed in the last two decades has also been used. It includes life stories and semi-structured interviews with former social work union board members and union activists, as well as documentary information from the social work trade union.

The dictatorship and the institutionalisation of social work in Portugal

The creation of the first social work schools and the legal recognition of the profession in Portugal happened in the 1930s as Oliveira Salazar's dictatorial project was putting down roots. Having been entrusted in 1928 with the Finance Ministry, Salazar's protectionism and austerity earned him the political recognition of the military, who, two years earlier, had brought the First Republic to an end. During that time Salazar continued to nurture a public image of a discreet, frugal, conservative, Catholic man, fully committed to the nation (Rosas, 1989, 1998).

In 1933, Salazar's leadership was strengthened when, as President of the Council of Ministers, he sought the approval of a new constitution, establishing what was to be known as the Estado Novo (Pinto, 1992). This new piece of legislation basically laid the constitutional ground for the regime to definitely reject democratic liberal government and multiparty parliamentarism, while establishing national corporativism, reinforcing colonialism and authoritarian rule and normalising state repression (Rosas, 1998).

To cement the moral conservativism of the dictatorship, the 1933 constitution sought to secure a series of privileges for the Catholic Church, an institution that ended up being a key ally of the regime (Pimentel, 2001). This social doctrine influenced the regime's concept of social work and welfare (Martins, 2010) and, under the new constitution, public welfare was not to be conceived as a right. Hence, the role of the state was merely supplementary to the private welfare organisations, particularly those dependent on the Catholic Church, private companies and corporativist structures.

The first social work school in Portugal was established in 1935, in Lisbon (Lisbon Institute of Social Service), and the second one in 1937, in Coimbra (Coimbra Social Normal School) (Martins, 2010). The Catholic Church was key in this process, particularly its laypersons' organisations, like the Portuguese

Catholic Action, the Noelist Movement and the OMEN (Organisation of the Mothers for the National Education) (Pimentel 2001). The education of social workers was set outside of university institutions[1] and its administration was entrusted to religious bodies – Mary's Franciscan Missionary Sisterhood oversaw Coimbra's school; Lisbon's bishopric administered the city's school (Martins, 2010). French and Belgian social work had a strong influence, shaping until the present-day the appellation of the profession and its professionals in Portugal: *social service*; *social assistants* (Branco, 2017).[2]

In 1939, a major step was taken towards the legal recognition of the profession when a government decree limited the use of the professional title of social worker (then verbalised as *assistant of social service*) to those who held diplomas in Social Service from those social work schools (Branco, 2015). That decree also set the doctrinal and ideological tone of the profession, addressing social workers as the 'labourers of social service' (Ministério da Educação Nacional, 1939), bestowed with a missionary commitment to assist the poor and guide them in the (regime's) *right* moral and ideological direction – something found frequently in contemporary European right-wing dictatorships, as Mabon-Fall (1995), Sunker and Otto (1997) and Lorenz (2014) have shown.

The Portuguese corporative state and the creation of the National Union of Social Workers (SNPSS)

The 1933 constitution legitimised what was to become the Portuguese Estado Novo corporativist system. The Estado Novo was, Garrido (2010) claims, an experience consistent with the European authoritarian corporativism of the earliest decades of the 20th century. Although without the backup of a large mass movement and purged of the voluntaristic and vanguardist imprint of fascism, the intent to build a corporativist system was one of the marks that took Salazar's rule closer to the dominant European fascist regimes of that time (Lucena, 1981; Pinto, 1990). Beyond its ideological breadth, Garrido (2010) argues, the Portuguese corporativist project tried to accommodate liberal economy under an authoritarian regime and to organise society in such a way that public order and social unrest could be disciplined and controlled. Domesticating capitalism and organising a collaboration between capital and work was what the Portuguese corporativist model sought (Garrido, 2010). In fact, Portuguese corporativism worked as a device meant to consolidate the regime, forming an instrument of social domination and mediation of socioeconomic interests (Rosas, 1998). In brief, the corporativist state was erected as part of a political strategy aimed to repress class–related social conflicts.

In order to absorb labour tensions and appease social conflicts, the Estado Novo strived to put in place a complex institutional structure (Freire and Ferreira, 2019) prioritising the mandatory organisation of economic activity while eradicating free labour unionism. To that purpose, a panoply of organisations was put together to prevent or replace collective action, civic and labour mobilisation suggestive of Marxism, anarcho–syndicalism and other forms of free unionism. This corporativist system relied on the compulsory integration of workers and employers of the industrial, fisheries, agricultural and commercial sectors, as well as corporative unions, into a horizontal scheme of representation, yet subjected to vertical political control (Freire and Ferreira, 2019). This pyramidal structure gathered in the base layer the sectoral organisations (guilds), the *Casas dos Pescadores* (Fishermen's Houses) and the *Casas do Povo* (Houses of the People, local structures meant to enforce basic welfare and healthcare services in rural areas to those who paid fees). A second tier was constituted, at the district territorial level, by guild federations, unions of Casas do Povo and labour union federations. At the top of the pyramid rested the corporations, constituted by regulation commissions, national boards and national institutes, all dependent on the political power (Freire and Ferreira, 2019).

In this corporativist system, although the national labour unions presented as the outcome of the free initiative of the workers, their existence relied forcefully on state consent and control (unlike before the dictatorship). A key mark of the corporativist project was the annihilation of free labour unionism and its replacement by an arrangement of over 420 unions politically endorsed and organised by the regime (Freire and Ferreira, 2019).

Although the first Portuguese national union of social workers was founded 15 years after the creation of the first school, and at a time when the corporativist system was already in place, it was nonetheless a product of that very same resolve to tame socio–professional representation, control the labour movements and prevent wider social mobilisation. In 1950, when there were about 150 social workers (Martins, 2017), the Social Assistants, Family Educators and Other Social Service Professions was brought into being as a corporative trade union under the tutelage of the Ministry of Corporations and Social Welfare (Martins, 2002). The first president of the union was Maria Luísa Ressano Garcia, a social worker from the OMEN and the *Mocidade Portuguesa* (Portuguese Youth) medical centre, procurator to the Corporative Chamber in the period 1957–61.[3] In 1959, Maria Helena Beltrão, a former director of the Portuguese Red Cross, was president of the social work union.[4]

In its earliest stage, the union was focused on organising professional improvement actions, and from 1956 to 1962 published the first Portuguese social work journal (*Cadernos de Serviço Social*). The union also arranged group spiritual retreats, reflecting the influence of the Catholic Church on the profession. A major sign of professional adherence to Catholicism was when the social work union became a member of the Catholic International Union for Social Service in 1951 (Martins, 2002, 2010).

During this phase, the national social work union conveyed a politically neutral image of professional practice, despite the obvious connivance with regime values. Such allegiance to the Estado Novo's authoritarian and conservative project was acknowledged in the union's statutes, a document that stated the rejection of 'any form of activity, internally or externally, contrary to the interest of the Portuguese Nation'.statutes also proclaimed that the union's interests were to be subordinated to the 'superior interest of national economy', therefore, class struggle as a means to attaining labour rights was disavowed (Martins, 2017, p 48).

At this stage, initiatives to improve the working conditions and salary of social work professionals can hardly be discerned (Martins, 2002). In 1968, the union name was changed to *Sindicato Nacional de Profissionais de Serviço Social* (SNPSS – National Syndicate of Social Service Professionals). This alteration reflected a series of changes that the profession had been facing in the 1960s, namely the admission of men, from 1964 onwards (Fernandes, 1985), and the rearrangement of social work-related professions (Branco, 2015). According to Rosa (1979), these changes represented a subtle turn in the involvement of the union, more concerned now with the protection of careers and the individual labour rights of social workers, yet far from a class-oriented movement.

In 1968, following a fall from a chair, Salazar was relieved of the office of president and replaced by his *dauphin*, Marcello Caetano, in what was seen by opposition sectors as an opportunity to reverse dictatorial measures (Rosas, 1998). Nonetheless, the authoritarian nature of the regime prevailed and its colonial policy was maintained at a time when Portugal was fighting wars on three fronts, in Angola, Mozambique and Guinea-Bissau. It was in this context that the legislation regulating the functioning of corporativist unions became the subject of changes (Barreto, 1990). Caetano's reforms allowed for freer union elections to take place and, through 1968–71, at least 30 union boards (one tenth of the national number of trade unions) were unfavourable to the regime (Barreto, 1999).

The changes in union legislation, coupled with other social and political facts, prepared the ground for the upcoming transformation of the Portuguese social work union, pushing it further away from the regime while promoting new claims and approaching other working-class and services union structures.

Renovation (with)in the National Union of Social Workers in the 1970s

The changes happening in the SNPSS after 1970 should be seen in the light of the larger sociopolitical transformations of the 1960s. In the second half of that decade opposition movements brewed and became radicalised. If, at the dawn of the 1960s, only a handful of social workers were active in political resistance to the regime (Martins, 2017), later on, a growing numbers of social workers were gradually mobilised as they joined progressive Catholic groups, anti-colonial movements, left-wing banned political organisations and the labour movement (Martins, 2021; Silva, 2021).

The politicisation of Portuguese social work resulted very much from the initial involvement of social workers and social work students in opposition movements that frequented the feminine unitary collectives (like the Democratic Women's Movement or the international women's movement GRAAL) and the progressive Catholic organisations (like *Pragma* or *Confronto*) (Santos and Martins, 2016b). Those organisations, mostly in the form of cultural cooperatives, were created in the mid-1960s by progressive Catholics with connections to the student and worker movements. Operating openly as well as clandestinely, they fostered critical reflection and political dialogue between a diverse set of social and professional groups and personalities discontented with the regime (Lopes, 2007). Progressive Catholic associations also contributed to the mobilisation of more radical resistance organisations, including those involved in armed actions, like the Revolutionary Brigades, where social workers ended up militating (Lindim, 2012; Silva, 2019a, 2021).

The involvement of a few social work professionals in the democratic opposition led to their participation in the elections of 1969 and 1973. This involvement was intrinsically connected to the subsequent political turn in the social work union. Following the political installation of Marcello Caetano, a national parliamentary election was scheduled to take place in 1969, allowing the presentation of alternatives to the regime's single-party list. Seizing the opportunity, the opposition gathered around a common list, the CDE (Democratic Electoral Commission), mobilising workers and trade union structures across Portugal (reflecting the impact of the new legislation that eased state control). As far as social work is concerned, some of its professionals were integrated in the CDE's political commission and, immediately after, a few ended up participating in the SNPSS's administrative structure (Martins, 2017). By gathering together several sectors of the democratic opposition and resistance to the dictatorship, the CDE brought progressive Catholics and communists closer together.

The change in the SNPSS started to gain momentum in 1970, when, following an internal election, some progressive and Left-leaning social workers joined the new board. By that time, the social work union membership had risen to a historic figure: 1,097 social workers had graduated by 1970 (Martins, 2021) and, in 1973, 827 professionals were unionised (Ferreira et al, 1992). This period saw a series of progressive SNPSS boards (Martins, 2017). Under progressive leadership, the social work union challenged the long-standing orientation established by the Estado Novo corporativist policy. Besides the political reorientation of the union, a new style of governance reliant on collegiality was adopted, seeking greater professional representation and participation. Union action was directed to meeting the salary demands and professional status of social workers (Rosa, 1979), and a network of delegations and sub-delegations representing a variety of services where social workers functioned was installed (Ferreira et al, 1992). This turn prompted a distancing from the legitimacy bestowed on the profession by the dictatorship. The union relinquished the idea that social workers should operate as conscious and active cooperants of the Estado Novo. Moreover, the union defied the notion of professional (political) neutrality that had permeated Portuguese social work from the late 1950s onwards, influenced by positivist and functionalist methods originating from the US. Instead, the SNPSS held that social work was to be seen as a profession and social workers were requested to recognise their condition as working class and were encouraged to join the struggle of other workers. These pronouncements should be understood in light of the gradual awareness of critical thinking currents, sparked by the dialogue between progressive Catholicism and Marxism and Paulo Freire's pedagogy (Santos and Martins, 2016a).[5]

The SNPSS's political turn became more pronounced in 1973 following another internal electoral dispute that brought forth two distinct professional projects: one based on progressive ideals fuelled by younger generations of social workers, and another, more conservative, backed by an older professional elite who contested trade union unicity and disavowed collaboration with other workers' unions.

The clash was won by the former, the young social work vanguard (Martins, 2017, p 53). Documentary and oral sources collected from some of the protagonists show what could be envisaged as a rank-and-file process (Reisch and Andrews, 2002) where, still under the grasp of an authoritarian repressive regime, a group of young social workers took control of the main professional collective organisation and, from within, led the effort to politically reorient the profession (Silva, 2019b; Matos-Silveira et al, 2020).[6] The moment was recalled by former board members in these terms:

> A list of old faces was running – all well known as *the great* social workers of the time – and there was this list of young, unfamiliar, yet loud, social workers. The election was highly disputed and we won it. ... It was absolutely amazing, because everybody was thinking the well-known social workers would win. (Board member, interviewed in 2016)

> We won the election ... against a conservative list. It was quite an achievement because we were younger, we were rookies. Most of us had graduated not a long time ago. ... The other list had people with status. ... It was a very important election ... in a moment when

people craved for change. … The professional body had accepted us, showing that in the core of the labour force, there was space to steer the change. (Board member, interviewed in 2016)

The change happening in the SNPSS took the union closer to the wider political struggles in Portuguese society. A major battle was taking place in the labour movement, where, infused by the legislative changes of the Caetano era, the now more autonomous but not yet free union structures strived to achieve full union freedom. After 1973, the SNPSS stepped up its participation in the clandestine unitary labour movement to the point of becoming a key partner of what was to become, after the fall of the Estado Novo, the Inter-Union General Confederation of Portuguese Workers – CGTP-IN.[7] Such proximity to the progressive clandestine union movement, per se a relevant challenger of the regime, pushed the SNPSS to develop alliances with the workers' struggles: "in a general assembly this question was asked and debated: 'do we want to be on the workers' side or on the bosses' and government side?'" (Board leader, interviewed in 2000).[8] Standing on the workers' side was the option taken, directing the union to negotiate collective labour contracts and rights in the private companies and public services where social workers were placed (Martins, 2017). In the words of another former board member, "we were converging with Portuguese society – although fragile and small, we had a political project that rejected the Estado Novo" (Board member, interviewed in 2016).

Besides aligning with the clandestine labour movement, the social work union reinforced its allegiance with the opposition movements and associations, particularly those circling around the progressive Catholic milieu. By turning into a politically engaged structure, the SNPSS also became an agent active in the politicisation of its constituents. A board member recalled her own experience as a representative of the union's role in raising social workers' political beliefs and ideological stands: 'participating in the clandestine inter-union movement made my political turn. That was where I connected the dots. … It was in those meetings that I heard from chemical and textile industrial workers stuff that I couldn't even dream of' (Board member, interviewed in 2016).

The SNPSS's political turn placed the union, its board members and closest collaborators under the radar of the political police, the DGS (*Direcção Geral de Segurança* – General Security Directorate). As a result, union activity was often marked by strategies to thwart police control, including holding meetings in secrecy and concealing the circulation of union information (Ferreira et al, 1992; Ferreira, 2004). Concerns over the safety of union members mounted as the SNPSS increased its participation in the inter-union movement, fuelled also by the arrests, in 1971, of labour union militants (Barreto, 1999; Martins, 2021).

Another key action was the involvement of the union in the Rato Chapel vigil, in Lisbon on the eve of 1 January 1973. This event showed the vitality of progressive Catholic opposition to the Estado Novo (Cardina, 2010), the adherence of some non-secular church figures and their willingness to openly confront the regime through public demonstrations of resistance and opposition (Azevedo, 2011). At the same time, the initiative showed the vigour of the regime's repression. The Rato Chapel vigil, intended as a peaceful gathering against the colonial war complemented by a 48-hour hunger strike (Lopes, 2007), ended up being violently repressed by the civil and political police. The rally, composed of people from different opposition backgrounds, was dispersed by a police charge, resulting in over 70 detentions (Pimentel, 2013). Students, clergymen, local parishioners, prominent intellectuals and academics participated in the vigil and among the detainees were some of the most important progressive Catholics, like Francisco Pereira de Moura, at that time a faculty member of the Lisbon School of Social Work (Almeida, 2008; Passarinho, 2012) and married to a social worker, Eugénia Pereira Moura, who had taken part in the 1969 elections backing up the CDE opposition list (Ferreira, 2004).[9] The repression that followed led to the detention, interrogation by the DGS and later sacking from the public services of two social workers and a social work auxiliary (Ferreira, 2004; Martins, 2002).

Aloof from the radical movements that were sweeping the profession in Western Europe (Steinacker and Sunker, 2009), the US (Reisch and Andrews, 2002) and, particularly, the UK (Bailey and Brake, 1975; Weinstein, 2011), Portuguese social work started gradually, often surreptitiously, to receive information about the critical movement that was looming in Latin America (Santos and Martins, 2016a; Eiras et al, 2017). Since the early 1970s the SNPSS had an important role in organising seminars and meetings to share the ideas coming from the Latin American Reconceptualisation Movement (LARM). The movement, notwithstanding its internal differences and reconfigurations (Netto, 1975), fought to change both the profession and society – a transformation rooted in progressive ideals and the refusal of traditional social work forms (Raichelis and Bravo, 2021). The proposals of the LARM fitted the transformative agenda of the SNPSS's leadership, especially after the 1973 union elections, and in March 1974 the union invited a prominent individual from the LARM, the Uruguayan Herman Kruse, to present a seminar on the fundamentals of the Latin American social work reconceptualisation project – an event that took place under the surveillance of the DGS (Martins, 2021).

Conclusion

As a consequence of the 25 April 1974 revolution, full union freedom was allowed. The generality of pre-revolutionary trade unions boards were confirmed in workers' assemblies, the SNPSS being no exception (Barreto, 1991). At the onset of the revolution, the previously clandestine coalition of progressive unions was legalised as the CGTP-IN, the SNPSS being among its affiliates. One of the flags held by the CGTP-IN was trade union solidarity, an option backed by the SNPSS board.

Diluted within the new common union structure, the SNPSS saw its role as a spearhead of the profession's political vanguard diminish. In the aftermath of the revolutionary events, disapproval of trade union solidarity grew within the SNPSS, especially among the critics of the revolutionary leftward drift, who questioned the radicalisation of union activity (Martins, 2021).

Fraught by the political conflicts of the post-revolutionary period, particularly the confrontation between different political projects and ideological views within the Left and centre-Left, internal fractures within the SNPSS mounted, pulling the social work union farther away from a unitarist syndicate project. In 1975 the SNPSS changed its name to Union of Social Service Technicians and, according to the newly revised statutes, a professional association was to be created. The Association of Social Work Professionals was formally established in 1978, assuming from that moment on a prominent role in the struggles for professional and academic recognition that marked part of the social work agenda in the late 1970s and 1980s (Negreiros, 1999; Martins, 2021).[10]

Although social work trade unionism did not cease to exist after the 1974 revolution, the union's political role and self-assumed stand as steerer of professional political militancy did not match that featured by the SNPSS in the 1970–74 period. Then, the social work union boards, composed of professionals who had no qualms about assuming an independent stand in regard to the authoritarian regime, when not of open confrontation with it, turned a means of corporativist labour and social control into an instrument of liberation, critical thinking and radical action.

Notes
[1]   In 1964 social work began to be taught at the public Higher Institute of Social Sciences and Overseas Policy, but was discontinued in 1969.
[2]   In the second half of the 1970s the terms social worker (*trabalhador/a social*), social work (*trabalho social*) and social intervenor (*interventor social*) were used by some professionals, students and educators (Matos-Silveira et al, 2020; Silva, 2019b, 2021).
[3]   Source: National Assembly, biographic records of procurators.
[4]   The Portuguese Red Cross and its Feminine Auxiliar Section (SAF), in 1947 run by the Maria Helena Teixeira Beltrão, were well aligned with the regime. The SAF's national council was composed of women of aristocratic extraction and the wives of high-profile Estado Novo politicians (Pimentel, 2001).
[5]   Readmitting professionals whose trajectories had put them at odds with the regime was another display of the SNPSS's intention of breaking with the status quo (Martins, 2017). Such was the case of Eugénia Varela Gomes, known for her involvement in a failed military attempt to overthrow the regime in December

1961 and for her activism in support of political detainees, being herself a former political prisoner (Cruzeiro, 2003).

[6] This union mobilisation bore similarities with rank-and-file movements in other international contexts, namely the case of the unionisation around socialist values seen in the 1930s in the US (Reisch and Andrews, 2002) and the convergence with working-class trade unionism found in the early 1970s in the UK (Joyce et al, 1988).

[7] The Inter-Union General Confederation of Portuguese Workers – CGTP-IN was created in 1974 as the result of the *intersindical* (inter-union) movement – a coalition of progressive labour union structures which began to take shape in 1970, following a series of clandestine meetings (Accornero, 2013), among which was the SNPSS (Ferreira, 2004).

[8] Similar stands could be found in other foreign social work unions of that time, like the UK's National and Local Government Officers' Association (NALGO), which tended to take social work's union action beyond strict professional claims, bringing them closer to the claims of other professional groups (Bogogno, 2021) and service users (Joyce et al, 1988).

[9] Eugénia Pereira de Moura presided over the social work union between 1963 and 1965 (SNPSS archives).

[10] The social work union was dissolved in 2010 and, in 2013, a new trade union was established, the Social Assistants' National Syndicate (Leite, 2013), soon after affiliating with the UGT (the Workers' General Union, a coalition of trade union organisations with connections to the social democratic and liberal political forces).

References

Accornero, G. (2013) 'Contentious politics and student dissent in the twilight of the Portuguese dictatorship: Analysis of a protest cycle', *Democratization*, 20(6), pp 1036–1055.

Almeida, J.M. (2008) *A Oposição Católica ao Estado Novo (1958–1974)*. Lisboa: Nelson Matos Edições.

Azevedo, A.C. (2011) 'Sob ventos de mudança: O impacto do Concílio Vaticano II na oposição dos católicos "progressistas" ao Estado Novo português (1965–1974)', *Horizonte*, 9(24), pp 1148–1168.

Bailey, R. and Brake, M. (eds) (1975) *Radical Social Work*. 1st edn. New York: Random House.

Barreto, J. (1990) 'Os primórdios da Intersindical sob Marcelo Caetano', *Análise Social*, XXV(105–106), pp 57–117.

Barreto, J. (1991) *Formação das Centrais Sindicais e do Sindicalismo Contemporâneo em Portugal (1968–1990) (dissertation for public trial for assistant researcher position)*. Lisboa: ICS.

Barreto, J. (1999) 'Intersindical', in Barreto, A. and Mónica, M.F. (eds) *Dicionário de História de Portugal*. Lisboa: Figueirinhas, p 290.

Bogogno, A.D.D. (2021) 'Serviço Social radical: a experiência do Reino Unido no transcurso dos anos 1970', in M.V. Iamamoto and C.M. dos Santos (eds) *A História pelo avesso: A Reconceituação do Serviço Social na América Latina e interlocuções internacionais*. São Paulo: Cortez, pp 45–67.

Branco, F. (2015) 'Itinerário das profissões sociais', *Análise Social*, 214, pp 44–72.

Branco, F. (2017) 'O Serviço Social como elemento substantivo de efectivação da Política Social', in M.C.P. Neves and A.B. Félix (eds) *Ética aplicada: Protecção social*. Lisboa: Edições 70, pp 49–72.

Cardina, M. (2010) Margem de Certa Maneira: O maoísmo em Portugal 1964–1974. PhD thesis. Universidade de Coimbra.

Cruzeiro, M.M. (2003) *Maria Eugénia Varela Gomes – Contra ventos e marés*. Porto: Campo das Letras.

Eiras, A., Yazbek, M.C. and Santos, C.M. dos (2017) 'Os movimentos contestatórios no Serviço Social iberoeuropeu e da América do Norte no período de 1960 a 1980', *Revista Em Pauta*, 15(40), pp 22–39.

Fernandes, E. (1985) 'Elementos para uma cronologia do Serviço Social em Portugal', *Intervenção Social*, 2–3, pp 143–148.

Ferreira, A. (2004) *O discurso da resistência ou a resistência do discurso – os assistentes sociais no movimento de oposição ao Estado Novo*. Available at: www.cpihts.com/Mulheres na resistencia.pdf

Ferreira, D., Couto, M. and Bizarro, M.M. (1992) *Estudos e Pesquisas – Estudo exploratório sobre a construção do conhecimento do Serviço Social em Portugal (1970–1974)*. Lisboa: ISSSL.

Freire, D. and Ferreira, N.E. (2019) 'Corporativismos: Experiências históricas e suas representações ao longo do século XX', *Tempo*, 25(1), pp 256–276.

Garrido, Á. (2010) 'Estado Novo e corporativismo', in M.M.T. Ribeiro (ed) *Outros combates pela História*. Coimbra: Universidade de Coimbra Press, pp 297–309.

Joyce, P., Corrigan, P. and Hayes, M. (1988) *Striking Out Trade Unionism in Social Work*. London: Macmillan.

Leite, M. (2013) O Estado e o associativismo profissional e sindical dos assistentes sociais em Portugal. MSW thesis. ISMT.

Lindim, I. (2012) *Mulheres de armas: Histórias das Brigadas Revolucionárias*. Carnaxide: Objectiva.

Lopes, J. (2007) *Entre as Brumas da Memória: Os Católicos Portugueses e a Ditadura*. Porto: Ambar.

Lorenz, W. (2014) 'Is history repeating itself? Reinventing social work's role in ensuring social solidarity under conditions of globalization', in T. Harrikari, P.-L. Rahuala and E. Virokannas (eds) *Social Change and Social Work*. Farnham: Ashgate, pp 15–29.

Lucena, M. (1981) 'Uma leitura americana do corporativismo português', *Análise Social*, 17(66), pp 415–434.

Mabon-Fall, A. (1995) *Les assistantes sociales au temps de Vichy*. Paris: Harmattan.

Martins, A. (2002) *Serviço Social Crítico Em Tempos De Ditadura*. Available at: www.cpihts.com/1o Congresso Nac. SS.pdf

Martins, A. (2010) *Génese, Emergência e Institucionalização do Serviço Social Português*. 2nd edn. Beja: Progresso.

Martins, A. (2017) 'Serviço Social em Portugal no fascismo: Oposição, resistência e ação sindical', *Revista Em Pauta*, 40(15), pp 40–56.

Martins, A. (2021) 'Processo de renovação do Serviço Social português nos anos 1970 na perspectiva histórico-crítica', in M.V. Iamamoto and C.M. Santos (eds) *A História pelo avesso. A Reconceituação do Serviço Social na América Latina e interlocuções internacionais*. São Paulo: Cortez, pp 345–366.

Matos-Silveira, R. et al (2020) 'Social work, contestatory movements and socio-professional struggles in the Iberian Peninsula in the 1970s', *Critical and Radical Social Work*, 9(1), pp 113–128.

Ministério da Educação Nacional (1939) *Decreto-lei nº 30:135*.

Negreiros, M.A. (1999) Serviço Social Uma Profissão em Movimento: A Dinâmica Académico-Profissional no Portugal pós-74. PhD thesis. PUC São Paulo.

Netto, J.P. (1975) 'La crisis del proceso de reconceptualizacion del servicio social', in Alayon, N. (eds) *Deafio al Servicio Social*. Buenos Aires: Humanitas, pp 85–105.

Passarinho, I. (2012) As formigas e os carreiros: Uma abordagem de inspiração biográfica aos percursos de aprendizagem e à construção identitária de Assistentes Sociais. PhD thesis. Universidade de Lisboa.

Pimentel, I.F. (2001) *História das Organizações Femininas no Estado Novo*. Lisboa: Círculo de Leitores.

Pimentel, I.F. (2013) *História da oposição à ditadura 1926–2974*. Porto: Figueirinhas.

Pinto, A.C. (1990) 'O salazarismo na recente investigação sobre o fascismo europeu: Velhos problemas, velhas respostas?', *Análise Social*, 108–109(4–5), pp 695–713.

Pinto, A.C. (1992) 'The new state of Salazar: An overview', in R. Herr (ed) *The New Portugal: Democracy and Europe*. Berkeley: University of California Press, pp 73–106.

Raichelis, R. and Bravo, M.I. (2021) 'The social work reconceptualisation movement in Latin America and the renewal in Brazil: The protagonist role of the Latin American Social Work Centre', *Critical and Radical Social Work*, 9(1), pp 31–45.

Reisch, M. and Andrews, J. (2002) *The Road not Taken – A History of Radical Social Work in the United States*. New York: Routledge.

Rosa, M.T.S. (1979) 'O S.S. e o 25 de Abril', *Pró-Intervenção Social*, pp 4–6.

Rosas, F. (1989) 'A crise do Liberalismo e as origens do autoritarismo moderno e do Estado Novo em Portugal', *Penélope*, 2, pp 98–114.

Rosas, F. (1998) *História de Portugal*. Lisbon: Estampa.

Santos, C.M. dos and Martins, A. (2016a) 'Tendências Críticas na formação do Assistente Social', in A. Martins et al (eds) *Serviço Social Portugal-Brasil: Formação e exercício em tempos de crise*. Campinas: Papel Social, pp 109–128.

Santos, C.M. dos and Martins, A. (2016b) 'The education of social assistants in Portugal: Trends in critical thinking', *Katálysis*, 19(3), pp 333–341.

Silva, P.G. (2019a) 'Radical experiences of Portuguese social workers in the vanguard of the 1974 revolution', *Journal of Progressive Human Services*, 30(3), pp 1–21.

Silva, P.G. (2019b) 'The radical turn of Portuguese social work during the democratic transition (1974–76)', *Critical and Radical Social Work*, 7(1), pp 7–23.

Silva, P.G. (2021) 'The relevance of biographic narratives for social workers' professional memory, reflexivity and identity', *Qualitative Social Work*, 20(5), pp 1374–1392.

Steinacker, S. and Sunker, H. (2009) '68 in der Sozialen Arbeit', in H.U. Krause and R. Ratz-Heinisch (eds) *Soziale Arbeit im Dialog gestalten*. Opladen: Verlag Barbara Budrich, pp 273–289.

Sunker, H. and Otto, H.U. (1997) *Education and fascism: Political identity and social education in Nazi Germany*. London: Falmer.

Weinstein, J. (2011) 'Case con and radical social work in the 1970s', in M. Lavalette (ed) *Radical Social Work Today*. Bristol: Policy Press, pp 11–25.

10

The radical roots of popular social work in Palestine

Michael Lavalette

Introduction

In this chapter I want to look at the roots of what we might term an 'organic' Palestinian popular social work. There is a growing interest in social work within the Palestinian Authority, but too often, I would suggest, this focuses on the introduction and implementation of formal international standards of social work practice, at the expense of a focus on specifically Palestinian traditions of collective, community welfare provision (see Lindsay et al, 2007; Faraj, 2019).

To put this in context, professional interpretations (and many academic histories) of social work often ignore the contested nature of the social work project (Payne, 2005). They suggest a unified profession which has developed and grown over time, reflecting a common origin, set of practices and methods and a shared value base. The chapters brought together in this collection immediately throw this conceptualisation into question. As Midgley (2001) points out, social work is divided by competing interpretations and traditions of what it can and should be (for him there is the *remedial* or *case-work* tradition, the *developmental* tradition and the *activist* or *radical* tradition). These are important, and different, perspectives within professional social work and speak to different values and political standpoints on the social work project. But they remain different approaches within the *institutions of the profession*, a social work primarily organised 'from above' to meet the demands of service providers, institutions and states.

Writing in an earlier article with Chris Jones, we drew on a concept developed by the American theorist and activist, Hal Draper (1966), to suggest that we could usefully consider social work as having 'two souls': one the official 'soul' of professional social work (divided as Midgley, 2001 notes) and another developing out of the alternative cultures, practices and struggles of oppressed, marginalised and class-based networks within capitalist society (Jones and Lavalette, 2013). Our suggestion was that there is, in addition to 'professional' social work, a different form of social work, one that I have termed elsewhere 'popular social work' (Lavalette, 2011). Popular social work has grown up to meet the needs and demands of people within the confines, restrictions and limits of class-divided society. Popular social work 'from below' emerges out of social movements or class-based networks in two types of situation: first, where states fail to provide services, or withdraw services, or the services provided by states are too demeaning, stigmatising or controlling; and second, during significant protest waves that set out to challenge the world as it is presently constructed.

This attempt to look for a popular social work 'from the bottom up' is heavily influenced by the work of a group of writers who collectively have become known as the 'British Marxist historians'.

From 1946 to 1956 the Communist Party of Great Britain brought a remarkable group of scholars together to study aspects of British development from a Marxist perspective. The group included such luminaries as Maurice Dobb (writing about the transition from feudalism to capitalism [Dobb, 1963]), Eric Hobsbawm (writing on the Industrial Revolution and beyond [Hobsbawm, 1962, 1975]), Rodney Hilton (studying feudalism [Hilton, 1973]), Christopher Hill (the English Revolution [Hill, 1975, 1980]), Dorothy Thompson (the Chartists, and especially the role of women in the Chartist movement [Thompson, 1986]), John Saville (the formation of the modern state [Saville, 1987]) and E.P. Thompson (on the early working-class movement and working-class cultures [Thompson, 1968, 1991]). Together this group pioneered an approach to history called 'history from below', whose influence would impact upon sociologists and historians across much of the 20th century. In his review and analysis of this group, Kaye (1984) suggests that, collectively:

> [they] stress the importance to historical studies of studying the experience of the lower classes, they also insist that the lower classes themselves have been active participants in the making of history, rather than merely its passive victims ... [they have a] decided emphasis on resistance and rebellion ... [but] although they emphasise lower-class struggles in their writings, they are not oblivious to, or unrealistic about, the (often inherent) limitations of lower-class modes of accommodation and incorporation. (Kaye, 1984, pp 229–230)

In the oft-quoted preface to *The Making of the English Working-Class* Thompson writes that part of his mission was to: 'Rescue the poor stockinger, the Luddite cropper, the "obsolete" hand-loom weaver, the "utopian" artisan, and even the deluded follower of Joanna Southcott, from the enormous condescension of posterity' (Thompson, 1968, p 12). One of the tasks Thompson set himself, therefore, was to rescue those who have been, to use the term popularised by socialist-feminist historian Sheila Rowbotham (1977), 'hidden from history'. For Thompson, Rowbotham and others, part of their mission was to rescue the voices of those who had been written out of history and, in the process, start to reassert the agency and resistance of the oppressed as they 'make history' in the circumstances they find themselves in. In part this meant rediscovering the struggles and rebellions of the poor and dispossessed – whether that was the 'social banditry' of pirates, brigands and primitive rebels written about by Hobsbawm (1971) or the more direct political assaults on the powerful encapsulated in the works of, for example, Hill (1975), Saville (1987) and Dorothy Thompson (1986).

But for E.P. Thompson part of the process of rescuing people from the 'condescension of posterity' was to develop an understanding of the alternative cultures, customs, rights and practices of dispossessed communities, and their ways of understanding, engaging in and shaping their world. In the collection of essays brought together as *Customs in Common* (Thompson, 1991), he looks at what he terms the 'moral economy' of the crowd during food riots, the opposition to moves to regulate life and work by the demands of 'regulated time', the struggle to defend holidays and leisure time from encroachment by a system based on commodified labour and the historic, often unwritten and unregulated, rights claimed by the poor and dispossessed.

Thompson's work was suggestive of the fact that working-class communities are not simply passive victims of an ever-encroaching state and commodified public sphere. Rather, they are constantly involved in a struggle to understand and interpret their world; to create alternative networks and institutions that reflect and protect their interests and try to meet their essential needs collectively; to establish physical and cultural spaces where alternative futures, of some kind, can be imagined.

I suggest that such an approach and orientation can help us to recover a rich history of 'popular social work', a history of communities and networks coming together to address, and to attempt to solve, the problems confronting marginalised and oppressed groups in society.

Let me give some examples. First, from 19th-century Britain, bodies like friendly societies, burial clubs, and self-funded schools developed when state provision was almost non-existent or highly punitive in form. These, of course, were contradictory and confused providers of services we should not idealise, but they were forged out of necessity to try to meet, in however limited a way, community needs. In working-class communities with a strong collective class identity (like many mining communities, for example) libraries and reading rooms, basic health provision, and social centres were forged to provide collective access to (albeit limited) services for all. These 'popular services' developed where the state had failed to provide, or where those services on offer were too stigmatising or demeaning. In practice, these provisions often excluded less well-organised and less skilled workers and their families. They commonly failed to survive sudden runs on their funds occasioned by widespread unemployment, or major strikes. But they were, nevertheless, attempts to meet basic needs, within the restrictions of class society.

A second set of examples can be drawn from the practical experiments in collective self-help developed in the midst of significant protest waves. For example, as part of the great protest wave of the late 1960s Ginsborg points to Italy where: '[I]t was in civil society ... that radical alternatives spread most rapidly: "red" markets, kindergartens, restaurants, surgeries, social clubs, etc. opened (and often shut) one after another. Their aim was to organise social life along quite different lines' (Ginsborg, 1990, p 323). In the same period in the US the Black Panther Party set out to provide programmes of 'survival pending revolution' in the urban ghettoes. These included: 'free breakfast programs for school children and food aid for families; schools, adult education, and childcare; medical care, medical research, and clothing; free plumbing, home maintenance, and pest control; and protective escort for the elderly and ambulance services; cooperative housing; employment assistance; free shoes' (Pope and Flanigan, 2013). More recently, in 2012, former 'Occupy' activists in New York provided relief to neighbourhoods smashed by Hurricane Sandy, when state responses proved inadequate. And, over the last few years, during the COVID-19 pandemic, there have been many examples of radical mutual aid projects established to meet community needs (see Lavalette et al, 2021).

It is this orientation, then, on popular social work, on welfare from below, that I want to look at in this chapter. It is, I would suggest, in the popular responses to community needs in the context of imperialist occupation and the creation of an aggressive settler-colonial state that we can start to identify a rich tradition of organic Palestinian social work.

Setting the context: Palestine, 'Nahad' and the establishment of a settler-colonial state

Any attempt to look at forms of popular social work in Palestine needs to locate that activity in its specific, historical context. Although Palestine has a long and tumultuous history, its present situation arose out of the end of the Ottoman Empire and the intervention of the British in the region after the First World War (Hourani, 1991; Rogan, 2017; Masalha, 2018).

At the turn of the 20th century the Ottoman (Turkish) Empire was under significant external and internal threat (McMeekin, 2015). The 'Young Turk' revolt of 1908 against the sultan brought the promise of greater autonomy for the Arab provinces and greater acceptance of Turkish–Arab equality (Sorby, 2005). This led to a process of 'Nahad', that is, an awakening of national consciousness in the Arab world. There was considerable agitation for greater Arab autonomy within the Ottoman Empire, especially in what was known as the 'fertile crescent' (broadly the Eastern Mediterranean coast and the rivers and valleys of the Nile, Jordan, Euphrates and Tigris – present-day Northern Egypt, Palestine, Lebanon, Jordan, Syria and Iraq). But dreams of greater autonomy were soon squashed. A demand for Syrian self-government was rejected in early 1909 and the Young Turks turned towards a process of 'Turkification' across the old Ottoman Empire. The repressive actions of the Young Turks fuelled Arab nationalism and laid the basis for the Arab Revolt of 1915–18.

When the Turks entered the First World War on the side of Germany, the British saw an opportunity to extend and deepen their Empire across what was then called the 'Near East'. For the British there were two main drivers. First, the region had a plentiful supply of the increasingly important commodity, oil. The importance of oil is evident when considering that British imports of oil products increased eleven-fold between 1900 and 1920 (Regan, 2017, p 4). The first oil field in the region was discovered in 1908 in present-day Iran.

Second, the area was strategically important. It linked Britain (and other European powers, especially France) to India and China. The opening of the Suez Canal in 1869 cut sailing times from Britain to India and from France to what was then called Indo-China dramatically. It also encouraged imperial intervention into East Africa and the Arabian Peninsula. As a result, the ports of Beirut, Haifa and Port Said grew in economic and strategic importance.

During the First World War the British worked with a number of Arab nationalist groups to foment rebellion in the region and undermine the Turkish war effort. The nationalist groups formulated a set of conditions under which they agreed to cooperate with the British. 'The Damascus Protocols, as these conditions were known, became the basis of the Husayn–McMahon Correspondence … winning [British] support for nothing less than an Arab state in the Mashriq [that is, present-day Palestine, Egypt, Syria, Israel, Lebanon, Jordan, Saudi Arabia, United Arab Emirates, Yemen and Iraq] after the war' (Chacraft, 2016, p 201). Thus, in the McMahon–Husayn Correspondence of 1915/16, the British actively encouraged Arab hopes for independence (Hourani, 1991). The Correspondence was an encouragement for Arab forces to rebel against their Turkish masters and join the British 'to liberate' their lands.

Yet these demands for independence came up against the second British policy perspective, encapsulated in the Sykes–Picot Agreement of 1916 (Barr, 2011). Signed by the French and the British, and with the support of the Russians, it detailed how they would divide the Middle East in the event of an Allied victory. The Agreement identified zones of permanent influence, with the French and British taking control of Arab resources, including oil. Palestine, under the plan, would fall under British control (Barr, 2011; Reagan, 2017).

At the same time the British signed a third agreement that would have significant ramifications on the country up to the present day. In 1917 the

British Government signed the 'Balfour Declaration'. The Declaration is short, but makes its position clear: 'His Majesty's Government views with favour the establishment in Palestine of a national home for the Jewish people, and will use their best endeavours to facilitate the achievement of this object.' The Declaration was 'motivated by [British] ... self-interest that coalesced with the ambitions of the Zionist movement'. For the British, the aim was to

> Integrate this project [of establishing a Jewish Homeland in Palestine] into the goal of sustaining empire without appearing to replicate imperialist expansionism and colonisation. They hoped that Zionist settlement would provide a convenient surrogate, effectively implementing colonisation under the guise of national reconstruction. Zionism ... became an important adjunct of British imperial strategy in the Near East. (Regan, 2017, p 9)

Zionism and Judaism are not the same thing. Zionism is a political philosophy of Jewish nationalism that developed in Europe in the late 19th century against a background of growing anti-Semitism. Central to Zionist thought was the belief that anti-Semitism was inevitable in Europe and so Jews and Gentiles should segregate. The best means for this to happen was to establish a distinct 'Jewish Homeland' (Weinstock, 1979; Rose, 1986). To create such a homeland meant courting the European powers to gain their backing. Zionist leaders offered themselves to German, French, Russian and Ottoman leaders, but it was the British who supported the plan most vociferously.

As the First World War drew to a close the Sykes–Picot Agreement and the Balfour Declaration were central to establishing British imperial support for a 'Jewish Homeland' in Palestine.

The Paris Peace Conference of 1919 began a process of dividing the post-war world, and by June that year a mandate system was put in place by a Covenant of the League of Nations. Article 22 of the Covenant stated that mandates would be held by 'advanced nations' to govern over peoples not yet ready to 'stand by themselves [in] ... the modern world' (Regan, 2017, p 73). The mandate system allowed the division of the Middle East in terms that broadly followed the Sykes–Picot Agreement. As a result, Palestine came under British Mandate.

In the inter-war years, with British support, there was a steady flow of European Jewish settlers who migrated to Palestine to fulfil their national aspirations. In the process, of course, they came into conflict with the national aspirations of the people whose land they were trying to take and claim as their own.

As Palestinians fought for their national independence from British imperial rule, Zionist organisations worked side by side with the British to suppress Arab political aspirations (Marshall, 1989). During the great Palestinian Revolt of April 1936 to May 1939 the British deployed 25,000 troops and squadrons of aircraft to crush the rebellion (Hughes, 2019). This was the largest anti-colonial war within the British Empire in the inter-war period. In Britain's counter-insurgency campaign they recruited various groups of European Jewish settlers to police, harass, arrest and intimidate Palestinian communities. Many of the regulations and draconian legal measures imposed by the British (such as detention without trial, the use of collective punishment, destruction of homes and villages, extensive use of checkpoints to monitor movement) continue to be used by the State of Israel against Palestinians today (Kelly, 2017; Hughes, 2019). What Hughes (2019) calls the 'pacification of Palestine' meant that by the outbreak of the Second World War, the British had 'broken the back' of Palestinian political and civil society, and this, in turn, cleared the way for the post-war triumph of Zionism. As Perry Anderson notes, Zionism was:

> A movement of European ethnic nationalism [which] became, inseparably, a form of European overseas colonialism. … The Jewish enclave in Palestine was distinctive in another respect too. From the start it was a settler society without a home country – a colony that never issued from a metropolis. Rather, it had a proxy imperialism behind it. British colonial power was the absolute condition of Jewish colonization. … Zionism depended completely on the violence of the British imperial state for its growth. (Anderson, 2001)

At the end of the Second World War Britain retained its mandate over Palestine. The end of the war also saw increasing numbers of Jewish survivors of the Holocaust arriving in the country. From 1944, in their pursuit of an independent Jewish state, several groups engaged in a series of attacks on British sites and military personnel. Faced with the growing rebellion, the British announced that they would end the mandate no later than August 1948.

As British rule ended, the United Nations (UN) proposed the partition of Palestine. The partition plan was opposed by all the Arab states as it gave 55 per cent of Palestine to the creation of a Jewish state and only 45 per cent of the land to the majority Palestinian population.

By 1948 the Zionists within Palestine had already created, under the British Mandate, the key agencies of the state, whose fighting forces, from the start, were far superior in quality, training and equipment when compared to the combined forces of the Arab armies who were opposed to the proposed partition of Palestine.

On 14 May 1948, Israel declared its independence and on 15 May the combined armies of Egypt, Syria, the Arab League, Transjordan, Iraq and

Lebanon entered the UN-designated 'Palestinian' sector. In response, the newly formed Israeli state pushed their forces deep into the Palestinian sector, embarking on what Israeli historian Illan Pappe (2006) calls the 'ethnic cleansing of Palestine'.

The outcome of the war was never in serious doubt. For Israel it was both a war for survival and a means for territorial enlargement beyond the proposed UN borders of 1947. It was successful in achieving both aims and, at the conclusion of the final armistice with Syria, in July 1949, Israel had expanded its territory from 55 per cent to 79 per cent of mandated Palestine (Morris, 2008).

The consequences of both the war and Israel's territorial expansion was devastating for the Palestinian Arabs, who not only had to endure invasion and occupation but were faced with victors who wanted them off 'their' land. It was, as Pappe (2006) has shown, a direct Israeli war aim to permanently remove the indigenous Arab population from the new Israeli state. Throughout 1947 and 1948 Israeli forces forcibly expelled Palestinians from their land in events known as the *Nakba* (the Catastrophe). An estimated 750,000 Palestinians were forced into permanent exile. The consequences of the murder, maiming and displacement of Palestinian communities in 1947/48 continue to reverberate across the Middle East today.

Resistance, welfare and popular social work

For over 100 years Palestine has been subjected to European colonisation and settlement. Throughout that time Palestinians have resisted and have adopted a range of strategies to fight for their freedom. From the earliest phase of British colonisation Palestinians opposed both the British presence and the British facilitation of Zionist settlement. Between 1919 and 1923, for example, there were six Palestinian congresses convened in opposition to the Balfour Declaration and regular demonstrations against Britain and European Jewish migration and settlement of Palestine (King, 2007). From this period, up until the present, Palestinians have engaged in all manner of resistance activities. The national liberation struggle has gone through different phases, with different dominant strategies and approaches, but resistance has been a constant (Lavalette, 2021).

Historically, as part of the resistance movement, a vast range of grassroots organisations (which today might be termed 'civil society organisations') emerged to meet people's social, cultural and welfare needs. Within many of these networks, women played a central role. In 1929 the Palestinian Women's Union (PWU) was set up (after nine women had been killed while protesting against the mandate in Jerusalem). The PWU was involved in a range of social, economic and political campaigns – including organising protests and demonstrations – but it also saw itself as a welfare organisation, providing support for the families, and especially the children, of those who had been killed, injured or imprisoned as part of the liberation struggle. Protesting the British presence and increased Zionist settlement also had a radicalising impact upon the activists of the PWU, leading them to challenge some older, restrictive cultural practices. There were networks of the PWU in Jerusalem, Haifa, Nablus, Tulkarem, Jenin, Acre, Ramallah and Bethlehem and they started to challenge: 'Forced marriage, virginity and honour codes, cloistering, polygamy and summary divorce' alongside issues of national liberation (King, 2007, p 87). During the First Arab Women's Congress of Palestine (1929), which met to protest farm evictions and Zionist settlement and demand an end to the British Mandate, a delegation was sent to meet the British High Commissioner (to protest, on behalf of the Congress, against collective punishment and the mistreatment of Palestinian prisoners). The women entered his office, sat down and 'simultaneously threw back their veils', which the British High Commissioner interpreted as a 'breach of Arab courtesies' (King, 2007, p 89)!

In 1933 two sisters in Yafa, Moheeba and Arabiya Khursheed, set up an organisation called *Zahrat al-Uqhawan* (the Chrysanthemum Flowers) (Alsaafin, 2014). This group originally started as a campaigning welfare network but, after Moheeda witnessed a young Palestinian boy being shot by British forces, the lines between welfare campaigning and liberation struggles merged. During the Nakba Zahrat al-Uqhawan 'provided invaluable medical services [for refugees and displaced communities], carried food, water and ammunition to the rebels [defending their land from Israeli armed forces], dug trenches and erected barricades ... [and] performed heroically in battle' (PLO, 1975, p 7).

After 1948, women played a central role in creating and establishing a range of popular social work organisations to support refugees. According to Palestine Liberation Organization (PLO) records, these included, among others, the Arab Child Welfare House, the Arab Women's Society, the Young Arab Women's Club and the Association for the Support of Wounded Militants. Such organisations provided immediate support to meet people's needs (medical support, addressing food and housing issues and providing support to orphans, for example). But these organisations also had a self-conscious educative and campaigning role within the refugee diaspora. Each has played an important role in helping Palestinian communities to understand their plight and their contemporary conditions, as well as acting as a key source of historical collective memory.

The General Union of Palestinian Women (GUPW) was formed in 1965 as an affiliate of the PLO. It organised political campaigns, lectures, seminars and cultural events and offered a range of support activities to families of prisoners and the martyrs. The GUPW was also involved in training women militarily. The growing involvement of women in these activities also, by necessity, led to GUPW networks establishing crèches and kindergartens to provide collective childcare for activists and their families.

In the period between 1968 (the Battle of Karamah) and 1982 (the defeat of the PLO in Beirut) the dominant strategy of the PLO was to support the armed national liberation struggle (Lavalette 2021). But, as part of this general 'revolutionary war' (as the PLO described it), there was significant civilian mobilisation of the Palestinian communities in the Occupied Territories and among the diaspora. Three networks are worth considering.

First, a number of Voluntary Work Committees (VWCs) were set up. Originating in Bir Zeit University (just outside Ramallah) but soon spreading across the West Bank, VWCs were set up by students to encourage academics and students to undertake voluntary work projects during their holidays and at weekends. The groups undertook manual labour such as road building or infrastructural works in the refugee camps or helped with olive harvesting, for example. But the groups also took over local libraries and held public meetings and events where they would discuss politics, or the work of important Arabic writers. The VWCs undertook a range of community and economic development projects and consciously worked to break down barriers between town and country, between intellectuals and workers and between men and women. As a result, they established connections that would play an important role in future resistance activities.

Second, Youth Committees (*al-Shabiba*) originated in Anabta refugee camp in early 1980. Al-Shabiba was set up by Adnan Milhem, who was a former student leader from An-Najah University in Nablus and who had spent a number of years in Israeli prison. According to Jamal (1980), these were set up as 'youth committees for social work'. Writing about their formation, Milhem (1983) argues: 'These committees ... are ... a realisation of a phenomenon that was always very well-known in our villages and towns, namely mutual aid. On this foundation, the youth committees have built ... a new meaning for social work.'

The Al-Shabiba movement quickly spread to other refugee camps. It trained young people in community organising with a focus on radical mutual aid and turned to address a number of issues confronting the refugee communities. Through their work they gained respect and political legitimacy. The group members were all from the camps, knew the issues facing the refugees (as they were their issues as well), were non-hierarchical and non-sectarian in operation and combined activism with politics and cultural and historical awareness.

Third, the Prisoners' Movement is worthy of consideration. Palestinians are one of the most imprisoned populations in the world. Inside the Israeli prison complex, they are very well organised through 'prisoners clubs'. The Clubs exist in each prison and are run by the Palestinian political organisations. They negotiate and make demands on the Israeli authorities and engage in a range of protests, including collective hunger strikes. The Clubs also work to support prisoners' families, to aid and support family visits and to support released prisoners back into their communities and into employment. One of the more moving events one can witness in a refugee camp is the whole community turning out to celebrate and welcome back 'one of their own': a party for a released prisoner returning after years inside Israeli prison.

The high point of radical welfare intervention undoubtedly came during the First Intifada (1987–93). On 8 December 1987 a new phase of rebellion was unleashed by ordinary Palestinians in Gaza, the West Bank and across Palestine. As King notes: 'The deaths of four Palestinians at an Israeli checkpoint ... in Gaza touched off a landslide of primarily nonviolent Palestinian resistance that had been in the making for generations' (King, 2007, p 1).

The First Intifada initiated a period of mass rebellion against Israeli rule. It involved demonstrations, strikes, protests, stone-throwing, withholding taxes, confrontation with Israeli troops and defiance of Israeli authority. Palestinians at all levels engaged in civil disobedience and 'non-cooperation' with any Israeli authorities and institutions. Years of pent-up frustration and bitterness at unemployment, poor housing, overcrowding, poverty, repression and abuse burst out across Palestine48 as Palestinians demanded their rights and their national independence. The Intifada involved old and young, men and women. It was organised and coordinated through locally based, elected 'popular committees', who would distribute papers and leaflets and appeals (*bayanat*) outlining protest events and actions. The popular committees saw themselves as the basic building blocks of an alternative state, the 'apparatus of the people's self-government', as Leaflet No 18 from May 1988 put it (King, 2007, p 229). As such, they started to organise all aspects of social life.

The involvement of women in the struggle was significant. Particularly important were the Women's Action Committees, a decentralised network operating across Palestine48 that encouraged local leadership and local initiatives as part of the movement. This allowed women in Gaza, or in the north of the West Bank in Nablus, Jenin and Tulkarem, or in remote villages, to play a part in the movement. The women: 'Participated in civil disobedience ... sheltered youth and defied soldiers ... participated in distributing secret communiques, delivered ... funds for social relief, visited prisoners and their families' (James, 2013, p 19).

The Intifada saw the creation alternative education and cultural centres, libraries and health and welfare networks. The very nature of the mass movement challenged 'old' or conservative ideas. For example, women played a significant role in public life in the towns and villages, confronting traditional cultural expectations. In Jenin, for example, a disability project was set up which directly challenged stigmatising concepts of disability as a curse. Instead, concepts of disability were reconstructed as consequences of oppression and colonialism, allowing 'social models of disability' to take hold (Jones and Lavalette, 2011). Schools closed, but classes took place in the streets, and the curriculum started to change – even subjects like geography and history began to be taught to reflect Palestinian realities.

In all the activities and networks discussed in this section we can see radical welfare developments and popular social work activities emerge out of Palestinian realities. These forms of practice have developed out of, and are enmeshed in, the popular struggles of the Palestinian national liberation movement. In each of the radical welfare projects and organisations there are young men and women, rooted in their neighbourhoods, thinking creatively about the needs of individuals, families and communities in the context of oppression and colonial settlement. It is in these networks and activities that we can witness a truly organic Palestinian social work.

Conclusion

Across the Palestinian West Bank and in the Gaza Strip the legacy of radical welfare networks, formed out of the national liberation struggle, continues to shape popular social work activities.

In the refugee camps, youth centres draw on the heritage on the Al-Shabiba movement to engage with the community and with young people in particular. They engage by using a variety of methods – often dependent on the availability of resources provided by volunteers or sympathetic sponsors. In Balata camp, near Nablus, the Yaffa Centre uses music, drama and community organising to engage young people and let them reflect on their plight and consider alternatives. In Jenin camp the Freedom Theatre group (set up during the First Intifada) puts on plays and dramas to promote cultural resistance to the occupation. In the Amari camp, near Ramallah, the youth centre uses sport as the means to engage young people and explore their history and culture. In the youth centre in the Tulkarem camp music, art and craft works are employed to engage and work with people.

Networks of prisoner organisations continue to monitor the arrest, harassment and oppression of Palestinian prisoners and their families. Prisoners' families are supported by the community, because prisoners are viewed as heroes and martyrs of the liberation struggle. Families are supported on visits, with material needs, with campaigns for prisoners and with release and post-release reintegration into the community.

Women's centres exist in most camps. They provide a space for women to meet, take part in classes and events, raise issues and problems and address political concerns (both about life in the camps and about the national struggle).

Support for those with a range of disabilities and traumas has increasingly been 'socialised', identified as the result of the occupation and, in this sense, a 'social problem', not a marker of individual failing or stigma. Recently the

Palestinian Social Work Union has been mobilising to support traumatised young people in Gaza, whose lives are affected by the regular bombings undertaken by Israeli forces. The Union has moved resources and people into Gaza to work with those deeply affected by the military strikes.

In most of these projects the 'leaders' or facilitators will be from the camps and will be undertaking good-quality work with individuals and groups. Yet few, if any, will have a formal social work qualification. Rather, they will be the inheritors and the contemporary practitioners of a popular social work that has emerged out of the long struggle for Palestinian liberation. We should celebrate them and their work and seek out what we, as social workers, can learn from them.

References

Alsaafin, L. (2014) 'The role of Palestinian women in resistance', Open Democracy. www.opendemocracy.net/en/north-africa-west-asia/role-of-palestinian-women-in-resistance/

Anderson, P. (2001) 'Scurrying towards Bethlehem', *New Left Review* 10, July/August. http://newleftreview.org/A2330

Barr, J. (2011) *A Line in the Sand: Britain, France and the struggle that shaped the Middle East* (London, Simon and Schuster).

Chalcraft, J. (2016) *Popular Politics in the Making of the Modern Middle East* (Cambridge, Cambridge University Press).

Dobb, M. (1963) *Studies in the Development of Capitalism (2nd edn)* (London, Routledge).

Draper, H. (1966) *The Two Souls of Socialism*. www.marxists.org/archive/draper/1966/twosouls/index.htm

Faraj, M.Y.M. (2019) The Social Work Profession in Palestine: Challenges and strategies for future development (University of Birmingham, Unpublished PhD thesis).

Ginsborg, P. (1990) *A History of Contemporary Italy: Society and politics: 1943–1980* (Harmondsworth, Penguin).

Hill, C. (1975) *The World Turned Upside Down* (Harmondsworth, Penguin).

Hill, C. (1980) *The Century of Revolution 1603–1714* (2nd edn) (London, Reinhold International).

Hilton, R. (1973) *Bond Men Made Free* (Bristol, Arrowsmith Publishers).

Hobsbawm, E. (1962) *The Age of Revolution 1789–1848* (London, Abacus).

Hobsbawm, E. (1971) *Bandits* (London, Abacus).

Hobsbawm, E. (1975) *The Age of Capital 1848–1875* (London, Abacus).

Hourani, A. (1991) *A History of the Arab Peoples* (London, Faber and Faber).

Hughes, M. (2019) *Britain's Pacification of Palestine* (Cambridge, Cambridge University Press).

Jamal, A. (1980) *The Palestinian National Movement: Politics of Contention 1967–2005* (Bloomington, Indiana University Press).

James, M.K. (2013) 'Women and the Intifadas: the evolution of Palestinian women's organisations', *Strife Journal*, Issue 1 (March). www.strifejournal. org/wp-content/uploads/2020/05/STRIFE_1_3_JAMES_M_18_22.pdf

Jones, C. and Lavalette, M. (2011) *Voices from the West Bank* (London, Bookmarks).

Jones, C. and Lavalette, M. (2013) 'The two souls of social work', *Critical and Radical Social Work*, 2(3): 381–383.

Kaye, H. (1984) *The British Marxist Historians* (Cambridge, Polity Press).

Kelly, M.K. (2017) *The Crime of Nationalism: Britain, Palestine and Nation-building on the fringe of empire* (Oakland, University of California Press).

King, M.E. (2007) *A Quiet Revolution: The first Palestinian Intifada and nonviolent resistance* (New York, Nation Books).

Lavalette, M. (2011) 'Social work in extremis: disaster capitalism, "social shocks" and popular social work', in M. Lavalette and V. Ioakimidis (eds) *Social Work in Extremis* (Bristol, Policy Press), pp 1–14.

Lavalette, M. (2021) *Palestinian Cultures of Resistance* (London, Redwords).

Lavalette, M., Ioakimidis, V. and Ferguson, I. (2021) *Social Work and COVID-19: International perspectives* (Bristol, Policy Press).

Lindsay, J., Faraj, Z. and Baidoun, N. (2007) 'The emergence of social work in Palestine: Developing social work in a situation of political conflict and nation building', in M. Lavalette and I. Ferguson (eds) *International Social Work and the Radical Tradition* (Birmingham, Venture Press), pp 163–187.

Marshall, P. (1989) *Intifada: Zionism, imperialism and Palestinian resistance* (London, Bookmarks).

Masalha, N. (2018) *Palestine: A four thousand year history* (London, Zed Books).

McMeekin, S. (2015) *The Ottoman Endgame: War, revolution and the making of the modern Middle East 1908–1923* (Harmondsworth, Penguin).

Midgely, J. (2001) 'Issues in international social work: Resolving critical debates in the profession' *Journal of Social Work*, 1(1): 21–35.

Milheim, A. (1983) 'A Picture of Life – The Sacrifice of Youth', *Al-Fajr* (25 January).

Morris, B. (2008) *1948: A history of the first Arab–Israeli War* (New Haven, Yale University Press).

Pappe, I. (2006) *The Ethnic Cleansing of Palestine* (Oxford, One World).

Payne, M. (2005) *Origins and Social Work: Continuity and change* (Basingstoke, Palgrave Macmillan).

PLO (1975) *The Struggle of Palestinian Women* (Beirut, PLO).

Pope, R.J. and Flanigan, S.T. (2013) 'Revolution for breakfast: Intersections of activism, service, and violence in the Black Panther Party's community service programs', *Social Justice Research*, 26(4): 445–470.

Regan, B. (2017) *The Balfour Declaration: Empire, the Mandate and resistance in Palestine* (London, Verso).

Rogan, E. (2017) *The Arabs: A history* (Harmondsworth, Penguin).

Rose, J. (1986) *Israel, The Hijack State: America's watchdog in the Middle East* (London, Bookmarks).

Rowbotham, S. (1977) *Hidden from History* (London, Pluto).

Saville, J. (1987) *1848: The British state and the Chartist movement* (Cambridge, Cambridge University Press).

Sorby, K. (2005) 'Arab nationalism after the | Young Turk revolution (1908–1914)' *Asian and African Studies*, 14(1): 4–21.

Thompson, D. (1986) *Chartists: Popular politics in the Industrial Revolution* (London, Ashgate).

Thompson, E.P. (1968) *The Making of the English Working Class* (Harmondsworth, Penguin).

Thompson, E.P. (1991) *Customs in Common* (Harmondsworth, Penguin).

Weinstock, N. (1979) *Zionism: False Messiah (revised edition)* (London, Pluto).

PART IV

Social work's complicity with institutionalisation and detention

11

Institutionalisation and oppression within the mental health system in England: social work complicity and resistance

Rich Moth

Introduction

This chapter begins by locating institutional oppression in the English mental health system within its wider sociopolitical and historical context. It does so by introducing the Gramscian notion of the 'integral state' to examine the dialectical interaction between the coercive, disciplinary and distributive functions of the capitalist state, and how the counterbalancing of these elements, in particular force and consent, shapes and reshapes welfare regimes over time. It goes on to apply this theoretical lens to a historical overview of forms of mental health provision in England from the Victorian asylum to contemporary neoliberal services. The chapter then explores the social work profession's engagement with these oppressive institutional systems and psychiatric practices, which has ranged from complicity to resistance. This Gramscian mode of analysis is utilised to examine some of the tensions and contradictions underpinning these divergent responses.

Social work, psychiatry and the integral state

The argument to be elaborated in this chapter is that social work's development (like that of psychiatry and other health and welfare occupations) should not be understood in terms of an autonomous 'professional project' or a spontaneous response to self-evident human need. Rather, state social work is better understood as a highly context-dependent form of institutional activity, conditioned by the nature of the welfare regime from which it emerges and within which it is situated (Harris, 2008). Moreover, welfare regimes are themselves historically variable, and continually shaped and reshaped by the wider political economy, the requirements of capital and the state and demands from below (Ferguson et al, 2002). The Gramscian notion of the 'integral' capitalist state usefully captures the mediatory role of this institutional formation as it seeks to manage these contradictory dynamics and competing pressures in the interests of capital (Gramsci, 1971; Thomas, 2009; Greener et al, 2019). The 'integral state' seeks to preserve social order and maintain the relative legitimacy of prevailing class relations (or hegemony) in capitalist society through a combination of securing popular consent and the deployment of force, though consent and coercion are not counterposed within this framework but instead regarded as dialectically interrelated (Thomas, 2009).

The welfare system is an important site of interaction between these tendencies toward coercion on the one hand and consent on the other. Here, the integral state's deployment of redistributive interventions to embed and strengthen consent is counterbalanced by the wielding of punitive and restrictive measures to discipline and regulate populations and maintain social order. At any specific historical moment, the particular 'mix' of force and consent utilised by the state within the domain of welfare policy is a contingent question shaped by wider contextual factors. This mix is, moreover, shaped and mediated by levels of resistance (Davies, 2010). The interaction of these dynamics accounts for the historically variable balance between care and control within the institutions and policy agendas of the welfare state which, in turn, shape the practices of state social workers as well as psychiatrists, nurses and other health professionals (Greener et al, 2019).

Having provided this brief overview of the integral state and its implications for welfare policy and social work practice, I will now turn to its application to the mental health system in England. As noted already, the operation of welfare regimes and the role within them of professions such as social work or psychiatry changes over time. The nature of this temporal process is usefully captured by the notion of 'conjunctural settlement' (Harris, 2008), which refers to the predominance of certain distinctive forms of welfare policy, practice and ideology during particular historical periods or 'moments'. This conjunctural approach recognises that the wider prevailing conditions of political and socioeconomic possibility play a crucial role in shaping the balance between consent, coercion and resistance tendencies within welfare institutions and these, in turn, provide orientation for professional practices. Applying this approach, it is possible to identify four conjunctural settlements in the mental health system in England. These are the custodial system of the Victorian asylum; the biomedical treatment system of the hospital; community care within the Keynesian welfare state; and neoliberal service reconfigurations (Moth, 2022).

The next section will offer an overview of these four conjunctural settlements, with a particular focus on the coercive and oppressive elements of these institutional systems. However, it should also be noted that, at each of these moments, subordinated ideas and practices were also present as forms of resistance challenging hegemonic ideas and interventions (this will be briefly explored in the final section of the chapter).

From the asylum to the hospital: institutional custodialism, eugenics and medicalisation

'Madhouses' were relatively small in number and scale until the early 19th century. However, the Victorian era saw the emergence and rapid expansion of a more centralised public asylum system[1] and a concomitant increase in the number of people confined in such institutions (Porter, 1987). The institutionalisation of those deemed 'mad'[2] was underpinned by, and closely integrated with, the broader Poor Law system. As Bartlett (1999) notes, the new system of county asylums was effectively integrated within the institutional framework of the Poor Law Amendment Act 1834, with 'pauper lunatics' constituting the vast majority of those confined under this legislation. A key role of this new array of Poor Law institutions, including the workhouse, public asylum and outdoor relief,[3] was to impose a new social discipline around wage labour (O'Brien, 2000). This foregrounds the coercive and regulatory functions of the integral state in the context of the emergence and development of industrial capitalism and its particular implications for poor people experiencing madness.

The design of the asylum system as well as its physical architecture was influenced by these wider sociopolitical conditions, reflecting the Poor Law workhouse, but also the barracks-like regimes of the new sites of industrial production, the factory and mill. Behind their grand facades, the asylum buildings modelled prisons both in terms of the concern with security and in the culture of staff (Busfield, 1986). This segregative institutional strategy has been characterised as custodialism (Scull, 1977), and this orientation was further legitimised by the widespread cultural associations of madness with 'danger' and violence that have remained prevalent since antiquity (Rosen, 1978). This justified the suppression and containment of 'pauper lunatics' and has endured across various historical periods[4] (Pilgrim and McCranie, 2013; Moth, 2022).

Asylum doctors (later to be known as psychiatrists) played a subsidiary organisational role in this Poor Law institutional system for much of the 19th century, with administrative authority ultimately residing with magistrates (Busfield, 1986; Bartlett, 1999). This was, in part, due to the limitations of the psychiatric knowledge base at this time (Pilgrim, 2008). However, by the latter part of the century biomedical conceptualisations began to become more established, with Henry Maudsley (a key figure in the development of British psychiatry) declaring 'mental illness' to be a brain disease (Burstow, 2015; Maudsley, 1867). With this change in psychiatric orientation, the institutional containment approach of the asylum increasingly came under challenge. Moreover, this period also saw a significant expansion of social policy intervention by the (integral) capitalist state (Lavalette and Penketh, 2003). In combination, these factors heralded a transition away from custodialism as the primary and dominant policy response to madness by the British state for most of the 19th century and towards an increasing focus on medicalisation and the biomedical management of mental illness (Moth, 2022).

By the early 20th century, the 'mad doctor' associated with the asylum began to be superseded by the psychiatrist located within the emergent hospital system. This new organisational model of provision, combining psychiatric hospital and outpatient clinic, was increasingly oriented to biomedical treatments. The opening in 1915 of the London hospital which took Maudsley's name was emblematic of this shift (Coppock and Hopton, 2000). The nature of the biomedical interventions offered in the new hospital settings was initially shaped by the success of the bacteriological paradigm within general medicine. This had led to the development, for example, of vaccines for cholera and antiseptics to reduce infections, and this influenced some psychiatrists who proposed that the causes of mental illness were located within the body (Scull, 2015). As a consequence, the early decades of the 20th century saw a significant expansion from the relatively limited range of physical treatment interventions then in use such as laxatives, and sedatives (for example, paraldehyde and chloral hydrate) (Rogers and Pilgrim, 2021). However, these new 'somatic' treatments were to expose psychiatric patients to a wide range of dangers and harms.

Foremost among these novel interventions were the shock therapies that emerged in the 1920s and 1930s. The first of these to emerge, insulin coma therapy, involved the deliberate administration of large doses of insulin to induce coma and sometimes seizures and convulsions in the patient. It was (incorrectly) believed that conditions (or rather labels) such as 'schizophrenia' could not coexist with epilepsy, so patients' physical responses to this intervention offered therapeutic benefit to those with such diagnoses. Soon after, a similar treatment offering an alternative means to produce these purportedly beneficial seizures, electro-convulsive therapy (ECT), was developed and widely adopted internationally. A third physical treatment that emerged at this time was psychosurgery. This involved the surgical procedure of lobotomy, removing sections of the frontal lobes of the patient's brain. The lack of evidence for the effectiveness of these treatments, the harms and deaths caused by these brutally invasive interventions and increasing controversy and resistance both from within psychiatry and particularly in wider society meant that by the 1960s the use of these somatic 'treatments' (except for ECT) had declined significantly (Scull, 2015).

But how was it possible that such damaging and injurious interventions could be sanctioned and implemented during this period? One important factor was the prominence of theories of hereditary 'degeneracy', in the late 19th century, that promulgated discriminatory ideas such as the greater liability of the poor to insanity, criminality and alcoholism, thereby dehumanising 'paupers' and other marginalised groups within the asylum system. Such ideas went on to underpin eugenics, a pseudo-scientific philosophy and reactionary political movement of the early 20th century that sought to shape social policy in order to ameliorate the purported ill-effects and threats to the nation-state from a 'tainted' gene pool among its population (Pilgrim, 2008). These notions of biological and racial inferiority were embraced by psychiatry, with advocates of eugenics (including Henry Maudsley) integral to the establishment of this new profession and its organisational centres in the UK such as the Institute of Psychiatry (Fernando, 2017; Gordon-Achebe et al, 2019). Eugenic theory was applied to asylum and hospital patients, providing justification not only for the brutal psychiatric treatments outlined earlier but also for programmes of sterilisation of the 'mentally ill' in many jurisdictions internationally (Burstow, 2015). The most notorious manifestation of eugenic ideology was the T-4 programme of extermination of asylum and mental hospital patients, referred to as 'useless eaters', in Nazi Germany from 1939 onwards (Scull, 2015) (see Chapter 6, this volume).

This overview of policy from the 19th to mid-20th century has highlighted the shift from the conjunctural settlement of the asylum to that of the hospital system. This foregrounds the contrast between the asylum, which served a more directly coercive function as part of a wider Poor Law strategy to inculcate wage labour discipline among the poor, and the establishment of the biomedical hospital system that represented a reorientation of these regulatory functions through 'medicalisation' by psychiatry (Cohen, 2016). Through these practices and ideational frameworks, psychiatry was thus able to offer the capitalist state a means to biomedically legitimise and depoliticise the social control of the poor, as well as women, racialised communities and sexual minorities (Ferguson, 2017). Moreover, psychiatry's association with eugenic ideas strengthened the profession's perceived legitimacy within the structures of the capitalist state during this period (Gordon-Achebe et al, 2019).

From community care to neoliberalism: from psychiatric abuse to malign neglect?

The preceding section has outlined a wide range of significant harms and forms of abuse that were experienced by people admitted to and confined within the asylum and early biomedical hospital regimes. A growing popular concern about these institutional abuses from the 1950s onwards coalesced with an emerging policy consensus for a more comprehensive welfare settlement in the post-Second World War period (Ferguson et al, 2002). This alignment was the outcome of an uneasy alliance between state monopoly capital and the labour movement as their interests converged around the construction of the Keynesian welfare state (Creaven, 2000). This emerging system of welfare provision created a context in which new approaches to the community treatment of those deemed mentally ill became both acceptable and feasible (Busfield, 1986).

In the immediate post-war period, hospitals for mental illness were reorganised to integrate with the new welfare state structure as part of the National Health Service (NHS). However, it was not until the early 1960s that community care reforms began to gather momentum. This was a time when concerns about the effects of institutionalisation and oppression in the mental health system were also emerging in the UK and internationally (Scull, 2015). This disquiet was crystallised in popular discourse through prominent critiques of psychiatric institutions such as Erving Goffman's (1961) *Asylums*. For Goffman, the psychiatric hospital was an example of a total institution which, like the prison or concentration camp, imposed social control on its inmates through forms of regimentation and 'mortification rituals' with dehumanising effects. Goffman's work foregrounded the harmful implications of institutionalisation and labelling in this setting and is often identified with a wider challenge to such institutional harms at this time, known as the anti-psychiatry movement.[5] Other contributors to this 1960s critique of mainstream psychiatry include philosopher Michel Foucault and 'renegade' psychiatrists R.D. Laing (from the Left) and Thomas Szasz (from the libertarian Right) (Scull, 2015; Sedgwick, 2015).

The anti-psychiatry movement initiated a high-profile critique of biomedical orthodoxy, challenging the dominant notion that the causes of mental distress were to be located in malfunctioning of individual biology and instead foregrounding the aetiological role of familial, institutional and social environments (Hopton, 2006; Rogers and Pilgrim, 2021). Also beginning to emerge during the 1960s and 1970s, a time of political foment characterised by high levels of resistance to racialised, gender, disability and LGBT oppression as well as resurgent labour movement struggles, was the service user/survivor[6] movement. This too played an important role in challenging medicalisation, custodialism and institutionalisation (Crossley, 2006; Survivors History Group, 2011; Beresford, 2012).

However, these pressures from below were not the only processes that contributed to the policy shift towards deinstitutionalisation which, though starting from the late 1950s, did not begin to gather pace until the 1980s. At the policy level two key provisions in the Mental Health Act 1959 began to enable the development of community services. These were a requirement for outpatient follow-up of patients who had been discharged after detention, and a legislated role for social work (Lester and Glasby, 2010). These were developed alongside the replacement of asylum admission with acute treatment in district general hospital (DGH) units. However, while there was an expansion of medicalised DGH units, there was not similar investment in community facilities (Rogers and Pilgrim, 2001). Residential provision, in particular, was neglected, due to the funding pressures experienced by local authorities (Busfield, 1986).

Nonetheless, by the 1980s, there had been some increase in the range of community mental health service provision, which included residential facilities such as hostels, group and nursing homes and NHS- and social services-run community mental health and day centres (Rogers and Pilgrim, 2001). There was also a more integrated role for social work within the newly emerging multi-professional community team structures (Bailey, 2012), and an expansion of spaces for relationship-based and therapeutically oriented practice (Moth, 2022). Moreover, progressive developments within the wider welfare state began to play a more prominent role within mental health services, such as a greater focus on group work and community development (Rogowski, 2020). Influenced by the social movements noted earlier, this period also saw the small-scale emergence of arenas of user-led provision and knowledge production (Beresford, 2016), alongside anti-oppressive, radical and democratising orientations among some health and welfare professionals (Ferguson and Woodward, 2009; McKeown, 2020).

Ultimately, however, the potentialities of the wider post-war expansion of Keynesian welfarism were not realised in the form of new, comprehensive and more inclusive community mental health services to replace the Victorian asylums. This was because, at the very moment when deinstitutionalisation processes began to accelerate, the economic crises of the mid-1970s began to unfold (Ferguson et al, 2002). Consequently, rather than service renewal, this moment was utilised by policy makers as an opportunity for public spending reductions, presaging the small-state fiscal reorientation of neoliberalism in the 1980s (Ferguson, 2017). A progressive policy rhetoric foregrounding the closure of the repressive institutions of the asylum and hospital masked the severely limited community support options made available to people with longer-term mental health needs.

As the Keynesian community care settlement transitioned into the neoliberal policy era, there was increasing recognition of the 'malign neglect' of mental health service users that characterised the policy agenda that followed deinstitutionalisation (Scull, 2019). This manifested in two particularly prominent ways. The first was the gendered displacement of care responsibilities for long-term service users onto predominantly female family members; the second was a trend towards 'reinstitutionalisation' as increasing numbers of people were placed in large-scale (often private sector) care settings (Scull, 2015) or confined within restrictive institutional environments such as forensic services and prisons (Fakhoury and Priebe, 2007; Kritsotaki et al, 2016).

These trends have remained prominent as neoliberal reform of community mental health services has unfolded since the early 1990s. This reform agenda is comprised of three interdependent elements. These are the reconstruction of service delivery through the creation of markets and imposition of market-oriented performance-indicator mechanisms, the repositioning of service users as consumers (in the context of the privatisation of risk and responsibility) and coercive and responsibilising forms of risk management (Moth, 2022). The latter is the outcome of the return to prominence of long-standing discourses of 'violence and danger' associated with mental health service users during the 1990s, which were promulgated through political and media institutions in the wake of deinstitutionalisation reforms (Warner et al, 2017).

As a result of these reconfigurations, the work of practitioners has increasingly focused on 'informational' practices of data collection for markets and risk management, with a concomitant reduction in the time available for relationship-based work. Consequently individual, group and community work-oriented interventions have been marginalised, and there is a growing emphasis on service user self-care, including the self-management of risk factors pertaining to mental health. Such risk-oriented requirements typically foreground 'compliance' with prescribed medications (thus reinforcing biomedical-model interventions), as well as parsimonious use of services. However, the converse of this responsibilisation logic is that when conduct is deemed to have fallen short of these norms, the imposition of punitive sanctions is warranted (Moth, 2022). The controversial Mental Health Act reforms that introduced pre-emptive detention, increased spending on secure institutions and restrictive community treatment orders, and a rise in the numbers of people with mental distress incarcerated in prisons bears witness to this trend (Lester and Glasby, 2010; Brown and Baker, 2012). Austerity measures since 2010, and associated funding cuts and resource constraints, have further embedded and intensified this direction of neoliberal policy reform. This manifests through intensified reinforcement of biomedicalisation strategies for risk management. The structural violence of austerity (Cooper and Whyte, 2017) is also visible in the form of the 'discharge deaths' of service users, linked with service cuts, and 'benefits distress' caused by welfare reform measures (Moth, 2022; Moth, forthcoming).

To recap, the role of pressure from below by labour and social movements in the post-war period oriented Keynesian welfarism, within significant limits,[7] towards a somewhat more redistributive and socially oriented strategy for the management of marginality (Davies, 2014). This was visible through an increase in spaces of relationship-based and community-focused support. However, this (relative) shift towards consent by the integral state was short lived, and has since been superseded by a significant reduction in direct (supportive) state intervention under neoliberalism. Instead, an indirect regulatory stance for producing and managing subjectivity has been established (Parker, 2014). This has taken the form of expectations of 'responsible' employment-focused conduct by users, reinforced through policy levers such as service or benefits conditionalities, but supplemented by a more directly coercive penal strategy applied to those who are unwilling or unable to conform to these policy injunctions (Moth, 2022).

Social work in the mental health system

The core argument of the chapter thus far has been that welfare regimes create enablements and constraints that shape (though do not determine) the forms of professional practice that take place within changing organisational settings. Various professional groups have played an important role in the management of mental health systems, most prominently magistrates in the 19th century and then psychiatry from the 20th century onwards. However, social work has also played a significant, though auxiliary, role in this system since the early part of the 20th century.

The establishment of mental health social work in England can be traced back to the 1920s, with the first appointment of a social worker at London's Tavistock Clinic, a key centre for psychodynamic practice, and the introduction of psychiatric social work training at the London School of Economics (Ramon, 2006; Long, 2011). However, it was with the introduction of community care in the post-war period that social work's presence began to significantly expand within this setting. But consideration of social work's role in the mental health system must inevitably confront the tensions and contradictions for the profession as it has navigated the historically variable tendencies towards coercion and consent within the institutions of the mental health system that have already been outlined. The following two sections will consider these vexed questions in more detail. The first examines social work's complicity with oppressive practices in this setting, while the second explores social work involvement in radical movements and resistance to harms and oppression in the system.

Social work complicity with oppressive practices

Psychiatric social work (PSW) was initially a numerically small professional grouping, though numbers increased from the 1920s to 1950s.[8] The predominant orientation among PSWs during this early period, up to the middle of the 20th century, was an acceptance of psychiatric authority and of their group's subsidiary position within a medically dominated institutional hierarchy (though most PSWs were located in community rather than hospital settings until the post-war reforms) (Ramon, 1985). PSW did not establish an independent knowledge base but drew on the psychiatric and psychodynamic concepts of the time, which were implemented through a case-work model (Timms, 1964). Indeed, this orientation and identification with psychiatry was utilised as a means to try to secure PSW's professional status (Ramon, 1985).

This theoretical and practical stance adopted by PSW generated a tendency towards the individualisation and psychologisation of clients' problems, including their experiences of mental distress. Consequently there was actually a reduction in the extent to which the social and environmental dimensions were incorporated in the professional worldview of PSW in the 1950s when compared with the profession's incipient phase in the 1920s. A further corollary of this organisational and ideational positioning was that PSW articulated only relatively limited support for later post-war community care reforms, and the profession tended to be somewhat uncritical of the dominant biomedical–somatic treatment approach[9] (Ramon, 1985). These factors, including the acceptance of a subsidiary professional identity and the limited independent professional organisation, neutered any potential for PSW to challenge the authority of psychiatry even as community care reforms offered conjunctural opportunities for the reorientation of dominant service philosophies and practices within an increasingly multidisciplinary setting. Consequently, PSW tended to align with the requirements of these medically dominated institutions and the regulatory and coercive demands of the integral state that underpin them (Ioakimidis and Trimikliniotis, 2020).

However, recent academic work has suggested a more complex relationship to psychiatry during this formative period, with the development of supplementary social 'treatments' by PSWs suggesting some degree of critical orientation towards medicalisation (Long, 2011; Broad, 2020). In her case study of the transition to community care following the 1957 Percy Report (the recommendations of which were implemented as the Mental Health Act 1959), Harrington (2016, p 146) notes how the increasing prominence of psychiatric social work in the local authority mental health service in Salford played an important role in promoting the shift from a custodial to therapeutic and relationship-based orientation within this setting.

Radical approaches and resistance

The era of psychiatric social work as a distinct professional grouping was effectively brought to an end in the early 1970s by the genericist orientation promoted in the Seebohm Report (Stewart, 2016). The new institutional arrangements meant that social workers experienced greater organisational independence from psychiatry in the new post-Seebohm social services departments. Consequently, though members of this professional group still experienced pressure to comply with psychiatric treatment decisions during this period, there was also a greater willingness to challenge extant institutional power structures. Many social workers became, to use Pearson's (1975) evocative term, 'saboteurs'. The implication here is that some began to adopt a more overtly humanitarian stance, based on the profession's ethico-political commitments, as a basis from which to critique pathologising institutional processes such as psychiatric labelling of service users.

As noted earlier, a key impulse underpinning this reorientation was the political radicalisation of the 1960s and early 1970s. This produced intellectual foment, exemplified by developments such as the 'rediscovery of poverty'. This challenged psychodynamic theory, then the dominant explanatory framework within mainstream mental health social work, and its tendency to individualise social problems. In combination with the influence of social movements for civil rights and anti-racism, women's liberation, LGBT rights and peace, as well as growing trade union militancy at that time (Lavalette, 2011), some social workers connected with what has been termed the profession's 'radical kernel'[10] (Ferguson and Lavalette, 2007). This inspired the formation of networks of activist social workers, most notably Case Con in 1970. The name of the collective was itself a critique of the 'case conference', an emblematic practice within mainstream social work, which it was argued reduced the structural problems facing service users to the 'victim blaming' of individual adjustment (Weinstein, 2011). Though these initiatives were taken up by a minority strand within social work, such radical initiatives nonetheless resonated more widely, shaping the broader ethico-political stance of the profession (Ferguson and Lavalette, 2007).

As well as inspiring activist practitioners, these wider political and liberation struggles in society formed a backdrop to the activism of welfare service users. A prominent example emerging at this time is the Mental Patients Union (MPU), the first mental health service user/survivor-led political campaign group in England (Durkin and Douieb, 1975; Spandler, 2006). The MPU sought to resist oppression in the mental health system in the form of confinement, compulsory treatment and over-medicalisation, demanding greater patient rights and autonomy (Durkin and Douieb, 1975). Moreover, the potential for practitioners to be allies of service-user struggles was illustrated by the role played by an activist social worker[11] in the MPU's formation.

The potential for such 'cross-sectional' alliances, that is, activist interventions bringing together service users/survivors, social workers and activists from other mental health professions, has been illustrated in a number of more recent interventions to challenge oppressive neoliberal mental health policy reforms (Moth and Mckeown, 2016). For instance, since 2010, cross-sectional campaigns led by users but involving social workers have included resistance to austerity-related closures of mental health resource centres in Liverpool, Cambridge and Salford (Moth et al, 2015), and a national campaigning alliance against 'psychocompulsion' and 'work cure' reforms in the welfare benefits system (McKenna et al, 2019; Moth and Lavalette, 2019).

However, such 'cross-sectional' alliances are not automatic, and there can be significant barriers to their development. They require recognition by social work activists of unequal survivor–worker power relations and a commitment to relational reciprocity and democratisation in such political engagements to address these dynamics (McKeown et al, 2014; Moth and McKeown, 2016). Nonetheless, commitments to such participatory forms of resistance may themselves prefigure alternative socially just welfare futures. In doing so, these activist interventions contest the profound limitations of the counterbalancing of regulatory self-help and coercion that is characteristic of the integral state's mental health policy interventions under neoliberalism. Instead, they offer possibilities to create spaces of redistributive justice in both a material and an epistemic sense. This orientation reduces the possibilities of such transformative activities being recuperated by neoliberal policy makers[12] (Davies, 2014) while, at a broader level, these inclusive forms of resistance have the potential to contribute to a wider progressive shift in the balance between force and consent in the integral welfare state.

Conclusion

This chapter has offered a historical overview of institutionalisation and oppression within the mental health system in England, and considered both complicity with and resistance to these processes by the social work profession. A Gramscian theoretical lens was utilised to foreground the role of the integral (capitalist) state in shaping the nature of welfare regimes and thereby creating the wider conditions for (though not determining) professional practices. A key implication of this integral state approach is that, while identifying the culpabilities of particular professions such as psychiatry in relation to historic and contemporary harms and abuses in mental health service contexts, and the complicity of social work, it also provides a means to go beyond this by identifying the causal processes within the wider capitalist system that underpin these oppressive dynamics. In doing so, it enables a focus both on the kinds of systemic (anti-capitalist) transformations ultimately necessary to transcend such institutional harms, as well as on the forms of political agency in the present that may contribute to the realisation of such ends. The chapter has concluded by identifying one such form of agency, cross-sectional alliances and solidarities between liberatory service user/survivor movements and radical social workers (as well as other activist professionals). Arguably, this orientation offers potential as a transformative strategy to inform ongoing challenges to malign neglect, enduring medicalisation, coercion and oppression in the neoliberal mental health system while also strengthening the conditions of possibility for alternative, socially just policy and practice responses to lived experiences of mental distress.

Notes

[1] This challenges Foucault's (1961) claims of a mid-17th-century 'Great Confinement' across Europe.

[2] The terminology for describing such lived experiences is contested and historically variable. I have tended to reflect contemporaneous terms in the various historical sections of this chapter, though I generally use the term mental distress (though also sometimes madness) to reflect my own positioning that rejects pathologising categorisations of 'mental illness' and 'mental disorder' (see Sapey et al, 2015, p 6, for further discussion of these debates).

[3] Such relief could take the form of financial support outside of the workhouse or forms of non-monetary support such as food or clothing (Fraser, 2017).

[4] For instance, the custodialism of Victorian legislation such as the Lunacy Act 1890 (Rogers and Pilgrim, 2001).

[5] Cultural interventions such as Ken Kesey's novel (and the associated movie) *One Flew Over the Cuckoo's Nest* were also important in the widespread dissemination of this critique.

[6] This term survivor has become a prominent form of collective self-identification and refers to survival from oppressive psychiatric systems (Beresford, 2012).

[7] However it should be clearly noted that the egalitarian, universalist and relational principles and potentialities of Keynesian welfarism were undermined, in practice, by underfunding, the reproduction of structural discrimination in its delivery mechanisms in relation to gender, 'race' and other social divisions, and a paternalist orientation towards service users. The significant limitations of mental health services during this period amply illustrate this tension (Ferguson et al, 2002; Beresford, 2016).

[8] As Bartlett (1999, p 4) and Harrington (2016, p 140) note, PSW has a complex lineage, with aspects of the role derived from that of the 'Poor Law relieving officers', who became 'duly authorised officers' under Mental Treatment Act 1930, then 'mental welfare officers' under the Mental Health Act 1959, before the role was again revised to create the Approved Social Worker role under the Mental Health Act 1983, the forerunner of the current Approved Mental Health Professional.

[9] It should be noted that eugenics influenced not only psychiatry but also social work during the early part of the 20th century (Jones and Novak, 1999), and this may have contributed to the blunting of social work's critique of biomedicalisation.

[10] This refers to the social justice-oriented welfare practices of the settlement movement and social reformers such as Clement Attlee and Sylvia Pankhurst that influenced social work in its late 19th- and early 20th-century formative years (Ferguson and Lavalette, 2007).

[11] Liz Durkin, a social work student on placement in the Paddington Day Hospital in London at the time when the MPU was formed there, played a significant role as an ally through organising and facilitating some of the activities of the group (Davies, 2005).

[12] Though it does not eliminate this possibility. A prominent recent example of recuperation is the recovery model, a progressive approach originating in the survivor movement, which has been appropriated and hollowed out by neoliberal policy makers as it has been integrated into mainstream mental health services (Recovery in the Bin, Edwards et al, 2019).

References

Bailey, D. (2012) *Interdisciplinary Working in Mental Health*. London: Palgrave Macmillan.

Bartlett, P. (1999) *The Poor Law of Lunacy: The Administration of Pauper Lunatics in Mid-nineteenth Century England*. Leicester: Leicester University Press.

Beresford, P. (2012) 'Psychiatric System Survivors: An Emerging Movement'. In N. Watson, A. Roulstone and C. Thomas (eds) *Routledge Handbook of Disability Studies*. London: Routledge, pp 151–164.

Beresford, P. (2016) *All Our Welfare: Towards Participatory Social Policy*. Bristol: Policy Press.

Broad, J. (2020) 'Working in cases: British psychiatric social workers and a history of psychoanalysis from the middle, c.1930–60'. *History of the Human Sciences*, doi: 10.1177/0952695120930914.

Brown, B. and Baker, S. (2012) *Responsible Citizens: Individuals, Health and Policy under neoliberalism*. London: Anthem Press.

Burstow, B. (2015) *Psychiatry and the Business of Madness: An Ethical and Epistemological Accounting*. London: Palgrave Macmillan.

Busfield, J. (1986) *Managing Madness: Changing Ideas and Practice*. London: Unwin Hyman.

Cohen, B. (2016) *Psychiatric Hegemony: A Marxist Theory of Mental Illness*. London: Palgrave Macmillan.

Cooper, V. and Whyte, D. (2017) 'Introduction: The violence of austerity'. In V. Cooper and D. Whyte (eds) *The Violence of Austerity*. London: Pluto Press, pp 1–34.

Coppock, V. and Hopton, J. (2000) *Critical Perspectives on Mental Health*. London: Routledge.

Creaven, S. (2000) *Marxism and Realism: A Materialistic Application of Realism in the Social Sciences*. London: Routledge.

Crossley, N. (2006) *Contesting Psychiatry: Social Movements in Mental Health*. London: Routledge.

Davies, J. (2010) 'Neoliberalism, Governance and the Integral State'. *Critical Governance Conference, University of Warwick, 13–14 December 2010*. Warwick: University of Warwick.

Davies, J. (2014) 'Rethinking urban power and the local state: Hegemony, domination and resistance in neoliberal cities', *Urban Studies*, 51(15): 3215–3232.

Davies, L. (2005) *Authentic Practice Works. Professional Social Work*. Birmingham: BASW.

Durkin, L. and Douieb, B. (1975) 'The Mental Patients Union'. In D. Jones and M. Mayo (eds) *Community Work Two*. London: Routledge and Kegan Paul, pp 177–191.

Fakhoury, W. and Priebe, S. (2007) 'Deinstitutionalization and Reinstitutionalization: major changes in the provision of mental healthcare'. *Psychiatry*, 6(8): 313–316.

Ferguson, I. (2017) *Politics of the Mind: Marxism and Mental Distress*. London: Bookmarks.

Ferguson, I. and Lavalette, M. (2007) 'The social worker as agitator: The radical kernel of British social work'. In M. Lavalette and I. Ferguson (eds) *International Social Work and the Radical Tradition*. London: Venture Press, pp 11–31.

Ferguson, I. and Woodward, R. (2009) *Radical Social Work in Practice: Making a Difference*. Bristol: Policy Press.

Ferguson, I., Lavalette, M. and Mooney, G. (2002) *Rethinking Welfare: A critical perspective*. London: Sage.

Fernando, S. (2017) *Institutional Racism in Psychiatry and Clinical Psychology: Race Matters in Mental Health*. Basingstoke: Palgrave Macmillan.

Fraser, D. (2017) *The Evolution of the British Welfare State: A History of Social Policy since the Industrial Revolution, 5th edition*. London: Palgrave Macmillan.

Goffman, E. (1961) *Asylums*. Harmondsworth: Penguin.

Gordon-Achebe, K., Hairston, D.R., Miller, S., Legha, R. and Starks, S. (2019) 'Origins of racism in American medicine and psychiatry'. In M. Medlock, D. Shtasel, N.H. Trinh and D. Williams (eds) *Racism and Psychiatry: Contemporary Issues and Interventions*. New Jersey: Humana Press, pp 3–19.

Gramsci, A. (1971) *Selections from the Prison Notebooks of Antonio Gramsci*. London: Lawrence and Wishart.

Greener, J., Hart, E.L. and Moth, R. (2019) 'Resisting the punitive state–corporate nexus: Activist strategy and the integrative transitional approach'. In E.L. Hart, J. Greener and R. Moth (eds) *Resist the Punitive State: Grassroots Struggles Across Welfare, Housing, Education and Prisons*. London: Pluto Press, pp 3–27.

Harrington, V. (2016) 'Integration in a Divided World: Salford Community Mental Health Services 1948–1974'. In D. Kritsotaki, V. Long and M. Smith (eds) *Deinstitutionalisation and After: Post-war Psychiatry in the Western World*. London: Palgrave Macmillan, pp 135–154.

Harris, J. (2008) 'State social work: constructing the present from moments in the past'. *British Journal of Social Work*, 38 (4): 662–679.

Hopton, J. (2006) The future of critical psychiatry. *Critical Social Policy*, 26 (1): 57–73.

Ioakimidis, V. and Trimikliniotis, N. (2020) 'Making Sense of Social Work's Troubled Past: Professional identity, collective memory and the quest for historical justice'. *British Journal of Social Work*, 50: 1890–1908.

Jones, C. and Novak, T. (1999) *Poverty, Welfare and the Disciplinary State*. London: Routledge.

Kritsotaki, D., Long, V. and Smith, M. (2016) 'Introduction: Deinstitutionalisation and the pathways of post-war psychiatry in the western world'. In D. Kritsotaki, V. Long and M. Smith (eds) *Deinstitutionalisation and After: Post-war Psychiatry in the Western World*. London: Palgrave Macmillan, pp 1–36.

Lavalette, M. (2011) Introduction. In M. Lavalette (ed) *Radical Social Work Today*. Bristol: Policy Press, pp 1–11.

Lavalette, M. and Penketh, L. (2003) 'The Welfare State in the United Kingdom'. In C. Aspalter (ed) *Welfare Capitalism Around the World*. Hong Kong: Casa Verde Publishing, pp 61–86.

Lester, H. and Glasby, J. (2010) *Mental Health Policy and Practice, 2nd edition*. Houndmills: Palgrave Macmillan.

Long, V. (2011) '"Often there is a good deal to be done, but socially rather than medically": The psychiatric social worker as social therapist, 1945–70'. *Medical History*, 55(2): 223–39.

Maudsley, H. (1867) *The Physiology and Pathology of Mind*. London: Macmillan.

McKenna, D., Peters, P. and Moth, R. (2019) 'Resisting the Work Cure: Mental health, welfare reform and the movement against psychocompulsion'. In M. Berghs et al (eds) *The Routledge Handbook of Disability Activism*. London: Routledge, pp 128–143.

McKeown, M. (2020) 'Love and resistance: Re-inventing radical nurses in everyday struggles'. *Journal of Clinical Nursing*, 29(7–8): 1023–1025.

McKeown, M., Cresswell, M. and Spandler, H. (2014) 'Deeply engaged relationships: Alliances between mental health workers and psychiatric survivors in the UK'. In B. Bursow, B.A. Lefrançois and S. Diamond (eds) *Psychiatry Disrupted: Theorizing Resistance and Crafting the (R)evolution*. Montreal: McGill/Queen's University Press, pp 145–162.

Moth, R. (2022) *Understanding Mental Distress: Knowledge, Practice and Neoliberal Reform in Community Mental Health Services*. Bristol: Policy Press.

Moth, R. (forthcoming) 'Traps, gaps and benefits distress: Theorising the social and psychological harms of neoliberal welfare reform'. Article in preparation.

Moth, R. and Lavalette, M. (2019) 'Social policy and welfare movements "from below": the Social Work Action Network (SWAN) in the UK'. In U. Klammer, S. Leiber and S. Leitner (eds) *Social Work and the Making of Social Policy*. Bristol: Policy Press, pp 121–136.

Moth, R. and McKeown, M. (2016) 'Realising Sedgwick's vision: Theorising strategies of resistance to neoliberal mental health and welfare policy'. *Critical and Radical Social Work*, 4(3): 375–90.

Moth, R., Greener, J. and Stoll, T. (2015) 'Crisis and resistance in mental health services in England'. *Critical and Radical Social Work*, 3(1): 89–101.

O'Brien, M. (2000) 'Class struggle and the English Poor Laws'. In M. Lavalette and G. Mooney (eds) *Class Struggle and Social Welfare*, London: Routledge, pp 13–33.

Parker, I. (2014) 'Psychotherapy under capitalism: The production, circulation and management of value and subjectivity'. *Psychotherapy and Politics International*, 12(3): 166–175.

Pearson, G. (1975) 'Making social workers: Bad promises and good omens'. In R. Bailey and M. Brake (eds) *Radical Social Work*. London: Edward Arnold, pp 13–45.

Pilgrim, D. (2008) 'The eugenic legacy in psychology and psychiatry'. *International Journal of Social Psychiatry*, 54(3): 272–284.

Pilgrim, D. and McCranie, A. (2013) *Recovery and Mental Health: A Critical Sociological Account*. Basingstoke: Palgrave Macmillan.

Porter, R. (1987) *Mind-Forg'd Manacles: A History of Madness in England from the Restoration to the Regency*. London: Athlone Press.

Ramon, S. (1985) *Psychiatry in Britain: Meaning and Policy*. London: Routledge.

Ramon, S. (2006) 'British mental health social work and the psychosocial approach in context'. In D. Double (ed) *Critical Psychiatry: The Limits of Madness*. Basingstoke: Palgrave Macmillan, pp 133–148.

Recovery in the Bin, Edwards, B.M., Burgess, R. and Thomas, E. (2019) 'Neorecovery: A survivor led conceptualisation and critique' [transcript]. Keynote presented at the 25th International Mental Health Nursing Research Conference, The Royal College of Nursing, London. Available from: https://recoveryinthebin.org/2019/09/16/__trashed-2/

Rogers, A. and Pilgrim, D. (2001) *Mental Health Policy in Britain*. 2nd edn. Houndmills: Palgrave Macmillan.

Rogers, A. and Pilgrim, D. (2021) *A Sociology of Mental Health and Illness*. 6th edn. Maidenhead: Open University Press.

Rogowski, S. (2020) *Social Work: The Rise and Fall of a Profession?* 2nd edn. Bristol: Policy Press.

Rosen, G. (1978) *Madness in Society*. New York: Harper.

Sapey, B., Spandler, H. and Anderson, J. (2015) 'Introduction'. In H. Spandler, J. Anderson and B. Sapey (eds) *Madness, Distress and the Politics of Disablement*. Bristol: Policy Press, pp 1–9.

Scull, A. (1977) 'Madness and segregative control: The rise of the insane asylum'. *Social Problems*, 24(3): 337–351.

Scull, A. (2015) *Madness in Civilization: A Cultural History of Insanity*. London: Thames & Hudson.

Scull, A. (2019) *Psychiatry and Its Discontents*. Oakland: University of California Press.

Sedgwick, P. (2015) [1982] *Psycho Politics*. London: Unkant Publishers.

Spandler, H. (2006) *Asylum to Action: Paddington Day Hospital, Therapeutic Communities and Beyond*. London: Jessica Kingsley Publishers.

Stewart, J. (2016) 'Child guidance and deinstitutionalisation in post-war Britain'. In D. Kritsotaki, V. Long and M. Smith (eds) *Deinstitutionalisation and After: Post-war Psychiatry in the Western World*. London: Palgrave Macmillan, pp 175–194.

Survivors History Group (2011) 'Survivors History Group takes a critical look at historians'. In M. Barnes and P. Cotterell (eds) *Critical Perspectives on User Involvement*. Bristol: Policy Press, pp 7–18.

Thomas, P. (2009) *The Gramscian Moment: Philosophy, Hegemony and Marxism*. Leiden: Brill.

Timms, N. (1964) *Psychiatric Social Work in Great Britain (1939–1962)*. London: Routledge and Kegan Paul.

Warner, J., Heller, N., Sharland, E. and Stanford, S. (2017) 'The historical context of the risk paradigm in mental health policy and practice: How did we get here?' In S. Stanford, E. Sharland, N.R. Heller, and J. Warner (eds) *Beyond the Risk Paradigm in Mental Health Policy and Practice*. London: Palgrave Macmillan, pp 1–16.

Weinstein, J. (2011) 'Case con and radical social work in the 1970s: The impatient revolutionaries'. In M. Lavalette (ed) *Radical Social Work Today*. Bristol: Policy Press.

12

A refugee crisis or a crisis of anti-immigrant politics? Hostile refugee reception, the pandemic and new solidarities in Cyprus

Nicos Trimikliniotis and Vassilis Tsianos

Introduction

This chapter examines the challenges for social work 'from below' when states do not meet basic needs in protecting refugees and asylum-seekers, or when states choose to neglect or even expel them, generating a racialised hostile environment. Focusing on Cyprus, the chapter examines how the processes of the long-drawn division of the country, known as the Cyprus problem, is entangled with issues pertaining to racial discrimination faced by asylum-seekers. Also, it explores the realities and potential for a progressive social work *in extremis* as praxis of solidarity. The measures imposed during the COVID-19 pandemic have reshaped the rights regimes for citizens and non-citizens, exacerbating racial ideologies and configuring new regimes of exception and derogation of rights. This has impacted intensively on the rights of non-citizens (asylum-seekers, refugees and migrants), with new border controls and other restrictions on their mobility. Moreover, the rise in numbers of arrivals of asylum-seekers has created greater demands for persons in need. As this chapter explains, social work has failed to meet the growing need for support, due to systemic reasons and government policy which has decided that it must remove benefits and services – which it brands as 'pull factors' – in order to curb 'illegal immigration'. This has reached crisis levels.

The history of social work in Cyprus since British colonial times is one of complicity rather than resistance. The protracted conflict, which led to the 1974 coup and the subsequent Turkish invasion, resulted in the continuing de facto division of the country. The financial crisis that hit Cyprus in 2012 and peaked in 2013, and the pandemic since 2020, have reshaped social work in multiple ways. This transformation is visible mainly in the context of social work with migrants and refugees.

The story of migration and asylum is very much at the heart of what is happening in this divided country, influenced by geographical factors, the de facto division of the country and the problematic Cyprus–Greece––Turkey triangle. This is the context within which social work 'from below' has emerged. State and private institutions that have traditionally and historically represented social work practice are either outright hostile or simply failing (again) in moments of necessity. In contrast, praxis-based solidarity via collective initiatives (socialities), manifested in the form of unofficial social work from below, have emerged out of a humanitarian crisis.

The pandemic and mass migration immigration, asylum and neo-racist xenophobia in Europe

During these strange and difficult pandemic times, Antonio Gramsci is often invoked, even in the most unlikely quarters. Gramsci's (1971, p 276) rather simplified historical schema of the long death of the 'old', where the 'new' is stillborn, contains plural temporalities and potentialities, despite the dangers it generates. 'Morbid symptoms' are inherent in the long and multidimensional crisis that take various forms (Sasoon, 2021). As Robert Boyer (2021) aptly points out, capitalisms (in the plural) are in the 'whirlwind of the pandemic', and this overturns the logics where the economy imposes its own logic on society, something that ceases during wars, great economic crises or pandemics.

The basic Gramscian idea is of the crisis of hegemony, the manifestation of which is authoritarian statism (Poulantzas, 2016) with 'policing of the crisis' (Hall et al 1978/2013). Today we speak in terms of radical disagreement, or dissensus characterised by authoritarianism, tensions, polarisations and contradictions of our time, which have further intensified during the pandemic and post-pandemic era. There is a major disagreement, best attributed as dissensus, around the refugee and immigration phenomenon as the central feature of the time (Trimikliniotis, 2020a; 2022; Parsanoglou et al 2022). 'Dissensus' refers to more than the mere opposite of consensus or unanimity and primarily refers to a social and ideological situation of fundamental disagreement over the meaning of the terms of the disagreement and not simply lack or absence of political consensus. The term encompasses the fundamental disagreement on the major issues pertaining to immigration and asylum and how to address these in society.

Immigration and asylum are key issues in social work that challenge how we understand and how we do social work when dealing with xenoracist and exclusionary policies, discourses and practices. Social workers as public servants –that is, state employees – are called upon to implement state policies. However, implementing xenophobic or racist, sexist or other exclusionary policy fundamentally contradicts the basic professional ethical standards as declared by the Global Social Work Statement of Ethical Principles.[1]

Counteracting such exclusionary tendencies is possible but difficult (Mascocha, 2015). Activism becomes crucial in 'challenging harmful political contexts' (Briskman, 2019) beyond and against state policies, in the current polarised era. Immigration is a major challenge for the 21st century. A key to understanding disagreement in politics generally stems from the fact that immigration (forced and voluntary) is a major factor in social transformation causing broader social changes. Migration results in challenges that shake and question taken-for-granted assumptions in what Papastergiades (2000) refers to as 'the turbulence of migration'.

The making of a detention-welfare humanitarian crisis in Cyprus: overcrowding, complicit social work and hostile environment

It is impossible to understand how the current asylum system operates in Cyprus without connecting the refugee asylum and welfare system in Cyprus to broader migration and asylum flows, particularly since the COVID-19 pandemic. Cyprus, an island republic with a complex history of conflict, is located in the south-easternmost region of the Mediterranean, geographically and historically adjoining Europe, Asia and Africa. The two main communities on the island are Greek Cypriots and Turkish Cypriots.

Asylum and migration to Cyprus must be understood within the context of the geographical position and turbulent political and historical setting of the island, in which ethnic conflict between the two communities has dominated over all other social and political issues since the 1950s.[2] After the Turkish invasion the division of the island in 1974 created a new 180km-long border. The northern area is the unilaterally declared 'Turkish Republic of Northern Cyprus' (TRNC), recognised only by Turkey and administered by the Turkish Cypriots with the backing of the Turkish army. The southern area has been under control of the Republic of Cyprus since1964 and is administered by Greek Cypriots. The two parts of the island are separated by a buffer zone known as the 'Green Line', an area under control of the United Nations.

The southern, Greek-Cypriot controlled, part of the island has seen massive economic growth. The 'Cyprus economic miracle' (Christodoulou, 1992) was premised on cheap labour provided first by displaced persons and then by migrant labour, on state intervention and on international opportunities in a service-based economy following the collapse of the Lebanon and the regimes of the former communist bloc in eastern Europe. The country has been de facto divided since 1974 but there is no recognised border but a mere ceasefire line. The opening of checkpoints allowing crossings in 2003, one year prior to the Republic of Cyprus's accession to the European Union (EU) in 2004, was an important moment allowing social contact and economic cooperation. Both parts of the island saw economic growth during this period, despite the rejection of the UN plan to reunite the county by the Greek-Cypriots . However, this was brought to an abrupt end by the financial crisis that hit Cyprus in 2012. Even though the Republic of Cyprus is now enjoying economic growth, there has been a significant rise in inequality, poverty and precarity. In the northern part of the island, a collapse of the Turkish lira, mass inflation in Turkey and the energy crisis are causing major social and economic uncertainty.

In 2020, the situation of 'third-country nationals' and asylum-seekers changed suddenly and drastically with the outbreak of the COVID-19 pandemic: the number of applications halved, as pandemic restrictions made travelling harder for asylum-seekers, and the Republic of Cyprus refused to accept applications for three months. There was prolonged detentions, overcrowding and reception conditions deteriorated. There was a sharp rise in poverty and homelessness in community as the state failed to support asylum-seekers and migrants. In 2021 the number of applications returned to the level in 2019. Arrivals increased further in 2021 and 2022 saw the largest recorded numbers of irregular entry and asylum applications.

The island's location and history, the division and the buffer zone separating north and south attracted flows of migrants from Africa and the Middle East, who managed to enter the territory under the control of the Republic of Cyprus through unguarded points of the buffer zone. Upon the outbreak of the pandemic, the government introduced measures which would hardly have been seen as acceptable before. These included the suspension of the asylum system; pushbacks on land and at sea; the forced transfer of all asylum-seekers into camps and the conversion of the camps into closed centres; the placement of barbed wire at certain points along the buffer zone for the first time; and the policies that resulted in reducing the standards of the reception conditions to make the country less attractive. The numbers of asylum-seekers dropped significantly in 2020, even though government rhetoric about rising numbers continued unabated. With the relaxing of the pandemic measures, the lockdown and slowdown of the world economy increasing poverty and desperation of closure of more other routes to Europe led to an increase in the numbers of irregular entry. Also, the collapse of the Turkish Lira made living conditions for the refugees and migrants in the northern part of the country under the control of the unrecognised Turkish Republic of Northern Cyprus, mostly on student visas but illicitly working, unliveable. Many of them moved to areas under the Republic of Cyprus and applied for asylum (Trimikliniotis et al, 2023).

Before the pandemic, in spite of ministerial claims boosted by media reports, little evidence could be found that Cyprus had become a new route to the EU (Trimikliniotis, 2000b). Cyprus is an island state; it is not a member of the European Schengen Area; and the island is not thought of as a genuine geographical Eastern Mediterranean route to the EU. In 2021, as in 2019, there was an increase in the number of asylum applications in comparison to previous years, but the reasons for this rise are rather more complicated than the conspirator versions of 'hybrid war' by Turkey that are offered by the Republic of Cyprus government and amplified by a complicit media. There is some validity to the argument that restrictions numbers of asylum-seekers entering the EU, particularly in the way they were achieved, may well have had a disproportionate impact on EU border countries, such as Cyprus. However, this fails to explain why Cyprus is favoured as a route in comparison to other destinations which are closer and more accessible to continental Europe and where there are better prospects for a new, secure life and work. Asylum-seekers may choose Cyprus as a destination due to rising tensions and wars in countries of the Middle East and Africa, along with repressive measures by their regimes; or for other reasons. As people get more desperate and other destinations seem more difficult to reach, Cyprus is likely to see a further rise in migrant and asylum-seeker numbers. Cyprus is currently facing an increase in numbers of irregular entry and asylum applications, whilst other countries in EU have seen a decline. However, this must be relativised and scrutinised in context of the Government's decade-long refusal to adopt a migrant integration plan, the blockage of legal routes of entry and a cumbersome and bureaucratic asylum system with years-long delay in making asylum determinations. Cyprus' geographical location and the unrecognised regime in the north makes it a location for seeking refuge. The country is insufficiently prepared for the current developments. The country's asylum and immigrant labour systems are in serious need of reform, together with a necessary broader reform of the EU's Dublin Regulation. This explains why the tough anti-immigration rhetoric, policies and barriers in form of deterrent measures on land and at sea (including illegal pushbacks) – in short, the creation of a hostile environment – has not dented asylum-seekers from seeking refuge in Cyprus.

The pandemic revealed and widened the gaps in the healthcare system, which essentially excluded several categories of third-country nationals. Non-governmental organisations (NGOs) complained about major gaps in migrants' access to information about the pandemic and insufficient access to emergency care. Migrants and asylum-seekers faced disproportionate fines for failure to comply with the lockdown and movement restrictions. Although NGOs attempted to bridge some of these gaps by providing translations of pandemic measures and regulations and contacting the health authorities on migrants' behalf, they also experienced access problems themselves. During the pandemic remarkable acts of solidarity towards asylum-seekers and refugees emerged on the part of various informal groups.

Studies reveal that refugees face a serious housing problem, poverty, and difficulties in accessing benefits and rights – in violation of the basic reception conditions required by Cypriot and EU law. After the pandemic has come a humanitarian crisis (Demetriou and Trimikliniotis, 2021a; 2021b; 2021c). The pandemic restrictions led to the disruption of recreational activities for unaccompanied children in shelters, who were left alone with nothing to do. Information on protective measures was supplied to them only by NGOs. Unaccompanied minors who entered Cyprus during the first wave of the pandemic were denied access to asylum or to reception conditions. The pandemic complicated the processing of deportations of undocumented migrants, leading to the overcrowding of the police detention facilities, which were unprepared for the sudden increase in numbers and lacked health protocols (FRA, 2021a, 2021b, 2021c; Trimikliniotis, 2020b, 2020c).

The historical development of social services in Cyprus: complicity, failure and exclusion

In theory, social services must be made available to all those in need, irrespective of ethnicity, nationality or citizenship. Social welfare services (SWS) are obliged to accommodate and provide welfare benefits for asylum-seekers, as per the relevant Laws and EU reception condition Directives, and asylum-seekers may apply for social benefits, provided that they cannot meet their basic needs such as housing, food, clothes and monthly bills. Social workers employed by the SWS make an assessment the immediate needs of accommodation, food and/or psychosocial support. However, asylum-seekers face extreme poverty following their application for benefits, as the system is not automated and there are long delays in the provision of benefits.

Prior to the pandemic there were few studies on social work with refugees and migrants. Further development of professionalism in social work was called for, and gaps in the provision of social services for asylum-seekers and refugees were mentioned (Spaneas et al, 2018). However, various reports from those working with asylum-seekers did provide comprehensive critiques of failure, gaps and complicity in official social welfare and social work provision. Since the pandemic, the situation has become desperate for asylum-seekers, due to extreme homelessness, poverty, despair and overcrowding in reception centres,[3] as well as anti-immigration that is both rampant in the media and inflated by politicians and public office-holders (Demetriou and Trimikliniotis, 2022).

This is the current context in which social work operates in Cyprus. But this must be placed in a longer historical perspective. As with most other colonial contexts, the failures and complicity of social work in Cyprus must be located in the history of social services which were imposed from the top down, rather than a grassroots creature born of popular demand. Within the Cypriot colonial context, social work emerged as the product of a contradictory balance between 'social care' and 'social control' (Ioakimidis and Trimikliniotis, 2019a; 2019b). Essentially, British colonial social work theories, policies and practices were imported to Cyprus as tools to contain the discontent of the working classes and, more specifically, to tackle 'antisocial' behaviour among the poorest sections of the population, as demonstrated by colonial reports and decrees dealing with the issue of juvenile delinquency in some of the most impoverished areas of the island. By 1946, the British authorities had prioritised the establishment of a probation system infused by Victorian moralism and colonial oppression. Child labour and widespread poverty devastated the largest section of the island's population. Despite the strict religious ethos in both communities (Greek-Cypriots and Turkish-Cypriots), an increasing number of young people, totally alienated by their harsh living conditions and lack of prospects, engaged in petty crime and defiance of colonial rule. Nonconformity among many young people became particularly dangerous for the authorities, especially when seen in the context of anti-colonialism. Political activism was explicitly highlighted in the first report evaluating the need for an 'effective' probation system in Cyprus. Childcare, child adoption laws, social insurance and public benefits for the 'deserving destitute', which provided a totally new dimension in social work, were introduced in the 1950s during the last phases of British colonial rule. The profession was eventually modernised and relocated within the framework of a newly developed central welfare office. These developments embraced the international optimism of the time, which saw social work as an important tool for social development and psycho-social empowerment within a social democratic welfare state. It was hoped that the idea of generic social work linked to personal social services would help the profession to move away from politically ambiguous probation projects. The British colonial authorities saw welfare measures as tools that would contain labour agitation and 'help to divert the Greeks from their persistent calls for Union with Greece' (Triseliotis, 1977: 23). This is the basis of social work's history of complicity in Cyprus to serve the ultimate political aims and an ethos determined by those in power. However, the labour movement, aligned to the Left, developed an alternative, albeit elementary, social work from below, based on class solidarity, which was instrumental in the drive for reforms in favour of the working class (Ioakimidis and Trimikliniotis, 2019a; Neocleous, 2022).

Professionally speaking, postcolonial social work was a development of the colonial system in the communally organised newly independent republic. However, as with other institutions in Cyprus, it was shaped by the ethnic conflict in the 1960s, the war and the de facto partition since 1974 (Triseliotis, 1977; Ioakimidis and Trimikliniotis, 2019a).

Social work, in the immediate aftermath of war in 1974, centred on relocation, reconstruction and rapid economic development, due to the mass displacement of Greek-Cypriots from the northern part of the island. Things changed with the rapid economic growth based on mass tourism and services, financialisation and urbanisation, which saw the emergence of a different country from the poor, rural one of the 1950s. By the late 1980s migrant labour would take up the low-skilled jobs that Cypriots refused to do. Migrant workers were seen by policy makers as temporary 'working hands', not permanent workers. With the Republic of Cyprus's accession to the EU in 2004, policy makers thought that EU workers would replace third-country nationals. However, EU workers were employed in addition to third-country national migrant labour – the latest census of population shows that 21 per cent of all workers are third-country nationals.[4] Cheap migrant labour allowed the extension of the accumulation regime and played a massive role in economic development (Michael et al, 2005). It is a system brought about by the 'migration state of exception', which added another layer to the Cypriot states of exception (Trimikliniotis et al, 2012; Trimikliniotis, 2013): The notion of state of exception is a regime based in the logic of necessity in an exceptional situation requiring extraordinary measures that result in suspension of ordinary law and result in derogation of rights. This has taken a particular and prolonged form in the context of the Cyprus conflict (Constantinou, 2008; Trimikliniotis, 2018).

Today, poverty and exclusion are prevalent among the migrant and asylum-seeker population. Despite international scholarship documenting the importance of social work with asylum-seekers against racism (Masoscha, 2015), in Cyprus, state-based social work practice as well as research has neglected these populations for years.

Another solidarity in the time of pandemic: socialities and mobile commons

The emergence of solidarity towards refugees, asylum-seekers and migrants during the pandemic arose because of what is proving to be a humanitarian crisis, certainly exacerbated by the state's failure or refusal to act (asylum and welfare services). It is a kind of social work 'from below', to be sharply distinguished from the institutionally cultivated or officially sponsored practice of established charities and well-funded voluntaristic NGOs. The latter operate as classic quangos, in the sense that they function essentially as long arms of the state, always complicit in official anti-immigrant and anti-asylum policy. In the current climate of generating anti-immigrant moral panics (Hall et al, 2013[1978]) and a hostile climate (Goodfellow, 2019), these officially sponsored NGOs are merely replicating what the ministry instructs, leaving masses of asylum-seekers without help (Demetriou and Trimikliniotis, 2022). Alternative social work has emerged as activist networks in opposition to and defiance of the government-led anti-immigrant policy and discourses, and this type of social work has allowed a solidarity in praxis to emerge.

In this sense, the three-tiered functionalist taxonomy of solidarity offered by Prainsack and Buyx (2017) fails to capture the realities on the ground. Nonetheless, to locate the situation in Cyprus, we first critically examine the current debates over solidarity. Before the COVID-19 pandemic, Prainsack and Buyx (2017) aptly argued that there is a complex relationship between solidarity and pandemics, that is, pandemics do not automatically foster solidarity. They argue that 'rather than only celebrating solidarity where we see it happen, we need to build institutions and circumstances that can make solidarity stable and lasting' based on 'strong and well-funded public infrastructures' that increase 'the resilience of societies in times of crisis'. Prainsack (2020) examined how the COVID-19 crisis affected solidarity during the first months of the pandemic. She distinguished solidarity from 'other types of support and pro-social practice', locating solidarity as manifested at different levels: 'at the inter-personal level, the group level, or at the level of legal and contractual norms'. Drawing upon findings from ongoing studies on personal and societal effects of the COVID-19 crisis, she argues that:

> While forms of inter-personal solidarity have been shifting even during the first weeks and months of the crisis, the importance of institutionalized solidarity is becoming increasingly apparent. The most resilient societies in times of COVID-19 have not been those with the best medical technology or the strictest pandemic containment measures, but those with good public infrastructures and other solidaristic institutions. (Prainsack, 2020, p 124)

There is no automatic or guaranteed solidarity that emerges under difficult or oppressive circumstances, as this is contingent on a number other crucial social, cultural, ideological and political factors: solidarity is born not *in abstractum* but out of historic relations. Solidarity cannot be understood unless placed in a conflict-based societal paradigm of antagonistic social and political relations. However, hegemonic projects of the ruling blocks strive for social order and ideologically for the promotion of national-social cohesion promoting 'national solidarity'.

Solidarity is seen differently by the various sociological schools, as 'the concept of solidarity is applied to social theory and politics with different meanings and connotations' (Stjernø, 2005, p 2). Back in the mid-19th century, first it was Charles Furrier and Pierre Leroux, who were precursors of socialist and Marxist thought on solidarity. Then, Auguste Comte saw solidarity as a remedy for the increasing individualisation and atomisation of society, which he considered detrimental to the well-being of the collective.

There are also religious routes and readings of solidarity via Judaism, Christianity and Islam. Christian scholars such as Thomas Aquinas stressed community and fellowship between all humans as a key normative principle for the organisation of communal life. In the works of the famous Arab Muslim scholar Ibn Khaldun, 'asabiyah' is 'a systems approach to human cooperativeness and group solidarity' (Gierer, 2001).

Solidarity is invoked by different quarters today, but juridically it is a somewhat neglected concept. Even though it is elevated as a fundamental principle in EU law, as one of 'the foundations of a united Europe ... laid on fundamental ideas and values ... which the Member States' are obliged to act upon: 'The principle of solidarity of the European Union is a fundamental principle based on sharing both the advantages, i.e. prosperity, and the burdens equally and justly among members. The principle of solidarity is often used in the context of social protection' (EurWORK, 2011).

Mitas (2016) points out that of the 'three deities of the modern pantheon (freedom – equality – solidarity/fraternity)', the third was the least fortunate. Despite debates about the meaning and limits of freedom, and the depth and breadth of equality, solidarity remained the invisible aspect of the triptych. The few times when it was discussed, solidarity was seen either as a simple natural feeling (something, in short, indifferent to legal cohabitation) or as a voluntary duty: something that in law is a contradiction.

Marxists and other critical and conflict perspectives are generally critical of functionalist approaches to solidarity. However, solidarity is a crucial term within a class paradigm and is a key concept in workers' struggles and history. This is located as praxis within the processes of struggle as a manifestation of class consciousness, and took specific forms as means of international solidarity. Marx and Engels discuss the solidarity of their times, but they view this type of solidarity within the emancipatory project of the working classes and subaltern peoples. This is the working-class solidarity that transcends nations and borders, a bond that generates internationalism, contra the solidarity of the bourgeoisie, the class enemy. It is the solidarity of one class contra the solidarity of another. This perception of solidarity is not the same as a functionalist national solidarity that often predominates in public debates.

Mitas (2016) proposes a radical alternative reading of the philosophical foundation of solidarity, which performs a critical function. His approach criticises theories that deny (or conceal) the binding texture of solidarity, and proposes a perspective which reads the historical-social conditions that give rise to solidarity. He argues that solidarity represents 'a fundamental principle of justice, a condition of the possibility of legal cohabitation worth mentioning'. Also, he aptly sees it as 'an inherent principle of constitutional law', which enshrines specific regulatory content which acquires an affirmative dimension that requires independence for each and every one, which in turn requires everyone to contribute to the independence of others. Mitas (2016) proposes a Marxian-inspired reconstruction of the Kantian logic in terms of 'a fundamental right-to-debt binary' constructed as: citizens' demand for life independence is commensurate with a debt of solidarity they owe to each other, and the state demands the contribution of citizens to consolidate social solidarity towards debt for the consolidation of institutions of a substantial a welfare state.

Solidarity cannot be viewed as a fetishised or sanctifying category that exists, but as the emergence of multiple socialities in specific conjunctures. Drawing on Sitas (2004, 2008, 2010), who has illustrated this based on struggles and lives in South Africa, together with Parsanoglou and Tsianos (Trimikliniotis et al, 2016) we have illustrated but a fragment of what already exists: 'We are witnessing modes of livelihoods which are kinds of socialities, solidarities and connectivities long experienced in the Global South, the East and what was thought of as "backward Rest" and not in "the West" or the "Global North"' (Hall 1992). Solidarity in this sense is a manifestation of socialities as forms of consciousness whereby a deeper sense is externalised as praxis, not *in abstractum*. Of course, solidarity can be cultivated and enhanced as a product of socialisation processes. The 'ideological apparatuses', that is, institutions specialising for the purposes of reproduction, can enhance or undermine such processes. This is a dialectic where contested ideas are fought over: whose solidarity, whose boundaries, whose definition and delineations and what kind of solidary? E.P. Thompson (1964, p 13) notes various instances of solidarity as historic processes within class struggles. From the early days of industrial revolution, workers formed socialities built by their own senses of community in their daily lives and struggles: Thompson (1964, p 583) invites us to 'imagine the solidarity of the community' and 'the extreme isolation of the authorities'.

As Tony Negri (2003, p 77) has it: 'Consciousness rises up – not as a utopian element, but as a real one – as consciousness of collective antagonism, or rather, of antagonistic collectivity. As we have seen, time is collective and productive essence.' The Marxian and Marxist conception of solidarity is not classless, but class centred, born out of the class struggles and culture of community derived via resistance and through the development of class consciousness vis-à-vis the opposing class, and this is inseparable from internationalism. Here internationalism is a 'duty' derived from the recognition that this is a precondition for emancipation.[5] In the political activism of Marx this is more than apparent, and is adopted by the founding declaration of the First International, which finishes by underscoring that 'the emancipation of the working classes requires their fraternal concurrence', and in the slogan, now inscribed on Marx's grave, 'Proletarians of all countries, unite!' (Marx 2000[1864]).

The story, however, does not stop there. Inevitably class is entangled with race, gender, coloniality and migration in a manner that makes consciousness, sociality and solidarity complex and contested, even among the subaltern. For instance, race and class oppression had wide acceptance, not only by the bourgeoisie, but also within the working class. Hence, Ron Ramden (2017, p 507) spoke about race and class oppression being incorporated within and shaping 'a national working-class consciousness'. Exclusionary politics ensured that 'there ain't no black in the Union Jack', in the emblematic book title of Paul Gilroy (1987). The starting point is E.P. Thompson's classic work on 'the making of the English working class' as a cultural formation through their own experiences as 'embodied in traditions, value systems, ideas and institutional forms' (Thompson, 1964, p 10–11). Pitched against the racism and class oppression via the practices and policies of British capital which 'received the general endorsement of the white working class', Ramdin (2017, p 504) illustrates the processes in cultural terms, as Black people have been in Britain since Roman times, as the 'Blackmores' presence dates from 1555.

Gender here is no peripheral matter to be subordinated to race or class. It is a dimension of oppression and identity and a vector of social organisation. Gender, coloniality and migration under capitalism generate complex dimensions of exploitation and oppression, but these must read in context via the specific immigration and accumulation regimes. Black feminist thought, as well as not quite White feminist thought, has been critical of the ways anti-racism and equality struggles tend to marginalise gender issues (Anthias and Yuval-Davis, 1992). Bordering processes, intersectionality and transnational belonging require that we search specifically for socialities, alliances and solidarities that emerge from struggles in specific contexts (Yuval-Davis et al, 2019; Anthias, 2020). Speaking then in general terms is not only 'nebulous' but 'a subterfuge in the political rhetoric to hide the fact that it is missing or on the decline in the real world' (Stjernø, 2005, p 2) or, even worse, to conceal the fact that the nationalist working class wants a subordinate and docile migrant working class in the labour hierarchy. Moreover, the politics of solidarity cannot hide the real difficulties on the ground in forging alliances when complex dimensions of oppression, exploitation, power relations and hierarchies, competing ideological and political projects and priorities are manifested in social divisions, fragmentations, precarisation and antagonisms, are in fact fracturing the unity in action and solidarities flowing from the consciousness of a mythical 'unitary working class'.

Precarity has become a key feature in the processes, rendering the precariat a protagonist in the current post-Fordist world (Standing, 2011). This generates highly fluid, transitional, uncertain and contradictory situations. Different processes emerge via the destruction of old 'unities' or assumed unities, generating and reassembling new forms of subjectivities and resistance are transforming social struggles and movements as we have known them (Trimikliniotis et al, 2016). This was apparent prior to the mass exodus from conflict zones in Syria, the Middle East and northern Africa –often described as the 'Mediterranean refugee crisis', whereby the eastern Mediterranean became the most populous route for refugees to enter the European borders in their desperate journey to the prosperous EU core. In previous work, the realities of the eastern Mediterranean boundary triangle illustrate infinite survival struggles, articulations and claims in precarious spaces that can be illuminating in different ways. In the current debates, dominated by alarmist binaries between regimes of humanitarian compassion and military crusades against smugglers, the reading of such struggles may offer some pointers for alternative approaches. Such readings can provide us with insights into the processes of precarity routing, sharing and 'commoning' to prevail over borders of immigration surveillance, suppression and violence. Escape is both resistance and survival (Papadopoulos et al, 2008). This where 'solidarity' must be connected to 'mobile commons':

> It is the reconstruction and reconnection of the fragmentations or disjointed fractures in the specific forms of praxis that allows for the particular to be 'captured' as theoretical snapshots allowing for both politics and theory to emerge. The notion of *mobile commons* allows us to locate the trail, the marks or scratches punctuated on the global canvas of precarity of people constantly on the move, as precarity is deeply punctuated in their *modus operandi*. Labour then is not confined to work or the work place; labour is a force or energy propelling us 'forward' or 'back and forth' that is derived from our vitality-as-existence (survival, pleasure and revolutionary imagination): it is propelling forces of labour forward in opposition to the sense of death shaping the sphere of praxis – thus time (of labour and struggle) is '*morphologized*', that is, it takes a particular shape and form, or it is *spatialized*. (Trimikliniotis et al 2016, p 137)

Solidarity and social work from below during the pandemic

The question of socialities and solidarity is an empirical one derived from the concrete situation in the current polarising context of anti-immigration hysteria launched by the government in Cyprus (Trimikliniotis, 2020b; Demetriou and Trimikliniotis, 2022), which has resulted in the shrinking of the democratic public sphere, imposing all sorts of pressures on civic organisations for civil society action (Demetriou and Trimikliniotis, 2021). We are witnessing solidarity towards migrants and refugees in Cyprus during the pandemic years which seems to be emerging as part of the social 'magma' (Castoriadis, 1994). From the outset of the pandemic, solidarity, as opposed to the repressive logic of the restrictive measures imposed, was the alternative, a creative potential, drawing on the resources of communities across the globe (Ioakimidis, 2020).

At an activistic level, solidarity practices emerged immediately with the lockdown, as various small local initiatives began to converge to create a country-based initiative. This is neither a charity-based approach, nor one that relies on the state. As state policy became repressive, with the arrest and mass encampment of asylum-seekers, and flatly refused to offer any support to migrants and asylum-seekers, more action-based initiatives grew. In this sense, we are witnessing in the polarised context of Cyprus a 'reassembling [of] the social', which forces us to rethink our sociological terms (Latour, 2005, p 261). All this in opposition to the hegemonic racist and anti-migrant discourses which justify the policies of encampment, marginalisation, neglect and abandonment versus the various manifestations of solidarity of praxis. 'Actor-networks' are creatively engaging in the process of making spaces for praxis.

> 'I find amazing that we can connect with people from so many different backgrounds: we work together because we have a common purpose, and we all bring our own perspectives, ideas and resources! Also, what is amazing is that we connect with so many youngsters who have just finished their studies but are unemployed and refused to be drawn to the set ways of their conservative parents who don't see the mass poverty, hunger and homelessness of migrants as *their* problem. We connect across generations, something I never saw before!' (Interview with activist JA, 30 January 2022)

But what is at the heart of these sentiments expressed by one of the activists?

> 'We are dealing with a revolt of the young. This is what I can deduce from what I was told by a young woman in her late 20s or early 30s who joined via WhatsApp and became active in collecting and delivering basic goods to asylum-seekers who are homeless and freezing during this unusually cold winter. After finishing her university studies, she is happy just to get some income to get by and do activistic work. As she told me: "I cannot just get a regular office job and pretend that nothing is happening around me! I am unemployed now, but I simply need some income to carry on what I am doing. Is this too much to ask?"' (Interview with activist JA, 30 January 2022)

Facing the humanitarian crisis, the state is refusing to provide support, but also blames asylum-seekers and migrants for their plights. The Minister for the Interior regularly describes asylum-seekers as 'irregular migrant flows … an illegal invasion of people in the government-controlled areas, as part of Turkey's moves to change Cyprus' demographics'.[6]

Social work from below has emerged in defiance and in opposition to such extreme policies and rhetoric. Activists see how precarious living in squalor and misery, in camps or in the community, forces many African asylum-seekers and refugees to take up any jobs in exploited and low-skill areas is the reality for many.

It is apparent that the praxis of solidarity as a manifestation of sociality and consciousness emerges via alliances between those committed to collective and individual praxis and those in need themselves. Breaking and overcoming barriers and ethnic borders produces a specific 'time and space for solidarity', in the words of Agustin and Jorgerberg (2016), contra the pessimism of our times: the crisis of (state) solidarity produces 'a solidarity as a political action which enhances alternatives to existing policies on refugees and asylum seekers' (Agustin and Jorgerberg, 2019, p 129). The colonial and postcolonial subaltern speaks and creates in late Althusserian terms this is a product of the 'aleatory materialism of the encounter' to produce what is so far an uncharted terrain (Althusser, 2006).

A simple typology summarising these processes makes apparent that an osmosis is at work that brings together persons from different national, ethic and social backgrounds, as well as from different perspectives. What is crucial is how the vast majority draw on migration experiences and knowledge. Many activists are migrants themselves. Mostly they are settled migrants from different countries: a retired social worker from the UK, a doctor, many students (both Cypriot and foreign); refugees and asylum-seekers who are active; settled migrants with shops or restaurants; persons from the diaspora bringing to Cyprus their own experiences and knowledge of activism from abroad. One activist who comes from Thessaloniki was very active in solidarity work with refugees who were stuck in Edomeni in Greece during the Greek refugee crisis. Now he is a student residing in Cyprus and one of the most persistent and reliable activists, willing to defy the authorities and take risks to deliver basic necessities to refugees, even during the lockdown period.

Another cohort are workers and retired persons who identify with the Left. As one woman activist told us: "If we don't do something now to support refugees and migrants in need what sort of Left-wing people are we? Where is our internationalism? If you are on the Left you are anti-racist and must show your support when another human is in need!" (Interview with activist AL, 30 January 2022). She regularly collects and distributes food and clothing and is an organiser. Another activist has been an organiser since her student years; now a teacher, she is one the most active organisers.

A third cohort is organised around the Catholic religious charity Caritas. However, unlike the middle-class Red Cross, which has simply failed or refused to distribute the supplies it has stockpiled in its storage rooms, they have been among the most active in offering support via the 'dignity centre',[7] which offers free a supermarket and an evening centre, organises soup kitchens, mobilises support and distributes food and clothing.[8]

A fourth cohort is around groups of anarchists, who have also been active in providing shelter and support during the current crisis.

This is a process still in in the making; new groups are emerging, both formal and informal. As the crisis takes on new shapes and forms due to the pandemic, economic crises, wars, conflicts, refugeehood and dispossession in the world, and as racialised border regimes generate a hostile environment, resistance manifests itself in different forms of socialities and solidarities.

Conclusion

We have shown that the story of official (that is, state centred) social work in Cyprus since colonial times has been one of complicity rather than resistance. This has been shaped by the protracted conflict that has resulted in the coup, invasion and continuing de facto division of the country, the financial crisis (that hit Cyprus late) and the pandemic crisis. This is a process of reshaping social work, both the complicit practice and the non-state social-work-as-resistance based on initiatives from below. Currently, 'migration and asylum' is a crucial socio-political issue in this divided country located at the crossroads of continents in the eastern Mediterranean and in a problematic triangle with Greece and Turkey. This social work *in extremis* has emerged through initiatives from below and beyond state and established (private) institutions and complicit state-funded quangos, which are either outright hostile or simply failing (again) at moments of necessity like the pandemic crisis. Praxis-based socialities are manifested in the form of solidarity work emerging from a humanitarian crisis. The initiatives *in extremis* have emerged in the context of activists' encounter with an internationalist outlook, new migrant/refugee socialities and mobile commons via active engagement on the ground. This is a process of remaking radical social work and politics from below.

The turmoil as well as the symptoms of love, epidemics and multiple socialities (among them, one that can be termed solidarity) are there, but they are neither automatic nor mechanically constructed. They have emerged at a time when the state refused or collapsed. We have seen this even in the most extreme circumstances, as 'social work in extremis' (Lavalette and Ioakimidis, 2011). In pandemic and post-pandemic times, as wars, conflicts, environmental and economic crises ensue, new manifestations of social work *in extremis* as a praxis of solidarity from below are emerging. This inspires hope in a hopeless world.

Notes
1   See www.ifsw.org/global-social-work-statement-of-ethical-principles/#:~:text= Social%20workers%20must%20not%20allow,workers%20must%20act%20w ith%20integrity
2   After the coup by the Greek junta and local paramilitaries, the Turkish invasion and the de facto division of the island in 1974, the regime in the north unilaterally declared independence as the Turkish Republic of Northern Cyprus (TRNC) in 1983; so far, only Turkey has recognised it.
3   Such as CyRC, 2021, 2022; Demetriou and Trimikliniotis, 2021a, 2021b, 2021c).
4   The total number of foreign nationals amounts to 193,300 and corresponds to 21.1 per cent of the total population, Cyprus Statistical Service (2021) *Census of Population and Housing 2021: Preliminary Results*, 18 May 2022, www.pio.gov. cy/en/press-releases-article.html?id=27965#flat.
5   This is apparent, inter alia, in Part II, 'Proletarians and Communists', of *The Communist Manifesto*.
6   Kades (2022) 'Cyprus has no choice but to fence off green line: Interior minister', *Cyprus Mail*, 16 October.
7   www.facebook.com/DignityCentreNicosia
8   caritascyprus.org/

References

Agustin, Ó.G. and Jorgerberg, M.J. (eds) (2016) *Solidarity Without Borders: Gramscian Perspectives on Migration and Civil Society Alliances*. London: Pluto Press.

Agustin, Ó.G. and Jorgerberg, M.J. (2019) *Solidarity and the 'Refugee Crisis' in Europe*. London: Palgrave Macmillan.

Althusser, L. (2006) *Philosophy of the Encounter: Later Writings, 1978–1987*. Edited by O. Corpet and F. Matheron. London: Verso.

Anthias, F. (2020) *Translocational Belongings: Intersectional Dilemmas and Social Inequalities*. London: Routledge.

Anthias, F. and Yuval-Davis, F. (1992) *Racialized Boundaries: Race, Nation, Gender, Colour and Class and the Anti-Racist Struggle*. London; New York: Routledge.

Boyer, R. (2021) *Οι καπιταλισμοί στην δίνη της πανδημίας* (Capitalism in the Midst of the Pandemic). Athens: Polis.

Briskman, L. (2019) 'Challenging harmful political contexts through activism', in S.A. Webb (ed) *The Routledge Handbook of Critical Social Work*. London: Routledge, pp 549–559.

Castoriadis, C. (1994) 'The logic of magmas and the question of autonomy', *Philosophy & Social Criticism*, 20(1–2): 123–154. doi: 10.1177/ 019145379402000108

Christodoulou, D. (1992) *Inside the Cyprus Miracle, the Labours of an Embattled Mini-Economy*. Minneapolis: University of Minnesota.

Constantinou C. M. (2008) 'On the Cypriot States of Exception', *International Political Sociology* 2: 145–164.

CyRC (2021a) *Addressing Housing Needs of Vulnerable Asylum Seekers/Refugees in the Community*, Report funded by the US Department of State Embassy in Cyprus; implemented by the Cyprus Refugee Council.

CyRC (2022) *Country Report: Cyprus*, Cyprus Refugee Council, The Asylum Information Database (AIDA), coordinated by the European Council on Refugees and Exiles (ECRE), updated in April 2022. Available from: https://asy lumineurope.org/wp-content/uploads/2022/04/AIDA_CY_2021update.pdf

Demetriou, C. and Trimikliniotis, N. (2021a) *Migration: Key Fundamental Rights Concerns – Bulletin 1 – 2021, Fundamental Rights Agency of the EU*, Cyprus Report for the European Union Agency for Fundamental Rights, 1 October and 31 December 2020.

Demetriou, C. and Trimikliniotis, N. (2021b) *Migration: Key Fundamental Rights Concerns – Bulletin 2 – 2021, Fundamental Rights Agency of the EU*, Cyprus Report for the European Union Agency for Fundamental Rights, 1 January and 30 June 2021.

Demetriou, C. and Trimikliniotis, N. (2021c) *Migration: Key Fundamental Rights Concerns – Bulletin 3– 2021, Fundamental Rights Agency of the EU*, Cyprus Report for the European Union Agency for Fundamental Rights, 1 July and 30 September 2021.

Demetriou, C. and Trimikliniotis, N. (2021d) *Legal Environment and Space of Civil Society Organisations in Supporting Fundamental Rights*, Cyprus, Report for the Fundamental Rights Agency of the EU, January. Available from: https://fra. europa.eu/sites/default/files/fra_uploads/franet_cyprus_civic_space_2021.pdf

Demetriou, C. and Trimikliniotis, N. (2022) *Migration and Asylum during the Age of the COVID-19 Pandemic: A Report on Cyprus*, Friedrich-Ebert-Stiftung (FES) July. Available from: https://library.fes.de/pdf-files/bueros/ zypern/19499.pdf

EurWORK (2011) 'Solidarity principle', EurWORK European Observatory of Working Life, Eurfound.

FRA (2021a) *Migration: Key Fundamental Rights Concerns – Bulletin 1 – 2021*, Fundamental Rights Agency of the EU, 1 October and 31 December 2020, Migration: Key Fundamental Rights Concerns – Bulletin 1 – 2021, European Union Agency for Fundamental Rights (europa.eu).

FRA (2021b) *Migration: Key Fundamental Rights Concerns – Bulletin 2 – 2021*, Fundamental Rights Agency of the EU, 1 January and 30 June 2021, Migration: Key Fundamental Rights Concerns – Bulletin 2 – 2021, European Union Agency for Fundamental Rights (europa.eu).

FRA (2021c) *Migration: Key Fundamental Rights Concerns – Bulletin 3 – 2021*, Fundamental Rights Agency of the EU, 1 July and 30 September 2021. Available from: https://fra.europa.eu/en/publication/2021/migration-key-fundamental-rights-concerns-bulletin-3-2021

Gierer, A. (2001) 'Ibn Khaldun on solidarity ("asabiyah") – Modern science on cooperativeness and empathy: A comparison', *Philosophia Naturalis* 38: 91–104.

Gilroy, P. (1987) *There Ain't no Black in the Union Jack: The Cultural Politics of Race and Nation.* London: Hutchinson.

Goodfellow, M. (2019) *Hostile Environment: How Immigrants Became Scapegoats.* London: Verso Press.

Gramsci, A. (1971) *Selections from the Prison Notebooks.* London: Lawrence and Wishart.

Hall, S. (1992) 'The West and the rest: Discourse and power', in S. Hall and B. Gieben (eds) *Formations of Modernity.* Cambridge: Open University and Blackwell, pp 275–295.

Hall, S., Critcher, C., Jefferson, T., Clarke, J. and Roberts, B. (2013 [1978]) *Policing the Crisis, Mugging, the State and Law and Order* (2nd edn). London: Routledge.

Ioakimidis, V. (2020) 'Η παγκόσμια αλληλεγγύη την εποχή της πανδημίας', Διαδράσεις σε Καραντίνα, 26 April. Available from: https://dialogos.com. cy/diadraseis-i-pagkosmia-allileggyi-tin-epochi-tis-pandimias/

Ioakimidis, V. and Trimikliniotis, N. (2019a) 'Social work and the Cyprus problem: The challenges of reconciliation in de facto divided and crisis-ridden society', in J. Duffy and J. Campbell (eds) *International Perspectives on Social Work and Political Conflict.* London: Routledge, pp 79–93.

Ioakimidis, V. and Trimikliniotis, N. (2019b) 'Imperialism, colonialism and a Marxist epistemology of "critical peace"', in S.A. Webb (ed) *The Routledge Handbook of Critical Social Work*, Abingdon: Routledge Handbooks Online, pp 560–571.

Latour, B. (2005) *Reassembling the Social: An Introduction to Actor-Network-Theory*, Oxford: Oxford University Press.

Lavalette, M. and Ioakimidis, V. (eds) (2011) *Social Work in Extremis: Lessons for Social Work Internationally.* Bristol: Policy Press.

Marx, K. (2000[1864]) *International Working Men's Association,* Marx & Engels Internet Archive (marxists.org) 2000. Available from: www.marxists.org/archive/marx/works/1864/10/27.htm

Masocha, S. (2015) *Asylum Seekers, Social Work and Racism.* Basingstoke: Palgrave Macmillan.

Michael, M., Hadjiyiannis, C., Stephanides, M., Christofides, L. and Clerides, S. (2005) 'Οι οικονομικές επιδράσεις των ξένων εργατών στην Κύπρο' (The economic consequences of the presence of foreign workers in Cyprus) *Δοκίμια Οικονομικής Πολιτικής* No 10–05 December. Available from: www.ucy.ac.cy/erc/documents/DOP10-05.pdf

Mitas, S. (2016) *Η αλληλεγγύη ως θεμελιώδης αρχή δικαίου.* Athens: Sakis Karagiorgas Foundation.

Negri, A. (2003) *Time for Revolution.* London: Bloomsbury.

Neocleous, G. (2022) *Κοινωνικά κινήματα ως φορείς αλλαγής, Μια κοινωνική ανάλυση του λαϊκού εργατικού κινήματος στην Κύπρο* (Social Movements as Carriers of Social Changes: A Social Analysis of Popular Labour Movement in Cyprus). Athens: Iambos.

Papadopoulos, D., Stephenson, N. and Tsianos, V. (2008) *Escape Routes: Control and Subversion in the Twenty-First Century*. London: Pluto Press.

Papastergiadis, N. (2000) *The Turbulence of Migration: Globalization, Deterritorialization and Hybridity*. Cambridge: Polity.

Parsanoglou, D., Spyropoulou, G., Trimikliniotis, N. and Tsianos, V. (2021) 'Η μεταναστευτική/προσφυγική κινητικότητα στα χρόνια της πανδημίας: η κρίση πριν και μετά' ('Migration/refugee mobility in the years of pandemic: the crisis before and after)', in A. Kapsalis, V. Koumarianos and N. Kourachanis (eds) *Κοινωνική Πολιτική και Αυταρχικός Νεοφιλελευθερισμός την Περίοδο της Πανδημίας* Covid-19 (Social Policy and Social Policy and Authoritarian Neoliberalism in the Period of the Covid-19 Pandemic). Athens: Topos.

Poulantzas, N. (2016) *State, Power, Socialism*. London: Verso.

Prainsack, B. (2020) Solidarity in Times of Pandemics, *Democratic Theory* 7(2: 124–133. www.berghahnjournals.com/view/journals/democratic-the ory/7/2/dt070215.xml

Prainsack, B. and Buyx, A. (2017) *Solidarity in Biomedicine and Beyond* (Cambridge Bioethics and Law). Cambridge: Cambridge University Press.

Ramdin, R. (2017) *The Making of the Black Working Class in Britain*. London: Verso.

Sassoon, D. (2021) *Morbid Symptoms, Anatomy of a World in crisis*. London: Verso,

Sitas, A. (2004) *Voices that Reason: Theoretical Parables*. Pretoria: University of South Africa Press.

Sitas, A. (2008) *The Ethic of Reconciliation*. Durban/New Delhi: Madiba Press.

Sitas, A. (2010) *The Mandela Decade 1990–2000: Labor, Culture and Society in Post-apartheid South Africa*. Pretoria: Unisa Press.

Spaneas. S., Cochliou, D., Zachariades, A., Neocleous, G. and Apostolou, M. (2018) 'The living conditions of asylum-seekers in Cyprus', Report for UNHCR Office in the Republic of Cyprus, 2018. doi: 10.13140/ RG.2.2.16208.05121

Standing, G. (2011) *The Precariat: The New Dangerous Class*. New York: Bloomsbury.

Stjernø, S. (2005) *Solidarity in Europe: The History of an Idea*. Cambridge: Cambridge University Press.

Thompson, E.P. (1964) *The Making of the English Working Class*. London: Vintage Press.

Trimikliniotis, N. (2013) 'Migration and free movement of workers: EU Law, Crisis and the Cypriot States of Exception', *Laws* 2(4): 440–468.

Trimikliniotis, N. (2020a) *Migration and Refugee Dissensus in Europe: Borders, Insecurity and Austerity*. London: Routledge.

Trimikliniotis, N. (2020b) *Cyprus as a New Refugee 'Hotspot' in Europe? Challenges for a Divided Country*, Report for Friedrich-Ebert-Stiftung.

Trimikliniotis, N. (2020c) 'COVID, re-racialisation of migrants and the "refugee crisis"', in M. Lavalette, V. Ioakimidis and I. Ferguson (eds) *Social Work and COVID-19*. Bristol: Policy Press, pp 137–144.

Trimikliniotis, N., Ioakimoglou, E. and Pantelides, P. (2012) 'A political economy of division, development and crisis: Envisioning reunification beyond the Cyprus economic miracle', in N. Trimikliniotis and U. Bozkurt (eds) *Beyond A Divided Cyprus: A State and Society in Transformation*. New York: Palgrave Macmillan, pp 217–247.

Trimikliniotis, N., Parsanoglou, D. and Tsianos, V.S. (2016) 'Mobile commons and/in precarious spaces: Mapping migrant struggles and social resistance', *Critical Sociology* 42(7–8): 1035–1049. doi: 10.1177/0896920515614983

Trimikliniotis, N. (2018) 'The proliferation of Cypriot states of exception, The Erosion of Fundamental Rights as Collateral Damage of the Cyprus Problem', *Cyprus Review* 30(2) Fall: 43–84.

Trimikliniotis, N. (2022) 'Migration and asylum: "Dissensus" as a sociological concept in European politics', in A. Sitas, S. Damodaran, A. Pande, W. Keim and N. Trimikliniotis (eds) *Scripting of Defiance: Four Sociological Vignettes*. New Delhi: Tulika Press, pp 56–90.

Triseliotis, J. (1977) *Social Welfare in Cyprus*. London: Zeno.

13

Institutionalisation of certain children and mothers in Ireland: reflections on the 'troubled history' of child welfare social work

Caroline McGregor

Introduction

The premise of this book is that 'by engaging with both the oppressive and resistant histories of the social work profession, this book aims to contribute to a more nuanced and fulsome account of our profession's history'. In this chapter, the role of Irish social work in relation to institutionalisation and mass incarceration is explored to contribute to this work. A history of the present perspective, derived from the work of Michel Foucault, scaffolds this work (Skehill, 2007). Such an approach recognises continuities and discontinuities between past and present in terms of 'dominant' and 'minority' discourses. It implies a view of history as a fluid and nebulous phenomenon that looks and feels differently depending on the perspective from which we view it. A history of the present approach rejects revisionism, whereby we judge the past from the vantage point of the present. It is an approach that facilitates the capturing of a complex and contradictory history that shows both positive and negative forces. Such an approach avoids defensivism, denial or blame and promotes critical constructive analysis of history which informs the present and the future.

The chapter begins with a brief note on the history of institutions for women and children in Ireland, directing the reader to sources to explore this theme in further depth, followed by a section focusing on the 'received history' of child welfare in Ireland. This is followed by a commentary on the *Final Report of the Commission of Investigation into the Mother and Baby Homes* (2021) (FRCIMBH) for illustration. A number of themes pertinent to the report are explored that impacted on the context of social work during the latter part of the 20th century. The discussion emphasises the importance of a critically informed historical perspective that captures the complex and contradictory nature of practice. It highlights the need for further critical analysis of the role of the social work profession in practices of institutionalisation and deinstitutionalisation that often led to systematic abuses, human rights violations, treatment of certain children and their mothers as objects of control rather than subjects of care and widespread evidenced abuse, neglect and discrimination, especially towards women who had children outside of marriage ('unmarried mothers') and their 'illegitimate' children.

A note on mass institutionalisation and incarceration of women and children in Ireland during the 20th century

Institutional care was the dominant form of 'welfare' for children in need ('illegitimate', poor, destitute, subject to neglect or abuse) and mothers (mostly 'unmarried mothers' as well as destitute parents) in Ireland throughout the 20th century (Raftery and O Sullivan, 1999; Reidy, 2009). These institutions included workhouses (welfare homes), county homes, Magdalen Laundries, industrial schools, reformatories, Mother and Baby Homes and related institutions (Earner-Byrne, 1997, Earner-Byrne, 2003; Glynn, 2015). Most of the 'institutions' – except the state workhouse and associated institutions – were run by religious orders, many supported by the state through a capitation fee system to deliver these services. This history of institutionalisation in Ireland is complex and warrants separate critical analysis in itself. Buckley and McGregor argue that 'for many children who grew up in institutions in Ireland, their experience was objectification, lack of power and absence of a champion for their human rights' (Buckley and McGregor, 2019, p 1068). This is borne out in personal testimonials and multiple critical analyses (Doyle, 1989; Raftery and O' Sullivan, 1999; Maguire and Ó'Cinnéide, 2005; Tyrell, 2006; Keenan, 2012).

Three major themes are highlighted by Buckley and McGregor (2019) regarding institutional care in Ireland during the 20th century to help capture the complexity of context. These are: the link between institutions and economics (Buckley 2013); issues relating to parentage and gender (see, for example, Luddy and Murphy, 1990; McAvoy, 1999; Kennedy, 2004); and the symbiotic relationship between the state and the church (Whyte, 1980; Inglis, 1987; Kenny, 2000; Buckley and McGregor, 2019). Further important themes to consider include: the role of religious orders in the delivery of core social services (Clear, 1987), histories of childhood and categorisation of children (Maguire, 2009; Buckley, 2013; Luddy and Smith, 2014) and counter-practices of deinstitutionalisation'. In Ireland, the latter relates especially to adoption from institutions under the legislation of the Adoption Act 1952 as well as in violation of that legislation through secret, coerced, forced and/or illegal adoption (Milotte, 1997; Maguire, 2002; McCaughren and McGregor, 2018). Practices of fostering and boarding out, less scrutinised to date, also need consideration.

In these histories there is a complex web of influences that shaped practices of institutionalisation in Ireland during the 20th century. While care should be taken to avoid generalisation, the evidence we have compellingly confirms that child welfare was mostly controlled via a symbiotic and powerful relationship between the Catholic Church organisations and state systems, at local and national level. The power of patriarchy and moralism pervaded society and its effects were felt most harshly by women who were deemed to go outside of the 'ideal' of motherhood and womanhood – such as by having children outside of wedlock in a context where marriage has special protection (to this day) in the Irish Constitution – and by the children born as 'illegitimate', a word used up to the 1980s in Ireland.

This history is very much alive to present-day social work practice. 'Retrospective disclosure' of abuse has become a major current practice, with focus on child welfare, incorporating responses to persons abused within institutions, still very much in its infancy (Mooney, 2018). Adoption social work services are intrinsically focused on persons in the present seeking information and tracing of their pasts in a complex and contested context (McCaughren and McGregor, 2018). The need to intrinsically examine the connection between social work and the Catholic Church, especially, in Ireland is described as an ethical imperative for present-day practice by Flynn (2021). The need for an enhanced awareness of the need to know and understand the past, to respond in the present, is palpable. The publication of the FRCIMBH has intensified this necessity for greater attention to history, as it has illuminated social work's troubled and complicit history with regard, specifically, to the institutionalisation and incarceration of certain children and mothers in Ireland. There is much to be learned from this illustrative example, as is discussed in this chapter. To contextualise this consideration, the next section reflects on 'received' histories – that which is 'known' to date – of child welfare social work in Ireland.

'Received history' of child welfare social work in Ireland

Three dates marked the main historical developments in child protection and welfare services in the mid- to late 20th century: 1970, 1980 and 1991. In 1970, there was a major inquiry into industrial schools as the dominant form of institutional care (*Kennedy Report*, 1970). It was also the year marking the development of a comprehensive welfare system, including state child welfare, under the Health Act 1970. The publication of a report on a *Task Force on Child Care Services* (1980) consolidated the move away from institutional care and towards family support and community-based care and services. The introduction of new legislation in 1991 that replaced the 1908 Children Act (in place since before Ireland became independent from Britain) and its relevant amendments sets the historical context for present–day practice (see Burns and McGregor, 2015; Devaney and McGregor, 2017).

Skehill (1999a, 1999b, 2000, 2003, 2004), criticised histories of the development of child protection and welfare in Ireland at that time for presuming too linear, gradual and progressive a connection between these key moments. Skehill argued that while these 'key moments' were pivotal, there was much that went before this. For example, there was a statutory child welfare practice in boarding traced back to 1862. This included support to some children in institutions, placed there by the state, and a small number of 'children's officers' were employed from the 1940s onwards, some of whom were qualified social workers. Social workers were employed in Ireland from the beginning of the 20th century (Kearney and Skehill, 2005). Most employment up to 1970 was in welfare departments, hospitals (as almoners or psychiatric social workers) and some community settings. However, social workers were also working in the fields of child welfare, adoption and support to 'unmarried mothers'. As far back as the mid-1930s, organisations such as the Joint Committee of Women's Societies and Women Social Workers were calling for legal adoption and support for unmarried mothers and Inspectors of Boarded Out children (predecessors to statutory social work) were instrumental in advocating against institutionalisation and lack of regulation of children in foster care (boarded out) throughout the mid-20th century.

Skehill (2004) argued that social work was mainly a 'minority' discourse, separated somewhat from the dominant institutional practices of the state and church. This minority development was depicted as vacillating between the influences of secular, mostly UK-based, training in social work vis-à-vis the dominant religious organisations, socio-spiritualism and a symbiotic relationship between church and state in Ireland. While practices and experiences of institutionalisation feature strongly in Skehill's historical accounts of social work, they most often provided critical context to the 'majority' discourse. Insufficient attention was paid to the relationship between dominant institutions such as industrial schools, reformatory schools, Mother and Baby Homes, county homes and related institutions involved in the accommodation of certain categories of children and mothers. However, as is discussed later, this separation from the development of professional social work from dominant institutional practices must be questioned from the vantage point of the present. Thus we have another 'received history' to challenge in the 21st century.

Just like the first 'received history', much of what has already been presented remains factually correct. Historically, and in the present, social workers are generally not employed within institutional settings. Up to 1970, most 'residential workers' were members of the religious orders who either directly owned and ran the homes or did so on behalf of the state alongside a mix of lay workers, trained and untrained. Two distinct pathways of training have evolved since the 1970s in the field of residential child care, and later 'social care' alongside professional social work. Perhaps this distinctiveness has reinforced the distancing from social work with histories of institutionalisation and has led to less focus to date on the role of the profession and individuals within it. However, while only few social workers were employed within the institutions, they/we interacted with them in child welfare practice, work with 'unmarried mothers', engagement in deinstitutionalisation practices such as adoption and fostering and in the general development of the child welfare and protection system in Ireland, especially since 1970. As discussed in the next section, this engagement has been thrown into sharp focus with the publication of a report relating to one such type of institution, 'Mother and Baby Homes' in Ireland.

2021 *Final Report of the Commission of Investigation into Mother and Baby Homes*

Facing up to a troubled and contradictory history

The publication of the 2021 FRCIMBH points to the need to radically rethink, re-engage with, reflect on and redress the role of the social work profession in the history of institutionalisation and the incarceration that was part and parcel of this. This relates to Mother and Baby Homes, county homes and related institutions. Chapters 1 and 2 of the FRCIMBH summarise the details of the law and policies underpinning the Mother and Baby Homes, county homes and related institutions covered by the Commission (Commission of Investigation into Mother and Baby Homes, 2021). The Mother and Baby Homes were established from 1927 as a 'service' for women who were deemed to be 'first time offenders' in Irish policy (although some women who had two or more children were admitted). Women were usually required to work for two years afterwards within the homes and their children were most often adopted, many illegally (Buckley and McGregor, 2019). The homes were either direct state provision (from the workhouse and county home system) or provided by religious orders, supported by state funding. The Commission to investigate the homes was set up in 2015 following the discovery by local historian Catherine Corless of the burial of 796 children in a septic tank in a Mother and Baby Home in Tuam, Co. Galway (Buckley and McGregor, 2019). Deaths and children's burials in institutions, lack of consent to adoption, harsh and inhumane treatment of women and denial of access to information about the whereabouts of children born in the homes are some of the themes resonating in the FRCIMBH. There is evidence of discrimination on the grounds of race, disability, class, gender, patriarchy, mental health, moralism and judgementalism. The testimonies from witnesses in the report provide in-depth evidence of the lack of empathy that was so often shown towards women and children. The lack of attention to sexual crime through assault of women and sexual abuse of children is stark. The language and terminology used in the report itself, and in relation to past practices, needs to be critically interrogated. Questions have also been raised about the accuracy of representation of the people's testimonials and concerns about the destruction of original 'Confidential Committee Material'.

Apart from the range of issues to consider, a comprehensive analysis of the FRCIMBH is not possible at present because the report itself has been contested on a number of grounds and an alternative version of the executive summary has been produced from a human rights perspective. Therefore, reference to the report is used here as a trigger for critical reflection about the role and nature of social work that can inform present-day understandings and future practices. Taking on board the limitations of the evidence provided, the learning from the report challenges the profession, and those working within it past and present, to engage more critically and assertively with a troubled past and a contradictory position as both a beacon of change and a reinforcer of dominant norms and practices leading to discrimination and human rights violations.

Social worker(s) are mentioned approximately 600 times in the report. This relates mainly to the later periods covered, from 1960 onwards. As noted in the report, by 1971 there were 831 social workers in Ireland and by 1980, this had increased to 3,680 (FRCIMBH, Ch 12, p 21). At least eight different aspects of social work/social work-related practice during 1970 feature in the report: adoption, local authority children's officers, community care social workers, social workers employed in specific institutions/voluntary organisations, hospital social work (almoners), social work in services for unmarried mothers, social workers in residential care and probation officers. The efforts of the Inspectors of Boarded Out children prior to 1970 – whose work is detailed in Skehill (2004) – in promoting greater use of family-based care and more regulation of child welfare are noted. So too is the work of the Joint Committee of Women's Societies and Women Social Workers, referred to earlier.

It is clear from the recurrence of the theme in the report, that there is an underlying assumption that the increased presence of professionally qualified social workers in the system had a direct impact on changing cultures and practices relating to mothers and children. Many references are made to how the increase in professional social workers led to a change in attitudes and options for women and their children. References are also made to the lack of understanding about the trauma and impact of adoption (for example) in the absence of social work and the way in which social workers offered women alternatives and support to maintain their children, through the 1970s and 1980s in particular. The 'tension' between the dominant views of the religious orders and professional social workers is also referred to, with various examples given of competing discourses as practices changed through the 1970s and 1980s. Indeed, there are many examples of commentaries that acknowledge the greater involvement of social work as bringing often transformative change in practices with mothers and their children.

However, there are also a many references in the report to instances where social workers were found to be complicit in the practices of the time by their actions or inactions. Failure to protect from harm and abuse recurs. There are also examples of social workers, up to the 1980s, showing a judgemental and harsh attitude to women in the homes. And a reference is also made, again during the 1980s, to a worker being dishonest with a mother, implying that they would support her to live independently but then, without her consent, having her sent to a home. A reading of the report requires us to reflect on the impact of the dominant discourse about the preference of foster care over institutional care which, in hindsight, were too 'taken-for-granted'. For example, the report contains many examples of abuse within foster care, often when children were boarded out from the homes. While the majority of alterative care in Ireland continues to be via foster/kinship care, with many favourable reasons to support this, the tacit 'acceptance' of this form of care raises the question of what might have been missed in terms of a more critical interrogation of practices, mostly led by social work, with regard to inspection and support for children in foster care in the past.

While there are many unknowns still to uncover, and issues about the evidence within the report to be addressed adequately, there is sufficient evidence to conclude that Irish social work, just like the discipline in many other jurisdictions (Hering and Waaldijk, 2006; Lorenz, 2007; Hauss and Schulte, 2009,), has what Ferguson et al (2018) call 'horrible histories' to contend with. The underlying assumptions about the relationship between social work and institutional care as somewhat separate or insignificant needs further interrogation. This includes critical examination of social work's role in the practices linked with 'deinstitutionalisation' or 'alternative' practice – such as adoption which was intrinsically connected with the practices of placement/confinement of women in the mother and baby institutions, concealment of adoptions, falsification of information and illegal adoptions.

It seems that we have a long and complex road ahead for social work in Ireland in order to continue the process of learning and critical reflection triggered by the FRCIMBH. We need to be self-critical and reflective about this evidence of our contradictory role, which is unique neither to the mother and baby institutions, nor to Ireland.

Discussion

An apology from the Irish Association of Social Workers in response to the FRCIMBH was an important first step in acknowledging

> times when the social work profession did not provide compassionate support, failed to uphold basic human rights, and failed to challenge the social and institutional injustices, which caused such devastation

in the lives of women and children. We have heard the powerful and brave testimonies of the survivors. The IASW will now reflect on how we can best respond to what we have learned and continue to learn from the survivors. (IASW, 15 Feb 2021)

This marks the beginning of a new history of our present that takes responsibility for our role within the complex domain of institutional care for children in Ireland.

First, this must begin with attention to *the needs and interests of those directly impacted upon by the past practices*. Many people in the present are still very much affected by their past and their experiences are diverse and complex. This includes people who were in the institutions as mothers or children, their families, adoptees, adoptive parents and those disclosing retrospective abuse. The hurt, trauma and injustice transcend generations. A life-course perspective is essential to recognise the long-lasting impact of childhoodmotherhood experience through adulthood, the continuation of trauma intergenerationally and the massive impact on many individuals with regard to their health and well-being (see McGregor and Dolan, 2021).

Second, we need to *face up to and critically interrogate 'received histories'*. Academics and policy makers should reflect on past histories, to ask how much was seen and not seen or said and not said that shaped and influenced 'knowledge' and 'assumptions' about our past. For example, the histories relating to Boarding Out and foster care in Ireland (Skehill, 2004) should be revisited to acknowledge the level and severity of abuse that the Commission's report has exposed within some foster homes and the limited governance and regulation of the same, despite the technical existence of regulation processes. There is an urgent duty and responsibility for the profession to 'write in' a fuller, more accountable, nuanced and honest record of the contested and contradictory role of social work in these flawed and exposed systems.

Third, we must make *learning history in social work education* central, not peripheral. Social workers need to be knowledgeable about their own history and historical context. We need to engage with the duality of oppression and transformation that features in our complicated and complicit histories. This can be done within a wider ecological frame that recognises the complex layers of context influencing the different moments of history and time and the need for historical and restorative justice. This can help to situate the role of social work vis-à-vis other power forces within the ecosystem, including individual micro-level practices within families (including fathers and wider family networks) and dominant practices of religious-run services and state-supported practices. It can also situate social work as a product of the time, fundamentally connected to society and social context. Social workers need to engage critically with that 'time' and 'context'. Opportunities to reflect on what powers social work had, and what it didn't have, vis-à-vis other power forces can inform critical reflection (McGregor, 2016). Just because social work was, relatively, a minority discourse vis-à-vis the power of the state and church did not render it powerless to act under the limited regulation and legislation that did exist.

And at the same time, those who practised during this time need space and attention to contextualise the opportunities and challenges of practice of the time. Going back to a history of the present approach, this approach should be neither revisionist or simplistic. We need to create space for honest dialogue that gives life to the nature of practices during the moments of time. Avoiding a defensive stance will open up opportunities for truth and reconciliation that enable us to recognise, for example, that while much of the identity associated with the institutions discussed connects with a dominant discourse of misuse of powers across a range of domains, other identities, like those related to 'home' and 'care' (Edwards, 2017), need to be acknowledged. Experiences, whether they are about time spent in institutions or about abuse or harm experienced, require action-oriented responses from social workers individually and the profession collectively. We need to be upfront and brave about naming our own poor or uniformed practices, or failures to practise, and to create conditions for critical reflection within the profession in partnership, through citizenship practices, with those directly affected and their wider communities.

Conclusion

Social work, given its skills and value base, is well placed to lead on development of opportunities for further research, critical dialogue and engagement between those who practised and those who experienced practice relating to the mass institutionalisation of women and children in Ireland. The 'child welfare' system in Ireland for many decades was based not only on an 'architecture of containment' (Smith, 2007), but on an objectification of certain children, young people and mothers, to the point where many of their basic rights as citizens were denied and violated. This is not to say there were not examples also of empathic and subjective responses, but these can be fully brought to the fore only within an honest, open and frank engagement with a troubled and very troubling history. Reflecting on the experiences of many women and children in the institutions discussed, it seems that a lack of empathy in practices of institutionalisation led to the objectification of the 'unmarried mother' or 'illegitimate child' rather than subjectifying their personhood as individual women and children. We have an opportunity, in redressing and correcting the history of child welfare social work and institutional care in Ireland, to promote empathy with and subjectification of those affected by practices of institutionalisation. This includes a focus on practices in other countries where institutionalisation and mass incarceration continue to be used for women and/or children, as well as current practices within Ireland with families in Direct Provision, another form of inappropriate institutional care for another category of marginalised children and families (for persons who are asylum seekers). After all, the promotion of subjectivity, within the social, is deemed to be one of the defining and persistent features of social work (Philp, 1979; Parton, 1991; Skehill, 2004; McGregor and Dolan, 2021).

References

Buckley, S.A. (2013) *The Cruelty Man: Child Welfare, the NSPCC and the State in Ireland, 1889–1956,* Manchester: Manchester University Press

Buckley, S.A. and McGregor, C. (2019) 'Interrogating institutionalisation and child welfare: The Irish case, 1939–1991', *European Journal of Social Work,* 22(6): 1062–1072.

Clear, C. (1987) *Nuns in Nineteenth-Century Ireland*, Dublin: Gill and Macmillan.

Commission of Investigation into Mother and Baby Homes (2021) Final Report of the Commission of Investigation into Mother and Baby Homes, Dublin: Department of Children, Equality, Disability, Integration and Youth.

Devaney, C. and McGregor, C. (2017) 'Child protection and family support practice in Ireland: A contribution to present debates from a historical perspective', *Child and Family Social Work*, 22(3): 1–9.

Doyle, P. (1989) *The God Squad*, London: Corgi.

Earner-Byrne, L. (2003) 'The boat to England: an analysis of the official reactions to the emigration of single expectant Irish women to Britain, 1922–72', *Irish Economic and Social History*, 30: 52–70.

Earner-Byrne, L. (1997) *Mother and Child: Maternity and Child Welfare in Dublin, 1922–60*, Manchester: Manchester University Press

Edwards, D. (2017) *Cultural Autobiographical and Absent Memories of Orphanhood: The Girls of Nazareth House Remember*, London: Palgrave Macmillan.

Ferguson, I., Ioakimidis, V. and Lavalette, M. (2018) *Global Social Work in a Political Context: Radical Perspectives*, Bristol: Policy Press.

Flynn, S. (2021) 'Literature on professional social work and controversies surrounding Roman Catholicism in the Republic of Ireland: adapting the dynamic model', *Journal of Religion and Spirituality in Social Work: Social Thought*. DOI 10.1080/15426432.2021.1978124

Glynn, E. (2015) 'Magdalene matters', in R. Barr, S.A. Buckley and L. Kelly (eds) *Engendering Ireland: New Reflections on Modern History and Literature*. Newcastle upon Tyne, Cambridge Scholars Publishing, pp 32–52.

Hauss, G. and Schulte, D. (eds) (2009) *Amid Social Contradiction*, Opladen and Farmington Hills: Barbara Budrich Publishers.

Hering, S. and Waaldijk, B. (2006) *Guardians of the Poor – Custodians of the Public: Welfare History in Eastern Europe 1900–1960*, Opladen; Farmington Hills: Barbara Budrich Publishers.

Inglis, T. (1987) *Moral Monopoly: The Catholic Church in Modern Irish Society*, Dublin: University College Dublin Press.

Irish Association of Social Workers (2021) IASW Statement on Report of the Commission into the Mother and Baby Homes. https://www. iasw. ie/IASWStatement_ReportCommission_MotherBabyHomes

Kearney, N. and Skehill, C. (2005) (eds) *Social Work in Ireland: Historical Perspectives*, Dublin: Institute of Public Administration.

Keenan, M. (2012) *Child Sexual Abuse and the Catholic Church*, Oxford: Oxford University Press.

Kennedy, E. (1970) Reformatory and Industrial Schools System Report 1970, chaired by District Justice Eileen Kennedy. Dublin: Stationery Office.

Kennedy, P. (2004) *Motherhood in Ireland: Creation and Context*, Cork: Mercier Press.

Kenny, M. (2000) *Goodbye to Catholic Ireland*, London: Templegate.

Lorenz, W. (2007) 'Practicing history: Memory and professional contemporary practice', *International Social Work*, 50: 597.

Luddy, M. and Murphy, C. (eds) (1990) *Women Surviving: Studies in Irish Women's History in the 19th and 20th Centuries*, Dublin: Poolbeg Press.

Luddy, M. and Smith, J.M (eds) (2014) *Children, Childhood and Irish Society: 1500 to the Present*, Dublin: Four Courts Press.

Maguire, M. (2002) 'Foreign Adoptions and the Evolution of Irish Adoption Policy, 1945–52', *Journal of Social History*, 36(2): 387–404.

Maguire, M. (2009) *Precarious Childhood in Post-independence Ireland*, Manchester: Manchester University Press.

Maguire M. and Ó'Cinnéide S. (2005) '"A good beating never hurt anyone": The punishment and abuse of children in twentieth century Ireland', *Journal of Social History*, 38(3): 635–652.

McAvoy, S. (1999) 'The regulation of sexuality in the Irish Free State, 1929–1935', in G. Jones and E. Malcolm (eds) *Medicine, Disease and the State in Ireland, 1650–1940*, Cork: Cork University Press, pp 253–266.

McCaughren, S. and McGregor, C. (2018) 'Reimagining adoption in Ireland: A viable option for children in care?' *Child Care in Practice*, 24(3): 229–244,

McGregor, C. (2016) 'Balancing regulation and support in child protection: Using theories of power to develop reflective tools for practice', *Irish Social Worker*, Spring, 11–16.

McGregor, C. and Dolan, P. (2021) *Support and Protection across the Lifecourse: A Practical Approach for Social* Work, Bristol: Policy Press.

Milotte, M. (1997) *Banished Babies: The Secret History of Ireland's Baby Export Business*, Dublin: New Island Books.

Mooney, J. (2018) 'Adult disclosures of childhood sexual abuse and section 3 of the Child Care Act 1991: Past offences, current risk', *Child Care in Practice*, 24: 245–257.

Parton, N. (1991) *Governing the Family*, London: Macmillan Education.

Philp, M. (1979) 'Notes on the form of knowledge in social work', *Sociological Review*, 1: 83–111.

Raftery, M., and O'Sullivan, E. (1999) *Suffer the Little Children: The Inside Story of Ireland's Industrial Schools*, Dublin: New Island Books.

Reidy, C. (2009) *Ireland's 'Moral Hospital': The Irish Borstal System, 1906–1956*, Dublin: Irish Academic Press.

Skehill, C. (1999a) *History of Social Work in the Republic of Ireland*, Lampeter: Edwin Mellen Press.

Skehill, C. (1999b) 'Reflexive modernity and social work in Ireland: A response to Powell', *British Journal of Social Work*, 29: 797–809.

Skehill, C. (2000) 'An examination of the transition from philanthropy to professional social work in Ireland', *Research on Social Work Practice*, 10(6): 688–704.

Skehill, C. (2003) 'Social work in the Republic of Ireland: A history of the present', *Journal of Social Work*, 3(2): 141–59.

Skehill, C. (2004) *History of the Present of Child Protection and Welfare Social Work in Ireland*, Lampeter: Edwin Mellen Press.

Skehill, C. (2007) 'Researching the history of social work: Exposition of a history of the present approach', *European Journal of Social Work*, 10(4): 449–63.

Smith, J.M. (2007) *Ireland's Magdalen Laundries and the Nation's Architecture of Containment*, Manchester: Manchester University Press.

The Task Force on Child Care Services (1980) Final Report to the Minister for Health, Dublin: Stationery Office.

Tyrell, P. (2006) *Founded on Fear: Letterfrack Industrial School, War and Exile*, edited by D. Whelan, Dublin: Irish Academic Press.

Whyte, J.H. (1980) *Church and State in Modern Ireland 1923–1979*, Dublin: Gill and Macmillan.

PART V

Survivor perspectives and contemporary reflections

14

Facing the legacy of social work: coming to terms with complicity in systemic inequality and social injustice

Bob Pease

Introduction

As the contributors to this volume illustrate, social work has a troubled history. It has been complicit in the internment of Japanese Americans during the Second World War, apartheid in South Africa, the stolen generations and refugee detention in Australia and dictatorships in Nazi Germany, Franco's Spain and in Argentina and Chile, to name just a few of the case studies in this book. The premise of the book is that the profession has an ethical obligation to acknowledge this history and to learn from it. Only then can it chart an ethical future free of the legacy of the past. Ferguson (2019) notes that this 'horrible history' involved social workers actively colluding with oppressive policies of the state. In other instances, they acquiesced or remained silent in the face of policies and practices that reproduced oppression.

How do we understand this accommodation to injustice? Did it involve ignorance and lack of awareness of what they doing? Did they believe that they were 'doing good'? What does this mean for present-day complicity with injustice? How culpable are current social workers for inaction against injustice?

Can social work become a radical profession?

Those of us who are part of the radical tradition of social work have sought to find a way that social work can be revitalised to address the contradictions arising from the state organisation of the profession through progressive, radical, critical, anti-oppressive and structural forms of theorising and practice. Since the emergence of the radical critique of social work in the 1970s, there have been ongoing debates about the limitations and potential of alternative forms of practice to bring about significant social change and about whether social work could become a radical profession. There were numerous dimensions to the radical critique of social work. The major elements of it were: (i) social work is a social control mechanism that 'cools out' clients and keeps them submissive; (ii) social work is a professional elitist activity that is more concerned with its own self-interest than with meeting client needs; (iii) social work's values foster conformity to middle-class norms; (iv) social work individualises and pathologises problems that are social and political in character; and (v) social work operates in a theoretical vacuum in that it lacks an adequate knowledge base (Bailey and Brake, 1975; Galper, 1975; Corrigan and Leonard, 1978).

Notwithstanding this critique, many proponents of radical social work are positive about the future of the profession. Ife (1997) argues that social work is radical by its nature and can make an important contribution to social justice and human rights. Briskman (2013) asserts that professional associations in social work can take a strong social justice stance and Ferguson (2009, p 81) proclaims that 'another social work is possible'. However, Hearn (1982) reminded social workers in the early 1980s that radical social work was not antisocial work. It was always a part of social work and it operated within the professional tradition of social work. While we can find inspiring examples of radical social workers individually and collectively opposing social injustice, there are few examples of professional social work associations and organisations taking a progressive stand on social justice issues. In fact, as Reisch and Andrews (2002) demonstrate, radical social workers were often punished by their professional associations for challenging systemic injustice. While many social workers distance themselves from professional associations and there are radical caucuses in the profession, is it possible for social work as a profession to become radical, given its location in the state?

The tensions between the social justice project and the professional project are sometimes expressed as that of 'dual loyalty', in terms of the conflict between social workers' allegiance to the state that employs them and to the vulnerable people they work with (Briskman, 2019). Flynn (2021) frames this tension between social workers' desire for social justice and their repressive role as agents of the state as a paradox. However, Olson (2007) challenges the espoused view of many social workers that the profession of social work is primarily organised around social justice. Rather, he argues, it is the professional project that is at the heart of social work and this project is at odds with social justice. The profession endeavours to conflate these two projects, but it usually results in social workers espousing social justice but doing something else. While some social workers embrace radical perspectives, this is in opposition to professionalisation and social workers' employing agencies that thwart social justice.

Brady et al (2019) argue that social work needs to move beyond what they call the 'myth of the radical profession'. They say that we should not overestimate social work's progressive history and we should acknowledge social work's contradictory practices in relation to social justice. In their view, social work has never been committed to radical social change. They are doubtful that social work as a profession can transform the structures and practices that oppress people. This would seem a valid concern when it is rare for the official canons of the profession through its associations and codes of ethics to even espouse radical forms of social change.

Recently, Maylea (2021) has argued more strongly that social work cannot be reformed because it is unable to address the fundamental flaws which characterise social work: theoretical tensions within the profession, professionalisation, inability to atone for historical abuses and lack of capability to respond to contemporary challenges such as climate change, institutionalised racism and violation of human rights in mental health settings. Consequently, for Maylea, the profession must be abolished. I return to this issue later in the chapter.

Under the cover of kindness

Twenty-five years ago, Margolin (1997) argued that social workers deny to themselves that their espoused social justice imperatives obscure the role that their professional activities play in the surveillance of oppressed people. Margolin's critique was harsh in arguing that social workers presented themselves as empowering while practising power on behalf of the state. Social workers were told that they ignored the exercise of power and that they practised a form of amnesia about the historical role of the profession in subordinating vulnerable populations to the norms of the state. When writing about the then contemporary times, Margolin argued that social work's preoccupation with reflectiveness and concern about victim blaming and social control did not address social work's surveillance functions and the imposition of dominant values on the lives of those it aims to serve.

The very process of critical reflection by social workers about the social control aspects of their profession was seen by Margolin as yet another way that social workers avoid the more fundamental challenges to their profession. In fact, he argues, the self-criticism of social work itself supports the legitimacy of the profession as a whole because, while it encourages critical reflection upon itself, this critical reflection does not extend to interrogation of the premises upon which the profession rests. Similar to Maylea (2021), the implication of Margolin's analysis would seem to be that social work should cease to exist, or at least in its present form as an apparatus of the state.

Many social work educators responded defensively to Margolin's charge that social work's discourses of empowerment and critical reflection masked their own exercise of power and manipulated them into the machinery of the state. Mullaly (1998), in his review of the book, argues that Margolin does not do justice to the progressive forms of social work of which he is a proponent. He rejects the view that social work is only about social control, and objects to what he sees as Margolin's self-righteous and patronising tone. In an extensive critique, Wakefield (1998) also takes exception to the notion that social work's goodness is a myth and what he sees as Margolin's narrow understanding of social work as case-work. It is true that Margolin does not address structural approaches and community work. However, these approaches are not immune from the kind of critique Margolin makes of case-work (Occhiuto and Rowlands, 2019).

I can understand why many social work educators responded defensively to the critique. When I first read Margolin in the early 2000s, I was very unsettled by it. Were my own efforts to forge a radical and pro-feminist practice in social work complicit with the overall disciplinary functions of the profession? As unsettling as it was, much of what Margolin argued about the covert political functions of social work rang true to me, and I think that his analysis is as relevant today as it was when he first wrote it.

Social work in and against the state

Social work historians who trace the history of the profession as solely a progressive response to need ignore the regulatory roles that have always been part of social work. In most countries, social work is embedded in apparatuses of the state. While some Marxists believe that there is very little potential for progressive social workers to contribute to social change, others believe that there are opportunities for social workers to subvert neoliberal prerogatives and develop forms of progressive practice within the state (Vickers, 2015). Early radical social workers argued that the state was semi-autonomous and reflected the balance of class struggles at particular moments in time (Corrigan and Leonard, 1978). This, in their view, opened up opportunities for radical social workers to enact practices outside the surveillance of the state.

The state received critical attention by radical social workers in the 1970s and 1980s. However, in the last 40 years there has been little theorising of the state in the writings of radical and critical social work (Feldman, 2020). The unstated assumption underpinning traditional social work is either that the state is liberal and progressive, or it is a neutral mechanism capable of being used for different ends by different people. Without analysis and critical engagement with the state, radical and critical social work will be read by some as resting upon the same premises.

We can understand the state through a Marxist lens as a tool used by the ruling class to serve their economic interests (Vickers, 2019). We can also see it through a Gramscian perspective that argues that the state functions more as an ideological apparatus to perpetuate dominant cultural values and ideas (Wallace and Pease, 2019). Alternatively, we can make sense of it through a Foucauldian framework that sees the state as a form of governmentality that governs the conduct of populations through disciplinary techniques and functions (King, 2020). All of these theories recognise the repressive dimensions of the state. If we are to develop more radical forms of social work practice that avoid complicity with injustice, we must understand the relationship between the state and the profession.

One of the mechanisms of the state's control of social work is through the regulation of the profession, which in many countries takes place through registration (van Heugten, 2011; Macias, 2016; Heron, 2019; McCurdy et al, 2020). Professional associations, as apparatuses of the state, also shape the curriculum in social work education. Many radical critics have argued that increasing emphases on the professionalisation of social work have contributed to the profession's neglect of social justice (Brady et al, 2019; Occhiuto and Rowlands, 2019; Kim, 2020).

Social work has become one of the institutions through which neoliberalism functions to shape subjectivities of both workers and clients (Wallace and Pease, 2019). Heron (2019), writing in the Canadian context, documents the ways in which the profession's competency standards reinforce neoliberal imperatives and colonial knowledge that take social work further away from social justice aspirations. She questions whether critical reflection and interrogation of dominant epistemologies are possible, given the entrenchment of Western knowledge and neoliberal values.

Is critical reflection enough?

Critical reflection is increasingly encouraged in social work as a counter-hegemonic practice (Flynn, 2021). One of the claims of critical reflection is that it creates the opportunity for social workers to strengthen the social justice imperatives of the profession and to enact practices more consistent with critical social work (Fook and Gardner, 2007).

While critical reflection encourages practitioners to think critically about power relations, it generally does not encourage them to locate their experience in the context of class, gender, race and sexuality social divisions (Swan, 2008). Heron (2005) argues that issues of power and privilege are either generally neglected or insufficiently theorised in many discussions about critical reflection. She encourages greater focus on the power relations operating in practice, the subject positions that social workers occupy and their personal and professional investments in becoming a particular kind of social worker.

How do race, class, gender and sexuality influence the process of critical reflection?

Briskman (2017), for example, argues that in order to revitalise radical social work, social workers should be more reflective about the ways in which Western paradigms permeate the profession. It has been noted by many commentators that social work as a profession is based on colonial framings of knowledge and professional purpose that marginalise Indigenous knowledge and culture (Occhiuto and Rowlands, 2019; Dittfield, 2020). Social workers have been slow to turn a decolonial lens upon themselves to enable them to acknowledge their complicity with the profession's reliance upon Eurocentric knowledge.

It was clear to me as a social work educator that many students had not addressed their own privileged positioning. This is true of many social work educators and practitioners as well. While many social workers have been exposed to anti-oppressive approaches to practice, they know more about oppression than about privilege and complicity and their own social location in relations of power. Consequently, many have argued that the concept of privilege should be included more substantially in social work curricula (Vodde, 2001; Barnoff and Moffat, 2007; Pease, 2010; Todd, 2011).

However, critical reflection on unearned privileges is not enough if it does not extend to critical analysis of the subject position of the social worker as 'innocent expert' (Occhiuto and Rowlands, 2019). The subjectivity of the innocent expert fosters an illusion that social workers can escape the power relations they are embedded within. This idea of innocence is usefully informed by James Baldwin's notion of racial innocence (Bussey, 2020). Similar to Baldwin's observation of so-called 'good' White people's complicity in racial subordination, social work's disavowal of its history of complicity in social injustice involves a refusal to acknowledge uncomfortable truths. Baldwin's focus on the way that innocence functions as a form of covert racism that perpetuates White supremacy is relevant to understanding social work's complicity with domination. Racial innocence also involves a disavowal of history. As Baldwin so aptly put it in an interview in the *New York Times* in 1962: 'Not everything that is faced can be changed but nothing can be changed until it is faced.'

Todd (2011) demonstrates the dangers in thinking that critical reflection as a technique can address the structural and systemic form of privilege and injustice that social workers face. She illustrates the tendency for us to focus on racism and other forms of oppression that are 'out there' in the wider society and fail to address the more subtle ways in which various forms of privilege and complicity are reproduced through so-called progressive practices. Are radical and critical social workers an example of what Todd calls the 'good white subject'? Do we seek to portray radical forms of social work as 'good social work' that is free of political and ethical dilemmas?

The emancipatory language and transformational frameworks of critical reflection hide the reality that it functions as another form of surveillance of social workers, fostering in them a greater capacity to self-manage within the dictates of neoliberalism (Gilbert, 2001). Fejes (2013) suggests that critical reflection is a form of confession that uses reflective techniques to shape the self. While it promises transformation and emancipation, it actually becomes a normalising practice that enables individual social workers to solve problems within the constraints of the workplace because it is unable to address conferred privilege and systemic injustice.

Critical reflection rarely addresses the challenges faced by social workers employed by the state and the statutory responsibilities that social workers have to exercise (Rankine, 2018). While critical reflection focuses on interrogating power relationships impacting on clients, social workers, educators and professional associations also need to turn the critical gaze more upon the social work profession itself so as to become more aware of its historical complicity with injustice (Macias, 2016).

Critical reflection fosters a heroic and a hopeful narrative of social work that is potentially able to move beyond oppressive relations of power that social workers are embedded within. Can social workers respond ethically to the histories of pain and harm caused by the profession's complicity with systemic injustice?

All conceptions of radical social work hold out a conception of hope, a belief in a more hopeful future for the profession that is beyond complicity and social control. Hope can fuel action in the present. But what if our sense of hope reinscribes privilege and oppression? Maudlin (2014) suggests that by focusing on a more hopeful and anticipated future we can take attention away from complicity in the present. Hope can create the false notion that we can transcend our complicity. Rather than trying to avoid complicity, we should recognise that it is inevitable, and consequently we should learn to live with it and deal with it in our lives (Zembylas, 2020). Another way of expressing this is Haraway's (2016) notion of 'staying with the trouble'.

Facing complicity in social injustice

I have written previously about the position of social workers occupying contradictory class locations and the privilege of those who occupy male, White, heterosexual, cis-gendered, able-bodied locations (Pease, 2010; Pease, 2022). I have also emphasised the value of the concept of complicity as an important part of understanding such locations (Pease, 2016). Complicity keeps the focus on the practices that reproduce privilege and oppression rather than some individualistic notions of privilege which are more to do with the self.

One way of understanding the complicity of members of privileged groups with normative and exploitative practices is through the scholarship on epistemologies of ignorance (Sullivan and Tuana, 2007). Members of privileged groups, even when they have good intentions, can reproduce social inequalities through various forms of ignorance. The way in which epistemologies of ignorance operate is that members of privileged groups generally do not know the extent to which they do not know. Gilson (2014) suggests that epistemological ignorance is connected to the ideal of invulnerability, and that both work to enable members of privileged groups to deny systemic privilege and oppression. To be successful in maintaining vulnerability, one must shut oneself off from being affected by the experience of others (Pease, 2021). To address this, Gilson encourages the development of 'epistemic vulnerability', which increases the capacity of people to learn from others, as it not only opens us up to knowing facts at a cognitive level but also allows us to experience emotional and embodied responses.

The concept of complicity identifies our past and present responsibility for our part in injustice and provides a moral imperative to address these responsibilities. In this view, people are structurally complicit when they either consciously or unconsciously reproduce unjust social structures (Aragon and Jagger, 2018). Are we still culpable, however, if we are unconscious of reproducing injustice? We have a moral imperative to critically reflect on our complicity that harms others and to become more aware of the role we play in reproducing oppressive social arrangements. The implication is that we should then transform ourselves and the oppressive social practices we participate in.

Aragon and Jaggar (2018) identify different levels of injustice: interpersonal, institutional and structural injustice. These different levels of injustice are linked to different levels of complicity. In this framework, social work's complicity with the injustices documented in this book operates at all levels. While individual social workers can and do enact interpersonal injustice with other individuals, and while social work is complicit also in structural injustice through its acceptance of normalised social practices, it is at the institutional level where its collective practices are enacted through codes of ethics, competencies and the statutory regulation of its affairs.

In the critical studies of Whiteness, the concept of complicity has been more fully interrogated than in social work. When Applebaum (2007) talks about White people reproducing racist practices, while seeing themselves as morally good, she could equally be talking about social workers (most of whom in the global North are White). Like 'good white people', social workers see themselves as part of the solution to social problems, while denying that they are part of the problem that needs to be addressed.

As social workers tend to see themselves as part of the professional-managerial class (Ehrenreich and Ehrenreich, 1979; Pease, 2022), notwithstanding their ethical imperative to 'do good', they will find, like all relatively privileged groups, that complicity and privilege are not easily recognised. They cannot assume that just because they espouse principles of human rights and social justice they can transcend systems of privilege and oppression. The notion of good intentions is one of the ways in which complicity is denied. Just as Applebaum (2017) encourages White people to interrogate their self-conception as good people, so should social workers be encouraged to examine the ethos of 'doing good' that masks social work's complicity in injustice.

Conclusion

Wilson (2017) encourages social workers to revisit Wendy Brown's (1999) notion of left melancholy to help us as a profession to understand our history. Otherwise, social workers are doomed to remain unrealistically optimistic as we allow ourselves only to remember certain knowledges and practices of our profession. We disavow unpopular understandings and feelings in order to keep our idealised conception of our profession alive. As long as we see ourselves only as good people doing good work, we will remain defensive towards knowledge that challenges the premises of our work. If we do not acknowledge the failures of our profession and the reality that we cannot act in the world without causing harm as well as good, we will not move forward. Wilson (2017) suggests that social work should take a reparative stance towards our history, acknowledging that we have done harm and recognising that no form of knowledge (including critical knowledge) can ensure that we can always predict the outcomes of our professional work.

Do some radical and critical expressions of social work provide us with comfort by helping us to maintain a sense of progress in addressing oppression and privilege? Do they encourage us to keep alive a form of optimism that negates the lessons of our history? This is not a problem of critical theory; it is more that some social work theorists may not have drawn deeply enough from it.

Rossiter (2001) writes about her search for a site of innocence in social work, a site where she could teach students how to do some form of critical social work. This would enable her to overcome her suspicions about 'doing social work' and address the painful experience of her contradictory relationship to the state. Such an endeavour would enable her to forget the troubled history of social work and her own complicity with that history that conceals oppressive relations and ideologies.

Rossiter's search for some innocent space resonated strongly with me. I always felt ambivalent about social work, even though I located myself in the critical tradition of the profession. In my teaching in social work, I would tell students that it was important not to identify too closely with a professional social work identity. I would encourage them to think outside of social work and not limit their political aspirations of social justice work to the hours of paid social work practice. I encouraged them to think beyond social work in terms of critical sources of knowledge and philosophical principles. In effect, I was encouraging them to develop an identity beyond social work.

While I have published on radical and critical social work, most of my publications and research have not been located within professional social work. Is my theoretical and activist work on men's violence prevention, undoing privilege, interrogating hegemonic masculinity and global warming and so on part of social work? I had not thought of it in that way as I wrote, spoke publicly to others and engaged in activism.

The political philosophy of Deleuze and Guattari (1988) has in recent years inspired me to re-theorise professional identities. From their perspective, all identities impose rigid boundaries on our subjectivities and our practices, and constitute what they call majoritarian forms of power and domination. We may understand social workers' resistance to a professional identity as 'becoming minoritarian'. By minoritarian, Deleuze and Guattari are not referring to specific groups of people but to processes of subversion of the dominant majoritarian identities that shape social workers. In this view, in order to resist oppressive power relations, social workers should move to the margins to create another consciousness and sensibility that challenges professional social work identity. This will involve becoming outsiders in the profession.

If the state and professionalism are not compatible with radical social work, then it can only function in alternative organisations outside of the state (Reisch, 2019). Lavalette (2019) distinguishes between official 'state-directed social work' which is shaped by the priorities and needs of the state and what he calls 'popular social work'. Popular social work is outside of the professional boundaries of social work and is constituted by progressive social movement politics, which may or may not involve social workers. For Lavalette, radical social work is part of state-directed social work in that it is engaged in practices in and against the state.

Many social workers work in organisations that are part of the not-for-profit sector. However, many such organisations are funded by the state and their activities are consequently regulated by the state. Smith (2017) has identified how the anti-violence movement has ceased to be a social movement and has become more of a network of state-funded organisations that has become co-opted by the state. Consequently, state-funded non-profit organisations function as part of the state and constitute what INCITE (2017) calls the 'non-profit industrial complex'. So, popular social work, as social justice organising, would also be outside of much of the non-profit sector.

As the relationship between social work and the carceral state, which coercively manages poor communities and communities of colour, is made more explicit, we see calls for an anti-carceral politics for social work (Kim, 2020; Jacobs et al, 2021). Such a politics poses perhaps the most significant challenge that social work has faced, that of abolition. As the movement for defunding the police grows, the place of social work as part of the carceral state has also been brought more into focus, as it has been proposed that social work should become more integrated with police departments

(James-Townies, 2020; Baines, 2021). If social work is to be part of the resistance to punitive measures against the poor and the oppressed, and deal with its complicity in injustice, it may need to question the unquestionable, its role within the carceral state. If it is to take seriously reparation, solidarity, decolonisation and accountability, it will need to explore what an abolitionist stance in relation to social work might entail. This may open up new spaces for social workers to face and come to terms with the legacy of social work's past.

Acknowledgements

I would like to thank Carolyn Noble, John Fox, Russell Shuttleworth, Ian Hyslop and the editors for their constructive comments on an earlier version of this chapter.

References

Applebaum, B. (2007) 'White complicity and social justice education: Can one be culpable without being liable?', *Educational Theory*, 57(4): 453–467.

Applebaum, B. (2017) 'Comforting discomfort as complicity: White fragility and the pursuit of invulnerability', *Hypatia,* 32(4): 862–875.

Aragon, C. and Jagger, A. (2018) 'Agency, complicity and the responsibility to resist structural injustice', *Journal of Social Philosophy*, 49(3): 439–460.

Bailey, R. and Brake, R. (eds) (1975) *Radical Social Work*, London: Edward Arnold.

Baines, D. (2021) 'Soft cops or social justice activists: Social work's relationship to the state in the context of BLM and neoliberalism', *British Journal of Social Work*, https://doi.org/10.1093/bjsw/bcab200

Barnoff, L. and Moffatt, K. (2007) 'Contradictory tensions in anti-oppressive practice in feminist social services', *Affilia*, 22(1): 56–70.

Brady, S., Sawyer, J. and Perkins, N. (2019) 'Debunking the myth of the "radical profession": Analysing and overcoming our professional history to create new pathways and opportunities for social work', *Critical and Radical Social Work*, 7(3): 1–18.

Briskman, L. (2013) 'Courageous ethnographers or agents of the state: Challenges for social work', *Critical and Radical Social Work*, 1(1): 51–66.

Briskman, L. (2017) 'Revitalising radical social work', *Aotearoa New Zealand and Social Work,* 29(2): 133–136.

Briskman, L. (2019) 'Challenging harmful political contexts through activism', in S. Webb (ed) *The Routledge Handbook of Critical Social Work*, London: Routledge, pp 549–559.

Brown, W. (1999) 'Resisting left melancholy', *Boundary 2,* 26(3): 19–27.

Bussey, S. (2020) 'Imperialism through virtuous helping: Baldwin's innocence and implications for clinical social work practice', *Journal of Progressive Human Services*, 31(3): 192–209.

Corrigan, P. and Leonard, P. (1978) *Social Work Practice under Capitalism: A Marxist Approach,* London: Macmillan.

Deleuze, G. and Guattari, F. (1988) *A Thousand Plateaus: Capitalism and Schizophrena,* London: Bloomsbury.

Dittfeld, T. (2020) 'Seeing white: Turning the postcolonial lens on social work in Australia', *Social Work and Policy Studies,* 3(1): 1–21.

Ehrenreich, B. and Ehrenrich, J. (1979) 'The professional-managerial class', in P. Walker (ed) *Between Labour and Capital,* Sussex: Harvester Press, pp 5–45.

Fejes, A. (2013) 'Foucault, confession and reflective Practices', in M. Murphy (ed) *Social Theory and Educational Research: Understanding Foucault, Habermas, Bourdieu and Derrida,* London: Routledge, pp 52–66.

Feldman, G. (2020) 'Social work and the state: Perspectives and practice', *Social Policy Administration,* 55(5): 879–890.

Ferguson, I. (2009) 'Another social work is possible: Reclaiming the radical tradition', in V. Leskosek (ed) *Theories and Methods of Social Work,* Ljubjana: Faculty of Social Work, University of Ljubjana, pp 81–98.

Ferguson, I. (2019) 'Responding to political polarization: The new social work radicalism', in S. Webb (ed) *The Routledge Handbook of Critical Social Work,* London: Routledge, pp 476–501.

Flynn, S. (2021) 'Revisiting hegemony: A Gramscian analysis for contemporary social work', *Irish Journal of Sociology,* 29(1): 77–96.

Fook, J. and Gardner, F. (2007) *Practising Critical Reflection: A Resource Handbook,* London: Open University Press.

Galper, J. (1975) *The Politics of Social Services,* Englewood Cliffs: Prentice Hall.

Gilbert, T. (2001) 'Reflective practice and clinical supervision: Meticulous rituals of the confessional', *Nursing and Health Care Management Issues,* 36(2): 199–205.

Gilson, E. (2014) *The Ethics of Vulnerability: A Feminist Analysis of Social Life and Practice,* New York: Routledge.

Haraway, D. (2016) *Staying with the Trouble: Making Kin in the Chthulucene,* Durham: Duke University Press.

Hearn, J. (1982) 'Radical social work: Contradictions, limitations and political possibilities', *Critical Social Policy,* 2(1): 19–34.

Heron, B. (2005) 'Self-reflection in critical social work practice: Subjectivity and the possibilities of resistance', *Reflective Practice,* 6(3): 341–351.

Heron, B. (2019) 'Neoliberalism and social work regulation: Implications for epistemic resistance', *Canadian Social Work Review,* 36(1): 65–81.

Ife, J. (1997) *Rethinking Social Work: Towards Critical Practice,* Melbourne: Longman.

INCITE (eds) (2017) *The Revolution Will Not Be Funded: Beyond the Non-Profit Industrial Complex,* Durham: Duke University Press.

Jacobs, L., Kim, M., Whitfield, D., Gartner, R., Pancichelli, M., Kattari, S., Downey, M., McQueen, S. and Mountz, S. (2021) 'Defund the police: Moving towards an anti-carceral social work', *Journal of Progressive Human Services,* 32(1): 37–62.

James-Townies, l. (2020) 'Why social work cannot work with police', *Slate,* slate.com.

Kim, M. (2020) 'Anti-carceral feminism: The contradictions of progress and the possibilities of counter-hegemonic struggle', *Affilia: Journal of Women and Social Work*, 35(3): 309–326.

King, J. (2020) 'Pedagogy and power through a Foucauldian lens', in C. Morley, P. Ablett, C. Noble and S. Cowden (eds) *The Routledge Handbook of Critical Pedagogies for Social Work,* London: Routledge, pp 143–152.

Lavalette, M. (2019) 'Popular social work', in S. Webb (ed) *The Routledge Handbook of Critical Social Work*, London: Routledge, pp 536–548.

Macias, T. (2016) '"Between a rock and a hard place": Negotiating the neoliberal regulation of social work practice and education', *Alternative Routes,* 26: 251–276.

Margolin, L. (1997) *Under the Cover of Kindness: The Invention of Social Work,* Charlottesville: University Press of Virginia.

Maudlin, J. (2014) 'The abandonment of hope: Curriculum theory and white moral responsibility', *Journal of Curriculum and Pedagogy*, 11(2): 136–153.

Maylea, C. (2021) 'The end of social work', *British Journal of Social Work,* 51: 772–789.

McCurdy, S., Sreekumar, S. and Mendes, P. (2020) 'Is there a case for the registration of social workers in Australia?', *International Social Work,* 63(1): 18–29.

Mullaly, B. (1998) 'Book review of *Under the Cover of Kindness*', *International Social Work,* 41(4): 535–536.

Occhiuto, K. and Rowlands, L. (2019) 'Innocent expertise: Subjectivity and opportunities for subversion within community practice', *Journal of Progressive Human Services*, 30(3): 197–210.

Olson, J. (2007) 'Social work's professional and social justice projects: Discourses in conflict', *Journal of Progressive Human Services*, 18(1): 45–69.

Pease, B. (2010) *Undoing Privilege: Unearned Advantage in a Divided World,* London: Zed Books.

Pease, B. (2016) 'Interrogating privilege and complicity in the oppression of others', in B. Pease, S. Goldingay, N. Hosken and S. Nipperess (eds) *Doing Critical Social Work*, Sydney: Allen and Unwin, pp 89–103.

Pease, B. (2021) 'Fostering non-anthropocentric vulnerability in men: Challenging the autonomous masculine subject in social work', in V. Bozalek and B. Pease (eds) *Post-Anthropocentric Social Work: Critical Posthuman and New Materialist Perspectives*, New York: Routledge, pp 108–120.

Pease, B. (2022) *Undoing Privilege: Unearned Advantage and Systemic Injustice in an Unequal World,* London: Zed/Bloombury.

Rankine, M. (2018) 'How critical are we? Revitalising critical reflection in supervision', *Advances in Social Work and Welfare Education,* 20(2): 31–46.

Reisch, M. (2019) 'Critical social work in the US: Challenges and conflicts', in S. Webb (ed) *The Routledge Handbook of Critical Social Work,* London: Routledge, pp 35–45.

Reisch, M. and Andrews, J. (2002) *The Road Not Taken: A History of Radical Social Work in the United States,* Philadelphia: Brunner-Routledge.

Rossiter, A. (2001) 'Innocence lost and suspicion found: Do we educate for or against social work?', *Critical Social Work,* 2(1): 1–6.

Smith, A. (2017) 'Introduction: The revolution will not be funded', in INCITE (eds) *The Revolution Will Not Be Funded: Beyond the Non-Profit Industrial Complex,* Durham: Duke University Press, pp 1–18.

Sullivan, S. and Tuana, N. (eds) (2007) *Race and Epistemologies of Ignorance,* New York: State University of New York Press.

Swan, E. (2008) 'Let's not get too personal: Critical reflection, reflexivity and the confessional turn', *Journal of European Industrial Training,* 32(5): 385–399.

Todd, S. (2011) '"That power and privilege thing": Securing whiteness in community work', *Journal of Progressive Human Services,* 22(2): 117–134.

van Heugten, K. (2011) 'Registration and social work education: A golden opportunity or a Trojan horse', *Journal of Social Work,* 11(2): 174–190.

Vickers, T. (2015) 'Marxist approaches to social work', in J. Wright (ed) *International Encyclopedia of the Social and Behavioral Sciences* (2nd edn), London: Elsevier, pp 663–669.

Vickers, T. (2019) 'Marxist social work: An international and historical perspective', in *The Routledge Handbook of Critical Social Work,* London: Routledge, pp 24–34.

Vodde, R. (2001) 'De-centering privilege in social work education: Whose job is it anyway?', *Race, Gender and Class,* 7(4): 139–160.

Wakefield, J. (1998) 'Foucauldian fallacies: An essay review of Leslie Margolin's Under the Cover of Kindness', *Social Service Review,* 72(4): 545–587.

Wallace, J. and Pease, B. (2019) 'Responding to neoliberalism in social work education: A neo-Gramscian approach', in S. Webb (ed) *The Routledge Handbook of Critical Social Work,* London: Routledge, pp 663–669.

Wilson, T. (2017) 'Repairing what's left in social work, or when knowledge no longer cuts', *British Journal of Social Work,* 47(5): 1310–1325.

Zembylas, M. (2020) 'Re-conceptualising complicity in the social justice classroom: Affect, politics and anti-complicity pedagogy', *Pedagogy, Culture and Society,* 28(2): 317–331.

15

'We want social workers to hear our story': learning from parents whose children were taken away

Guy Shennan

Introduction

This chapter has its origins in an unexpected encounter that took place in 2017. I was attending a narrative therapy conference and heard a keynote presentation entitled ' "I'll always be a Mum": young women talk about finding peace after their children are adopted'. After the three young women had spoken, we listened to a small number of conference attendees reflect on what they had heard, in the role of 'outsider witnesses', an interesting practice from narrative therapy (Carey and Russell, 2003). As I listened, I mused on my own role and realised that I had more than one that was relevant to that moment. While I was attending the conference primarily as an independent practitioner and trainer specialising in the solution-focused approach (Shennan, 2019), I was also at that time the Chair of the British Association of Social Workers (BASW), and I had formerly practised as a social worker in the system that these young women had been subject to. While I was also a witness to the parents' account, rather than being fully outside of it, I felt as if I was somewhere in 'the space between' the positions of insider and outsider (Corbin et al, 2009). I was implicated, in a way that the other mental health professionals there (I did not come across any other social workers) were not.

During their presentations, one parent said, "I think it's really important for social workers to see what's going on", and another that she wanted social workers to hear their story. Afterwards, I spoke to the two clinical psychologists who ran the service that was supporting the parents, and through them to the parents themselves. I explained my role with BASW and that this meant I should be able to help their story reach more social workers. I later interviewed two of the parents, some of the material from which appeared in a magazine article (Shennan, 2017–18), and I co-wrote a blog post with one (Shennan and Karen, 2018),[1] both of which pieces I shall draw from in this chapter. Before presenting the main themes that emerged from these interviews, I will share some reflections on and experiences of the problematic nature of the social work system and practices of which I have been a part. In the final section of the chapter, I will consider ways in which we might respond to such histories – and present examples – of controlling and complicit social work.

Reflections on social work's contradictions

Social work, as practised in the UK in the early part of the 21st century, had a huge impact on the lives of these young women and their children. It might have had different effects in another time and place. Social work is not unchanging and monolithic; there is no underlying essence of social work that remains constant over time (Shennan, 2020). It has always been a contested activity, from the beginnings of modern social work in the late 19th century. Before he was prime minister of the UK, Clement Attlee was a social worker and social work lecturer, and, writing about different visions of social work, he contrasted 'the tone of suspicion' running through the work of the influential Charity Organisation Society with his belief in the need for social workers to place trust in the people they serve (Attlee, 1920, p 65). In his article describing Attlee's time in social work, Dickens (2018) sets out the prevailing social policy context that included two schools of thought about poverty and welfare, labelled individualist and collectivist, respectively. The individualist view, of which the Charity Organisation Society were leading exponents, saw individuals as responsible for themselves and their families and the conditions in which they lived, and while charities would provide help to the poor assessed as deserving it, others would be left to the mercies of Poor Law relief. In contrast, the collectivist view placed more emphasis on social conditions and the structural causes of poverty. Collectivists, including Attlee, argued for a greater role for the state, including public services based on notions of entitlement and citizenship.

The individualist–collectivist spilt is a simplification, as there would have been differences within each school of thought and overlaps between the two. All the same, a simple bifurcation is a useful way to mark two general positions and a range of differences between them. Another useful two-way division has been proposed between 'official' and 'popular' social work (Jones and Lavalette, 2013; Lavalette and Ioakimidis, 2017). Official social work refers to the professionalised practices of state-directed social welfare, which have dominated modern conceptions of social work in the UK, since the development of the post-war welfare state in particular. The notion of popular social work, problematic though it might be (McDermott, 2014), alerts us to other possibilities for the provision of help that arise from a grassroots community solidarity.

It was official social work that I was entering upon becoming a social worker in the late 1980s, although within this I was to experience another division. The social work I was taught at university, which I was able to try out in my practice placements, was different from, and did not prepare me for, what I was expected to do once qualified and employed in an English social services department. Ten years before I qualified, Bill Jordan had written that it sounded 'simpleminded to talk of social work as "helping people"; yet it is difficult to find a better way of describing what social workers try to do' (Jordan, 1979, p 1). This fitted what I learned while training, but did not describe what I was to do later. Though I was initially a generic social worker, the overwhelming majority of my work was with children and families, and much of it could be characterised as assessing, policing and anxious surveillance, rather than helping.

Two brief stories will illustrate the system I had joined and its influence upon me. I was allocated a family in which the parents had great difficulties in managing the behaviour of their teenage son, David, who attended a special school for children with emotional and behavioural difficulties. I was recently qualified and eager to do social work as Jordan described it. It was challenging work but rewarding, finding ways of getting alongside David and his parents, the latter in particular being willing to work with me. I then received a report that David's father had hit David, causing some bruising. When I spoke with David's father, he told me how he had lost his temper with David and was remorseful about having hit and hurt him. A child protection case conference was convened, the first one I had attended. This was in the early days of parental participation in such meetings, and David's father was able to attend only at the beginning and the end. After he left the meeting near its beginning, having talked about what had happened and expressed regret again, the manager who was chairing the conference said: "I wouldn't trust him as far as I could throw him." I was astonished by this comment, which appeared to come from nowhere, but I was to learn that it represented a general position taken towards parents, that they were not to be trusted and posed a danger to their children. I liked to think I resisted taking such a position, though I think the next story indicates how my perspective shifted at least in part from an outsider to an insider one.

Three or four years later, I was working with a family where court proceedings were underway. Mary's drinking had badly affected her parenting, which was one of the reasons for her children being removed from her care. The plan for the youngest was that she would be adopted, while the older children would remain in long-term foster care. However, Mary was contesting the proceedings and wanted her children returned to her. In many ways she seemed to be getting her life back together, and there had been no reports of her drinking for some time, but the department's view remained firm that care orders were needed and the youngest child should be adopted. I wondered what the court would think. Then Mary phoned one day, sounding clearly drunk. I leapt from my desk, in order to immediately visit her, knowing that seeing her in this state would provide strong evidence for our case. A mature student social worker on placement in my team was sitting opposite, and, though all these years later I do not recall her words, that she was troubled by the alacrity with which I set off to see Mary is a clear memory. I imagine she had yet to develop an insider perspective.

I retained enough of an outsider status to be troubled myself by the system I was working in, feelings I shared with others and which became almost mainstream with the publication of research studies that led to calls for a 'refocusing' of services away from investigative child protection and towards family support (Department of Health, 1995). My own route out of that system was via training in solution-focused practice (Shennan, 2019), which showed me the possibility of a more service-user-led approach. This led me to the narrative therapy conference, and the encounter with the parents who had fallen foul of this system, which never was refocused and was now as much in need of a humane alternative as ever (Featherstone et al, 2014; Featherstone et al, 2018).

Main themes of the interviews

Reading the interviews again, over four years later, the overall image I am left with is of two young people entering adult life and approaching parenthood, with hopes and dreams and the motivation to turn them into a reality, who, when they needed support, found instead that the state services they encountered provided the opposite. "It felt like a constant battle against them, forever fighting, responding, battling against them, rather than them ever helping me, giving support" (Helen).

They were battles that were to end with their children being permanently removed from their care, yet from the bleakness of those moments these young women were able to talk again about renewed hopes, however buffeted they had been by the storms they had gone through. Early 21st-century official social work in the UK had been a major part of those storms, a social work that had buffeted rather than buttressed. In this section I shall disentangle from this overall image several themes that arose in the interviews, including the women's resistance to these storms, before a final section that considers how social workers and others can complement this with their own resistance.

Beginning with hopes, one thing that stood out in the interviews, as well as the women's hopes themselves, was the lack of any signs of interest in these hopes from the social workers involved once concerns arose. Before they had children, both women were clear about the kind of parents they wanted to be.

'I wanted to do a lot of things with my daughter and there's things I wanted to encourage her to get into.' (Karen)

'I didn't want my child to ever have the life that I had to live. I wanted to give them that different life and be a friend to them as well as a parent, and discipline, without too much, and boundaries and routines.' (Helen)

They shared this hope – or intention – that their parenting would be different than they had experienced. "I was looking forward to being able to do things differently than how I was brought up, being close with my child and also having discipline there. For me I had no boundaries and I didn't want that for my child. I was looking forward to doing that differently" (Karen). It did not appear that they were asked about their hopes as parents once services were involved, yet a suggestion by Karen indicates, it seems to me, that this might have been a helpful approach: "I think they should initially ask parents, what type of parent do you want to be, and then help them to achieve that ... Everyone has an idea and it's not always achievable. I mean, it is achievable, but it's not always easy to achieve it."

In that last sentence can be detected the hope-related qualities of motivation and determination. These qualities also appeared at other times, including before parenthood – "I felt like I have to step up now and I have to move forward and become the best person I could possibly be" (Helen) – and during Helen's ordeal following her second child being removed into care, when she exerted great efforts to improve matters – "I also got myself counselling, with three different therapists ... I put myself onto parenting and domestic violence courses, anything I could put myself on". Helen arranged all these services for herself, as at that time she was not experiencing any support from her social worker, and she was not actually aware that social workers could help with such things.

This takes us to what I believe is the central message that emerges from these accounts, which was the nature of the response the parents received from the state social services once they were in difficulties and concerns arose. This is summarised in this stark comment by Karen in our blog post: 'After being in the care system myself, and having a child at 18, *I was automatically put under assessment*, which lasted for two years.' In our interview, Karen reported that a social worker "actually said that almost every parent who's been in care will either be in assessment units or foster placements and most of them go into assessment units". Far from Bill Jordan's conception of social work as 'helping', this type of 'assessment' that one is 'automatically put under' has a chilling sound to my ears. There were liberal mentions of assessment throughout:

'I felt social workers tried to use everything against me in a sense, because ... I think my gran was talking to her and she had an assessment with my grandma, and she came up with some really silly things.' (Karen)

'I was also under assessments, I don't know what it was called now. It was like a parenting assessment, so there was a lady who sort of assessed my parenting pre-birth.' (Karen)

'We then went to an assessment centre for two months, and then my younger son went into care.' (Helen)

Karen found one of her earlier social workers supportive, partly as she "tried to avoid me going into an assessment unit", which adds to the sense that these are not places a parent would want to be in.

The effects of feeling under assessment at all times were starkly described:

'I was nine months pregnant and was having to go to meetings and it was almost impossible. My immunity was down a lot, and running from meeting to meeting was not easy.' (Karen)

'I felt like there was a lot of pressure on me and I was in a constant state of panic and trying to keep up with everything because I knew that obviously children get taken away. I found that probably influenced me and brought me down, made me feel quite depressed and anxious, that didn't help, made it harder.' (Karen)

Various types of assessment are mentioned – psychological, risk, parenting – but what do not appear to have been assessed were support needs and the type of support that might have helped. The omnipresence of assessment appeared to be matched by the absence of support, yet support is surely what is needed for young parents, living with a grandmother because of their own parents having difficulties, or experiencing domestic abuse.

When the courts decided that their children should be adopted, this was of course devastating for the parents. Helen made clear how this loss was added to by the sudden ending of a whole range of intense contacts: "It just went from all of this contact, all of this, to nothing, no communication with anybody, and everything stopped. My solicitor stopped contacting me, the social worker stopped contacting and even my therapy stopped at the same time."

Once Helen and Karen's children had been adopted, it seems the services had no continuing need to be in contact with them. Featherstone et al (2014, p 4) rightly challenge this instrumental view of parents, asking why we don't engage with mothers and fathers as subjects in their own right, and questioning the ethics of 'rescuing children and leaving their parents behind in a society riven by inequalities' (Featherstone et al, 2014, p 3). This connects with one of Helen's final messages that she wanted social workers to hear, which was that they "need to realise that whatever decision they're making about children, it's got huge consequences for everyone involved, and if it's easier to get support, then actually why are you not doing that?" Why indeed? And this ethical question needs to be posed not only, or even primarily, to individual social workers, but to the politicians and policy makers who have pushed adoption in particular in recent years (Hill, 2018).

Perhaps most moving to hear was Helen seeking to put into words her feelings of loss, supported and echoed by Karen:

'Sometimes I feel it would be easier if my children actually died, rather than being removed, because they're out in this world. I have no idea who they are, who they're becoming and I'm not part of their life. I'm grieving, it's constant grieving, you're always going through it and it's not like you can go to a grave and know that that's where your kids are. Any time you think of them, you know they're out there and it just makes it so much harder.' (Helen)

'It's one of the hardest things to ever admit to, but I think that almost everyone I've spoken to has said that, and I feel like that as well. It's hard.' (Karen)

'I don't wish for a second my child had died, but sometimes the pain, that pain … I just feel like, when you lose someone you know, they've gone, whereas we've lost our children but they've not gone, and they're going to become adults who we would not have ever expected them to be.' (Helen)

Yet they retained or renewed a sense of hope. With the service that supported them and arranged the conference presentation where I met them, they engaged with another narrative practice, the Tree of Life (Lock, 2016). Helen explained how this is used as a response to a trauma, in which "you draw a tree and the roots are where you're from, your background, the ground is where you're at now, like what's going on, then the trunk of the tree is your strengths … and then the branches are your people around you, and the fruits and leaves are your hopes and dreams". They also talked about the storms of social services involvement and the effects of these on their trees, yet they always maintained a focus around their hopes and dreams:

'I hope that when she's old enough that if she does want to contact me that I can show her that I have been doing these things and that I've always tried my best to involve her even though she's not there in a sense.' (Karen)

'My hopes and goals are that I can become the woman that my children deserve to have as a mother.' (Helen)

Conclusion

A complicating factor in considering how to deal with the history of complicity illustrated in this chapter is that it is situated in the present.

This is what is happening in state-directed children's social work right now in the UK and in similar forms elsewhere in the world. What is needed most urgently therefore is change, and one way to deal with this history of complicity is by describing and working towards a future of the type of social work practice that should replace it.

A useful entry point is suggested by the four aspects of radical social work practice outlined by Ferguson and Woodward (2009, p 153):

- radical practice as retaining a commitment to good practice;
- radical practice as 'guerilla warfare' and small-scale resistance;
- radical practice as working alongside service users and carers;
- radical practice as collective activity and political campaigning.

The first of these of course begs the question of who determines what counts as good practice, though the authors make a sound case for following the desires of many social work educators and practitioners for practices that are both relationship and values based. Another way to determine good practice is to link this with the third aspect in the list, of working alongside service users and carers, and to learn from what parents tell us would be helpful.

I noted earlier the overall wish of the parents I interviewed for more support to be available, and the specific suggestion of asking parents about their hopes as parents and their ideas for achieving this. Other suggestions made, which will be relevant to social work generally, but especially in the context of statutory powers, were for social workers:

- To be open and transparent: "That transparency of being able to build that trust and the more you're open and explain things to somebody, the more likely they're going to be able to be open and honest with you."
- To explain clearly: "Just make it more easy to understand ... the words that they use."
- To be clear about what is needed: "If someone had said to me, 'You are going to lose your children if you do not open your mouth, yeah?' I would have opened my mouth!"
- To treat parents as individuals; a plea that was made several times, indicating the proceduralisation and standardisation of approach which now grips social work so hard (Fenton, 2016), and the negative impact of this on service users: "Social workers should consider that every parent has different styles, and to help support them in doing that, rather than just sticking to strict guidelines of how parenting should be."

Another potential link between the four aspects of radical practice listed here would be to see following service users' wishes regarding practice as acts of resistance, rather than solely practising according to the imperatives of state employers. Whether these would be small scale or not is another matter, given the moral courage needed to resist 'organisational professionalism', and to act from an 'occupational professionalism' (Fenton, 2016). The latter draws on knowledge arising from understanding the service user's issues, while in the former, organisational rules and procedures are the main source of knowledge (Liljegren, 2012, p 308). That practising in ways more aligned to occupational than organisational professionalism is possible can be seen in texts by people in or close to practice (Rogowski, 2013; Turbett, 2014).

Given the difficulties involved in working in ways that resist current authoritarian child welfare practices, collective activity is crucial. This includes workers coming together and being active in their trade unions, professional associations and campaigning groups such as the Social Work Action Network. What is also needed is for social workers to work collectively with service users and people with lived experience, both to campaign for the changes that are necessary and to assist in the development of new forms of welfare provision. In the child welfare field that has been the focus of this chapter, such groups and alliances already exist, examples in the UK including the Reframe Collective, the Parents, Families and Allies Network, and Parents Advocacy and Rights. The types of help that such parent-led initiatives are developing are important in their own right and can also prefigure more wholesale shifts in practice away from a complicit and towards a more progressive social work.

I believe it is also important to find models of practice that will be congruent with and enable such social work, an essential feature of which, in my view, is to be not only responsive to but led by the wishes of service users. I believe that solution-focused and narrative approaches have something to offer in this respect. Solution-focused practice is led by the hopes of the people being supported (Shennan, 2019), while narrative practitioners have been developing various ways of working collectively (Denborough, 2018). David Denborough (2008) describes the use of collective narrative documents, which respond to collective trauma through written testimonies of hard times that communities have experienced, and the ways in which those communities have actively responded to them. Adding in a little inspiration from the Tree of Life and the solution-focused attention to hopes, perhaps all those who wish to see change in this area – social workers, service users, academics, students and others – can create documents together, of the hard times of social work complicity, the resistance to this and our hopes and dreams of something better. This book is of course already an example of this.

Note
[1] Karen is a pseudonym, as is Helen, the name used for the other parent in the magazine article and this chapter.

References

Attlee, C. (1920) *The social worker*. London: Bell.

Carey, M. and Russell, S. (2003) 'Outsider-witness practices: Some answers to commonly asked questions', *The International Journal of Narrative Therapy and Community Work*, 1: 12–29.

Corbin Dwyer, S. and Buckle, J. (2009) 'The space between: On being an Insider-Outsider in qualitative research', *International Journal of Qualitative Methods*, 8(1), 54–63.

Denborough, D. (2008) *Collective narrative practice: Responding to individuals, groups and communities who have experienced trauma*. Adelaide: Dulwich Centre Publications.

Denborough, D. (2018) *Do you want to hear a story? Adventures in collective narrative practice*. Adelaide: Dulwich Centre Publications.

Department of Health (1995) *Child protection: Messages from research*. London: The Stationery Office.

Dickens, J. (2018) 'Clement Attlee and the social service idea: Modern messages for social work in England', *British Journal of Social Work*, 48(1): 5–20.

Featherstone, B., White, S. and Morris, K. (2014) *Re-imagining child protection: Towards humane social work with families*. Bristol: Policy Press.

Featherstone, B., Gupta, A., Morris, K. and White, S. (2018) *Protecting children: A social model*. Bristol: Policy Press.

Fenton, J. (2016) 'Organisational professionalism and moral courage: Contradictory concepts in social work?', *Critical and Radical Social Work*, 4(2): 199–216.

Ferguson, I. and Woodward, R. (2009) *Radical social work in practice: Making a difference*. Bristol: Policy Press.

Hill, A. (2018) 'Adoption a "runaway train often breaching rights of birth parents"', *The Guardian*, 18 January. Available at: www.theguardian.com/society/2018/jan/18/adoption-has-become-runaway-train-social-workers-cannot-stop

Jones, C. and Lavalette, M. (2013) 'The two souls of social work: Exploring the roots of "popular social work"', *Critical and Radical Social Work*, 1(2): 147–165.

Jordan, B. (1979) *Helping in social work*. London: Routledge and Kegan Paul.

Lavalette, M. and Ioakimidis, V. (2017) '"Popular" social work in extremis: Two case studies on collective welfare responses to social crisis situations', *Social Theory, Empirics, Policy and Practice*, 13(2), 117–132.

Liljegren, A. (2012) 'Pragmatic professionalism: Micro-level discourse in social work', *European Journal of Social Work*, 15(3): 295–312.

Lock, S. (2016) 'The Tree of Life: A review of the collective narrative approach', *Educational Psychology Research and Practice*, 2(1): 2–20.

McDermott, D. (2014) 'The two souls of social work: Exploring the roots of "popular social work" – popular or radical social work?', *Critical and Radical Social Work*, 2(3): 381–383.

Rogowski, S. (2013) *Critical social work with children and families*. Bristol: Policy Press.

Shennan, G. (2017–18) 'A constant grieving', *Professional Social Work*, December 2017–January 2018: 19–20.

Shennan, G. (2019) *Solution-focused practice: Effective communication to facilitate change (second edition)*. London: Bloomsbury.

Shennan, G. (2020) 'Practising social work', in T. Bamford and K. Bilton (eds) *Social work: Past, present and future* (pp 97–113). Bristol: Policy Press.

Shennan, G. and Karen (2018) 'Re-telling a young mother's story'. Chair's Blog, British Association of Social Workers. 7 June [Blog]. Available at www.basw.co.uk/media/news/2018/jun/chairs-blog-re-telling-young-mothers-story

Turbett, C. (2014) *Doing radical social work*. Basingstoke: Palgrave Macmillan.

16

Decolonisation and critical social work pedagogies

Caroline Bald and Akudo Amadiegwu

Introduction

There is much said about social work's complicity in state violence globally, as in systemic intergenerational trauma resulting from ideologically driven social policy – from stolen babies in Spain and Ireland, to institutional racism inherent from Nazi Germany, to apartheid in South Africa, to First Nations oppression (Garner, 2010; Bhatti-Sinclair, 2011; Bartoli, 2013). With each exposed scandal, there is both justified outcry that a profession purporting to stand for social justice should be involved in such brutal subjugation and a reluctance or push-back to scrutinising social work as a whole. It has caused many to ask if social work, by its very nature, is the apparatus of the state of the day. If social justice statements are comforting fig leaves soothing a profession's moral conscience, it may indeed be that social work can only truly decolonise by untying its tether to power altogether. Or is a binary view of social work as state or anti-state too simplistic? Is abolitionism a spectrum that social work has always been engaged in, giving space for daily micro and macro resistances within the system?

This chapter considers both the labour which has gone into exposing social work's complicity with oppression and the ways in which decolonisation might be achieved. The focus is on social work education as a space for resistance and activism. The specific focus which follows is on the structural design of social work education as perhaps a lesser-explored area of resistance – who enters social work education, who teaches and the constructed classroom. The chapter considers as a case study the march to professionalisation experienced across social work in England and, specifically, the politically conferred power that regulatory bodies with registration machinery have over the agency to resist. Is decolonisation compatible with professionalisation?

We acknowledge the intense labour engaged in decolonisation. Questioning if we have come far enough or if more is achievable does not diminish these efforts. The emotional labour of resistance is acknowledged, and the push-back or strength of the backlash is perhaps a testament to how disorientating the resistance to state power has been. There nevertheless remains a curious logic of construction which we will attempt to unpick: whether the binary of social work as 'social – work' will ever allow for full emancipation from state control or whether we must be content with the dualism within social work to help and protect.

Decolonisation

> Who is heard and who is not defines the status quo. Those who embody it, often at the cost of extraordinary silences with themselves, move to the centre; those who embody what is not heard ... are cast out. By redefining whose voice is valued, we redefine our society and its values. (Solnit, 2017, p 18)

An uncredited photograph on social media captures a shop-window sign telling customers 'we are open, the door is just very heavy'. It is a representation of the space social work education now inhabits – physically open, acknowledging its flaws yet unwilling or unable to replace its underpinning, its positional power as an instrument of the state. It begs the question: is the very nature of social work always going to mean there is a door too heavy for some to open, albeit it furnished with signs of inclusion?

While calls to decolonise education have a long history, there has been renewed argument since the murder of George Floyd and the Black Lives Matter global movement. This chapter considers the ethics of inclusion through a discourse analysis, questioning whether there has been engagement with change and a wholesale opening of doors, or if promises of transformation have been bureaucratised to the level of reading list representation. Lastly, I consider whether having a door means that social work, in being *work*, is by its very nature impossible to decolonise without deconstruction.

One of my (Caroline) first responsibilities when becoming a social work educator some five years ago was the arrangement and management of student placements. Two hundred days of in-practice or clinical learning placements accounted for about half of student learning on social work programmes in England. During this time, students would often approach me at the beginning of term or as I was matching them with their placement. I was soon struck by the commonality of their queries: the personal in practice. Students would approach me, most often in the corridor, to whisper "I am a care leaver", "I have a criminal conviction" or "I am a carer". The whisper jarred. I heard their quiet acceptance that their experience was a problem, but also that it might preclude them in some way from social work – the personal was something to be overcome. The majority were working-class, Black women concerned that their knowledge was not valued in social work education (Yosso, 2005).

Later hearing responses such as "we'll need to limit their database access", "it depends", "they knew the course was full time", "should they be studying social work?" in turn seemed to want to educate me, as an educator, that real-life experience was problematised by the "way we do things" and, crucially for the students, weaponised into being something other, to be whispered in corridors. In those whispers, a recognition of difference and the negative social work education in England's focus on student *suitability* becomes a pedagogical lens through which the colonisation of social work remains very much alive through 'think well'.

This chapter is a reflective exploration of the duty critical social work pedagogy has to decolonisation – from accessing our classrooms, to a connected curriculum. The chapter draws on my reflection as a social work educator in England and my doctoral research exploring social work admissions decision making based on *suitability*. I consider whether it is possible for social work education to ever fully acknowledge, let alone address, its role in reproducing inequality.

Much has been written about decolonisation and the necessity of social work education to address and atone for the profession's histories of complicity. It is not my intention to diminish the hard work that has gone into, and continues to go into, addressing privilege and restorative teaching. However, it is my observation through educator experience and research that there remains much to be done, and I would encourage educators to consider not only practice implications but the practice of education itself – the structures, language and power dynamics which either help or hinder our efforts towards full inclusion. In the end, I question whether social work education by its very nature will always risk performativity toward employment, and perhaps it is time that we consider *social work education's* relationship with *work* itself.

Drawing on global social work education literature on decolonisation, this chapter will consider the commonality of lessons learned, concerns and suggested next steps. This chapter is not intended as a summary of decolonisation efforts globally, though it will signpost. My concern is more in relation to what remains undone, the elephant in the room, so to speak: is the very nature of social work education such that there is an inevitability of teaching 'do good', with educators as the experts on what this means and practice pressures to show how it's done, negating student experience; or, worse still, simply commodifying knowledges all over again in the name of doing good?

Decolonising the university

The history of social work education has been one of increasing removal from street-activism roots. Calls to professionalise social work began in the early 1900s, in part attempting to gain traction in service negotiation. The push from inside the profession followed an already established path of cross-public-sector education, with teaching, nursing, midwifery and, most recently, policing becoming university-based education. A degreed social work was presented as giving social work as a discipline its rightful status. From the 1980s, curiously in parallel and contrast with growing calls for widening participation – a movement acknowledging the emancipatory relevance of representation in higher education – mechanisms were growing to protect this status, to restrict or filter social work education access and content. Some might say, in truth, by seeking status in universities as the infrastructure of empire, the profession held its own feet to the fire of Euro-capitalist centricity (Bhambra et al, 2018).

Decolonisation without definition

It would be true to say that the definition of decolonisation is contested. While most recently universities in the UK have heralded evidence of decolonisation by reviewing reading lists, it ought to be more clearly acknowledged that decolonisation is a process which frames colonisation as not accidental but a series of investments in maintaining power, with education mechanisms providing both agency and credibility. To separate decolonisation from the violence of colonisation is to silence the symbolic and actual violence in and through which it worked (Icaza and Vazques, 2017).

Decolonisation itself should be considered a broad spectrum of root-and-branch responses to the colonisation of knowledge and space. Mbembe (2016) centres on the root of education – its location, education's epistemological centring of specific knowledges. He asserts that there is a need to critique dominant Eurocentricity, citing 'the fight against what Latin Americans in particular called epistemic coloniality' (Mbembe, 2016, p 5). The term ethnocentric describes an attitude or policy giving priority to the culture and viewpoint of one particular ethnic group – White European in Mbembe's view – to the exclusion of others. Therefore, an ethnocentric curriculum reflects the culture of one ethnic group, often dominant White culture. For example, organising the curriculum of social work theory ethnocentrically, Bhopal (2018) warns, risks student assignments being written from the unacknowledged assumption of Whiteness. To add cultural contextuality to an ethnocentric curriculum is arguably tokenism. Students hearing of cultures valuing community caring for a newborn as an adjunct to attachment theory risks presenting cultural difference or the other, rather than questioning the misogynist ethnocentricity inherent in a theory focusing on maternal care. The function of decolonisation should be to deconstruct theory so as to reconstruct from a global social work perspective. The question is whether English practice is ready to hear social work students who have never heard of Bowlby, and therein lies the staying power of colonised knowledges, an echo to Ball's (1994) 'Little Englandism', which he used to describe the way White British culture presents past glories and the creation of the other.

Reminding of Freire's (1970) warning about the risks of relying on education restricted to the rote learning of specifically Euro-American male theorists, reflecting the credibility of universality, the academy is all too willing to afford only pale–male–stale. All too often, social work academics undertake their review of reading lists at a point in the year when energies are ebbing. The inclusion of critical theorists rarely displaces mid-century stalwarts, despite repeated concern as to their validity. Is it enough to provide a counter argument to Eurocentric knowledges, or does that continue to uphold attachment theory, for example, as a dominant worldview, while race- and gender-aware counter knowledges are included – but only as bit parts, all too often relegated to the cutting floor of the student's mind in the race to remember for performative assignments – or, worse still, tick the marking schema's performative criticality box?

This ordering of knowledge, what we teach as well as how we include order and emphasis, is captured in Bhambra and colleagues'(2020) call for a shift to connected sociologies. She too considers an epistemological concern for knowledge not being linear, but highlights the space given to ordering knowledge, such as historically locating in student minds older as origin and origin as truth. Bhambra presents the process of decolonisation as a structural reconfiguration – with space to deconstruct the curriculum, for example, and reconstruct it with a renewed ordering of knowledge. It is curious to consider the social work curriculum as an example of decolonisation praxis. While in England the curriculum is not prescribed as it is for other professional educations such as nursing, clarity is given by the professional regulator, Social Work England, about what students ought to learn, presented as headings in the form of a Professional Capabilities Framework. In many ways this allows for individual providers to develop and deliver curricula relevant to decolonisation. However, this does appear to be on a continuum with regulatory authority and power being retained through the threat of inspection and revalidation of the provider. This area of scrutiny is under-researched, with many social work academics speaking in terms of 'don't ask, don't tell'.

Bhambra (2014) noted that there is 'no connection where there is no reconstruction; and no understanding remains unchanged by connection' (Bhambra, 2014, p 5). To therefore make connection with decolonisation means to engage with the necessity and possibilities of reconstruction. However, in social work, in part argued to embed professionalisation, there is emphasis on consistency – a pull away from curriculum-level reconstruction. It was evident when establishing a new social work master's course, for example, when the regulatory body rejected calling the new degree by an alternative name, Social Work and Human Rights, that the absence of written guidance does not diminish inferred agency. To do so was argued to be potentially confusing, and might imply a point of difference from other providers – the latter argument reinforcing an unsaid expectation that social work education content or emphasis should be comparable across providers, and that content should reflect configured narratives – with no room for legitimate reconstruction beyond a dedicated module and course theme. However, there remains a concern-causing pause to avoid getting what you might wish for – as Nancy Fraser might say, capitalism finds a way to eat its own tail. How far is social work education from being provided with a prescribed curriculum, like that in teaching – heralded as a standardisation improvement mechanism no doubt, challenging those epistemological connections that Bhambra argues as being key to growing particular forms of understanding; whose understanding notwithstanding.

Pete (2018) presents decolonisation as the application of epistemological knowledges in the form of pedagogy or methodologies of teaching. Echoing Freire's centring conscientisation, Pete argues for a more 'complete conversation' which centres story, allowing for reflexivity and relatability – 'of telling the story then engaging in a critical examination of "how you have come to know what you know"' (Pete, 2018, p 174). For me as a social work educator, there is at least a moment once a year where I am heavily reminded of the knowledge in the classroom, my teaching about trauma becoming increasingly trauma informed while still not fully acknowledging that the expertise is in and of the classroom. The pedagogical rupture reminds me, as an educator, of the fundamental value of intersectional and complete conversations, as well as of the symbolic violence inherent in the traditional classroom set-up of screen and desk, a structural limitation embedded in learner expectation on campus, and a structural inequality undermined by the move to online learning due to the COVID-19 pandemic, renewing interest in physicality, the how and where of pedagogy (Beesley and Devonald, 2020; McFadden et al, 2020; Rowbotham, 2020).

Finally, to develop the construction of decolonised learning, social work education must acknowledge positionality – as mentioned, the knowledge or capital in the classroom – but, in addition, crucially, while also addressing the 'incomplete narratives' evident in the academic body, the lecturers (Icaza and Vazques, 2017).

> A university that engages in *positioning its knowledge* practices is a university that reveals the intersectional conditions of *knowledge production* and that shows unequivocally how the axes of differentiation along race, class and gender have *been essential* for establishing the canon and, concurrently, how the canon has been essential to reproduce these *axes of discrimination*. (Icaza and Vazques, 2017, p 119; original emphasis)

Icaza and Vazques (2017) reinforce the centrality of the knowledge in the room; that teaching is meaning making and that enabling reflexivity is based on the academy's skills to encourage and hold difficult conversations in a safe space. Some might consider this to be something that social work education does well. The education and training standards encourage professional reflection, if not reflexivity, as a key capability integral to practice. Student social workers are encouraged to work through arguments from a critical perspective, drawing on their own experience. However, in turn, students must routinely bring their deliberations back to relevance to social work practice, assuming a knowledge of what 'social work' is – and, crucially, is not. In this lies concern for what can be described as learning under the bright lights of assessment. Student social workers are being burdened with critique under the impression that their views are afforded equal value, while to err has already been presented as jeopardising the marking schema. When researching student social worker professional well-being, students were asked about their experiences of help seeking, with the word 'fear' repeatedly used to explain why help was either not sought earlier or not sought at all (Bald and Howells, 2017; Finch, 2017). In a relatively short time, students had gleaned learning which advised them against help seeking, that to seek help would in some way speak negatively to their professional capacity. Closer review noted intersectional differences, and, while the sample was too small to be representative, it echoed increasing evidence of negative experiences of social work education by minority students (Azzopardi and McNeill, 2016; Harms Smith and Rasool, 2020; Sangha, 2021). The importance of placing the burden of decolonisation on the academy, not on the student, cannot be underlined more clearly. All too often, social work education conflates relationship-based values with mutual responsibility to do the work. Unlearning is difficult and takes time, with limited to no space provided in contemporary university workload measurement tools for meta reconstruction.

For some in their first year studying social work, framing 'fear' as an unconscious learned response is part of a construction that I refer to as 'think right'. Grown out of the 'think well' narrative, 'think right' is a pervasive message representation of what social work means and what social work does, evident long before a student decides to apply to a social work education provider. Admissions to social work education courses is an under-researched area of pedagogy. Considered to be outside the classroom, there is limited reflection on the learning gleaned through navigating the classroom door, heavier for some, to revisit the shop window image. As with Stan Cohen's river, entering a classroom into which you cannot see is one of social capital – a conceptual understanding of what social work might look like and a personal alignment with that understanding. To apply for training draws on a range of capital, including narrative capital, an ability to verbalise relevant to circumstance or to talk the talk. What academics rarely do is go outside the door to check what it looks like from the other side: cultural references to social work, course web pages, open door policies to engagement. We assume a role of ensuring that only the right people are admitted onto our courses and that our courses remain available only to those who demonstrate that they 'think right'. The level of scrutiny in social work education courses in England is higher than that for employment. Doctoral research findings show that academics are enabled to ask applicants openly about criminal convictions in open interview sessions, the literature highlighting how brutalising an experience that can be. The Social Work England education and training standards centre suitability as a key conceptual framework for admissions decision making, without construction. They position the test of suitability as common sense – signifying only that applicants need to meet measures of 'health, good character and conduct', before positioning this statement immediately ahead of reference to criminal records, thereby positioning suitability as a vetting out, a gatekeeping framework.

In colonising social work education, social work practice in the UK has notable differences along lines of race – be it working in child protection (Bernard and Harris, 2016), mental health (Walker, 2020) or Gypsy, Roma and Traveller communities (Cemlyn, 2008), to give examples.

Where to?

Decolonisation within the social work context includes the decentralisation and reconstruction of knowledge production, beyond surface-level change (Crampton, 2015), to incorporate 'new knowledges' which reinvent the world (Marais and Marais, 2007; Bhambra et al, 2018). However, Marais and Marais (2007) decry the minimal effort to incorporate 'silenced knowledges' that originated from the global South into mainstream social work discourse. Previous attempts to make social work education and service delivery culturally appropriate were carried out within the context of the dominant Western ideologies. Brydon (2012) argues that, internationally, the social work curriculum has been constructed on Western ideals that are held to be universal.

The social work curriculum in the UK is all-encompassing and goes beyond the classroom experience, to include practice placements. As is widely acknowledged, the curriculum is inherently Eurocentric. This presents a narrow view of the world, taught to generations of aspiring social workers as authoritative, and, ultimately, informs their practice and service provision. However, Pinar (2004) argues for a cultural change, with the incorporation of personal stories into the curriculum. This, he posits, has been identified as the most effective approach educators can use to sensitise their students to issues regarding social justice. It is on this premise that this chapter proceeds to proffer a solution to the issues outlined earlier, exploring different ways to incorporate not just personal stories but other knowledges and worldviews into the social work curriculum.

Personal stories are not just limited to case studies in written text but include personal accounts of lived experiences shared by service users, which recognise them as experts in their quotidian lives. They also include stories shared by students of their experiences on placements, and the 'self' they bring into social work, without feeling the need or pressure to fit in or separate their authentic self from the 'professional' self they present. Rajan-Rankin (2015) highlights the invisibility that Black students in particular feel when they are on placements. This discourse, which is subsumed under 'neo-liberalist ideals of professionalism'(Rajan-Rankin 2014) that the social curriculum promotes, renders students powerless and voiceless to share their own narratives, for fear of being misconstrued as either racist or unprofessional (Rajan-Rankin, 2015).

Ways and approaches

A decolonised social work curriculum can be achieved in multiple ways. I will explore two approaches for the purposes of this discourse. The first approach is the Reggio Emilia Pedagogical Approach, which encourages teachers to engage in active learning and sustained, shared thinking with children. This approach is rooted in early years pedagogy; however, I have benefited from this approach both as a teacher and as a student. I admit that I am partial to this approach because of my background in early years education, and it has influenced my teaching and social work practice. I have found the approach to be effective in a range of social work practice, from sharing communication skills with parents to brain injury-related social work, as it recognises service users as 'experts' in their own lived experiences.

In this context, this approach would involve the co-construction of knowledge by teachers and students in collaboration, where the student is an active participant and 'owns' the knowledge and the teacher is a co-learner and co-collaborator. The curricular approach therefore would not be a top-down approach where the teacher/lecturer only shares knowledge from the Westernised curriculum, but instead where the teacher encourages active participation from the student, who takes ownership of the knowledge. Students then bring knowledge from their cultural background and placement experience and both teacher and learner become co-learners, co-collaborators and co-constructors of knowledge (or knowledges).

It is imperative to acknowledge the challenge, as Brydon (2012) rightly highlights, in the acceptance and incorporation of other worldviews into one's pre-existing frame of reference. Admittedly, this can be challenging for the academic, irrespective of race, who has to accept, incorporate and filter where necessary other belief systems, values, idioms and practices into the pre-existing, albeit Westernised, frame of reference, while ensuring high-quality teaching and making judgements regarding suitability, standardisation and sustainability. In practical terms (that is, if you asked me for a how-to guide), the skill of 'sustained shared thinking' can be used to surmount this difficulty. Drawn from early years pedagogy, sustained shared thinking was introduced to promote creativity and critical thinking, and was designed to support a child's metacognition and emotional, social and personal development (Brodie, 2014). In this context, this would involve the sharing of thinking between the social work student and lecturer (Siraj and Asani, 2015) in a collaborative effort with the aim of developing the student's critical thinking skills with support from others (Brodie, 2014), which shows sustained learning over time (Purdon, 2016). The learning process is a continuum, as the Reggio Emilio Approach also advocates continuous professional development and lifelong learning; therefore the learning process is ongoing and rapidly evolving.

An example of welcoming other worldviews is in child raising/caregiving practices within other contexts. Students being encouraged to share their own non-Western experiences or perspective can aid in the understanding and perceptions of the caregiving relationship. The Western lens is based on Bowlby's (1958) Attachment Theory, which studies the caregiver/child relationship, the caregiver being mostly the mother. However, in many contexts, it literally 'takes a village to raise a child'. The child may be raised first by the grandmother, whose caring duties may start from what is traditionally known in Eastern Nigeria as 'omugwo', a custom that involves the postpartum and nursing care of both mother and child (Onyeji, 2004; Moscadino et al, 2006; Umunna, 2012), effectively raising the child supported by a host of relatives. Critical feminists argue that the social construction of the mother as the primary caregiver results in certain women being problematised, punished and policed for lack of adherence to the White middle-class parenting ideal (Dominelli, 2002), thereby neglecting the mother's needs (Buchanan, 2013). Duschinsky, Greco and Solomon (2015a) further argue that this approach is politically motivated and serves an agenda which is patriarchal and unfair (Contratto, 2002) and places a premium on White middle-class parenting, to the detriment of other cultures (Duschinsky et al, 2015a) that may be multi-generational and that influences their idea of parenting (Croll, 2006).

Bhugra and Gupta (2011) assert that good practice must be culturally appropriate and give due consideration to issues that relate to diversity, including gender, religion and sexual orientation. Practice placements are an avenue for students to develop and express a decolonised mindset and cultural awareness, especially when supporting ethnic families. Culture, in this regard, is not necessarily in relation to demographic or geographic locations, but an expression of conscious choice, identity or representation (Ray and Srinivas, 2012) and dearly held values and norms (World Health

Organisation, 2020). Therefore, it is imperative for practice placements to create an enabling environment for students to develop these skills.

Drawing from my own placement experience, this requires the interrogation of dominant discourse through the lens of critical social work (Fook, 2016), which helped me to challenge the linear thinking or the inference or even belief that there is one way of creating knowledge, in this instance, the Western view (Fook, 2012). I had an ethical dilemma when supporting B., a 13-year-old South Asian girl with mental health challenges. B.'s name and identity have been anonymised in line with the Data Protection Act 2018. B., in contravention of her treatment plan, did not comply with the meal arrangements of the hospital, she just wanted food provided by her parents at mealtimes. This was concerning, considering her body mass index and general health and well-being. Adopting the stance of a 'researcher in practice' (Schon, 1983) helped me to create a new way of understanding and not just to accept established knowledge.

The Western perspective was concerned with the nutritional value and calorific content of the meals, and rightly so. However, it was imperative to understand who B. was, her identity, which in this regard refers to B.'s perception of herself and her place in the social order (Fook, 2016). Europeans have a higher body mass than contemporary South Asians, whose body mass, comparatively, is generally lowerfrom birth – a characteristic that even persists generationally after emigration to different countries of the world, including the UK (Wulan et al, 2010; Yajnik, 2003; Pomeroy et al, 2019). The highest national rates of thinness and stunting in the world are recorded in South Asia (UNICEF, 2010, p 6). The onset of puberty for South Asian girls is between ages 10 and 12, and they experience rapid growth, reaching full adult height by the age of 15 (UNICEF, 2010). However, the concept of adolescence is regarded as a Western construct, as girls of age 15 and women are jointly categorised as 'women of reproductive age' in light of their gender, sexuality and reproductive ability (UNICEF 2010, p 2). Hicks (2015) argues against this view of gender as a set of cultural practices that reduces the person to just a role or identity, and he reiterates the feminist argument that gender is a social relationship, largely due to the promotion of hierarchy, which is reinforced through daily interactions.

Studying food habits is imperative, because of the significant role it plays in the identity of a society and understanding their culture, due to its connection with other aspects of culture (Arnott, 2011). In South Asian communities, food and sharing meals symbolises kinship, and is important in the establishment of intergenerational social and kin relations (Janowski and Kerlogue, 2007); it strengthens familial and communal relationships (Leong-Salobir, 2011), with close links to religion (Arnott, 2011). Among South Asian migrant families such as B.'s, food signifies ethnic identity and serves as a means of connection to 'home' (Vallianatos and Raine, 2008). In some South Asian communities, fasting, which includes partial restriction of and total abstinence from food, is traditional, and a religious practice that may be misconstrued, if viewed from a Western perspective, as starving to death (Arnott, 2011).

I am mindful that this may be a generalised view of South Asian communities, but the purpose of this discourse is to highlight and underscore the meaning and importance of food to B., beyond the Western lens. As D'sylva and Beagan (2011) succinctly put it, 'food is culture but it's also power'.

Integrated learning model

Another approach would be to adopt aspects of the integrated learning model (Picciano, 2017). This model was designed for online learning but can be adapted to suit blended learning, which incorporates face-to-face interactions in the classroom. It is a pedagogical approach that involves a co-construction of knowledge between the student and lecturer. Learning is a social activity which is concerned not only with the quality of subject content but also with the social and emotional development of the student. Students are encouraged to contribute to the discourse and engage in dialectical questioning and reflection, leading to the development of new knowledges. The process is fluid and collaborative.

In this context, the decolonisation process permeates every strand of the Integrated Learning Model and, by extension, the whole curricular offering of social work education, both in and out of the classroom, through to assessments and also practice placements. It interrogates preconceived ideas and ideals, and subject content and the student's learning. An advantage of this model is that it is flexible, which is needed as the learning evolves.

Picciano (2017) refers to content as a major driver of instruction, with its mainly linguistic delivery whereby the teacher speaks and the students listen, and the teacher writes and then the students write. However, this must not be the case. When adapted to suit a decolonised curriculum, the subject/content includes knowledge from different parts of the world, including the global South. I have carefully curated research from the global South in this chapter, especially in B.'s case described earlier, and the richness and wealth of knowledge presents a perspective different from the norm but opens a whole new world.

This learning model is concerned not just with the curricular content but also with the social/emotional support of the student. This is derived from constructivist thought, which views teaching and learning as social activities. Picciano (2017) emphasises the importance of the social and emotional development of the student at different levels of education, even at graduate level. The delivery of the decolonised curriculum should encourage open and honest conversations where students can make contributions without fear of being tagged as racists or being misconstrued (Rajan-Rankin, 2015). This model also encourages independent learning where students can carry out research from other parts of the world. Dialectal questioning takes the Socratic approach, where the teacher uses skilled questions to assess the student's knowledge and facilitate critical thinking. This also helps in reflection, which has been written about extensively in social work.

Social work is an international professional and, as I always emphasise to my students, the degree earned from the University of Essex can open up opportunities in South Africa, Australia, America, Canada and in different parts of the world. The decolonisation movement is burgeoning globally, from the Indigenous thinking of the Aborigines and Native Americans increasingly pushing for recognition in Australia and America, respectively (Brydon, 2012), through to the resistance movement characterised by 'Rhodes must fall' in South Africa (Kessi et al, 2020).

The curriculum must therefore be a reflection of the international appeal of the profession, otherwise we would be doing students a great disservice.

Conclusion

We are mindful that this chapter has been written through the lens of two social work academics, one Black, one White. We have reflected on the nature of 'Blackness' and 'Whiteness' as socially constructed labels foisted on us, which we adopt as identification. However, race is not a feature of our personal identity or how we view ourselves. Indeed, being Black was not an issue until Akudo immigrated to the UK or Caroline emigrated to South Africa. However, we are increasingly mindful of the importance of this symbolisation, as students find resonance and acceptance because of what we each represent either in look, stories or language.

The pedagogical approaches we have referenced in this chapter are the Reggio Emilia Approach, with origins in the town of Reggio Emilio in Italy, and the works of the American professor Anthony Picciano. Our view of decolonisation is not of a complete erasure of Western ideas but of an opportunity to bring together a fusion of ideas to learn about and uphold the rights of a person, a people, in order to contribute to and create a new body of knowledge about the rapidly changing world around us.

What we both agree on is there being a need to move how decolonisation is practised into an everyday understanding of the power of language, knowledge and skills. As Bhopal (2018) affirms, we do not live in a post-racial society in the UK and, as such, much remains to be addressed in undoing the harms caused in colonising social work education.

References

Arnott, M.L. (2011) *Gastronomy: The Anthropology of Food and Food Habits*. Berlin: Walter De Gruyter Mouton.

Azzopardi, C. and McNeill, T. (2016) From cultural competence to cultural consciousness: Transitioning to a critical approach to working across differences in social work. *Journal of Ethnic & Cultural Diversity in Social Work*, 25(4): 282–299.

Bald, C. and Howells, A. (2017) Professionalising social work education without losing our soul: A critical reflection on the role and purpose of practice placements in the context of Teaching Partnerships. *Journal of Practice Teaching & Learning*, 15(3): 75–87.

Ball, S. (1994) *Education Reform: A Critical and Post-structural Approach*. Milton Keynes: Open University Press.

Bartoli, A. (2013) *Anti-racism in Social Work Practice*. St Albans: Critical Publishing Ltd.

Beesley, P. and Devonald, J. (2020) Partnership working in the face of a pandemic crisis impacting on social work placement provision in England. *Social Work Education*, 39(8): 1146–1153. https://doi.org/10.1080/02615479.2020.1825662.

Bernard, C. and Harris, P. (2016) *Safeguarding Black Children: Good Practice in Child Protection*. London: Jessica Kingsley Publishers.

Bhambra, G.K. (2014) *Connected Sociologies*. London: Bloomsbury Academic

Bhambra, G. and Nisancioglu (2018) *Decolonising the University*. London: Pluto Press.

Bhambra, G.K., Nişancıoğlu, K. and Gebrial, D. (2020) Decolonising the university in 2020. *Identities*, 27(4): 509–516.

Bhatti-Sinclair, K. (2011) *Anti-racist Practice in Social Work*. Basingstoke: Macmillan.

Bhopal, K. (2018) *White Privilege: The Myth of a Post-racial Society*. Bristol: Policy Press.

Bhugra, D. and Gupta, S. (eds) (2011) *Migration and Mental Health*. Cambridge; New York: Cambridge University Press.

Bowlby, J. (1958) The nature of the child's tie to his mother. *International Journal of Psycho-Analysis*, 39(5): 350–373.

Brodie, K. (2014) *Sustained Shared Thinking in the Early Years: Linking Theory to Practice*. London: Routledge.

Brydon, K. (2012) Promoting diversity or confirming hegemony? In search of new insights for social work. *International Social Work*, 55: 155–167.

Buchanan, F. (2013) A critical analysis of the use of attachment theory in cases of domestic violence. *Critical Social Work*, 14(2): 19–31.

Cemlyn, S. (2008) Human rights and Gypsies and Travellers: An exploration of the application of a human rights perspective to social work with a minority community in Britain. *The British Journal of Social Work,* 37(1): 153–173.

Contratto, S. (2002) A feminist critique of attachment theory and evolutionary psychology. In M.B. Ballou and L.S. Brown (eds) *Rethinking Mental Health and Disorder: Feminist Perspectives*. New York: Guildford Press, pp 29–47.

Crampton, A. (2015) Decolonizing social work 'best practices' through a philosophy of impermanence. *Journal of Indigenous Social Development*, 4(12): 8–11.

Croll, E.J. (2006) *The Intergenerational Contract in the Changing Asian Family*. Oxford Development Studies 34: 473–491.

Dominelli, L. (2012) *Feminist Social Work Theory and Practice*. Basingstoke: Palgrave.

D'Sylva, A. and Beagan, B.L. (2011) 'Food is culture, but it's also power': the role of food in ethnic and gender identity construction among Goan Canadian women. *Journal of Gender Studies*, 20: 279–289.

Duschinsky, R., Greco, M. and Solomon, J. (2015a) The politics of attachment: Lines of flight with Bowlby, Deleuze and Guattari. *Theory, Culture & Society*, 32: 173–195.

Duschinsky, R., Greco, M. and Solomon, J. (2015b) Wait up! Attachment and sovereign power. *International Journal of Politics, Culture, and Society*, 28: 223–242.

Finch, J. (2017) *Supporting Struggling Students on Placement: A Practical Guide*. Bristol: Policy Press.

Fook, J. (2012) *Social Work: A Critical Approach to Practice*. 2nd edn. London; Thousand Oaks: SAGE.

Fook, J. (2016) Critical reflectivity in education and practice. In B. Pease and J. Fook (eds) *Transforming Social Work Practice: Postmodern Critical Perspectives*. London: Routledge, pp 195–210.

Friere, P. (1970) *Pedagogy of the Oppressed*. London: Penguin Books.

Harms Smith, L. and Rasool, S. (2020) Deep transformation toward decoloniality in social work: Themes for change in a social work higher education program. *Journal of Progressive Human Services*, 31(2): 144–164.

Hicks, S. (2015) Social work and gender: An argument for practical accounts. *Qualitative Social Work*, 14: 471–487.

Icaza, R. and Vazques, R. (2017) Intersectionality and Diversity research in Higher Education, *Tijdschrift voor Orthopedagogiek* (Special Issue on Diversity in Academia), edited by H. Jansen, 7–8: 349–357.

Janowski, M. and Kerlogue, F. (eds) (2007) *Kinship and Food in South East Asia*. Copenhagen: Nordic Institute of Asian Studies.

Kessi, S., Marks, Z. and Ramugondo, E. (2020) Decolonizing African Studies. *Critical African Studies*, 12: 271–282.

Leong-Salobir, C. (2011) *Food Culture in Colonial Asia: A Taste of Empire*. London: Routledge.

Marais, L. and Marais, L. (2007) Walking between two worlds: An exploration of the interface between Indigenous and first-world industrialized culture. *International Social Work*, 50(6): 809–20.

Mbembe, J.A. (2016) Decolonizing the university: New directions. *Arts and Humanities in Higher Education*, 15(1): 29–45.

McFadden, P., Russ, E., Blakeman, P., Kirwin, G., Anand, J., Lahteinen, S., Baugerud, G. and Tham, P. (2020) COVID-19 impact on social work admissions and education in seven international universities. *Social Work Education,* 39(8): 1154– 1163. https://doi.org/10.1080/02615 479.2020.1829582.

Moscardino, U., Nwobu, O. and Axia, G. (2006) Cultural beliefs and practices related to infant health and development among Nigerian immigrant mothers in Italy. *Journal of Reproductive and Infant Psychology*, 24: 241–255.

Onyeji, C. (2004) Igbo rural women in Africa as creative personalities: Musical processing of socio-economic solidarity. *Journal of Musical Arts in Africa*, 1: 84–101.

Pete, S. (2018) Meschachakanis, a Coyote Narrative: Decolonizing Higher Education. In G.K. Bhambra, D. Gebriel and K. Nişancıoğlu (eds) *Decolonizing the University*. London: Pluto Press, pp 173–189.

Picciano, A.G. (2017) Theories and frameworks for online education: Seeking an integrated model. Online Learning 21. Available at: http://olj.online learningconsortium.org/index.php/olj/article/view/1225

Pinar, W.F. (2004) *What is Curriculum Theory?* Mahwah: Lawrence Erlbaum Associates.

Pomeroy, E., Mushrif-Tripathy, V., Cole, T.J., Wells, J.C.K. and Stock, J.T. (2019) Ancient origins of low lean mass among South Asians and implications for modern type 2 diabetes susceptibility. *Scientific Reports* 9: art 10515. Available at: https://link.springer.com/content/pdf/10.1038/s41 598-019-46960-9.pdf

Purdon, A. (2016) Sustained shared thinking in an early childhood setting: an exploration of practitioners' perspectives. *Education*, 3–13(44): 269–282.

Rajan-Rankin, S. (2014) Self-identity, embodiment and the development of emotional resilience. *British Journal of Social Work*, 44: 2426–2442.

Rajan-Rankin, S. (2015) Anti-racist social work in a 'post-race society'? Interrogating the amorphous 'other'. Available at: www.researchgate.net/ publication/281488401_Anti-racist_social_work_in_a_'post-race_soci ety'_Interrogating_the_amorphous_'other'

Ray, K. and Srinivas, T. (2012) *Curried Cultures: Globalization, Food, and South Asia*. Berkeley: University of California Press.

Rowbotham, J. (2020) Students pass judgement on online learning: 'never again'. *The Australian*, 5 December.

Sangha, J. (2021) What are the experiences of Black, Asian and minority ethnic students in relation to their progression on an undergraduate social work course in one university in England? *Social Work Education*, 0: 1–20.

Schön, D.A. (1983) *The Reflective Practitioner*. London: Temple Smith.

Siraj-Blatchford, I. and Asani, R. (2015) The role of sustained shared thinking, play and metacognition in young children's learning. University of Wollongong, Faculty of Social Sciences – Papers (Archive). Available at: https://ro.uow.edu.au/sspapers/1486/

Solnit, R. (2017) *The Mother of All Questions*. London: Granta.

Tamburro, A. (2013) Including decolonization in social work education. *Journal of Indigenous Social Development*, 2(1): 1–16.

Umunna, D. (2012) Rethinking the neighborhood watch: How lessons from the Nigerian village can creatively empower the community to assist poor, single mothers in America. *American University Journal of Gender, Social Policy & the Law*, 20: 847.

United Nations Education Fund (2010) A continuum of care for adolescent girls in South Asia: Defining the issues, synthesizing evidence, and working towards a policy agenda. Available at: http://origin.who.int/pmnch/media/membernews/2011/adolescent_health_rosa.pdf

Vallianatos, H. and Raine, K. (2008) Consuming food and constructing identities among Arabic and South Asian immigrant women. *Food, Culture & Society*, 11: 355–373.

Walker, S. (2020) Systematic racism: big, black, mad and dangerous in the criminal justice system. In R. Majors, K. Carberry and T. Ransaw (eds) *The International Handbook of Black Community Mental Health*. Bingley: Emerald Publishing, pp 41–60.

World Health Organisation (2020) Embracing cultural diversity unlocks key resources for more inclusive health systems. BCI Hub. Available at: https://bci-hub.org/news/embracing-cultural-diversity-unlocks-key-resources-more-inclusive-health-systems

Wulan, S.N., Westerterp, K.R. and Plasqui, G. (2010) Ethnic differences in body composition and the associated metabolic profile: A comparative study between Asians and Caucasians. *Maturitas*, 65: 315–319.

Yajnik, C.S., Fall, C.H.D., Coyaji, K.J., Hirve, S.S., Rao, S., Parker, D.J.P. et al (2003) Neonatal anthropometry: The thin–fat Indian baby – The Pune Maternal Nutrition Study. *International Journal of Obesity*, 27: 173–180.

Yosso, T.J. (2005) Whose culture has capital? A critical race theory discussion of community cultural wealth, race. *Ethnicity and Education*, 8(1): 69–91.

17

Adoption social work practice in Ireland: critical reflections on present-day injustices

Claire McGettrick

Introduction

I am grateful to the editors for their kind invitation to contribute to this collection. This book is an important and timely intervention; it considers how social work practice has been complicit in historical injustices and examines instances where social workers have resisted human rights abuses in the past. Social work and the populations it serves can only benefit from a frank and honest engagement with its complex history. However, to do so successfully, the social work profession must also confront discriminatory practices in the present.

In this chapter I argue that in the adoption field in Ireland, oppressive social work practices are not a phenomenon that can be consigned to the past. Despite the profession's grounding in human rights and social justice principles, adoption social work practice often requires the execution of policies that are at odds with such values. So-called 'historical' injustices are perpetuated through the withholding of records from adopted people and the micro-management of those who wish to reunite with their families of origin. Conversely, it is noteworthy that social workers have been among the most vocal advocates for children's rights in intercountry adoption, often in the face of significant opposition (for example, O'Brien, 2009; Boland, 2014). Yet, social workers in the same field engage in practices that discriminate against adult adopted people. In this chapter I explore the possible reasons for this contradiction.

My work is grounded in three main perspectives, each of which informs this chapter. Firstly, I am an adopted person who grew up under Ireland's closed, secret adoption system. As a child, I had no contact with my mother or my family of origin. Although it is now almost 30 years since I first met my mother, I am still denied access to my full adoption file. In this chapter I share some of my personal experience with social work practice. It is the first time I have done so in a public forum; for several reasons (not least the intent behind this book), I believe that this is the right time and place to do so.

Secondly, my personal experience of inequality inspired me to become an activist and advocate, pursuing justice for people affected by Ireland's 'architecture of containment' (Smith, 2007). Over a 20-year period since the turn of the century my colleagues and I have gathered thousands of pages of documentary evidence and witness testimony from people affected by forced family separation, Mother and Baby Homes, Magdalene Laundries and other institutions.[1] Drawing on this expertise, I highlight some of the injustices that play out in present-day social work practice.

Thirdly, my personal experience, activism and advocacy work led me to enter the world of academia, where I examine and problematise adoption research paradigms. I am grateful to be funded by the Irish Research Council to conduct my doctoral research on the bodies of expert knowledge on adoption at the School of Sociology in University College Dublin. I advocate for a paradigm shift in social work practice as it relates to adopted people. By interrogating how and why adult adopted people must interact with social work practice in the first place, I hope to promote reflection among social workers about the role the profession plays in the private lives of people affected by adoption.

I conclude this chapter with a brief discussion of the important work being carried out in the Irish Association of Social Workers (IASW). In 2021, in response to the publication of Ireland's Mother and Baby Homes Commission of Investigation (MBHCOI) *Final Report*, the IASW issued a historic apology for the failings of the social work profession (IASW, 2021). This marked the beginning of a period of reflection in the Irish social work field about adoption and related issues. The IASW's efforts demonstrate the benefits for all concerned of collaborating with people impacted upon by human rights abuses.

While this chapter focuses predominantly on social work practice as it relates to adopted people in Ireland, much of it also applies to mothers, relatives and indeed social work practices in other jurisdictions.

A note about terminology

From the outset, it is necessary to correct a common misconception about so-called 'historical' injustices in Ireland.[2] The discourses surrounding our nation's treatment of women and children in the 20th century wrongly characterise such abuses as (a) exclusively institutional and (b) historical. James Smith (2007, p 2) defines Ireland's 'architecture of containment' in both concrete and abstract terms. In the case of the former, it comprised of a range of institutions, including industrial and reformatory schools, Mother and Baby Homes, Magdalene Laundries and adoption agencies. In its abstract form, this architecture took the form of the legislation (including adoption legislation) that underpinned the system, as well as the 'official and public discourses that resisted admitting to the existence and function of their affiliated institutions' (Smith, 2007, p 2). To date, however, state inquiries have taken a compartmentalised approach, investigating only (a certain number of) institutions and largely ignoring the abstract elements of Ireland's containment infrastructure, including the adoption system.

Forced family separation, whether institutional or otherwise, was central to Ireland's architecture of containment. In the Irish context, 'forced family separation' means the forcible separation of children from their families of origin through adoption, through the 'boarding out' system[3] or through institutionalisation. Contrary to the sworn testimony of mothers, and although the adoption system was not part of its remit, the MBHCOI *Final Report* alleged that it 'found very little evidence that children were forcibly taken from their mothers' (MBHCOI, 2021, p 9). Eight witnesses took judicial review proceedings to challenge the Commission's findings, and in December 2021, the Irish High Court declared that the MBHCOI had denied fair procedures to these survivors (Clann Project, 2021). As part of the settlement, the government deposited the High Court declarations in the Oireachtas[4] Library alongside the MBHCOI *Final Report*, and the impugned sections of the *Report* are now listed alongside it on the government's website (Government of Ireland, 2021). As evidenced in witness testimony gathered by the Clann Project[5] and submitted to the MBHCOI, forced family separation took on many forms. In some instances, children were taken by force from their mothers' arms; in others, women and girls were physically forced to sign adoption papers (see O'Rourke and McGettrick et al, 2018, pp 30–34). In other instances, forced family separation was less obvious, but no less real. To fully understand Ireland's particular system, it is crucial to recognise that adoption transcended class; social class and/or financial stability did not prevent a woman or girl from losing her child to adoption. In 1967, 97 per cent of all non-marital births in Ireland ended in adoption (Adoption Authority of Ireland, 2013, p 25). This statistic offers indisputable evidence that the system provided no choice apart from adoption to women and girls who were pregnant outside of marriage. *This is forced family separation*. While it is likely that, on paper at least, most adoptions in Ireland were technically 'legal', it is also the case that many mothers sought the return of their children before signing the final papers and, in most cases, they were rebuffed. Many subsequently (and *seemingly willingly*) signed final adoption papers, but there is little doubt that they had been forced down this path because they were denied the opportunity to exercise their right to change their minds within the allotted time frame. *This is also forced family separation*.

Ireland's closed, secret adoption system was – and still is – a constitutive element of the nation's architecture of containment. And, as with institutional abuses, injustice in adoption is wrongly treated as historic. The social construction of adoption also acts as a containment mechanism, often preventing adopted people from developing a class consciousness. Once an adoption order was sanctioned, all parties were expected to move on with their lives as if the child had been born to the adoptive parents (Darling, 2005, pp 186–187). Section 24(a) of the Adoption Act 1952 states that the adopted child was to be considered 'as the child of the adopter or adopters born to him, her or them in lawful wedlock' (Ireland, Adoption Act 1952). Thus, the silence and secrecy that pervaded the adoption system were also inculcated within the adoptive family itself. In some cases, adoptive parents hid their daughter or son's adoptive status from them (O'Rourke et al, 2018, p 81). Many adopted people, fearful of appearing disloyal, will wait until their adoptive parents have passed away before seeking out information or tracing (O'Rourke et al, 2018, p 80). Moreover, adopted people often feel obliged to conform to certain expected norms, for example, dutifully reporting a happy adoption experience (McGettrick, 2020, p 199). As a result, and notwithstanding their frustrations about being denied access to their information, relatively few Irish adopted people recognise that they are affected by 'historic' injustice. Thus, and despite ongoing revelations of illegal adoption practices (for example, Ó'Fátharta, 2021), it is a challenge for us as advocates to achieve recognition of adoption as one of the key elements of systemic human rights violations against women and children in Ireland.

Social work practice: a personal perspective

I was born in Dublin in 1973 and adopted through St Patrick's Guild Adoption Society (SPG), an adoption agency run by the Religious Sisters of Charity (RSC). I spent most of my first six weeks in St Patrick's Infant Dietetic Hospital in Temple Hill, Blackrock, an institution also run by the RSC. Although I have no memory of my first interactions with social work practice during my early weeks, I am keenly aware of the significance of these encounters, because they had a permanent impact on my life trajectory. As Hapgood (1984, p 68) argues, adoption social workers 'are engaged in a unique form of social engineering. ... The decisions taken by those responsible will profoundly influence the lives of all concerned'.

Like other adopted people, once my adoption order was ratified, the path my life would take was permanently altered. Assessments and decisions made by social workers and other personnel (both lay and religious) determined what family would raise me.[6] Had SPG chosen a different adoptive family, my life would have taken an entirely different course. I would have a different name; I would have grown up in another part of the country; my accent would not be the same. I would have shared my childhood with different siblings – people who are strangers to me now would have called me their sister. Or, I may have been an only child. I would not have gone to the same schools; I would not have the same circle of friends. As an adopted person, it is unsettling to know that my life path was determined by a set of anonymous social workers and other personnel, none of whom I have ever met. And, I have been repeatedly prevented from examining the documents that might reveal the basis upon which they came to their decisions.

The next time I encountered social work practice was in late 1992, when I visited SPG to ask for information about myself and to enquire about meeting my mother. SPG's director, Sr Gabriel Murphy, answered the door and brought me into her office. After asking me for identification, she left the room and returned with a small piece of paper containing my parents' non-identifying information – their ages, religion, occupations, build and hair colour. For 19 years I had known nothing about my background and these fragments of information were like treasure to me. After this short meeting, Sr Gabriel arranged an appointment for me to meet with a social worker. I was not informed of the purpose of the meeting, nor did I think to ask, such was my naiveté at the time.

'Olivia',[7] the lay social worker assigned to me at SPG was a nice woman; yet, over the course of several meetings with her, I could not escape the feeling that I was undergoing some form of assessment. Olivia did not disclose the purpose of our meetings, but my strong sense was that I should not say or do anything that might jeopardise the prospect of reunion. For example, I was afraid to appear overeager in case Olivia would think I was too pushy. Nobody had spelled out the rules, but I fully understood that SPG and this social worker held all the power. In recent years I have obtained some of my SPG records via data protection legislation. While the documents are heavily redacted, I have been able to access some of the notes Olivia made at the time of our meetings in 1992 and 1993. Details were recorded about aspects of my life, my motivations for searching, my reactions during conversations with Olivia and even my demeanour during meetings and phone calls. It seems that once I began making enquiries as an adult, I became a new object of knowledge for SPG, and the information gathered about me was being used to determine my suitability for reunion with my mother. As Foucault (1977, p 14) argues: 'the exercise of power itself creates and causes to emerge new objects of knowledge and accumulates new bodies of information'.

Foucault (1977, p 14) also contends that 'It is not possible for power to be exercised without knowledge, it is impossible for knowledge not to engender power'. This rings true of my experience with social work practice. During our first meeting, I asked Olivia if she could tell me my original name. After checking my file (held in a separate room), she told me my first name, but not my surname. I was happy to finally know my own name, but surely such information should have been provided as a matter of course? A file in which I am the central character – containing over 100 pages of documents about my identity, my original family, my early life, my adoption, the narrative of how I came to inhabit my adoptive identity and other records created long after my placement – was located somewhere in SPG's premises, but not only was I not permitted to have access, I literally was not allowed to be in the same room as it. Later, I learned my mother's name, but only because Olivia mentioned it in passing in a letter. I should have complained, but my lack of empowerment prevented me from even considering doing so. I also understood implicitly that compliance was my only option, because at that point I believed SPG was my only link to my mother.[8] SPG and their social worker had all the knowledge and, therefore, all the power.

Thankfully, Olivia was able to locate my mother, who was delighted to hear from me. For two months, my mother and I corresponded through SPG, and I remember feeling like I was in a sort of prison because our letters were being read before they were passed on. My mother and I met for the first time on 25 May 1993 in SPG's offices. Olivia told us that we should not exchange surnames or addresses until our second meeting and, astonishingly, we obeyed. In the years to come I would learn that my experience with social work practice is far from unique; indeed, it is mild in comparison what others have had to endure. Regrettably, in the 30 years since I embarked on my own search, adoption social work practice has not improved – instead, policies have become more discriminatory and practices have become more paternalistic.

Present-day injustices in social work practice

Most Irish adoption agencies have now closed, and in the majority of cases their records have been transferred to TUSLA, Ireland's Child and Family Agency. Since its establishment in 2014, this Agency has taken a highly restrictive approach to the release of personal information to adopted people. It is important to state that I do not take issue with the majority of rank-and-file social workers currently working in TUSLA. However, TUSLA social workers' adoption practices involve the execution of discriminatory and prejudicial policies which emanate from management level. Some social workers have been so troubled by these policies that they have secretly approached my colleagues and me to express their concerns. In one instance, several social workers asked a third-party intermediary to contact me personally to convey their disquiet. Furthermore, I acknowledge that some social workers have gone above and beyond the call of duty in their interactions with adopted people and their relatives.

Unfortunately, most adopted people I encounter experience TUSLA's policies and practices as discriminatory, obstructive and mistrustful. When an adopted person applies to TUSLA to access their personal records, the Agency undertakes a risk assessment to consider the 'harm' that may be caused by the release of such information (Ó'Fátharta, 2019). As will be discussed further, TUSLA's adoption policies also involve the unnecessary management of adopted people who are seeking to trace their families of origin.

Discriminatory policies and practices have a devastating impact on affected people. For example, Clann Project Witness 16 said she felt TUSLA treated her "as a threat to my mother, and that the social worker tried to keep us apart for as long as possible" (O'Rourke and McGettrick et al, 2018, p 96). Witness 8 said: "Throughout the time I spent researching my birth family I found the authorities from whom I sought assistance obstructive and unhelpful" (O'Rourke et al, 2018, p 97). Witness 68 said: "It has been the most daunting, depressing, miserable and lonely search. I have faced umpteen brick walls. … All I know is that it has worn me out" (O'Rourke et al, 2018, p 105).

Adoption social work practice: access to information

Under data protection law, Irish citizens, including adopted people, have the right to obtain their personal data. These rights were strengthened in 2018 with the introduction of the General Data Protection Regulation (GDPR) (European Union, 2016; Ireland, Data Protection Act 2018). However, data controllers in TUSLA, the Adoption Authority of Ireland and government departments routinely misinterpret the GDPR to deny adopted people access to their personal data. At TUSLA, data protection law is inextricably – and wrongly – intertwined with social work practice. This is well illustrated in TUSLA's *Access Requests Standard Operating Procedure Draft 2.2* (SOP) document (Child and Family Agency, 2021). According to the SOP:

If the response to a requester['s] application for information] diminishes another person's enjoyment of a right or freedom, it will give rise to adverse effects. … Consideration of its application should be guided by the requester and associated persons' circumstances. Consult with a Social Worker, as outlined at Appendix 1, if information required for the application of this restriction is needed.

Appendix 1 of the SOP asserts that: 'Privacy Officers alone are not equipped or expected to carry out a comprehensive assessment in this connection. Consult with a Social Worker if necessary in order to ensure the request is handled such as to facilitate demonstration of compliance in respect of the applicable data protection law.'

The 'applicable data protection law' does not require privacy officers to consult with social workers before records can be released to data subjects (European Union, 2016; Ireland, Data Protection Act 2018). Moreover, the legislation contains no special requirements for adopted people applying for their personal data. Neither does the law state that privacy officers are 'not equipped' to carry out assessments in relation to the release of information to adopted people. Nevertheless, according to TUSLA, its privacy officers must consult with social workers when they consider that the release of 'certain personal data may likely cause serious harm to the requester's physical or mental health or emotional condition' (Child and Family Agency, nd).

Using Freedom of Information legislation, I have obtained the National Adoption Service Consultation (NASC) form used by TUSLA's privacy officers when they consult social workers on the release of personal data.[9] When requested by a privacy officer, the social worker must provide a report using the NASC form. Although data protection law does not require the production of such information, the social worker must outline whether a trace for the person's family of origin has been initiated, and the status of that trace. The social worker is also required to provide their opinion as to whether the release of the individual's personal data will 'not give rise to serious harm', or whether it will 'seriously harm' the person's physical or mental health or their 'emotional condition'. The social worker must also set out the rationale for their assessment. Again, under data protection law, there is no obligation for data controllers to obtain this information before an individual's personal data can be released. TUSLA's policy on information release (implemented in part by social workers) is in breach of data protection law, unnecessarily intrusive and wrongly linked with social work practice, which results in discrimination against adopted people simply because they are adopted.

Adoption social work practice: tracing and reunion

Adopted people seeking to reunite with their families of origin report that TUSLA social workers seem preoccupied with their mental health status. Social work practice in this area involves excessive management of adopted people, requiring them to attend preparatory meetings and to fill out offensive questionnaires before their trace can commence. One adopted person who recently spoke to RTÉ radio recalled his experience with TUSLA's tracing service in 2014 (Liveline, 2022). When the person contacted the Agency, he was invited to attend a Preparation for Search Meeting, which was, according to TUSLA, 'the first step in commencing your search'.[10] The meeting lasted for six hours, from 10 am to 4 pm with an hour for lunch. Throughout the day, attendees were given several handouts, one of which was entitled 'Questions to think about?' In this handout alone, attendees were asked to consider a total of 22 invasive and demeaning questions, including:

- What do I see as my responsibilities for opening a door into the lives of other people?
- Am I prepared, once entering the search/reunion process, to be mindful of the other person's feelings?
- What obligations do I foresee when I enter this other family unit's world?
- How will this reunion affect everyone?

- Am I emotionally prepared if they are disinterested in me?
- Have I examined all the possible emotional states that I might end up experiencing, examining each of them in relation to myself as a person? How do I deal with anger? Joy? Frustration? Disappointment? Happiness? Fear?

It is not surprising that the adopted person reported his understanding of the meeting's purpose as follows: "The central message was 'maybe you shouldn't do this, I don't think you should do this' ... we're all there getting ready to start this exciting journey and ... we want to do this and [there is a] hidden message kind of not to."[11]

I cannot state with certainty whether TUSLA still requires adopted people to attend group meetings; however, several adopted people have reported in recent times that the Agency has obliged them to complete a questionnaire before their trace can begin. One such questionnaire, which was shared by an adopted person who traced within the past 12 months, has the following introduction:

> This questionnaire has been designed to assist you in considering the social and emotional factors that may be associated with the tracing process. It is important to think about your reasons for tracing, your expectations regarding this, and what you hope to achieve. It is important to note that the wishes of the person tracing and the wishes of the person being traced is [sic] balanced and respected.[12]

The questions adopted people are asked to answer include the following:

- Why do you wish to trace? How long are you considering it?
- What are your expectations/fantasies of your natural mother/father? Please describe them.
- How would you cope
  (a) if your natural mother/father is deceased?
  (b) if your natural mother/father cannot be located?
  (c) if your natural mother/father refuses to meet you?
  (d) if there is a re-union and your natural mother/father does not meet your expectations?
- How would you feel if your birth parents were unwilling to inform the children they have of their marriage, of your existence?
- What are the possible negatives that could arise in meeting your natural mother/father and how could they affect you?

These social work practices are inappropriate and intrusive on the lives of adopted people. Adopted people are asked to anticipate their feelings before they arise, with an implication that the adopted person has a duty to ensure that they will manage these emotions so as not to affect other people. The purpose of these interventions is clear – adopted people must be emotionally frisked before they are deemed suitable for reunion. It is worth pointing out that family history researchers or individuals who meet relatives through genetic genealogy services are not required to complete questionnaires or consider the emotional impact of their actions. Yet, adopted people are managed in this way purely because they are adopted. In the next section I discuss the possible reasons why many social work policies and practices involve the over-management of adopted people.

Thankfully, many adopted people are now aware that they can carry out their own traces, so they can circumvent TUSLA's controlling practices if they wish.[13] The adopted person who shared the questionnaire described earlier was told that he must complete the form before TUSLA would initiate his search, which would commence five weeks thereafter. Three weeks after submitting the questionnaire, the adopted person found his mother by conducting his own trace, and they now have a wonderful relationship with each other. However, not all adopted people know that they do not need to depend on TUSLA to meet their families of origin (particularly those who are not computer literate). Under the Birth (Information and Tracing) Bill, which is currently progressing through the Irish parliament, the Agency is nominated as the sole provider of tracing services (McGettrick, O'Rourke, and O'Nolan, 2022). Regardless of whether the Bill passes, a significant culture change is required to ensure that TUSLA social work practices no longer discriminate against affected people.

Adult adopted people and social work practice

I became an academic because my personal and professional experience led me to consider the main body of scholarly work on adoption as lacking in several respects. Mainstream adoption research does not always reflect the wide range of lived experiences, and thus, an increasing number of adopted people (myself included) are seeking to participate in the production of knowledge about adoption. My current research is focused on examining the role of expert bodies of knowledge in organising and regulating adoption systems and in shaping adoption policy. This role needs to be understood, because, as demonstrated in this chapter, it is through these bodies of knowledge that adopted people come to be known as a specific category of person, and how they are managed as a distinct social group.

In preparation for my doctoral research, I undertook a Bachelor of Social Science undergraduate degree at University College Dublin. I expressly chose modules that would prepare me for the road ahead, including social work modules. The knowledge and insight I gained from the social work courses led me to a crucial realisation: social workers are trained to help people in crisis. *However, adopted people are not in crisis by default.* I believe that this assumption, together with the discriminatory policies promoted by the Irish state and its agencies, is at the crux of why many adopted people experience current adoption social work practice as oppressive.

In *The Social Work Interview*, Kadushin and Kadushin (2013, p 238) ask: 'How do applicants become social work clients for the first time?' They continue:

> The applicant may have a problem for only a few months or as long as two years before deciding to seek social work services. … *When the applicant finally accepts that he or she has a problem and needs professional help,* it is usually the most difficult and painful step in the process. (Kadushin and Kadushin, 2013, p 238; emphasis added)

Adopted people engage with social work practice not because they have problems requiring 'professional help' – they do so because these professionals are appointed gatekeepers to the adopted person's access to their personal information and relationships with their families of origin. If social workers approach interviews with adopted people as if these individuals have problems requiring specialised intervention, it is hardly surprising that adopted people (who are simply seeking information or contact with family members) are interrogated as to the crisis levels of their emotional well-being.

Erica Haimes (a sociologist) and Noel Timms' (a social work professor) adoption study from the 1980s is also relevant to this discussion – for this adopted person at least, it is a hidden gem in adoption research (Haimes and Timms, 1985). The project examined the compulsory counselling requirement under the UK Children Act 1975, Section 26 of which granted adopted people in England and Wales the right to access their birth certificates. Under that legislation, people adopted prior to 1975 must attend a counselling session before obtaining their birth certificates. Haimes and Timms (1985, p 80–81) argue that:

> Adoption … presents problems for practitioners and for society as a whole. Consequently, adoptees also present a problem: we cannot place it or them easily. The uneasiness that is felt about the process is attributed to the individuals and extends to questioning their stability. In viewing adoptees potentially at least as damaged and in need of help, the psycho-pathological model attributes the uncertainty about adoption to the adopted people themselves.

According to John Triseliotis (1984, p 46), in the months prior to the enactment of the 1975 Act, strong opposition emerged against birth certificate access. Some raised 'the probability' of adopted people 'wrecking another person's life', so the counselling requirement was seen as 'a check or restraint against possible hasty actions by adoptees' (Triseliotis, 1984, p 46). Over 40 years later, Irish adoption policies and practices operate from the same premise. Crucially, in his analysis of the research carried out on the impact of the Children Act 1975, Triseliotis (1984, p 51) found that 'the calamities anticipated … [had] not materialized'. Indeed, as Haimes and Timms (1985, p 50) contend, 'instead of a picture of adoptees as "psychological vagrants" rushing around looking for a new set of family relationships, a more rational picture is available: that is, of adoptees seeking to place themselves socially'.

Adoption discourses in Ireland tend to characterise adopted people as highly emotional, fragile individuals. This is well illustrated in a recent advertisement for the position of 'Birth Information and Tracing (BIT) Intake and Information Manager' at TUSLA. Under 'Skills Required', the agency stated that applicants should have: 'Experience of working with clients, some of whom may be very distressed' (Child and Family Agency, 2022). In my professional experience, 'distress' is caused when TUSLA and other data controllers withhold information.

In fact, adopted people are not in a permanent state of distress; those seeking their personal data or reunion with their original families are generally emotionally robust, capable and resourceful: they have after all decided to apply their time and energy to making a significant enquiry about their origins. Adopted people have learned to be highly adept at navigating the complexities of their relationships with their adoptive and original families.[14] I do not suggest that forced family separation and other human rights abuses have no impact on adopted people's emotional and psychological well-being. Moreover, resilience is no justification for human rights abuses. However, the effects of these injustices are not universal – they vary from person to person, and they can change over time. How each adopted person elects to self-identify, how they decide to express their narrative or how they choose to come to terms with the ways in which they are affected are matters for them to determine for themselves. Yet, current discourses offer a one-size-fits-all framework: adopted people as 'damaged'.

Jo Woodiwiss (2015, p 183) argues that in the telling of our life narratives 'we are not free to tell any story'; instead, we must 'draw on those stories that are currently in circulation'. Woodiwiss (2015, p 183) further asserts that contemporary story-telling practices are dominated by a single narrative framework that is shaped by 'therapeutic culture, pop-psychology and self-help literature'. In navigating their adoption experience and constructing their narratives, many adopted people rely on self-help and popular adoption psychology literature, such as the work of Betty Jean Lifton (1979) and Nancy Verrier (1993). This is problematic, because under Lifton and Verrier's deterministic paradigm, adopted people are susceptible to mental illness, drug abuse, crime, promiscuity and a multitude of other pathologies. As

Woodiwiss (2015, p 185) argues, self-help literature confronts readers 'with a narrative framework within which to construct their own autobiographies' that 'not only encourages them to construct themselves as damaged and in need of healing, but makes it difficult to construct biographies that are not centered on damage'. This too contributes to the perception in social work practice that adopted people are, by default, damaged and in need of therapy and/or social work interventions.[15]

Conclusion

Should adoption social workers be involved by default in the provision of information and tracing services to adult adopted people? My position is that while social workers play a crucial role in our society, adult adopted people should not be forced to engage with social work practice simply because they are adopted. Moreover, for adopted people, trust in the social work profession is extremely low. In the past, social workers separated adopted people from their families of origin; in the present, social workers are the gatekeepers of their personal information, and they hold the power when it comes to reunion with family members. Many adopted people have had negative experiences with social work practice, both past and present, and much work needs to be done to repair relationships and build trust.

Following the IASW's apology on 15 February 2021, I engaged with the organisation via Twitter. I welcomed the apology and asked what the organisation planned to do on foot of it. I explained that past injustices continue in the present through social work practice, and urged social workers to challenge this discrimination. Two days later, Majella Hickey, a social worker and IASW board member, made contact with me. She explained that the organisation was anxious to ensure an appropriate follow-up to its apology. I had several constructive conversations with Majella, and these culminated in my being elected to the IASW Board of Directors in May 2021. I am now Chairperson of the IASW Adoption and Mother and Baby Homes Working Group. The IASW has already shown strong allyship with adopted people, for example, through the organisation's call for the removal of a mandatory and discriminatory 'Information Session' from the Birth (Information and Tracing) Bill[16] (IASW, 2022). The IASW is seeking to recruit adoption social workers to the Working Group, and discussions around further actions are ongoing.

Irish social workers are passionate about human rights and social justice. This is exemplified in the 'Social Workers 4 Change' campaign to reinstate the term 'human rights' in the Social Workers Registration Board (CORU) *Code of Professional Conduct and Ethics* (Social Workers 4 Change, 2022). With continued collaboration through the IASW Working Group, Irish adopted people and social workers can work together to address past and present injustices. I urge social workers to listen to adopted people and others affected by forced family separation. In line with their code of ethics, which requires them to 'promote social justice' and challenge 'negative discrimination and unjust policies and practices' (CORU, 2019, p 28), I encourage social workers to reflect on their current practices. By reckoning with the injustices in its past and its present, the social work profession can help to ensure that present-day practice complies with human rights and social justice principles. Such a transformation would not only provide an invaluable model of best practice, it would also represent an important measure of justice for both past and current failings.

Notes

[1] See: O'Donnell et al, 2013; O'Rourke and McGettrick, nd; McGettrick et al, nd; McGettrick et al, 2021.

[2] See also 'A Note About Language' in McGettrick et al (2022, pp 3–4).

[3] This was the term used for foster-care arrangements.

[4] Irish parliament.

[5] The Clann Project is a joint initiative by two voluntary organisations in Ireland, Adoption Rights Alliance and Justice for Magdalenes Research, in association with global law firm Hogan Lovells. Clann provided *pro bono* assistance to individuals affected by the institutional and forced family separation system to submit witness statements to the MBHCOI. The Clann Project spoke to 164 participants, and the project's Report drew from over 80 sworn witness statements. See: www.clannproject.org.

[6] According to Darling (2005, pp 185–6, 188), prior to the early 1970s, most church-run adoption agencies were staffed by religious personnel, and did not employ trained social workers. Documents in my file indicate that social workers (termed 'adoption workers') and religious personnel were involved in my adoption.

[7] Not her real name.

[8] In the early 1990s, adoption activist Enda Pyne developed a methodology for Irish adopted people to obtain their birth certificates, using genealogical research methods, however, I was unaware of this at the time. See: www.adoption.ie/records.

[9] TUSLA Ref: FOI-0015-2022. On file with the author.

[10] Correspondence from TUSLA dated 8 January 2014 (see McGettrick et al, 2022, pp 85–8).

[11] See McGettrick et al (2022, pp 85–8).

[12] On file with the author.

[13] See: www.adoption.ie/records

[14] With thanks to Katherine O'Donnell and Maeve O'Rourke, who helped me to recognise this.

[15] See also McGettrick (2020).

[16] See McGettrick et al (2022).

References

Adoption Authority of Ireland (2013) *Annual Report 2013*. Dublin: Stationery Office.

Boland, R. (2014) 'Changes to adoption law have shattered my hopes of becoming a parent', *Irish Times*, 8 March. Available at: www.irishtimes.com/life-and-style/people/changes-to-adoption-law-have-shattered-my-hopes-of-becoming-a-parent-1.1716740

Child and Family Agency (2021) 'Access Requests Standard Operating Procedure Draft 2.2'. Dublin: Child and Family Agency. Available at: www.tusla.ie/uploads/content/SOP_Access_2.2.pdf

Child and Family Agency (2022) 'Birth Information and Tracing (BIT) Intake and Information Manager – Grade VIII'. Dublin: Child and Family Agency. Available at: https://tusla-candidate.wizzki.com/LiveJobs/JobApply/80356?source=1&externalAgency=-1&fbclid=IwAR1eomhTb_IDyIHVKC4s4KeVnPuO7WSkRVgKFw2F7HYoaAlcekWWPa4QIbE

Child and Family Agency (nd) *Outcomes of Tracing*. Available at: www.tusla.ie/services/alternative-care/adoption-services/tracing-service/outcomes-of-tracing/

Clann Project (2021) Irish High Court Declares that Mother and Baby Homes Commission of Investigation Treated Survivors Unlawfully. Available at: http://clannproject.org/wp-content/uploads/Clann-Press-Release_17-12-21.pdf

CORU (2019) *Social Workers Registration Board Code of Professional Conduct and Ethics*. Available at: https://coru.ie/files-codes-of-conduct/swrb-code-of-professional-conduct-and-ethics-for-social-workers.pdf

Darling, V. (2005) 'Social work in adoption: Vignette', in N. Kearney and C. Skehill (eds) *Social Work in Ireland: Historical Perspectives*. Dublin: Institute of Public Administration, pp 184–195.

European Union (2016) 'Regulation (EU) 2016/679 of the European Parliament and the Council of 27 April 2016 on the protection of natural persons with regard to the processing of personal data and the on the free movement of such data, and repealing Directive 95/46/EC', *Official Journal of the European Union*, L 119: 1–88.

Foucault, M. and Brochier, J.J. (1977) 'Prison talk: An interview with Michel Foucault', *Radical Philosophy*, 16: 10–15.

Government of Ireland (1952) *Adoption Act*. Dublin: Stationery Office.

Government of Ireland (2018) *Data Protection Act*. Dublin: Stationery Office.

Government of Ireland (2021) *Commission of Investigation into Mother and Baby Homes and Certain Related Matters*. Dublin: Stationery Office. Available at: www.gov.ie/en/publication/316d8-commission-of-investigation/

Haimes, E. and Timms, T. (1985) *Adoption, Identity and Social Policy: The Search for Distant Relatives*. Aldershot: Gower.

Hapgood, M. (1984) 'Older child adoption and knowledge base of adoption practice'. In P. Bean (ed) *Adoption: Essays in Social Policy, Law and Sociology*. London: Tavistock, pp 54–82.

IASW (2021) IASW statement on Report of the Commission into the Mother and Baby Homes. Available at: www.iasw.ie/IASWStatement_ReportCommission_MotherBabyHomes

IASW (2022) IASW calls for removal of mandatory information session from Adoption Bill. Available at: www.iasw.ie/PressRelease_RemovalMandatory_InfoSession_AdoptionBill

Kadushin, A. and Kadushin, G. (2013) *The Social Work Interview*. New York: Columbia University Press.

Lifton, B.J. (1979) *Lost and Found: The Adoption Experience*. New York: The Dial Press.

Liveline. (2022) 'In need of dialysis – Adoption story – Naming meat and vegetable products'. RTÉ Radio One, 18 February.

MBHCOI (2021) *Mother and Baby Homes Commission of Investigation Final Report*. Dublin: Department of Children, Equality, Disability, Integration and Youth.

McGettrick, C. (2020) '"Illegitimate" knowledge: Transitional justice and adopted people', *Éire–Ireland* 55(1–2): 181–200.

McGettrick, C., O'Donnell, K., O'Rourke, M., Smith, J.M. and Steed, M. (2021) *Ireland and the Magdalene Laundries: A Campaign for Justice*. London: I.B. Tauris/Bloomsbury.

McGettrick, C., O'Donnell, K., O'Rourke, M., Smith, J.M. and Steed, M. (nd) 'Justice for Magdalenes Research'. Available at: www.jfmresearch.com

McGettrick, C., O'Rourke, M. and O'Nolan, L. and O'Donnell, K. (2022) 'Birth Information and Tracing Bill 2022: Briefing note and amendments'. Dublin: Clann Project. Available at: http://clannproject.org/wp-content/uploads/Clann_A8A-Briefing-Note_Information-Tracing-Bill_28-02-22.pdf

O'Brien, V. (2009) 'The potential of Ireland's Hague Convention legislation to resolve ethical dilemmas in inter-country adoptions', *Irish Social Worker*, Summer, pp 13–19.

O'Donnell, K., Pembroke, S. and McGettrick, C. (2013) 'Magdalene Institutions: Recording an Oral and Archival History'. Available at: http://jfmresearch.com/home/oralhistoryproject/

Ó'Fátharta C. (2019) 'Tusla considers damage release of personal information can cause', *Irish Examiner*, 16 July. Available at: www.irishexaminer.com/news/arid-30937257.html

Ó'Fátharta C. (2021) 'Mother and Baby Homes Report fails to fully address the issue of illegal adoptions', *Irish Examiner*, 14 January. Available at: www.irishexaminer.com/opinion/commentanalysis/arid-40206575.html

O'Rourke M. and McGettrick C. (nd) 'Clann: Ireland's Unmarried Mothers and their Children: Gathering the Data'. Available at: http://clannproject.org

O'Rourke, M., McGettrick, C., Baker, R. and Hill, R. (2018) *Clann: Ireland's Unmarried Mothers and their Children: Gathering the Data: Principal Submission to the Commission of Investigation into Mother and Baby Homes.* Dublin: Justice for Magdalenes Research, Adoption Rights Alliance, Hogan Lovells. Available at: http://clannproject.org/wp-content/uploads/Clann-Submi ssions_Redacted-Public-Version-October-2018.pdf

Smith, J.M. (2007) *Ireland's Magdalen Laundries and the Nation's Architecture of Containment.* Notre Dame: University of Notre Dame Press.

Social Workers 4 Change (2022) 'Reinstate "human rights" into the CORU Social Work Code of Professional Conduct and Ethics'. Available at: https://my.uplift.ie/petitions/reinstate-human-rights-into-the-coru-soc ial-work-code-of-professional-conduct-ethics

Triseliotis, J. (1984) 'Obtaining birth certificates'. In: P. Bean (ed) *Adoption: Essays in Social Policy, Law and Sociology.* London: Tavistock, pp 38–53.

Verrier, N.N. (1993) *The Primal Wound: Understanding the Adopted Child.* Baltimore: Gateway Press.

Woodiwiss, J. (2015) 'What's wrong with me? A cautionary tale of using contemporary "damage narratives" in autobiographical life writing'. In: K.W. Shands, G.G. Mikrut, D.R. Pattanaik and K. Ferreira-Meyers (eds) *Writing the Self: Essays on Autobiography and Autofiction.* Mölnlycke: Elanders, pp 183–201.

Index

References to tables appear in **bold** type.